Legal Problems of Religious and Private Schools

Ralph D. Mawdsley

Fourth Edition

Education Law Association

Disclaimer

The Education Law Association (ELA) is a private, nonadvocacy, and nonprofit association of educators and attorneys. The opinions expressed in this publication are those of the author and do not represent official views of the Association.

Printed in U.S.A
ISBN 1-56534-101-5

Published by
Education Law Association
300 College Park - 0528
Dayton, OH 45469
(937) 229-3589

DEDICATION

To Alice, my wife, who has provided continuous encouragement and support in my writing endeavors, and to our two sons, Jonathan and James, who have been the beneficiaries of education at religious K-12 schools and at private universities.

About the Author

Ralph D. Mawdsley is Professor and Chair, Department of Counseling, Administration, Supervision, and Adult Learning, Cleveland State University, Cleveland, Ohio. Prior to accepting this position, he spent twelve years as Professor of Education Law, Administrative Counsel, and Vice President of Human Resources at Liberty University. His K-12 teaching and administration experience includes twelve years as a public and private school teacher and superintendent. In addition to his Ph.D. from the University of Minnesota, he earned his J.D. from the University of Illinois. Dr. Mawdsley is admitted to the practice of law in Illinois and Minnesota.

He has published over 230 articles, books, and book chapters in the area of education law. Among his publications are several other ELA monographs, including *Academic Misconduct: Cheating and Plagiarism*, *Pupil Transportation and the Law*, *Legal Aspects of Plagiarism*, and *Free Expression and Censorship: Public Policy and the Law*. Dr. Mawdsley has served on the ELA Board of Directors and was elected Vice President of ELA in 1999. Since 1988, he has authored the "Employees" chapter of the *Yearbook of Education Law*, published annually by ELA. He has served since 1985 as a member of the Editorial Advisory Committee of *West's Education Law Reporter*.

Preface

For years, those of us interested in education other than that offered by government have debated the appropriate identification for such education. While the label "nonpublic education" would seem to work, defining a term as a negative has a disadvantage; the label suggests that the term is being defined by what it is not (not public) rather than being defined by its own characteristics and distinctiveness. The term "private education" would appear to be a logical choice, but this term has its own limitation. Although "private education" would seem to apply to all nongovernment education, those involved in religious schools, clearly the largest component of nongovernment education in the United States, have been concerned that the label does not communicate the religious distinctiveness of many schools. Hence, in selecting the title for this book, now in its fourth edition, the author continues to use the terms "religious" and "private" separately to reflect that nongovernment education has both sectarian and nonsectarian characteristics. Nonetheless, in many cases, legal issues apply equally to both sectarian and nonsectarian schools. For the sake of efficiency in this book, a distinction between the two kinds of schools will be made only where legal differences occur; otherwise, the term "nonpublic" will be used.

Religious and private education offers parents and students distinctive educational opportunities. For over 350 years, religious and private schools have been part of the fabric of American life. From home instruction to world-prominent universities, these schools have provided parents and students with pedagogical and philosophical choices. Despite the ebb and flow of legislative and judicial pressures on religious and private schools to look like public schools, such schools have, by and large, fought the good fight to maintain their distinctiveness.

In the almost two decades since the first edition of this book, legal problems facing religious and private schools have undergone many changes. Constitutional issues are still important, but the nature of the arguments has changed. Protection of religious beliefs, once advocated under the free exercise clause, are now argued under the free speech clause, using the rubric of religious expression. The establishment clause, a longstanding limitation on government-religion interaction, now permits government resources to be available on religious school premises. Changes in constitutional interpretation reflect the organic nature of the Constitution and highlight the transient nature of rights created and defined by our judicial system.

In an era where deregulation has become a popular mantra, it should not be surprising that state control over education has had its own form of deregulation. Diminished state regulation of religious and private schools is not inconsistent with state legislative efforts to increase parent choice through such means as charter schools, vouchers, and tax credits.

A climate among the states, though, that is more favorable toward forms of education other than the traditional public school system does not mean that religious and private schools will be free of legal problems. Not surprisingly, the amount of litigation involving religious and private schools has increased significantly since the last edition of this book. We live in a litigious society and, increasingly, students, parents, and teachers use the legal system as the venue to address complaints. As a result, judges in secular courts are being asked to determine how much of the law that applies to public schools should also apply to religious and private schools.

The author hopes that this edition will be of assistance to teachers and administrators in recognizing legal problems and in developing preventive strategies to resolve these problems before they end up in court. Not only did religious and private schools (K-12 and higher education) offer the first education in America, but they continue to serve as the benchmarks for quality education. To those who labor in the classrooms to provide quality education and to those who labor in the courtrooms to protect the distinctiveness of religious and private schools, I offer my sincere gratitude.

Ralph D. Mawdsley
May 2000

Contents

Chapter I

TORT LIABILITY

Charitable Immunity

The almost universal doctrine of charitable immunity was traditionally justified at one time because of the altruistic nature of the activities of charities and because the imposition of liability would be unfair when the organization received no benefit from its works.[1] However, the trend since World War II in most states has been the total or partial abrogation of charitable immunity.[2] Charitable immunity protected not only groups rendering charity but nonprofit service organizations generally, such as hospitals, churches, and schools and colleges. The reasons for abolition of charitable immunity in most states have generally been twofold: (1) charities are no longer low budget, marginal operations but are significant operations with large numbers of employees;[3] and

1 *E.g., see* Cox v. DeJarnette, 123 S.E.2d 16, 22 (Ga. Ct .App. 1961) (immunity has purpose of preserving "eleemosynary funds so as to enable the charity to carry out its beneficent purposes"). *See The Quality of Mercy: "Charitable Torts" and Their Continuing Immunity*, 100 Harv. L. Rev. 1382, 1383-84 (1987); Canon and Jaros, *The Impact of Changes in Judicial Doctrine: The Abrogation of Charitable Immunity*, 13 Law & Soc'y Rev. 969, 973 (1979). *See also* RESTATEMENT (SECOND) OF TORTS § 895 E comment c (1965); G.G. AND G.T. BOGERT, HANDBOOK OF THE LAW OF TRUSTS, 469 (5th ed. 1973).

2 *See* Annotation, *Tort Immunity and Nongovernmental Charities-Modern Status*,25 A.L.R.4th 517, 522-615 (1983) (at least sixteen jurisdictions have abrogated charitable immunity for all kinds of charitable institutions; twelve have abrogated immunity for charitable institutions like hospitals; and five have abrogated immunity for charitable institutions other than hospitals. Six states maintain partial immunity for all kinds of charities; ten maintain partial immunity only for institutions like hospitals; two maintain partial immunity for institutions other than hospitals). *See also The Quality of Mercy*, *supra* note 1 at 1385.

3 Foster v. Roman Catholic Diocese of Vermont, 70 A.2d 230 (Vt. 1950); Adkins v. St. Francis Hosp., 143 S.E.2d 154 (W.Va. 1965); Parker v. Port Huron Hosp., 105 N.W.2d 1 (Mich. 1960). *See* Barr v. United Methodist Church, 153 Cal. Rptr. 322, 331 (Cal. App. 1979) where the "business" of a charity in operating retirement homes was described as not only fulfilling "spiritual concerns" but was also identified as "commercial activities" requiring "primarily business decisions." *See also*, Albritton v. Neighborhood Ctrs. Ass'n for Child Dev., 466 N.E.2d 867, 870-71 (Ohio 1989) ("a policy exempting a charitable organization from having to compensate for harm caused by it is equivalent to requiring an injured individual to make an unwilling contribution to that organization in the amount which would be due him had he been injured by a noncharitable entity. Such coerced donations are inimical to the whole concept of charitable donations and service.")

(2) the risk of crippling verdicts can be minimized and controlled through the purchase of liability insurance.[4]

Regardless of any statute conferring partial or complete immunity,[5] courts have tended to consider the doctrine of charitable immunity as a judicial creation originally and thus subject to abolition by state courts when persuaded that public policy would demand such abolition.[6]

Notwithstanding the existence of a viable defense of charitable immunity in a state in the past, courts have demonstrated great imagination in circumventing the defense to find assets to satisfy a tort judgment, namely, waiver of exemption,[7] a business enterprise beyond the statutory nonprofit purposes,[8] property held by the charitable institution but subject to property taxes,[9] and liability to the extent of liability insurance coverage.[10] The abiding lesson from a study of the erosion and abolition of charitable immunity is that the doctrine can be suddenly invalidated with potentially disastrous results for the charitable institution. It is thus no surprise to find courts encouraging the purchase of liability insurance.[11]

---

4 Rakavic v. Croatian Cultural Club, 430 N.Y.S.2d 829, 837-38 (N.Y. App. Div. 1980); Mississippi Baptist Hosp. v. Holmes, 55 So.2d 142 (Miss. 1951); Darling v. Charleston Community Mem'l Hosp., 211 N.E.2d 253 (Ill. 1965); Myers v. Drozda, 141 N.W.2d 852 (Neb. 1966). *See* Kornhauser, *An Economic Analysis of the Choice between Enterprise and Personal Liability for Accidents*, 70 Calif. L. Rev. 1345 (1982).

5 *See* English v. New England Med. Ctr., Inc., 541 N.E.2d 329 (Mass. 1989) (statute limiting liability for charitable institutions to $20,000 in case where jury award had been $350,000 upheld over right to jury trial, equal protection, and substantive due process objections); Cotton v. Catholic Bishop, 351 N.E.2d 247 (Ill. App. Ct. 1976); Helgendorf v. First Baptist Church of Danville, 510 N.E.2d 659 (Ill. App. Ct. 1987) (in loco parentis statute interpreted as removing public school teachers from liability for ordinary negligence in "discipline and conduct of the schools" applied also to parochial schools and day care personnel).

6 Hungerford v. Portland Sanitarium and Benevolent Ass'n, 384 P.2d 1009 (Or. 1963); Pierce v. Yakima Valley Mem'l Hosp. Ass'n, 260 P.2d 765 (Wash. 1953); Roman Catholic Church v. Kennan, 243 P.2d 455 (Ariz. 1955).

7 Brown v. City of Pittsburgh, 186 A.2d 399 (Pa. 1962).

8 Kasten v. YMCA, 412 A.2d 1346 (N.J. Super. Ct. App. Div. 1980); Kirby v. Columbian Inst.,243 A.2d 853 (N.J. Super. Ct. App. Div. 1968).

9 Mack v. Big Bethel A.M.E. Church, Inc., 188 S.E.2d 915 (Ga. Ct. App. 1972); Baptist Mem'l Hosp. v. Couillens, 140 S.W.2d 1088 (Tenn. 1940).

10 Fairall v. Sisters of the Third Order of St. Francis, 198 N.E.2d 15 (Ill. App. Ct. 1962); Cox v. DeJarnette, 123 S.E.2d 16 (Ga. Ct. App. 1961). In an interesting conflict of laws case, a federal appeals court has affirmed the reduction from $155,000 to $20,000 of the judgment against a religious association because a Massachusetts statute provides that charitable institutions tort liability "shall not exceed the sum of twenty thousand dollars." Mason v. Southern New England Conference Ass'n of Seventh-Day Adventists, 696 F.2d 135 (1st Cir. 1982); MASS. GEN. LAWS ANN. ch. 231, § 85K. *See also,* English v. New England Med. Ctr., Inc., 541 N.E.2d 329 (Mass. 1989).

11 Ricker v. Northeastern Univ., 279 N.E.2d 671 (Mass. 1972); Mink v. University of Chicago, 460 F. Supp. 713 (N.D. Ill. 1978).

In today's litigious society it is probably advisable for a nonpublic school to have its own liability coverage, or to be covered under an umbrella policy of a parent organization. The amount of coverage should not be determined in a casual and off-hand manner, but should reflect each organization's risk factors, such as: the age group serviced; total number of students; size of facilities and state of their repair; nature of high risk activities; kind of punishments used, especially corporal punishment; number of related nonprofit organizations of similar purpose or mission;[12] and the extent of student medical coverage.[13] School liability coverage should be a careful, collaborative effort by the school's administration, the school's attorney, and an insurance agent.

Exculpatory Clauses

Educational institutions are generally responsible for the safety of persons who use their premises. This responsibility translates into a concept referred to as Standard of Care. As will be evident throughout this chapter on tort liability, Standard of Care is a fluid concept, and its definition can be affected by a wide range of variables. However, rather than wait for a court to determine whether a school has demonstrated an appropriate Standard of Care toward an injured party, school officials would generally much prefer to prevent litigation in the first place. To the extent that schools can limit liability prior to an injury

---

12 Under the concept of ascending liability, the tortious acts of one organization, e.g., a school, can be imputed to a related organization with a similar mission, e.g., a church, even though both are incorporated separately. *See* E. Gaffney, Jr. and P. Sorenson, Ascending Liability in Religious and Other Nonprofit Organizations (1984).

13 Unlike liability insurance, medical insurance coverage is keyed to status, not fault. Although parents of students in nonpublic schools tend not to be as litigious-minded as their public school counterparts, they will be understandably concerned about who will pay the expenses resulting from an injury involving a school function. When nonpublic schools do have medical insurance, the coverage may be secondary to that of the parents. But where using the parents' insurance policy as primary coverage will reduce the maximum policy limit, parents may be reluctant to use their own medical coverage if they believe the school was at fault. *See* Seals v. Loftis, 614 F. Supp. 302 (E.D. Tenn. 1985) (in case under IDEA, school district required to reimburse parents $99.70, the amount by which the lifetime maximum had been reduced when the district improperly required the parents to utilize their private medical coverage). *See also*, Coleman v. Academy of Sacred Heart, 650 So.2d 265 (La. Ct. App. 1994) (parents permitted to proceed with tort claim resulting from physical education injury to their child against school and its insurers, despite claim that parents had agreed to a settlement offer); Marshall v. Caddo Parish Sch. Bd., 743 So.2d 943 (La. Ct. App. 1999) (school district required to pay for unnecessary medical treatment that resulted when plaintiff's special education student injured his head and neck in a minor bus accident).

occurring, they will have reduced the time and expense connected with litigation.

In the broadest sense, exculpation of liability can refer to any means that reduce or eliminate the legal basis for a lawsuit. Most states have some degree of statutory immunity for certain kinds of governmental functions performed by public entities—a classification that would also include public schools.[14] However, such immunity would not apply to nonpublic schools, although state legislatures can choose to limit liability in certain areas as a means of encouraging participation by members of the public.[15] For most nonpublic schools, exculpation of liability will depend on releases and other similar, contractual-type provisions.

The contractual nature of nonpublic education lends itself to efforts to reduce or eliminate standard of care, and hence, liability for subsequent injury. Such efforts to exculpate liability by one-time releases, hold harmless clauses, or general contractual language, are common in nonpublic institutions and not uncommon in public ones.[16]

---

14 Very few states still recognize sovereign immunity as a total defense. *Compare* Pruett v. City of Rosedale, 421 So.2d 1046 (Miss. 1982) (sovereign immunity abolished prospectively) *with* Bego v. Gordon 407 N.W.2d 801 (S.D. 1987) (sovereign immunity prohibits lawsuits against school districts). Even where total sovereign immunity has been abolished, a state often preserves restrictions on lawsuits. *E.g., see,* Coonse v. Boise Sch. Dist., 979 P.2d 1161 (Idaho 1999) (school district liable only for acts involving malice or criminal intent, or reckless, willful and wanton conduct); Brady v. Board of Educ. of City of N.Y., 602 N.Y.S.2d 892 (N.Y. App. Div. 1993) (placement of behaviorally disabled students in public schools a discretionary function and, therefore, governmental immunity applied to school district); King v. Little Rock Sch. Dist., 782 S.W.2d 574 (Ark. 1990) (state immunity applied to school district lease of two school buses because under governmental immunity statute, school district required to purchase liability insurance only on buses that it owned); Robinson v. Indianola Mun. Separate Sch. Dist., 467 So.2d 911 (Miss. 1985) (immunity for discretionary acts such as choice of location and construction of school building); Overcash v. Statesville City Bd. of Educ., 348 S.E.2d 524 (N. C. Ct. App. 1986) (immunity waived only as to injuries covered by insurance); DeKalb County Sch. Dist. v. Borden, 339 S.E.2d 356 (Ga. Ct. App. 1987) (immunity waived to extent of insurance dollar coverage).

15 *See, e.g.*, Ohio Rev. Code §§ 2305.381, 2305.382 where the state legislature granted qualified immunity from all tort claims for uncompensated athletic coaches, managers, instructors, umpires and referees involved in sports programs. However, this immunity does not apply to "interscholastic varsity or junior varsity organized competition." *See also*, Fla. Stat. Ann. § 234.02(3) where parents, guardians and other responsible adults providing transportation in private cars for school activities have same protection from liability as school district employees acting in the scope of their employment.

16 For samples of releases for different purposes *see* 12 Les Collegii 7-8 (Fall, 1988). In addition to using release forms for traditional school events such as athletics and field trips, these forms have currently been extended to such events as Prom Night activities. Although a release is generally considered in the context of parental permission for students to participate in activities, elements of a release are also present in reverse in parent opt-out programs where, by statute in some states, parents must grant consent in order for students to participate in medical or health related counseling. *See, e.g.*, N.Y. Pub. Health § 2504. *See also*, Altman v. Bedford Cent. Sch. Dist., 45 F. Supp.2d 368 (S.D. N.Y. 1999) where the court, in interpreting this statute, refused to create a general parental opt-out requirement for regular public school classroom teaching.

All exculpatory language cases have in common the key element of informed consent.[17] Informed consent has three aspects of cognition:[18] knowledge of the activity; comprehension (understanding) of the risks; and application (understanding) of risks to persons granting the consent.[19] Although courts generally will not use these exact terms, informed consent can be a permissible defense for an institution where the elements of both knowledge and understanding are present.[20]

Judicial response to exculpatory language varies with the age of the participant or the nature of the activity—the younger the participant, the more dangerous the activities, and the more potentially hazardous the risks to the participants, the more closely scrutinized will be the exculpatory language. Such language pertaining to risks of serious injury or death may be considered a violation of public policy, and may therefore be unenforceable[21] or may be interpreted in such a restrictive manner that enforcement of the exculpatory language could hardly ever occur.[22] In *Porubiansky v. Emory University*,[23] the

---

17 The concept of informed consent has a fairly universal meaning in most legal contexts. Thus, the regulatory definition of "informed consent" under Family Educational Rights and Privacy Act (FERPA) as it applies to consent to release educational records is equally apposite to tort liability: "informed consent" is "the knowing consent of an individual or his legally authorized representative so situated as to be able to exercise free power of choice without undue inducement or any element of force, fraud, deceit, duress or other form of constraint or coercion." 45 C.F.R. § 46.103 (c). For discussion of the concept of "informed consent" in tort liability case, *see* Whitlock v. Duke Univ., 637 F. Supp. 1463 (M.D.N.C. 1986).

18 *See* B. Bloom, Taxonomy of Educational Objectives, Handbook I: Cognitive Domain (1956);' Ford, Design for Teaching and Training 80-220 (1978).

19 *See* Helms v. Chicago Park Dist., 630 N.E.2d 1016 (Ill. App. Ct. 1994) (in upholding summary judgment for defendant, the court noted that plaintiff, rendered quadriplegic as a result of a fall from rings at a Ring Station, could not claim a duty to warn by defendant where the Station had a picture and instructions how to use the rings and the plaintiff had used the rings in the past without incident).

20 *E.g., see* Holmes v. Health & Tennis Corp. of Am., 659 N.E.2d 812 (Ohio Ct. App. 1995) (in reversing a summary judgment for the defendant and remanding for trial, the court, in ruling that a release form in a membership contract was not adequate to eliminate liability for a person injured while weightlifting, noted that "the party waiving his right to recover must make a conscious choice to accept the consequences of the other party's negligence.")

21 *See* Restatement of Contracts Second, § 512; Williston on Contracts, § 1750 A (3d ed. 1961). Minors are not able to sign enforceable releases because they are not legally competent. However, parents may sign a hold harmless agreement whereby they agree to indemnify the school in the event the minor sues for damages. Enforceability of hold harmless agreements will depend on state law. *See also*, Kyriazis v. University of W. Virginia, 450 S.E.2d 649 (W.Va. 1994) (anticipatory release signed by rugby player was unenforceable as a matter of public policy because there was not an equal bargaining position between the parties).

22 *See* Scroggs v. Coast Community College Dist., 239 Cal. Rptr. 916, 919 (Cal. Ct. App. 1987) (release signed by deceased prior to scuba diving course did not destroy wrongful death action by widow. "Any contract, intending to limit or destroy a cause of action which belongs to the heirs, should be construed with an abundance of caution.").

23 275 S.E.2d 163 (Ga. Ct. App. 1980).

court determined consent forms signed by adults to receive reduced cost dental care from a university hospital were a violation of public policy because the hospital held itself out to perform a service and the purchaser was subject to the institution's superior bargaining power. The basis for this decision was that, since lawyers as a state licensed profession cannot exculpate liability, dentists should not be able to do so either.[24] To the extent that the professional nature of services is controlling, this case would have no effect on education since teaching, even though subject to state licensure, has never been accorded the same measure of professional accountability and is normally not subject to the same degree of statutory and regulatory licensure as are the other two professions.[25]

Where exculpatory language occurs as a clause within printed forms, it will normally be interpreted according to the law of contracts on the theory that the clause is part of a quid pro quo (usually an exchange of money for services). Like any contract, these exculpatory clauses, frequently referred to as releases, raise questions regarding adequacy of consideration for the release. In *Penrod v. Branson R-IV Public School District*,[26] a student, injured while riding in a teacher's automobile on a field trip, received a $48,000 settlement by the teacher and, in turn, executed a release "for all other persons and organizations who are or might be liable for all claims for all damages."[27] Against a claim that the school district should not be included as part of the release because the district had extended no consideration, the court observed that the injured party had received payment for his promises, even if the promises extended to a third party.

A similar issue is whether a parent's signature on a release should serve as a bar to a negligence claim by a minor child. In

---

24 *Id.* at 169. For an indication that states are acting to give complete protection to medical informed consent agreements, except in cases of fraud, deception or misrepresentation, *see* Whitlock v. Duke Univ., 637 F. Supp. 1463 (M.D. N.C. 1986), interpreting N.C. Gen. Stat. § 90-21.13.

25 Professional accountability in the legal and medical professions is cognizable under legal and medical malpractice theories, but courts have consistently refused to recognize educational malpractice as a basis for a legal claim. *See generally* VALENTE, EDUCATION LAW: PUBLIC AND PRIVATE, II 269-274 (1985). *See also*, Houston v. Mile High Adventist Acad., 872 F. Supp. 829 (D. Colo. 1994) (student's claim for failure to protect students, institute disciplinary procedures, and supervise parents and teachers amounted to educational malpractice which was not cognizable in Colorado).

26 916 S.W.2d 866 (Mo. Ct. App. 1996).

27 *Id.* at 867.

Aaris v. Las Virgenes Unified School,[28] a California court upheld dismissal of a cheerleader's claim for injury suffered during a cheerleading practice. In finding a consent to participate and release of liability form signed by the student's mother to be enforceable, the court observed that "[i]t is well established that a parent may execute a release on behalf of his or her child."[29]

As in all contracts, the language of exculpatory clauses is critical. In *Sivaslian v. Rawlins*,[30] a student injured in a sky diving course was not barred from bringing an action in negligence despite a "release and hold harmless" provision absolving operators and instructors of the sky diving school "from any and all manner of actions" because the release did not specifically mention the school's negligence, fault, or carelessness in instruction. In an earlier case in the same jurisdiction,[31] also involving a sky diving school, a court found a general release not to prohibit an injured participant's cause of action because the release did not specifically waive the failure by the teacher to instruct and the failure of the teacher to comply with FAA rules pertaining to securing a medical certificate from plaintiff prior to participating in sky diving. Similarly, in a California case involving a scuba diving course,[32] a release signed by a decedent student lacked specific language indicating that he assumed all risks of the activity.[33]

Exculpatory clauses can be enforceable as long as they are unambiguous. In *Bellefonte Insurance Company v. Queen*,[34] a court found as a matter of law that parents of a child killed after being struck at a crosswalk by a school bus were prevented from filing a lawsuit against the school board because of a "Special Release" they had executed. Despite the parents' claims that they had never intended to release the school board from all claims, the court found "unambiguous" the release of claims:

> ...we do hereby release acquit and discharge the School Board ... from all claims and demands, actions and causes of action, damages, costs, loss of services, expenses and compensation ... and any and all-known

---

28 75 Cal. Rptr.2d 801 (Cal. Ct. App. 1998).

29 *Id.* at 805.

30 451 N.Y.S.2d 307 (N.Y. App. Div. 1982).

31 Gross v. Sweet, 407 N.Y.S.2d 254 (N.Y. App. Div. 1978).

32 Scroggs v. Coast Community College Dist., 239 Cal. Rptr. 916 (Cal. Ct. App. 1987).

33 The release waived liability for "any accidents, illness, injury or death, or other consequences arising or resulting directly or indirectly form participation in SCUBA diving ..." *Id.* at 917.

34 431 So.2d 1039 (Fla. Dist. Ct. App. 1983).

> and unknown, foreseen and unforeseen damages and the consequences thereof ....[35]

Likewise, in *Batting v. Hartford Accident and Indemnity Co.,*[36] parents had no action against a Catholic school for retarded children. The court responded to the parents' claim that the school had not performed a quasi-contractual obligation to secure adequate medical services, allegedly causing their child's comatose condition, by finding a complete defense in the parental signature to the application form releasing the school "from any and all liability of every nature, kind and description as a result of any injuries, hurt or damage sustained by the child herein described." Similarly, in *Poskozim v. Monnacep*, a sky diving student who broke his leg unsuccessfully alleged that the instructor had negligently approved the boots he wore.[37] Despite the *Poskozim* court's statement that "exculpatory agreements are not favored by the law,"[38] the court found "unambiguous" the language in the release exculpating the defendant school districts from "all such personal injuries, conscious suffering...resulting from or in any way connected with or arising out of instruction, training, and ground or air operations ...."[39] But, the court went on to add, even had there been misconduct in approving plaintiff's boots, "such conduct would be characterized as instructional and the instant exculpatory agreement is explicit in its exculpation of all matters having to do with instruction."[40]

Specific language in a release can be supplemented by the injured party's knowledge. In *Whitlock v. Duke University,*[41] an experienced ocean diver suffered organic brain damage after participating in a simulated, experimental deep dive program. The diver had signed a consent form advising him of the risks of lung collapse, production of fluid, hearing loss, inflammation of the ear, and sinusitis, as well the risk of decompression sickness, including death, disability, and joint pain. Even though organic brain damage was not listed, plaintiff diver admitted he knew there existed such a risk associated with decompression. This knowledge of plaintiff seemed to be important because the

---

35 *Id.* at 1040. See also the consent and release form in Aaris v. Las Virgenes Unified Sch., 75 Cal. Rptr.2d 801, 805 (Cal. Ct. App. 1998).

36 482 F. Supp. 338 (W.D. La. 1977), *aff'd* 608 F.2d 119 (5th Cir. 1979).

37 475 N.E.2d 663 (Ill. App. Ct. 1985).

38 *Id.* at 665.

39 *Id.* at 664.

40 *Id.* at 665.

41 637 F. Supp. 1463 (M.D. N.C. 1986).

scientist in charge of the program stated that "all risks pertaining to deep diving that had occurred in the past were included on the informed consent form" but organic brain damage was not "because it was not a normal condition for experimental deep diving."[42]

In a more unusual set of facts a teacher who broke her arm when she fell off a donkey during a faculty-student donkey basketball game was found to have consented to the risk when the donkey ball company fulfilled its contract by instructing the participants prior to the game that donkeys buck and put their heads, down causing people to fall off.[43] On the other hand, a release signed by a teacher having her car repaired in the school's auto mechanics shop could not forestall a negligence action where a rather comical set of mishaps to the car could have occurred only in the absence of adequate teacher supervision.[44]

Occasionally releases may involve situations other than personal injuries. In *Petock v. Thomas Jefferson University,*[45] a student was legally bound by a signed agreement whereby the university permitted him to withdraw in exchange for his release (actually a withdrawal) of his civil rights ADEA claim against the university.[46] In two similar cases a student and faculty member were unsuccessful in their defamation actions based on evaluations performed on them by the institutions. In *Baker v. Lafayette College,*[47] a faculty handbook provision providing for annual evaluations not only was consented to when the faculty member signed his contract but gave the college an absolute privilege to distribute those evaluations to persons in the faculty review process. In *Kraft v. W. Alanson White Psychiatric Foundation,*[48] a student enrolled in a two-year training program who was denied a certificate of successful completion had actual knowledge of, and thus consented to, the catalog provisions stating the program was monitored and persons could be dismissed, which plaintiff should have reasonably understood

---

42 *Id.* at 1469.

43 Arbegast v. Board of Educ. of S. New Berlin Cent. Sch., 490 N.Y.S.2d 751 (N.Y. 1985).

44 Steffen v. Baker, 398 N.Y.S.2d 355 (N.Y. Civ. Ct. 1976).

45 630 F. Supp. 187 (E.D. Pa. 1986).

46 The court's emphasis that the plaintiff-student, "an experienced attorney," drafted the agreement suggests that courts are less disposed to find justiciable claims based on coercion or duress in signing a release when the person executing the release is represented by an attorney. *Id.* at 190-91.

47 504 A.2d 247 (Pa. Super. Ct. 1986).

48 498 A.2d 1145 (D.C. App. 1985).

to mean granting a certificate would occur only if the program was completed successfully.

Reliance upon exculpatory language in applications, handbooks, or field trip forms is ill-advised as a substitute for adequate instruction and supervision and safe equipment and facilities. However, exculpatory language and terms of the information communicated may play a vital role in the educational function. School officials need to be aware that constructing and relying on exculpatory clauses presents three levels of analysis. At the first level, schools need to determine whether clauses which seek to exculpate liability, as opposed to merely inform of risks, are readily enforceable in their jurisdiction.[49] At the second level, schools must determine the effect of specific exculpatory language on their clientele. School officials who seek to remove all liability for instruction, supervision, and safety certainly face some policy problems: whether a school's contract with parents should bind them to tuition payments while, at the same time, eliminating responsibility for injury to students; whether exculpatory language projects a less-than-caring image of the school; and whether parents may seek to negotiate changes in exculpatory language in exchange for gifts of money or services. At the third level, school officials must be aware of the levels of cognition represented by informed consent. However much adults may understand the exculpatory language, and thus find their claims limited or eliminated, the policy behind the voidability of minor contracts is that they are presumed not capable of the understanding necessary to render their contracts enforceable.[50] A better course of action would always be for schools to dedicate their energies toward providing a safe educational environment and eliminating the instructional and supervisory problems that form the basis for negligence actions.

Even though schools should not unduly rely on exculpatory language there are several reasons why releases may be helpful. First, depending on the jurisdiction, releases may protect the institution from liability. Second, releases may place students, at least the older secondary students and college students, on notice regarding their responsibilities. Third, releases may make injured parties aware they were informed regarding certain risks

---

49 *See supra* notes 16 and 17 and accompanying text.

50 *See* Shine v. Wabash R.R. Co., 132 N.E.2d 41 (Ill. 1956); Vladimer v. Mt. Vernon Hebrew Camps, Inc., 172 N.E.2d 283 (N.Y. 1961).

and therefore prevent a lawsuit being filed or at least provide leverage for a more equitable settlement. Fourth, releases may bolster an assumption of risk affirmative defense.

Legal Requirements

Tort Theories

Educational institutions are not insurers of the safety of their students.[51] Liability for torts in general must be predicated upon at least one of three theories: strict liability; intentional acts; and negligence. The legal theory pursued determines the elements necessary to sustain the burden of producing evidence to avoid dismissal of a complaint or summary judgment for defendant school and school personnel.[52] In line with judicial rejection of the insurer approach to education, courts have consistently refused to impose a strict liability theory on educational institutions, that is a theory of recovery which does not require proof of fault and breach of duty of care.[53] Even where a court considers a product to be dangerous, rather than impose a strict

---

51 Swanson v. Wabash College, 504 N.E.2d 327 (Ind. Ct. App. 1987); District of Columbia v. Doe, 524 A.2d 30 (D.C. App. 1987).

52 A plaintiff may fail in his complaint either because a statutory or other legal standard prohibits the lawsuit, e.g., Willis v. Dade County Sch. Bd., 411 So.2d 545 (Fla. Dist. Ct. App. 1982) (sovereign immunity), or because there were insufficient allegations or presentation of facts to meet the legal standard, e.g., Charpentier v. St. Martin Parish Sch. Bd., 411 So.2d 717, 821 (La. Ct. App. 1982). ("In any event, plaintiffs failed to prove that defendant's allegedly negligent conduct even occurred. In fact, the evidence shows that it didn't. Having failed to prove this, plaintiffs are unable to prove that any conduct and/or omission of defendant was a cause-in fact of Gwen's injuries. Third, there is no need to proceed on to a determination of defendant's duty and whether that duty was breached.")

53 *See* Belkin v. Middle County Cent. Sch. Dist., 691 N.Y.S.2d 84 (N.Y. App. Div. 1999) (playground equipment built for children according to specifications, but on which an adult was injured, not dangerous); Fallon v. Indian Trail Sch., 500 N.E.2d 101 (Ill. App. Ct 1986) (trampoline not intrinsically dangerous so as to impose strict liability); Dibortolo v. Metropolitan Sch. Dist. of Washington Township, 440 N.E.2d 506 (Ind. Ct. App. 1982) (physical education class not inherently dangerous setting). Strict liability is normally imposed by courts or legislatures on activities which are inherently dangerous. Indiana Belt Harbor R.R. Co. v. American Cyanamid Co., 517 F. Supp. 314 (N.D. Ill. 1981) (shipping hazardous and toxic substance); Caparole v. C.W. Blakeslee & Sons, Inc., 175 A.2d 561 (Conn. 1961) (pile driving); Peet v. Dolese & Shepard Co., 190 N.E.2d 613 (Ill. App. Ct. 1963) (storage and use of explosives); Proud v. W.S. Bills & Sons, Inc., 255 N.E.2d 64 (Ill. App. Ct. 1970)(excavations). State Worker Compensation statutes are classic examples of a strict liability approach to providing a remedy for injured employees. Employee remedy does not hinge on the issue of fault but on statutory employment questions: Warthen v. Southeast Oklahoma State Univ., 641 P.2d 1125 (Okla. Ct. App. 1981) (causal connection between employment and injury); Lockwood v. Independent Sch. Dist. No. 877, 312 N.W.2d 924 (Minn. 1981) (inclusion of injury within the statute); Cameli v. Pace Univ., 516 N.Y.S.2d 228 (N.Y. App. Div. 1987) (control of employee as requirement for employment relationship); Graczyk v. W.C.A.B, 229 Cal.Rptr. 494 (Cal. Ct. App. 1986) (scholarship athlete not employee); Davis v. New York City Bd. of Educ., 445 N.Y.S.2d 626 (N.Y. App. Div. 1981); Board of Educ. of City of Chicago v. Chicago Teachers Union, Local No. 1, 427 N.E.2d 1199 (Ill. 1981) (amount of recovery).

liability standard, a court is more likely to stretch the requirements for negligence in order to permit recovery.[54]

Intentional torts require general intent to commit an act and include the common torts of assault and battery[55] and intentional infliction of emotional distress,[56] as well as the quasi-intentional tort of defamation.[57] Intent generally denotes that the actors desired to cause the consequences of their acts or that they believed the consequences were substantially certain to result from the acts, but mere knowledge and appreciation of risk, short of substantial certainty, is probably not equivalent to intent.[58]

---

54 *See* Cazasdor v. Greene Cent. Sch., 632 N.Y.S.2d 267 (N.Y. App. Div. 1995) (Despite facts in evidence that preservative in frogs had burned student's skin and was considered a "dangerous product," court held that facts supported damage recovery for negligence as foreseeable even though instructor had distributed eye protection and had washed frogs, and even though neither school nor supplier of preserved frogs were aware of any similar chemical burns such as those the plaintiff had experienced).

55 Black's Law Dictionary 147, 193 (4th ed. 1961) (assault is reasonable apprehension of a battery; battery is the unlawful touching of another). *See* Rodriguez v. Johnson, 504 N.Y.S.2d 379 (N.Y. Civ. Ct. 1986) (slapping by school bus matron); Gaspersohn v. Harnett County Bd. of Educ., 330 S.E.2d 489 (N.C. Ct. App. 1985) (spanking by school administrator with a paddle).

56 *Cf.* Kamp v. Board of Regents of Northwest Missouri State Univ., 644 S.W.2d 675 (Mo. Ct. App. 1982) (plaintiff's claim that university's refusal to recognize doctoral degree earned from newly accredited degree program at another institution failed to demonstrate that university's decision for purposes of emotional distress was "extreme or outrageous") *with* Ross v. St. Augustine College, 103 F.3d 338 (4th Cir. 1996) (court upheld $180,000 compen satory and punitive judgment for "A" student who received all "Fs" in her final semester after she testified on behalf of a faculty member in racial discrimination case that resulted in a $745,000 judgment against the college). However, the cause of action for intentional infliction of emotional distress is easier to state than to prove. *See* Russell v. Salve Regina College, 938 F.2d 315 (1st Cir. 1991) (even though student nurse had cause of action for breach of contract when college failed to honor weight loss contract, she had no intentional infliction of emotional distress claim regarding college's treatment of her obesity); Hammond v. Katy Indep. Sch. Dist., 821 S.W.2d 174 (Tex. Ct. App. 1991) (no action for intentional infliction of emotional distress because statements allegedly made by principal and school psychologist were not egregious and were made in scope of employment); Gmuer v. Garner, 426 So.2d 972 (Fla. Dist. Ct. App. 1983) (former community college employee had no cause of action for intentional infliction of emotional distress against president for sexually suggestive invitations because the claim was not recognized in Florida).

57 Black's Law Dictionary 505 (4th ed. 1951) (defamation includes common law torts of libel and slander). *See* Joseph v. Elam, 709 S.W.2d 517 (Mo. Ct. App. 1986) (judgment of $3,000 upheld by former Dean of Students against acting President in slander action where defendant untruthfully stated that plaintiff was an ex-convict).

58 *See* Gouger v. Hardtke, 482 N.W.2d 84, 89 (Wis. 1992) (the act of one student throwing a piece of soapstone in a classroom at another student, even with intent to hit the student, "is not so substantially certain to cause injury that a court may infer an intent to injure;" in this case, the presence or absence of "intent to injure" was critical as to whether plaintiffs had filed their complaint within the statute of limitations for intentional torts which was shorter than the statute for negligence); Pennsylvania Millers Mut. Ins. Co. v. Crews, 361 S.E.2d 657 (Ga.Ct. App. 1987) (school principal's testimony that when he spanked child he expected to cause pain, but not the physical injury resulting from the child twisting to avoid a second swat, was sufficient to make inapplicable insurance company's exclusion for intentional bodily injury intended by the insured).

By far, the most common tort theory is negligence that bases liability on standard of care derived from expectations of how persons should act in varying situations. Although common law negligence has a burden of proof less than intentional torts, some states have granted school personnel immunity from personal liability unless there is proof of wanton, reckless, or malicious conduct.[59] This statutory obligation, even though it increases the burden of producing evidence, does not affect a plaintiff's obligation to satisfy the four legal requirements of negligence, applicable to both public and nonpublic educational institutions: a legal duty; breach of the duty; proximate cause; and injury.

Negligence: Legal Duty

A legal duty is one "which the law requires to be done or forborne to a determinate person or the public at large."[60] Legal duties for schools are normally based on relationships[61] or on a statute.[62] The absence of a legal duty will be fatal to a plaintiff's negligence complaint. In *Hartman v. Bethany College*,[63] the college owed no duty to a seventeen-year-old student assaulted after meeting two males at an off-campus bar. "It would be

59 See, e.g., Ohio Rev. Code § 2744.03(A)(6).

60 Black's Law Dictionary 1039 (4th ed. 1961). Not all alleged injuries are remediable because courts will occasionally refuse to recognize a cause of action like educational malpractice where a student's educational deficiencies have been nondiagnosed or misdiagnosed or the student has been placed in the wrong setting. Houston v. Mile High Adventist Acad., 872 F. Supp. 829 (D. Colo. 1994) (cause of action for educational malpractice does not exist, whether framed as breach of contract, breach of fiduciary duty, fraud, or outrageous conduct); Sirohi v. Lee, 634 N.Y.S.2d 119 (N.Y. App. Div. 1995) (Columbia University not liable as a matter of law for quality of educational environment promised and for false representation because these claims were subterfuge for educational malpractice). *See also*, the more frequently cited and older cases, Peter W. v. San Francisco Unified Sch. Dist., 60 Cal.App.3d 814 (Ct. App. 1976); Smith v. Alameda County Social Service Agency, 90 Cal. App. 3d 929 (Ct. App. 1979); Paladino v. Adelphi Univ. 454 N.Y.S.2d 868 (N.Y. App. Div. 1982); Pietro v. St. Joseph's Sch., 48 U.S.L.W. 2229 (N.Y. Sup. Ct. 1979). However, *see* Savino v. Board of Educ. of Sch. Dist. No.1, 506 N.Y.S.2d 210 (N.Y. App. Div. 1986) (failure to warn parent of psychological problems of student did not constitute educational malpractice and therefore claim not dismissable).

61 Toure v. Board of Educ. of City of New York, 512 N.Y.S.2d 150 (N.Y. App. Div. 1987) (duty toward student the same as that owed by a reasonably prudent parent); Boltax v. Joy Day Camp, 493 N.Y.S.2d 590 (N.Y. App. Div. 1985) (no duty owed to trespasser injured in pool at night after climbing over fence). The relationship between a school and its students creates a duty to protect. *See* Davis v. Monroe County Bd. of Educ., 526 U.S. 629, 119 S. Ct. 1661 (1999) (in a Title IX liability case that follows duty to protect under negligence, a school district can be liable for peer harassment under a deliberate indifference test).

62 Rodriguez v. Inglewood Unified Sch. Dist., 230 Cal. Rptr. 823 (Ct. App. 1986) (duty to protect students flows from compulsory attendance statutes); Scott v. Independent Sch. Dist. No. 709, 256 N.W.2d 485 (Minn. 1977) (duty to protect student based on statute requiring wearing of goggles in certain courses).

63 778 F. Supp. 286 (N.D. W.Va. 1991).

inconsistent with the case law in this area to impose a duty upon colleges to supervise students when they leave the college campus for non-curricular activities. It would also not be consistent with the settled expectations of students, parents or colleges."[64] Likewise, in *Laiche v. Kohen*,[65] elementary school coaches and their schools owed no duty to a 110-pound eighth grader whose leg was fractured when fallen on during a scrimmage football game by another 270-pound eighth grader. The court was "unable to find a basis for imposing on coaches a duty to their players to protect against the risk of injury from playing a football game with players of different weights."[66] At least five legal duties have been recognized: utilization of competent and proficient personnel;[67] adequate supervision,[68] adequate instruction;[69]

---

64 *Id.* at 291. *See also*, Ruiz v. Life Skills Sch., Ltd., 700 N.Y.S.2d 456 (N.Y. App. Div. 1999) (no duty of care after child has passed into custody of parents).

65 621 So.2d 1162 (La. Ct. App. 1993).

66 *Id.* at 1165.

67 This duty has most recently been addressed in causes of action called negligent hiring, supervision or retention of an employee. Nance v. Mathews, 622 So.2d 297 (Ala. 1993) (principal, nurse and supervisor of special education entitled to qualified immunity as to supervision and retention of aide); Greening v. School Dist. of Mallard, 393 N.W.2d 51 (Neb. 1986) (use of unlicensed employee for physical therapy not proximate cause of injury); Willoughby v. Lehrbass, 388 N.W.2d 688 (Mich. Ct. App. 1986) (negligent hiring or supervision claim rejected because hiring and supervision covered by governmental immunity); Fallon v. Indian Trail Sch., 500 N.E.2d 101 (Ill. Ct. App. 1986) (failure to investigate teacher credentials and teaching abilities or permitting unqualified teachers to continue teaching is not negligent hiring unless the student injury arises from a particular unfitness of an applicant); Doe v. Durtschi, 716 P.2d 1238 (Idaho 1986) (cause of action for negligent continuation of teacher existed where school district continued to employ teacher after knowledge of sexual abuse of children). Older cases approached the negligence of personnel competency from the more traditional aspects of failure to adequately instruct or supervise. O'Brien v. Township High Sch. Dist., 392 N.E.2d 615 (Ill. App. Ct. 1979) (attempted treatment of athlete by a student); Garber v. Central High Sch. Dist., 251 N.Y.S.2d 214 (N.Y. App. Div. 1937) (janitor supervising noontime gym activities); Nickley v. Skemp, 239 N.W. 426 (Wis. 1930) (failure of unlicensed nurse interns to recognize symptoms).

68 Velez v. Our Lady of Victory Church, 486 N.Y.S.2d 302 (N.Y. App. Div. 1985) (no liability for lack of supervision for desk toppling over in classroom where no notice of such occurrences in past); Smith v. Archbishop of St. Louis, 632 S.W.2d 516 (Mo. Ct. App. 1982) (liability for lack of supervision where second grader's paper costume came in contact with lighted candle); Levine v. Live Oak Masonic Housing, Inc., 491 So.2d 489 (La. Ct. App. 1986) (no liability for school for lack of supervision following two deaths from defectively wired air conditioner when student had ignored warnings about splicing wires).

69 Potter v. North Carolina Sch. of the Arts, 245 S.E.2d 188 (N.C. 1978) (liability incurred for failure to instruct student on use of fog machine); County of Riverside v. Loma Linda Univ., 173 Cal. Rptr. 317 (Cal. Ct. App. 1981) (liability for inadequate instruction of medical residents); Lawrence v. Grant Parish Sch. Bd. 409 So.2d 1316 (La. Ct. App. 1982) (failure to instruct student of hazards of using table saw without guard prevented school's assumption of risk defense. *But see* Koch v. City of Avon Bd. of Educ., 580 N.E.2d 809 (Ohio Ct. App. 1989) (physical education teacher and high school not liable for injury to student while performing squat vaults over vaulting horse where entire class had received lecture on use of the equipment and the applicable safety precautions and instructor had demonstrated the vaults for the students).

furnishing and maintaining safe equipment and safe premises;[70] and making and enforcing adequate rules.[71]

Duty of care can also be created by a special relationship. In *Kleinknecht v. Gettysburg College*,[72] the fact that a student had been actively recruited to play lacrosse was sufficient to create a duty of care for the College to have athletic trainers at fall semester practice sessions. Following the student's death by cardiac arrest at one of these practices, the court observed that

> [t]here is a distinction between a student injured while participating as an intercollegiate athlete in a sport for which he was recruited and a student injured at a college while pursuing his private interests, scholastic, or otherwise.... Had [deceased student] been participating in a fraternity football game, for example, the College might not have owed him the same duty or perhaps any duty at all .... [T]he fact that [the student's] cardiac arrest occurred during an athletic event involving an intercollegiate team of which he was a member does impose a duty of care on a college that actively sought his participation in that sport. We cannot help but think that the College recruited [deceased] for its own benefit, probably thinking that his skill at

---

70 Dristy v. Waterford Sch. Dist., 379 N.W.2d 428 (Mich. Ct. App. 1985) (school responsible for sidewalks outside school); Singer v. Sch. Dist. of Philadelphia, 513 A.2d 1108 (Pa. Commw. Ct. 1986) (school liable for absence of mat around vaulting horse); Bush v. Oscada Area Schs., 250 N.W.2d 759 (Wis. 1977) (classroom unsafe for laboratory experiment); Knight v. City of Philadelphia, 445 A.2d 778 (Pa. Super. Ct. 1982) (unsafe equipment). The hiring or posting of security guards does not in itself create a special duty of protection. Corcoran v. Community Sch. Dist., 494 N.Y.S.2d 747 (App.Div. 1985); Ferrara v. Board of Educ., 498 N.Y.S.2d 10 (N.Y. App.Div. 1986). School liability would be based only on reliance by an employee regarding safety of premises. *See* Carloe A. v. City of New York, 532 N.Y.S.2d 163 (N. Y. App.Div. 1988) (rape of teacher required to stay late after principal's assurances that custodian patrolled building).

71 Gathright v. Lincoln Ins. Co., 688 S.W.2d 931 (Ark. 1985) (duty of rule making did not require detailed supervisory safety program); Matteucci v. High Sch. Dist. No. 208, 281 N.E.2d 383 (Ill. App. Ct. 1972) (failure to enforce rules); Lynch v. Board of Educ. of Collinsville, 390 N.E.2d 526 (Ill. App. Ct. 1979) (failure to make and enforce rules).

72 989 F.2d 1360 (3d Cir. 1993). Generally, courts have been reluctant to base liability on special relationships, except in cases such as *Kleinknecht* where a quasi-contractual element was present. For judicial reluctance to use special relationship in child abuse situations, see Mawdsley, *Compensation for the Sexually Abused Student*, 84 Ed. Law Rep. 13 (1993); Sorenson, *School District Liability For Federal Civil Rights Violations Under Section 1983*, 76 Ed. Law Rep. 313 (1992). *See also* DeShaney v. Winnebago County Dep't of Social Servs., 489 U.S. 189 (1989) (state's knowledge of danger to a child in father's custody did not create special relationship between state and child so as to create duty to protect child); Rasivong v. Lakewood Community College, 504 N.W.2d 778 (Minn. Ct. App. 1993) (college as landowner where ethnic festival held had no special relationship with bystander at festival and thus no duty to protect that person from a criminal assault by an unknown third party).

> lacrosse would bring favorable attention and so aid the College in attracting other students.[73]

Special relationship can be a significant element in a plaintiff's case, but that relationship requires, as *Kleinknecht* indicates, an individualized knowledge of the practices and needs of students (or employees). For example, in *Chakuroff v. Boyle*,[74] a school district was liable to a worker in a woodworking class who had suffered injury from excessive dust and who had come to the attention of the district's superintendent by requesting a ventilation system. However, a special relationship can be more general and apply to a class of persons of whom plaintiff is a member. In *Petrie v. Louisiana Tech University*,[75] the university owed a duty to a student to warn him about a foreseeable risk, in this case striking a light pole at the bottom of a hill that school officials knew students used for sledding and had used in the past, resulting in severe injury (paraplegia).

However, a legal duty based on a special relationship requires more than participation in a school function. In *Albano v. Colby College*,[76] a private college was not liable for severe injuries to an eighteen-year-old student member of the college's tennis team while in Puerto Rico over spring break. The student had been injured after disobeying the coach's instructions not to drink excessively or leave the resort area. The court found dispositive that the student was an adult for purposes of consuming alcohol in Puerto Rico (legal age was eighteen in Puerto whereas legal age in Maine where college is located was twenty-one) and the injury did not occur on college premises. "[T]he mere ability to control—assuming that the coach or Colby College had such an ability here—does not give rise to a legal duty....The fact that the coach directed the students for their own safety to stay on the hotel grounds at all times and not to drink liquor to excess did not create 'a relationship of dependence' that would give rise to a legal duty where none existed to start with...."[77]

---

[73] *Kleinknecht*, 989 F.2d at 1368.

[74] 667 A.2d 1256 (R.I. 1995).

[75] 655 So.2d 659 (La. Ct. App. 1995) (the appeals court, in reversing the trial court's summary judgment for the university on the grounds that the light pole was obvious, noted that, "Universities guide many aspects of student life by undertaking to provide food, housing, and a wide range of extracurricular activities.") *Id.* at 666.

[76] 822 F. Supp. 840 (D. Maine 1993).

[77] *Id.* at 842.

Negligence: Breach of Duty, Reasonable Person, Foreseeability

The second requirement is a breach of legal duty. The determination of a breach is measured by the reasonable person (a retrospective test) and foreseeability (a prospective test) tests. The actual teacher whose conduct is at issue is measured against the hypothetical reasonable person's characteristics of "intelligence, physical attributes, perception and memory, and special skills."[78] The average school official will be assumed to be of average intelligence[79] and the burden will be on an injured plaintiff to prove that any alleged mental unfitness caused the injury.[80] Of course, students will also be assumed to have the average intelligence of persons of their age and maturity. In a Maryland case of first impression, *Hammond v. Board of Education of Carroll County*,[81] a state court of appeals determined that a sixteen-year-old female seriously injured while playing in her first high school football scrimmage was not entitled to any special warning regarding possible physical injury in football because as a person "at least of average intelligence" the risk of injury in voluntary contact sports is "common knowledge."[82] In *Levine v. Live Oak Masonic Housing, Inc.*,[83] two vo-tech students (ages eighteen and thirty-seven) were considered by the court to be "mature young men" and thus solely liable for two deaths ($130,000 damages) which resulted from their failure to heed the instructor's warning concerning not splicing wires on an air conditioner, repaired by the students and installed in a building destroyed by a fire determined to be caused by the improper wiring. Similarly, a high school student severely burned during a science laboratory experiment could not recover against the instructor because even though the students were average or below average in intelligence ("not the brightest") their conduct did not "conform to that which would be expected of a similarly situated child of the same age and with

---

78 E. Connors, Educational Tort Liability and Malpractice 9 (1981).

79 *E.g.*, Green v. Orleans Parish Sch. Bd., 365 So.2d 834 (La. 1979) (teacher's "reasonable man" intelligence reinforced by expert witness testimony).

80 *Fallon*, 500 N.E.2d at 481-82 (mentally handicapped employee hired by school may have some degree of unfitness but the unfitness is not justiciable unless it results in harm).

81 639 A.2d 223 (Md. Ct. App. 1994).

82 *Id.* at 226.

83 491 So.2d 489 (La. Ct. App. 1986).

the same capacity, discretion, knowledge and experience in creating the initial fire."[84]

Like intelligence, physical attributes can apply to both teachers and students. When two large male students began fighting in her class, a female teacher was justified in leaving the room to seek help from the principal next door.[85] Likewise, a teacher's use of a wrestling hold to compel an unruly and struggling student to the school office was permissible physical contact under state law,[86] and a teacher could recover a $6,000 compensatory and $23,000 punitive damages award against a student who had viciously attacked him when he caught the student smoking outside the building.[87] However, unnecessary or excessive physical contact between a large school employee and a smaller student can result in damages for the student.[88]

Perception and memory require school personnel to use their senses of observation and knowledge of past experience to "be alert to conditions which may be dangerous to participants, such as rowdyism, defective premises, lack of use of protective devices or safety equipment, and the age-skill experience of the participants in relation to the assumption of risks."[89] Perception and memory are not intuitive and reflect knowledge and experience regarding students and the educational process. Liability can result in a wide variety of situations that demonstrate lack of knowledge and/or experience about student safety. Some common situations include: use of a student teacher as a substitute teacher;[90] necessity of supervisory personnel in school or at a school event;[91] adequacy or appropriateness of

---

84 Rixmann v. Somerset Pub. Schs., 266 N.W.2d 326 (Wis. 1978) ($33,400 judgement against teacher reversed leaving student-plaintiff with only remedy for damages against two student lab partners).

85 Kim v. State of Hawaii, 616 P.2d 1376 (Hawaii 1980).

86 Willoughby v. Lehrbass, 388 N.W.2d 688 (Mich. Ct. App. 1986).

87 Anello v. Savignac, 342 N.W.2d 440 (Wis. Ct. App. 1983).

88 Rodriquez v. Johnson, 504 N.Y.S.2d 379 (N.Y. Civ. Ct. 1986) (damages awarded for school bus matron's slap on face of child talking loudly and moving about in his seat even though the slap itself was not an excessive use of force); Thomas v. Bedford, 389 So.2d 405 (La. Ct. App. 1980) (teacher liable for bruises to student's neck after he was squeezed by teacher about two hours after student had shot rubber band in face of teacher).

89 H. Hudgins, Jr. & R. Vacca, Law and Education: Contemporary Issues and Court Decisions 86 (1985).

90 Brahatcek v. Millard Sch. Dist. No. 17, 372 N.W.2d 680 (Neb. 1979).

91 Cook v. School Dist. UH3J, 731 P.2d 443 (Or. Ct. App. 1987) (complaint dismissed for failure to state cause of action even though court found that invitation to students of two schools to attend a game was sufficient to establish relationship giving rise to duty on part of school districts to take precautions to protect plaintiff from reasonably foreseeable acts of third parties); Comuntzis v. Pinellas County Sch. Bd. 508 So.2d 750 (Fla. Dist. Ct. App. 1987) (school had duty to provide supervisory person in cafeteria).

equipment;[92] responsibility for intentional acts by nonstudents against students;[93] awareness of student conflicts;[94] deviations from curriculum guides;[95] changing the standard rules of a game;[96] school or community problems such as racial unrest;[97] supervision of retarded students;[98] and dangerous premises discoverable upon examination.[99]

Special skills refer not only to skills which a faculty member has and can reasonably be expected to communicate to students,[100] but also to special skills possessed by a student which absolve or mitigate a faculty member's duty to instruct or supervise.[101] Not all activities require special skills. Thus, student paralysis resulting from a student's arching his back during a thirty second physical education class wrestling drill did not generate liability because a student arches his back naturally without having to be taught.[102] However, the assembling or operation of equipment by students usually assumes that they must be instructed in order to acquire the requisite skills.[103]

In summary then, the hypothetical reasonable person standard is an objective attempt to determine whether, in retrospect, a reasonable person with identified duties (teacher, administrator, coach) working with clientele varying in age and

---

92 Ausmus v. Board of Educ. of Chicago, 508 N.E.2d 298 (Ill. App. Ct. 1987) (furnishing too heavy bat to third grader).

93 Fazzolari v. Portland Sch. Dist. No. 1J, 734 P.2d 1326 (Or. 1987) (issue for jury presented as to whether school official's supervisory duty included warning students about sexual assaults in the area and taking preventive steps like trimming bushes near doorway).

94 Gammon v. Edwardsville Community Unit Sch. Dist., No. 7, 403 N.E.2d 43 (Ill. App. Ct. 1980) (knowledge of acrimonious relationship creates duty to prevent confrontation).

95 Larson v. Indep. Sch. Dist. No. 314, 289 N.W.2d 112 (Minn. 1980) (altering requirements for physical education gymnastics class).

96 Sutphen v. Benthian, 397 A.2d 709 (N.J. 1979) (increasing number of students in floor hockey game).

97 Raleigh v. Indep. Sch. Dist. No. 625, 275 N.W.2d 572 (Minn. 1978) (increased supervision required on school district field trip to film on Martin Luther King, considering racial unrest in some schools).

98 Foster v. Houston General Ins. Co., 407 So.2d 759 (La. Ct. App. 1981) (retarded child's running across street against light was foreseeable).

99 Adoin v. Evangeline Parish Sch., 376 So.2d 372 (La. 1979).

100 Potter v. North Carolina Sch. of the Arts, 245 S.E.2d 188 (N.C. 1978) (operation of fog machine); Lawrence v. Grant Parish Sch. Bd., 409 So.2d 1316 (La. Ct. App. 1982) (operation of electric power saw).

101 Paulsen v. Unified Sch. Dist. No. 368, 717 P.2d 1051 (Kan. 1986) (student had experience in prior woodworking class using table saw); Miles v. School Dist. No. 138, 281 N.W.2d 396 (Neb. 1979) (prior experience with jointer).

102 Green v. Orleans Parish Sch. Bd., 365 So.2d 834 (La. 1979).

103 Miller v. Macalester College, 115 N.W.2d 666 (Minn. 1962) (no instruction on assembling scaffolding); Brittan v. State, 103 N.Y.S.2d 485 (N.Y. 1951) (inadequate instruction on operation of physical fitness testing equipment).

skill levels under a variety of circumstances (classroom, field trip, day camp, athletic event) would have acted the same way as the defendants at trial. But school personnel liability is measured not only, in retrospect, by how they should have satisfied their duties (reasonable person) but the extent to which, in prospective, they should have anticipated the effects of their actions (foreseeability).

Foreseeability is determined by "the age, relationship, and physical characteristics of the parties involved; the gravity and probability of danger presented; and the necessity and utility of the actor's conduct."[104] Foreseeability is an extremely fluid concept, and to what extent a person's injury is foreseeable is often related to such factors as whether: the school had prior notice of similar incidents;[105] the injury or damages were intentionally inflicted;[106] a school rule or state statute was specifically directed to the misconduct which produced the injury or damages;[107] or students were engaging in voluntary activity

---

104 W. Valente, Law in the Schools 433 (3d ed. 1994).

105 Peschke v. Carroll College, 929 P.2d 874 (Mont. 1996) (college not liable where priest escorted drunk person, with gun stuck in belt from chapel and person later shot two cafeteria workers); Doe v. Howell, 441 S.E.2d 767 (Ga. Ct. App. 1994) (no evidence of prior forced sexual acts); Adams v. Caddo Parish School Bd., 631 So.2d 70 (La. Ct. App. 1994) (eruption of fight between two students waiting to see administrator after being taken to office by teacher for fighting did not create liability for school personnel or school district where a fight in the administrative area had never occurred within memory of longtime school employees); Carr v. Indian Lake School Dist., 496 N.Y.S.2d 950 (N.Y. App. Div. 1985) (no liability for injury to student's eye from thrown snowball where school had no notice of prior snowball throwing on school property); Brown v. City of New York, 516 N.Y.S.2d 22 (N.Y. App. Div. 1987) (no liability for stabbing where school had no actual notice of vicious propensities of student). *Contra* Phyllis P. v. Superior Court, 228 Cal. Rptr. 776 (Cal. Ct. App. 1986) (school's knowledge of sexual molestation of eight-year-old girl by another student created duty to notify parent and failure to do so created liability for emotional distress after girl was later raped by same student); Charkuroff v. Boyle, 667 A.2d 1256 (D. R.I. 1995) (prior contact between school and employee in woodworking class created duty to create safe premises).

106 Gragg v. Wichita State Univ., 934 P.2d 121 (Kan. 1997) (shooting fireworks on university campus by third party not foreseeable and, therefore, corporate sponsors owed no duty to control criminal act of third party); District of Columbia v. Doe, 524 A.2d 30 (D.C. Cir. 1987) (school not liable for intervening criminal act of rape of student). *But see* Doe v. Durtschi, 716 P.2d 1238 (Idaho 1986) (intentional act of teacher sexually molesting fourth grade student not defense to school district where cause of action was negligent hiring and retention).

107 Wilson v. Darr, 553 N.W.2d 579 (Iowa 1996) (church not liable for sexual abuse of child because it operated adequate training program for reporting abuse); Chambers v. St. Mary's Sch., 697 N.E.2d 198 (Ohio 1998) (failure of school to keep steps clear of snow and ice as per state administrative rule not negligence per se); Kavanaugh v. Orleans Parish Sch. Bd., 487 So.2d 533 (La. Ct. App. 1986) (statutory duty to provide "reasonably safe" environment did not apply to armed robbery of teacher where robbery could not have been reasonably foreseen from unrepaired hole in fence through which robbers entered); Scott v. Independent Sch. Dist. No. 709, 256 N.W.2d 485 (Minn. 1977) (statute requiring wearing of goggles in shop classes created liability even though injured student repeatedly took off goggles, despite numerous warnings from teacher). *Cf.* Eisel v. Board of Educ. of Montgomery County, 597

outside the school program.[108] In *Kleinknecht*,[109] the Third Circuit Court of Appeals reversed summary judgment for a private college as to a lacrosse player recruited by the College who collapsed and died of cardiac arrest during a practice scrimmage while no trainers were available at the practice field. In its decision. the Third Circuit Court of Appeals noted that

> [t]he type of foreseeability that determines the duty of care, as opposed to proximate cause, is not dependent on the foreseeability of a specific event ....Though the specific risk that a person like [deceased student] would suffer a cardiac arrest may not be foreseeable, the [plaintiffs] produced ample evidence that a life-threatening injury occurring during participation in an athletic event like lacrosse was reasonably foreseeable.[110]

However, in order for conduct to be foreseeable, even if it does not have to be specific, it still must be the kind that reasonable persons would agree could occur. In *Roe v. Catholic Diocese of Memphis, Inc.*,[111] the Diocese was not liable for the sexual assault by one four-year-old student on another in the restroom. While the court observed that a "freakish" accident could be foreseeable, conduct, however "vile and reprehensible between two adults," was "even more shocking and appalling" between two four-year-olds and, therefore, was not foreseeable.

Normally, an injury is not foreseeable if caused by an intervening intentional act. However, some courts have created an exception where schools, with knowledge of a student's suicidal tendencies, have failed to notify parents. Whether school officials acquire this knowledge from student class journals[112]

A.2d 447 (Md. 1991) (although state's Youth Suicide Prevention School Programs Act did not create statutorily based cause of action against school counselor who failed to intervene in a potential suicide, the court did find compatible with the Act a common law duty of reasonable care for counselors to prevent suicides when they have evidence of suicidal intent).

108 Swanson v. Wabash College, 504 N.E.2d 327 (Ind. Ct. App. 1987) (no liability by college where students voluntarily participated in recreational baseball and knew there would be no professional coaching assistance or supervision, or any written guidelines for play); Rhea v. Grandview Sch. Dist. No. JT, 694 P.2d 666 (Wash. Ct. App. 1985) (no liability for alcohol related death at release-day party where faculty advisor and principal had mere knowledge alcohol might be consumed and no district employee or agent was involved in planning or was present at party).

109 989 F.2d 1360 (3d Cir. 1993).

110 *Id.* at 1369, 1370.

111 950 S.W.2d 27 (Tenn. Ct. App. 1996).

112 Brooks v. Logan, 903 P.2d 73 (Idaho 1995).

or from past suicide attempts at school,[113] courts may consider a student's self-inflicted injury as foreseeable and require those officials to act affirmatively to contact parents. As one court expressed the issue, "[t]he risk of a child's death substantially outweighs the burden of making a phone call."[114] Knowledge of facts about suicide is important. A state appeals court decision in Wisconsin has upheld summary judgment for a school district where a student committed suicide by means of self-immolation at home, after the school had failed to follow the district policy of phoning parents at home or work when a student was absent from school.[115] In this case, the father had dropped his son at school but the child failed to attend his classes. Even though the parents claimed that they did not know their son had received five failing grades, had been removed from the basketball team for those grades, and had been very upset and had cried at school, no school personnel was aware of the student's intent to commit suicide. Hence, the court held that the student's suicide constituted an intervening, superseding cause that broke the chain of causation rendering the school district not liable for the student's death.

With school violence becoming more common, courts are not likely to permit school districts to avoid liability solely on the grounds that injuries were caused by intentional acts of a third party. All educational institutions have a duty to provide a safe environment, and whether they breach that duty will depend on past incidents, procedures in place to address violence, and response by school officials to the violence at issue.[116]

Negligence: Proximate Cause

In addition to creating duty of care, foreseeability is very much a key element in tying the first two negligence factors, duty

---

113 Wye v. Polk County Sch. Bd., 129 F.3d 560 (11th Cir. 1997).

114 *Id.* at 574.

115 McMahon v. St. Croix Falls Sch. Dist., 596 N.W.2d 875 (Wis. Ct. App. 1999).

116 For a good discussion of the issues, *see* Peschke v. Carroll College, 929 P.2d 874 (Mont. 1996) (court upholds jury verdict for college where one employee was killed and another injured with a gun by a drunk non-student, even though a priest had noticed when he escorted the person from the college chapel shortly before the shooting that the person had a gun in his belt, where the college had no past incidents of serious violence and where the person had been seen on campus in the past). *See also*, Gragg v. Wichita State Univ., 934 P.2d 121 (Kan. 1997) (university not liable for shooting of spectator at fireworks show where, even though university was located in high crime area, there was no evidence that crime level had posed security problems in past shows and law enforcement had no knowledge that assailant intended to shoot someone).

and breach of duty, to the third, proximate cause. Proximate cause is the logical and sequential connection "closely related in time, space or order"[117] between duty and breach of duty on one hand and injury on the other. There are three basic requirements in establishing proximate cause: (1) the injury would not have occurred "but for" the breach; (2) the injury must be the natural and probable result of the breach; and (3) there is no efficient intervening cause.[118]

The absence of proximate cause frequently plays a key role in a finding of no liability. In *Maness v. City of New York*,[119] a school district was not responsible for the murder of a junior high student outside the school during lunch break where the student's mother failed to prove that there had been inadequate supervision, in light of the intervening act by the boy who shot the student and the absence of anticipation that altercation between the two boys would result in injury. In *Griffith v. City of New York*,[120] a school whose nurse had denied treatment to a fourteen year-old girl with asthma was not responsible for the girl's subsequent serious injuries after the girl went home from school and fell from her apartment window. The court reasoned that once the child arrived at home, she came under the control and protection of her mother. In *Pedersen v. Joliet Park District*,[121] a student participating in a basketball game could not recover for injuries suffered in a fall when he offered no evidence that the floor was slippery from dust or wax. In *Levandoski v. Jackson County School District*,[122] a school was not liable for the murder of a thirteen-year-old girl who had skipped out of school between classes even though a school procedure required reporting deviations from the circulated absence list, and one teacher had failed to do so in a timely manner. In an egregious set of facts, a high school teacher was not the cause of a student's injuries in the wreck of an automobile driven by another person shortly after the teacher had falsely told the student that he had failed an advanced electronics test. The teacher's rather improbable explanation for deliberately giving the wrong

[117] E. Connors, Educational Tort Liability and Malpractice at 8 (1981).
[118] Greening v. School Dist. of Millard, 393 N.W.2d 51, 53 (Neb. 1986).
[119] 607 N.Y.S.2d 325 (N.Y. App. Div. 1994).
[120] 507 N.Y.S.2d 446 (N.Y. App. Div. 1986).
[121] 483 N.E.2d 21 (Ill. App. Ct. 1985).
[122] 328 So.2d 339 (Miss. 1976). *See also* Chavez v. Tolleson Elementary Sch. Dist., 595 P.2d 1017 (Cal. 1979).

information to the student was that he "wanted [the student] to know what it felt like to fail."[123]

Proximate cause, as the vital connecting element between breach of duty and injury, is more likely to be found by courts where a duty is well-recognized (such as in a state statute) or the conduct by school officials appears unreasonably indifferent to possible injury. For example, in California a school district was liable for injuries suffered by a child who was hit by a car after leaving school early because a California statute imposed on school districts the duty to "supervise at all times the conduct of the children on school grounds."[124] In *Toeller v. Mutual Service Casualty Insurance Co.,*[125] a bus driver who had excluded a student from his bus without notifying the parents or school authorities was liable for injuries suffered by the eleven-year-old when he was struck by a truck as he was riding his bicycle to school the next day.

A court supported a finding of proximate cause when a school counselor, notified that a student had threatened to commit suicide, failed to notify the student's parents and the student did, in fact, shortly thereafter commit suicide.[126] The state had a Youth Suicide Prevention School Programs Act,[127] and the court observed that "Maryland tort law should not treat an adolescent's committing suicide as a superseding cause when the entire premise of the Act is that others, including the schools, have the potential to intervene effectively."[128]

A junior college was eighty percent liable for injury to a high school student who slipped and fell on a liquid on a shop's concrete floor where the college's custodians had used wax rather than a skid-resistant material. Instructions for the wax stated that it was not to be used on concrete, other students had slipped on the floor in the past, and skid-resistant materials were available.[129]

---

[123] Rogers v. Retrum, 825 P.2d 20, 21 (Ariz. Ct. App. 1991).

[124] Hoyem v. Manhattan Beach City Sch. Dist., 58 5 P.2d 851 (Cal. 1978). *But see* Rogers v. Retrum, 825 P.2d 20 (Ariz.Ct. App. 1991) (although citing *Hoyem* as valid precedent for school liability for off campus students, the Arizona court distinguished *Hoyem* by finding that a high school did not breach its duty of supervision to a student injured in an automobile driven by a fellow student when the students had left school during the school day; the school had a policy permitting students to leave and enter the school during the school day).

[125] 340 N.W.2d 923 (Wis. Ct. App. 1983).

[126] Eisel v. Board of Educ. of Montgomery County, 597 A.2d 447 (Md. 1991).

[127] Md. Ann. Code, art. 7, §§ 7-4A-01 through 7-4A-06.

[128] *Eisel*, 597 A.2d at 454.

[129] Williams v. Junior College Dist. of Southwest Mo., 906 S.W.2d 400 (Mo. Ct. App. 1995).

Finally, in a case that pressed foreseeability and proximate cause almost to the point of strict liability, a school district was liable for serious cosmetic damage to a student's finger as she attempted to retrieve her coat thrown by another student on top of a 6' 5$\frac{1}{2}$" locker. The court reasoned that a $\frac{1}{16}$" protrusion on top of the locker on which the student caught her finger, a strand of a mop which had become caught on the protrusion, complaints to the principal by the girl and her mother regarding the girl's coat being thrown on top of the locker, a school rule prohibiting the throwing of coats, and the location of the locker outside the principal's office all added up to a logical connection between failure to maintain a safe school and the student's injury.[130]

Negligence: Injury

The fourth legal requirement in negligence action is an injury.[131] An injury must be real rather than imagined,[132] and courts are generally reluctant to award damages where there is not some form of physical contact or injury.[133] In *Phillips v. Lincoln County School District*,[134] an Oregon appeals court upheld summary judgment for a school district and its teachers where they required a student to use her given name in class and refused to permit her to use her nickname, "Boo." The court noted that "[w]e fail to see how a reasonable juror could find that such conduct constitutes an extraordinary transgression of the bounds of socially tolerable conduct."[135]

However, injuries, when they are cognizable, do not need to be substantial in order for a plaintiff to recover. In *Thomas v. Bedford*,[136] a fourteen-year-old student who had earlier shot a

---

130 Kinglsey v. Indep. Sch. Dist., Hill City, 251 N.W.2d 634 (Minn. 1977).

131 At least one state, Illinois, protects the right to recover for wrongs, declaring in article I, § 12 of its constitution: "Every person shall find a certain remedy in the laws for all injuries and wrongs which he receives to his person, privacy, property or reputation. He shall obtain justice by law, freely, completely and promptly."

132 *See* Sandlin v. Johnson, 643 F.2d 1027 (4th Cir. 1981) (damages and injunctive relief denied to parents of four children, who were among 22 of 23 children not promoted to third grade on the basis of reading level, as being beyond court expertise); Elias v. Youngken, 493 A.2d 158 (R.I. 1985) (no defamation in referring to employee as "terminated" so as to support claim of emotional distress).

133 *See* Gmuer v. Garner, 426 So.2d 972 (Fla. Dist. Ct. App. 1983) (no cause of action for intentional infliction of emotional distress allegedly resulting from odious, sexually suggestive invitations where there had been no physical contact).

134 984 P.2d 947 (Or. Ct. App. 1999).

135 *Id.* at 951.

136 389 So.2d 405 (La. Ct. App. 1980).

rubber band in the teacher's face received $500 damages when the teacher later found the student and gave him a "severe shaking." The presence of minor contusions on the student's chest, arm, and back demonstrated to the court that the teacher's conduct was less than reasonable. In *Rodriguez v. Johnson*,[137] a slap on a student's face which left no visible marks but made the child apprehensive about going to school resulted in a $250 award to the child's mother. Mere embarrassment or humiliation alone such as might be alleged to occur when a student is isolated or made to stand or sit in a corner or is required to sing or recite in front of the class would not be compensable.[138] However, teacher conduct which is "outrageous" or "beyond all possible bounds of decency" could be the basis for intentional infliction of emotional distress.[139]

Defenses to Tort Liability

Consent/Assumption of Risk

Defenses to tort liability are a way of avoiding, or at least diminishing, liability. Two of the most common defenses to avoid all liability are consent and assumption of risk. The defense of consent is difficult to distinguish from assumption of risk and is probably best reserved for exculpatory language frequently found in releases, hold harmless agreements, and handbooks that were discussed under an earlier section, "Exculpatory Clauses." Under either consent or assumption of risk, the important concept is that an injured party has understood that certain behaviors could result in injury, and, notwithstanding that understanding, has continued with the pattern of behavior that resulted in injury. Technically, a person consents to (or assumes) a set of behaviors, which under the circumstances and risk level resulted in injury,

---

137 504 N.Y.S.2d 379 (N.Y. Civ. Ct. 1986).

138 *See* Jett v. Dallas Indep. Sch. Dist., 798 F.2d 748 (5th Cir. 1986), *aff'd in part* 491 U.S. 701 (1989) (humiliation or embarrassment stemming from transfer to a different position not significant enough to support claim for constructive discharge); Irving v. J.L. Marsh, Inc., 360 N.E.2d 983 (Ill. App. Ct. 1977) (humiliation not compensable).

139 *See* Russell v. Salve Regina College, 890 F.2d 484, 487, 488 (1st Cir. 1989) (court rejected obese student nurse's claim of intentional infliction of emotional distress based on college's using plaintiff to model hospital procedures incident to the care of obese patients, prolonged lectures and discussions about weight loss, and contract making continued participation in nursing program contingent on weight loss of two pounds per week; "the College's conduct may have been unprofessional, but we cannot say that it was so far removed from the bounds of civilization as not to comply with the test set forth in [Restatement of Torts (Second) of Torts] § 46 ["'extreme and outrageous conduct'"]).

rather than the injury itself because many persons might engage in the same behaviors, with the same risk level, without being injured.

Assumption of risk is an available defense where "none of the fault for injury rests with plaintiff, but where plaintiff assumes consequences of injury occurring through fault of defendant, third party, or fault of no one."[140] An important element of this defense is that a plaintiff must have known and appreciated the risk which resulted in injury.

Knowledge and understanding of a risk involved in an activity can be acquired in various ways. In some cases, the risk may be obvious as where a person runs into another player involved in a contact sport.[141] In other cases, understanding the risks may involve demonstrations, videos, and training camps, as are used for cheerleaders who participate in gymnastic stunts.[142]

Assumption of risk can function as a counterweight to the generally accepted duty of schools to maintain safe equipment and premises. In *Paone v. County of Suffolk*,[143] a person who chose to play basketball on a school's court and who was injured by stepping in a hole was precluded under assumption of risk from recovering damages. Where cracks and breaks in the surface of the court were clearly obvious, plaintiff was considered to have assumed the risk of stepping into a hole or depression.

The nature of a risk may affect the extent to which assumption of risk will be applicable. In *Struble v. Valley Forge Military Academy*,[144] a student, who had fired blanks from a toy cannon at Academy athletic events more than 200 times, recovered a $200,000 judgment against the school when his leg was severely injured by the flame from the gun's muzzle. Even though the student knew not to stand in front of the cannon when fired, he was not aware that an injury could occur when his leg was six inches to the side of the muzzle. The student's case was aided here because the Academy had not provided instruction in firing the cannon or supervision while the cannon was fired.

---

140 BLACK'S LAW DICTIONARY 157-58 (4th ed. 1961).

141 Sandler v. Half Hollow Hills W. High Sch., 672 N.Y.S.2d 120 (N.Y. App. Div. 1998) (girls' field hockey).

142 *See* Aaris v. Las Virgenes Unified Sch. Dist., 75 Cal. Rptr.2d 801 (Cal. Ct. App. 1998) (as a result of lectures, demonstration, and video, student had assumed the risk of injury suffered during a practice session, despite injured student's claim that she did not feel comfortable with the stunt and participated because of peer pressure).

143 674 N.Y.S.2d 761 (N.Y. App. Div. 1998).

144 665 A.2d 4 (Pa. Commw. Ct. 1995).

Some sets of facts simply do not warrant application of assumption of risk. In *Hoeffner v. The Citadel*,[145] a student who had experienced emotional difficulties and had thoughts of suicide reported these difficulties to the school physician. The physician continued to treat the student for unrelated medical problems despite noting ongoing depression and suicidal thoughts. Approximately four months after first going to the physician, the student hanged himself in his room. The parents filed suit for negligence in caring for their son and, following the trial court's instruction to the jury that the suicide could constitute evidence of assumption of risk, the jury returned verdict for the physician and the school. In reversing the verdict, the state supreme court observed that where a party has a duty to prevent a person from committing suicide,

> the very suicide which the defendant has a duty to prevent cannot constitute assumption of risk ... as a matter of law.... The defense of assumption of risk applies where the plaintiff assumes a risk of harm arising from the *defendant's* negligent or reckless conduct rather than his own. In the absence of express consent to assume the risk, the plaintiff's conduct can be said to imply assumption of risk where it is shown that he understood and appreciated a known danger created by the defendant, and then freely and voluntarily exposed himself to it. [In this case], it is clear that [the student's] act of suicide cannot establish that he assumed a risk of harm created by the defendant's negligence in caring for his mental health.[146]

Contributory/Comparative Negligence

A common defense to a negligence claim is contributory negligence, which is "an act or omission amounting to want of ordinary care on part of the complaining party, which occurring with defendant's negligence, is proximate cause of injury."[147] If the contributory negligence occurs in a state that recognizes comparative negligence, then some degree of negligence by the complaining party will serve to mitigate damages but will not

---

145 429 S.E.2d 190 (S.C. 1993).
146 *Id.* at 193 (emphasis in original).
147 BLACK'S LAW DICTIONARY 1185 (4th ed. 1961).

necessarily prevent recovery of damages. The measure of damages will be determined by deducting the percentage of the complaining party's negligence from the damages award.[148] In comparative negligence states, courts tend to carefully scrutinize apportionment of liability to school children.[149] However, in a non-comparative negligence state, any degree of negligence by the complaining party, no matter how small, will prevent recovery.[150] In states where contributory negligence is a complete bar to recovery, courts closely analyze the age of the child as well as other factors surrounding the injury. In *Sharpe v. Quality Education, Inc.*,[151] an appeals court reversed a summary judgment for defendant bus company and held that a nine-year-old student "was not contributorily negligent as a matter of law."[152] The result in *Sharpe* seemed to be aided by the facts of the case where the owner of a school bus failed to make necessary repairs even though the bus had a history of mechanical malfunctions, including stalling. The student was hit by a car while crossing a four lane highway to make a phone call for help.

Self-Defense and Restraint

There are few legal areas that appear to generate greater concern by citizens in general and educators in particular than the subject of self-defense. Certainly it is an area about which there is considerable confusion regarding what the law permits individuals to do in defending their own persons. School personnel are generally concerned about what measures they can take in defending themselves if assaulted by a student or what measures they can take in breaking up school fights. The dearth of reported cases regarding the use of self-defense in educational

---

[148] *E.g., see* Williams v. Junior College Dist. of Cent. Southwest Mo., 906 S.W.2d 400 (Mo. Ct. App. 1995) (college eighty percent liable for slippery substance on shop floor); Williams v. Cahill, 629 N.E.2d 1175 (Ill. App. Ct. 1994) (forty percent negligence of truck driver who hit bus turning around in highway placed at forty percent of $293,000 judgment); Lockett v. Board of Educ. for Sch. Dist. No. 189, 555 N.E.2d 1055 (Ill. App. Ct. 1990) (student forty percent negligent in lowering bus window below stop-line in violation of state rules and therefore $110,000 judgment reduced by $44,000).

[149] *E.g., see* Branch v. Stehr, 461 N.Y.S.2d 346 (App. Div. 1983) (new trial awarded where jury apportioned ninety percent fault to six-year-old child).

[150] *See* Arnold v. Hayslett, 655 S.W.2d 941 (Tenn. 1983) (in non-comparative negligence state, negligence of twelve-year-old student found to have been proximate or causative force in his own death and thus $40,000 award by trial court reversed).

[151] 296 S.E.2d 661 (N.C. Ct. App. 1982).

[152] *Id.* at 662.

settings indicates that either school personnel exercise admirable self-control or situations in which students are injured as a result of faculty self-defense do not result in student lawsuits against faculty members. The subject of self-defense raises three key questions regarding deadly force, retreat, and retaliation.

The term "deadly force" in self-defense does not necessarily mean that someone died but rather indicates power in action, regardless of whether an instrument was used or death occurred.[153] The amount of force that can be used in a school setting depends upon the age of the pupil, the nature of the attacker's action necessitating defense, and the action of the one attacked after the initial attack has ceased. The essential elements of self-defense are that a person does not provoke the difficulty and that there must be an impending peril without a convenient or reasonable means of escape.[154] The recommended policy of retreating from impending bodily harm before responding with deadly force may make sense in many social settings, but it is hardly applicable in a school setting where teachers and administrators have a legal duty to supervise students.[155] Some states, such as Minnesota, have codified the use of reasonable force to encourage the exercise of that duty:

> Reasonable force may be used upon or toward the person of another ... when used by a parent, guardian or teacher ... in the exercise of lawful authority to restrain or correct such child or pupil.[156]

In a violent age when students may be using weapons that are life-threatening, the general rule is that defensive force may be used commensurate with the force of the attacker.[157] In order to justify the use of force on the grounds of self-defense, it is not required to show that the use of force was necessary to protect

153 *Cf.* BLACK'S LAW DICTIONARY 773 (4th ed. 1961).

154 *See* McDonald v. Terebonne Parish Sch. Bd., 253 So.2d 558 (La. Ct. App. 1971) (smaller student who threw broom at larger pursuing student putting out the student's eye held to be reasonably acting in self-defense without using excessive violence). *Cf.* Hayes v. State, 142 So. 675, 677 (Ala. 1930).

155 Failure of a teacher to intervene to protect a student assaulted by another student can be the basis of a tort claim, Kim v. State of Hawaii, 616 P.2d 1376 (Hawaii 1980), as well as a school official's failure to anticipate confrontations between students, Collins v. Wilson, 331 So.2d 603 (La. 1976); Gammon v. Edwardsville Community. Unit Sch. Dist. No. 7, 403 N.E.2d 43 (Ill. App. Ct. 1980).

156 Minn. Stat. Ann. § 609.06.

157 *See* Dixon v. Winston, 417 So.2d 122 (La. Ct. App. 1982) (blow by male to female student's face causing blowout fracture of bone surrounding left eye was held reasonable where male reacted immediately to female quickly turning in her seat and striking him in side with a fork).

from imminent personal injury. It is sufficient if the necessity was real or apparent.[158] But the mere belief of the persons attacked is not sufficient to justify the use of force.[159]

In other than self-defense situations, the possible harm to students who are fighting, as well as to spectators, demands that a school official take some affirmative action in separating the students. In addition, teachers may find it necessary to remove students who are causing disturbances in class or to remove persons who are not students from the school setting.[160] This action may range from using a voice command toward the antagonists to using physical force toward one or both of the students.[161] It would be reasonable for school personnel to physically separate students by holding them or even physically pushing them apart, but there is no need for school officials to jeopardize their own physical safety or to wait until they are struck before responding with force.[162] However, it is not reasonable for a teacher to become an aggressor toward one of the fighting

---

158 *See* Landry v. Ascension Parish Sch. Bd., 415 So.2d 473 (La. Ct. App. 1982) (criminal conviction reversed for teacher who fled from student attempting to hit him with two-by-four piece of wood and who held a handgun at his side, pointed toward the ground, because the student was considered at all times to be the aggressor and the teacher was acting in self defense; in addition, teacher won civil suit to be reinstated to teaching position from which he had been terminated); Sims v. School Dist. No. 1, Multnomah, 508 P.2d 236 (Or. 1973) (jury verdict for teacher in civil case who sought to remove from classroom a disruptive student who physically resisted efforts to remove him from the room); Owens v. Commonwealth of Kent., 473 S.W.2d 827 (Ky. 1971) (criminal assault and battery conviction of teacher for using sneeze gun on students who had threatened her reversed and new trial ordered; "[w]hile we admit that the use of a weapon such as a 'sneeze gun' is unusual and not to be encouraged, nevertheless, in this instance, threats of bodily harm being claimed, it may be justified.")

159 Germolus v. Sausser, 85 N.W. 946 (Minn. 1901); Boston v. Muncy, 233 P.2d 300 (Okla. 1951). *See* Frank v. Orleans Parish Sch. Bd., 195 So.2d 451 (La. 1967) (court refused to accept self-defense claim of 6'2", 230 pound physical education teacher who squeezed and shook a 4'9", 101 pound boy breaking his arm). Generally, provocative words are not considered to warrant physical retaliation. *But see* Thomas v. Carter, 114 So.2d 736 (Miss. 1927) (provocative words justified physical defense).

160 Generally, teacher use of force to remove disruptive students has been upheld. *See Sims*, *supra* note 158; People *ex rel.* Hogan v. Newton, 56 N.Y.S.2d 779 (N.Y. Sup. Ct. 1945). *But see* Williams v. Cotton, 346 So.2d 1039 (Fla. Dist. Ct. App. 1977) (teacher found to have committed "negligent battery" for using excessive force in removing from classroom a sixteen year-old unruly and boisterous student disturbing other students).

161 Wallace v. Batavia Sch. Dist., 68 F.3d 1010 (7th Cir. 1995) (teacher and school district not liable for alleged injury to student's elbow where teacher twice had asked two students, screaming at each other in class, to stop screaming at each other and, when they refused to stop, teacher grabbed one student's elbow to push her toward the door).

162 Andreozzi v. Rubano 141 A.2d 639 (Conn. 1958) (teacher's striking student upheld where student, with clenched fists had blocked door); Willoughby v. Lehrbass, 388 N.W.2d 688 (Mich. Ct. App. 1986) (teacher justified in applying full nelson to compel struggling student to go to office); People *ex. rel.* Hogan v. Newton, 56 N.Y.S.2d 779 (N.Y. Sup. Ct. 1945) (teacher cleared of criminal charges of assault and battery resulting from scuffle when teacher sought to escort high school age boy using profanity off elementary school grounds).

students or toward a student who first assaults another and then retreats. Once belligerents are separated or an attacker is disarmed or otherwise neutralized, the reasonable justification for the use of physical force is gone. The existence of a discernible line between defense and aggression is a well-accepted rule.[163] Likewise, the longstanding common law rule that a person coming to the defense of another steps into the shoes of the person he is assisting is probably generally accepted.[164]

As long as school personnel address themselves to physically separating fighting students or to resisting student attackers with the least force necessary, there should be no legal liability for injuries to the students. Likewise there should be no reason why a student antagonist could not be held and conducted to the office if he refuses to go. It is preferable to restrain antagonists if they pose a possible threat to themselves or to others rather than release them too soon and risk serious injury.[165]

Field Trips

Field trips are legally troublesome for educators because normal school responsibilities are exacerbated by new ones, such as heightened supervision due to the nature of the place visited or potential problems attendant to transporting the students. Field trips involve four areas with potential legal implications: instructions, supervision, transportation, and emergencies.

Even though it is questionable whether an elementary or secondary school can exculpate its legal liability by using the standard field trip forms,[166] such forms could be altered to be made into information instruments. Field trip forms should focus on furnishing as much information as possible to the parent or guardian signing the form rather than using the form to hold the school harmless in cases of negligence. A good field trip form should contain the following kinds of detailed information:

---

163 *Germolus*, *supra* note 159. *See* Johnson v. Carthell, 631 S.W.2d 923 (Mo. Ct. App. 1982) (school bus driver who held one of two boys fighting on bus, but boy being held was struck in eye by the other, was liable for injury to boy whom he was holding).

164 *See* Minnesota v. Merdina, 25 Minn. 161 (1878). For a more recent case, *see* Johnson v. Carthell, 631 S.W.2d 923 (Mo. Ct. App. 1982) (school bus driver not entitled to governmental immunity [as was the school district] as result of holding one of students fighting on bus, thus permitting the other student to strike the student being held in the eye; complaint alleged that the student who struck the blow was the original aggressor in the altercation).

165 *See Willoughby*, *supra* note 162.

166 *See supra* notes 14-50 and accompanying text concerning exculpatory clauses.

I. Description of Field Trip
(identify place to be visited, method of transport, type and time of supervision, time and place of departure and return).

II. Objectives of Field Trip
(describe objectives and how they may relate to coursework in school: tour factory and observe automation, assembly line for history class; hike along river or in mountains or along seashore to observe flowers, erosion, birds, fish, soil for science class).

III. Necessary Provisions
(lunch, extra set of clothes, sturdy shoes, money).

IV. Instructions to be Given to Students by Parent and Teachers
1. the place to be visited (e.g., river, factory) is dangerous because (reason(s) supplied by school);
2. obey the teacher or leader;
3. stay in the group (if required);
4. any further instructions the teacher wishes to include.

V. By signing the form, I (parent or guardian) certify that I request and give my permission for ____________________ ______________ to go on this field trip. I have given the instructions required above, and I release the teacher, principal and school from all liability and waive any claims against them.

____

Parent Signature Date

The pivotal aspect of any field trip is undoubtedly the nature of supervision provided. Supervision includes not only the responsibility by adults on the trip toward the students, but the responsibility of the person in charge of the field trip to adequately instruct those adults doing the supervising. The number of adults to accompany students on a field trip is variable depending on the mental age of the students or other circumstances that would demand more adults. In *Foster v.*

Houston General Insurance Co.,[167] one adult teacher accompanying eleven retarded students from a school to a gymnasium three blocks away was considered inadequate when a student was struck by a car and killed while crossing a street. In *Foster*, two teachers were scheduled to accompany the students but one teacher was unable to leave because she was teaching a class, and so the other teacher was told to go on ahead. A total judgment of $65,000 for the student's death was directed against the two teachers only and not against the school district because of the teachers' failure to provide an adequate number of supervisory personnel. The *Foster* court did not indicate what constituted a satisfactory teacher-student ratio but did state that the students should have been interspersed among the teachers with at least one teacher available to stand in the street to be crossed and to halt traffic.

In *Raleigh v. Independent School District No. 625*,[168] the St. Paul, Minnesota school district sponsored the bussing of 1,200 high school students to a movie theater for the showing of the film "King" as part of Afro-American History week. The school district superintendent required a teacher-pupil ratio of 1:35. At the time of the field trip there had been racial tension at one of the St. Paul high schools. After the film, as students were departing the theater, a white student had her purse stolen and her arm slashed. The *Raleigh* court, in upholding a verdict against the school district, noted that the district is not liable for sudden, unanticipated misconduct of fellow students, but it is liable for sudden, foreseeable misconduct which probably would have been prevented had a teacher been present. School district liability was based upon the knowledge of racial tension plus lack of adequate supervision and organization at the theater.

Liability problems can also be encountered in field trip situations where special training should have been provided in anticipation of potential dangers. In the leading case involving field trips, *Cox v. Barnes*,[169] an eighteen-year-old high school senior drowned at a beach while on a one day senior outing. Prior

---

[167] 407 So.2d 759 (La. Ct. App. 1981).

[168] 275 N.W.2d 572 (Minn. 1978). The jury instruction on foreseeability was: "It is the duty of the school to use ordinary care and to protect its students from injury resulting from circumstances where such conduct would reasonably have been foreseen and could have been prevented by the use of ordinary care. There is no requirement of constant supervision of all the movements of all pupils at all times."

[169] 469 S.W.2d 61 (Ky. 1971).

to approving the field trip, the school principal told the seniors that swimming would be permitted only if they furnished their own lifeguard. They asked the physical education director, who was an excellent swimmer, to accompany them, which he did. The student drowned while attempting to swim toward a diving tank approximately forty yards from shore on which was attached a sign that read "Off Limits." The alleged acts of negligence by the two adults accompanying the field trip were as follows: permitting students to enter the water within one hour after lunch; violation of signs regarding swimming at one's risk; failure to check water conditions; permitting students to swim in cold water in street clothes; failure to have lifesaving equipment available; and failure to sit in the lifesaving stands. The court refused to find the teachers or school district liable, and unquestionably, the requirement by the principal that a lifeguard accompany the field trip was a deciding factor. In addition, the age of the students was a factor because an eighteen-year-old was considered old enough to read and obey signs. A similar result was reached in *Morrison v. Community Unit School District No. 1*[170] where a fifteen-year-old student drowned in a swimming pool. Courts appear willing to find that older students are more likely to appreciate risks associated with certain activities, and thus they require less direct supervision.[171] Where students on field trips are injured or killed by the intentional acts of another person, whether or not a student, appears to be immaterial; the courts seem to be willing to find school personnel and the schools not liable because of the intervening intentional cause.[172]

Whether the owners of the situs of the field are liable for injuries to students on field trips often depends upon whether the students are considered to be licensees or invitees. Usually school personnel request permission to visit a place, and thus students are considered to be licensees with the situs owner responsible only to warn or make safe dangerous conditions known to him.[173] However, if the students are present at a situs at the invitation of the owner, the duty of the owner is to warn or

---

170 358 N.E.2d 389 (Ill. App. Ct. 1976).

171 Moore v. Drummet, 478 S.W.2d 177 (Tex. Civ. App. 1972) (fifteen-year-old falling off horse); Arnold v. Hafling, 474 P.2d 638 (Colo. 1970) (high school student pushed by another student).

172 Mancha v. Field Museum of Natural History, 283 N.E.2d 899 (Ill. App. Ct. 1972); Sharp v. Fairbanks N. Star Borough, 569 P.2d 178 (Alas. 1971).

173 Hudgins & Vacca, Law and Education: Contemporary Issues and Court Decisions at 97; Connors, Educational Tort Liability and Malpractice at 56.

make safe dangerous conditions that he knows of or that he should have known of.[174] In an interesting set of facts even former students can be invitees when returning to their school. In *School Board of Palm Beach v. Anderson*,[175] a former student who was killed when he returned to get his records generated liability for the school. The presence of the student in the building for a legitimate function plus knowledge of racial disturbances in the school were sufficient notice to school officials to keep the premises safe. As a result of the licensee-invitee distinction it would be better for students to be invited to the situs of the field trip, but as a practical matter most field trips would never take place if schools waited for invitations. Thus the most effective supervisory strategy is proper instruction to those participating in the field trip regarding anticipated hazards and safety rules.[176]

The problem of transporting students on field trips is a never-ending source of concern to school officials. While school buses or common carriers would be preferable, such means of transportation are not always available, practical, or financially feasible. Where students provide their own transportation in private cars, the concern for the school is whether the drivers will be considered to be agents of the school. The creation of an agency will depend upon a number of variables: whether a private car was used with the permission and for the convenience of the school; whether such use was a standard school practice; whether the function for which the car was used was a sanctioned school activity; and whether the school reimbursed the driver for expenses.

In *Caston v. Buckeye Union Insurance Co.*,[177] an injured student was able to satisfy the bulk of his $314,650 judgment against the school's insurer because the private car in which the student was injured was considered to be a "hired automobile."

---

174 In Nunez v. Isidore Newman High Sch., 306 So.2d 475 (La. App. Ct. 1975) the invitee standard is stated: "An owner or occupier of lands or buildings must take reasonable and ordinary care to protect invitees from any dangerous conditions on the premises and inspect the premises for any possible dangerous conditions of which he does not know."

175 411 So.2d 940 (Fla. Dist. Ct. App. 1982).

176 Obviously safety rules need to take into consideration the nature of the hazards plus the age of the students. As the mental age decreases mere verbal instructions for a first-time trip without adequate supervisory personnel may not be enough. *Cf.* Foster v. Houston Gen. Ins. Co., 407 So.2d 759 (La. Ct. App. 1981) (verbal warning to mentally handicapped walking three blocks to gym for first time not adequate) *with* Patterson v. Orleans Parish Sch. Bd., 461 So.2d 386 (La. Ct. App. 1984) (verbal warning about keeping fingers out of door plus orderly procedure in taking students to bathroom was adequate for first grader).

177 456 N.E.2d 1270 (Ohio Ct. App. 1982).

Two factors appeared to satisfy the court that the private car driven by the student was a "hired automobile." First, the car was being used as a substitute vehicle for school buses which were not available for the field trip. Second, the school official had made a request for volunteer drivers. But the mere fact that students use their own cars to get to school-sponsored activities should not in itself create an agency relationship for the school.[178] However, if school transportation is provided by the school and an exception is made for one student, the result can be different.[179] Even an unauthorized use of a car for a field trip can create school liability if it can be shown that the school had knowledge of the unauthorized use.[180] Because of the likelihood that high school students would prefer driving their cars to off-school activities, a school should warn all drivers regarding the importance of having adequate liability insurance and of ascertaining whether there are any policy limitations on liability coverage. As often as possible schools should provide transportation and make the use of that transportation mandatory.

The legal status of student use of private automobiles for field trips might arguably be similar to use of student cars to travel from one campus to another or from the campus to a work site. In *Richards v. Hambright*,[181] a South Carolina vocational center adopted a driving/riding policy which required parental permission before students would be permitted to drive or ride in cars from the high school to the vocational center rather than use the school district's bus. Even though school district officials had failed to check parental permission passes the week that a student was injured in an automobile accident, the state supreme court upheld dismissal of the injured student's suit against the school district. Failure to check passes did not rise to the level of gross negligence so as to waive governmental immunity.

However, *Richards* raises the question of whether the absence of a school driving policy might in itself be a basis for liability. A Pennsylvania court in *Capuzzi v. Heller*[182] suggested

---

178 *See* Bradshaw v. Rawlings, 612 F.2d 135 (3d Cir. 1979); Rauls v. Dugas, 398 So.2d 630 (La. 1981) (students driving own cars on function related to school did not generate liability). *See also Foster*, *supra* note 176 (although teachers liable for lack of supervision, refusal of school to provide bus transportation did not make school liable).

179 Williamson v. Board of Educ. of Berne-Knox, 375 N.Y.S.2d 221 (N.Y. 1975).

180 Sumter County v. Pritchett, 186 S.E.2d 798 (S.C. 1971).

181 374 S.E.2d 296 (S.C. 1988).

182 558 A.2d 596 (Pa. Commw. Ct. 1989).

that absence of such a policy will not prevent a favorable school district judgment. In *Capuzzi,* students injured as a result of two vo-tech uninsured students racing in their cars between the high school and the vo-tech school alleged school district governmental waiver under "negligent entrustment" or "employee" theories.[183] In denying recovery, the school district found that the power of the school district to refuse students the ability to drive cars did not equate to negligently entrusting the students' own cars to themselves, and the lack of any control by the school district over student operation of their cars obviates any employment relationship. Because of the governmental immunity component, neither the *Richards* nor *Capuzzi* cases is directly applicable to nonpublic schools. But at least *Richards* seems to indicate that a school policy requiring a parental release before an automobile is used to transport students may be in the school's best interest. Such a policy may mean that the parent's insurer could become the primary insurer in the event of an accident, and parents who sign the permission forms could not sue and recover damages in their own names.

One of the options schools are increasingly considering for field trips is the leasing or rental of cars or vans. Such an option is not without legal problems. In *Whittington v. Sowela Technical Institute,*[184] a plaintiff recovered a judgement in excess of $300,000 on behalf of himself and his minor son for the death of his wife, a student at the institute, against defendant school and its insurer when insurance coverage in the rental company contract was limited to $10,000. The field trip on which the student was killed was mandatory for all students, the students received academic credit, and the van was driven by two accompanying instructors. The court predicated liability on the school's failure of its "duty ... to provide a driver qualified and trained in transporting a large group of students over a long distance on a heavily traveled interstate highway."[185] *Whittington* is a troublesome case because two of the most common reasons for using rental cars and vans are to eliminate the high cost of professional licensed drivers and to pass on the insurance risk to the renter's insurer.

---

183 *See* Pa. Stat. Ann. tit. 42 § 8501 et seq.
184 438 So.2d 236 (La. Ct. App. 1983).
185 *Id.* at 247.

Whittington is a helpful precedent to dispel the notion that schools can eliminate liability for field trips by classifying them as "joint ventures." In this case, the school district had argued that it should not be liable because the district and the students were engaged in a joint venture. However, the court dispensed with the argument by declaring that the facts of this case did not fit the definition of a joint venture.

> A joint venture is an undertaking by two or more persons to combine their property, capital, labor or skill in any combination of these elements in the conduct of a particular line of trade of general business for joint profits, thus creating the status of a partnership, although the facts do not show a formal partnership.[186]

How schools should prepare for and handle emergencies on field trips is a subject that does not get much attention. A frequent question is what to do with the flagrantly disobedient or unruly student on a field trip. The problem is obviously exacerbated if the trip is for several days. Sending a student home should be done only as an absolute last resort and then only if the parent has consented in writing in advance to pay for the cost of such a return, if a common carrier is used, and if the parent is contacted prior to placing the student on the common carrier. The risks associated with such a problem area have unquestionably contributed to many schools prohibiting field trips that last for longer than one day. Obviously, some emergencies can be anticipated and planned for. It could well be negligent for school personnel to not take a first aid kit on a field trip, especially if the trip is to a place removed from hospitals or fire departments. First aid equipment and accompanying trained personnel need to be taken on a field trip commensurate with the nature of the trip. It probably would be negligent for school personnel not to have a trained lifeguard at a swimming activity, a snake-bite kit on a hike to a rocky or marshy area, or a stretcher, splints, and an accomplished guide on a hike through mountainous terrain.

Medical Needs

A school's responsibility to meet the medical needs of students has been a persistent problem area. The problem has been heightened by the Individuals with Disabilities Education Act

---

186 *Id.* at 246.

(IDEA)[187] which requires certain health related services be performed by public school districts "to assist a handicapped child to benefit from special education."[188] Such health related services, which must be furnished or paid for by public schools, have been found to include psychotherapy,[189] clean intermittent catheterization (CIC),[190] maintenance of a tracheotomy tube,[191] and a climate controlled classroom.[192] The nature of services required under IDEA raises questions about the appropriate tort liability[193] standard as well as the unauthorized practice of medicine.[194]

Basically, school officials are expected to act as reasonable and prudent persons and to contact medical help when they learn that a student needs attention.[195] The obligations can be extended to notify a child's parents of medical problems needing treatment.[196] Unless specifically trained to do so, school officials are not expected to go beyond administering lifesaving first aid,[197] but they will be liable for excessive treatment.[198]

---

187 20 U.S.C. § 1401 et seq.

188 20 U.S.C. § 1401.

189 Max M. v. Illinois State Bd. of Educ., 629 F. Supp. 1504 (N.D. Ill. 1986).

190 Irving Indep. Sch. Dist. v. Tatro, 468 U.S. 883 (1984).

191 Cedar Rapids Community Sch. Dist. v. Garret, 526 U.S. 66, 119 S.Ct. 992 (1999). *See also*, Dep't of Educ., State of Hawaii v. Katherine D., 727 F.2d 809 (9th Cir. 1984).

192 Espino v. Besteiro, 520 F. Supp. 905 (S.D. Tex. 1981).

193 *See* Greening v. School Dist. of Mallard, 393 N.W.2d 51 (Neb. 1986) (negligence claim denied for lack of proximate cause even though EHA [IDEA] services [physical therapy] were performed by an unlicensed employee). *But see*, Orr v. Brigham Young Univ., 960 F. Supp. 1522 (D. Utah 1994) (injured former student entitled to go to trial as to whether the university trainer breached medical standard of care in diagnosing and providing treatment for injuries).

194 *See* People v. Shokunbi, 232 N.E.2d 226 (Ill. App. Ct. 1967) (person who claimed to be a metaphysician not involved in practicing medicine without a license where his claims of treatment and cures not directed toward the public).

195 Mogabgab v. Orleans Parish Sch. Bd., 239 So.2d 456 (La. Ct. App. 1970) (delay by coaches in calling a doctor created liability); Peck v. Board of Educ. of City of Mt. Vernon, 317 N.Y.S.2d 919 (N.Y. 1970) (refusal to excuse heat stroke victim from practice created liability). *See also*, Kleinknecht v. Gettysburg College, 989 F.2d 1360 (3d Cir. 1993) (college liable for failure to have trainer at fall semester lacrosse practice even though lacrosse is spring competition sport).

196 Wye v. Polk County Sch. Bd., 129 F.3d 560 (11th Cir. 1997) (parent had negligence claim where school officials failed to call parent after student had twice attempted suicide at school, and later committed suicide at home); Savino v. Board of Educ. of Sch. Dist. No. 1, 506 N.Y.S.2d 210 (App. Div. 1986) (parent had cause of action for negligence where school district with knowledge that child's psychological problems would worsen if left untreated, failed or refused to notify parent).

197 *See* Federico v. Order of St. Benedict in Rhode Island, 64 F.3d 1 (1st Cir. 1995) (claim of parents of student who died of asthma at boarding school that school nurse should have administered the drug, epinephrine, was rejected by court because Rhode Island statute governing nursing standards permitted this drug to be administered by a nurse only at the direction of a physician, which was not available here).

198 Welch v. Dumsmuir Joint Union High Sch. Dist., 326 P.2d 663 (Cal. 1958) (coach allowed a student to move an injured player off the field, thus aggravating the injury).

Concern about proliferation of drug use on campus has prompted many schools to require student prescription medications be kept in the office and to prohibit distribution of such medications. Where a school has determined that medications cannot be carried at school by students or where certain medications need to be kept in a controlled temperature environment, schools need an established policy for storing and/or administering these medications. There are several excellent forms for schools titled "Medication Administration at School," "Physician Statement of Need," and "Request for Medication Administration."[199] It has been recommended that these forms be submitted on an annual basis and that medications be stored in a locked area.[200]

One option that may not be available to nonpublic schools is prohibiting all student medications. In *Alvarez v. Fountainhead, Inc.*,[201] a federal district court issued an injunction prohibiting the private Montessori school from enforcing its "no medications" policy in refusing admission to a student because he would need to bring a handheld asthma inhaler to school. The court found the refusal to permit the student to bring his medication to school a violation of Title III of ADA. In addition to requiring admission of the student, the court ordered school personnel to undergo training in use of asthma inhalers. To prevent other students from having access to the inhaler, the school would keep it in a locked cabinet. Although plaintiffs' expert witnesses testified that the training was only one hour in length, the court included in its order a release and waiver by the parents that school staff would not be liable in administering the asthma inhaler, as long as they exercised reasonable care. At the present time, since religous schools are exempt from Title III of ADA, the result in *Alvarez* would apply only to nonsectarian private schools.

Although not at issue in *Alvarez*, the case introduces the larger question of school responsibility for supervising, monitoring, and administering medications kept in the school's office, especially if the school prohibits students from carrying their own medications. Should a school be responsible for monitoring the dosage for assuring timeliness of administration

199 Mary Jane Rapport, *Suggested Guidelines for Dispensing and Controlling Student Medications*, Legal Legislative Update, 8, No.4, 40-42 (ACSI Spring 1998).

200 *Id.* at 38.

201 55 F. Supp.2d 1048 (N.D. Cal. 1999).

of medications where the students cannot carry the medications with them because of a school rule? Although there appear to be no cases in this area, one can argue that school control over storing and administering medications creates some measure of duty to see that these medications are dispensed. Parental permission to administer medications should not necessarily be translated into immunity from liability for failing to notify students who have not appeared at the office for their medications. Even parent waiver of liability on a parental form regarding a school's failure to notify students may not eliminate the students' cause of action.

The administration of medicines or medical procedures are governed by state laws regarding the practice of nursing/ medicine.[202] The problem in schools is that students with disabilities may need medicines administered or medical procedures performed, and medically trained personnel may not be available.[203] To what extent can medicines or medical procedures be performed by school personnel who have not been medically trained?[204]

The extent to which non-medically trained school personnel can perform nursing/medical functions for special education students is largely inferential. Federal courts have declared that certain medical procedures do not constitute "medical services" under IDEA,[205] which means that public schools are responsible for providing them. The U.S. Supreme Court, in *Tatro v. State of Texas,*[206] upheld the provision of CIC by non-medically licensed personnel, in part because a state attorney general opinion had

---

202 *E.g. see* Va. Code Ann. § 54.1-2902.

203 *E.g. see* Va. Code Ann., § 54.1-2901 (certain medical procedures can be handled only be a nurse under a physician's direction). *See also*, Federico v. Order of St. Benedict in Rhode Island, 64 F.3d 1 (1st Cir. 1995) (asthma drug could not have been administered by school nurse except under direction of physician).

204 For a collaborative effort to define medical/nursing functions, see GUIDELINES FOR THE DELINEATION OF ROLES AND RESPONSIBILITIES FOR THE SAFE DELIVERY OF SPECIALIZED HEALTH CARE IN THE EDUCATIONAL SETTING (Council for Exceptional Children 1990). This publication is the joint product of a number of national education, nursing, and special education organizations and characterizes specific special education services in terms of who can provide them: "Physician Order Required"; "Registered Nurse"; "Licensed Practical Nurse"; "Certified Teaching Personnel"; "Related Services Personnel"; "Paraprofessionals." Of course, nothing in the publication should be interpreted as supplanting a state's definition of its own medical nursing practice statutes.

205 The IDEA does not require school districts to provide "medical services" (those provided "by a licensed physician") to students with disabilities, but does require physician services as a related service "for diagnostic or evaluative purposes." 34 C.F.R. §§300.25(a) and (b)(4).

206 468 U.S. 883 (1984).

interpreted the state's Medical Practice Act as permitting services such as CIC to be performed by persons acting under a physician's supervision, which had been interpreted to include school employees. In *Department of Education, State of Hawaii v. Katherine D.*,[207] the Ninth Circuit Court of Appeals held that a school district's providing a lay person to suction a tracheostomy tube was not a medical service under IDEA because parents had been trained to provide the service at home, and presumably, school personnel could be trained to provide the service at school.

A determination that services must be provided under IDEA leaves unanswered the question as to who must provide those services, a question that is very much tied to the law of each state. For example, where a state statute describes the practice of nursing as "administering medications, treatments, and executing regimens prescribed by licensed physicians, dentists, and podiatrists,"[208] the administration of even such services as CIC by persons who are not nurses could be considered the unauthorized practice of nursing.[209] If nursing practice is extended to include all acts "requiring substantial judgment and specialized skills,"[210] then a broad range of services required under IDEA, such as CIC[211] or suctioning a tracheostomy tube, might be considered to be the practice of nursing.[212]

The U.S. Supreme Court's decision in *Cedar Rapids Community School District v. Garret F.*[213] that full-time, one-on-one nursing services for a student in a public school is permitted under IDEA as a "related service" raises difficult issues of nurse availability and cost. Whether federal courts will invoke

---

[207] 531 F. Supp. 517 (D.Hawaii 1982), aff'd 727 F.2d 809 (9th Cir. 1984).

[208] Ohio Rev. Code Ann. § 4723.02(B)

[209] In Ohio, the penalty for unauthorized practice of nursing is a fine of $500 or imprisonment of not more than ninety days. Ohio Rev. Code Ann. § 4723.99. The only exception permitted on a trial basis was "the transfer of responsibility for the performance of a selected nursing activity or task from a licensed nurse to a trained unlicensed person working under nursing supervision in a selected situation [in a Mental Retardation/Developmentally Disabled county board facility]." Ohio Admin. Code § 4723-21-01(B).

[210] Ohio Board of Nursing, *Statement on Selected Activities of Nursing Assessment*, Prac-1006, Jan. 21, 1983.

[211] *See* Ohio Board of Nursing, *Statement on Catheter Maintenance*, Prac-1011, June 6, 1986 ("The procedures [regarding the maintenance of catheters] should only be performed by nurses who are specially trained").

[212] *See* Ohio Board of Nursing, *Statement on Protocols, Standing Orders and Preprinted Orders*, Prac-1007, April 24, 1986 (standing orders, which include life threatening as well as non-life threatening situations, are appropriate for nurses to implement).

[213] 119 S.Ct. 992 (1999).

the preemption doctrine[214] to prevent states from enforcing unlawful practice of nursing/medicine statutes, where unavailability of nurses requires use of non-medically trained teachers/administrators/aides, remains to be seen. Assuming that certain services must be provided by a nurse, the expense of a full-time nurse would be more than a teacher's aide. Even though cost can be a factor in providing services,[215] courts are not likely to permit school districts to save the expense of hiring a nurse, especially where the alternative would be offering education to the student in a location other than the regular classroom.

If non-medically licensed personnel provide nursing/medical-type services in schools, will the standard of care be measured by a ordinary, reasonable person standard or by a medical standard? In *Butler v. Louisiana Board of Education*,[216] a state appeals court held that a university biology instructor, who had taken blood samples from students for blood type analysis, could be tried under a medical standard of care. In this case, the instructor permitted students to take blood samples from each other while they were sitting on a stool. After her blood sample had been extracted, plaintiff fell forward off the stool breaking six teeth. The court observed that a college instructor who

> approves and undertakes to supervise a project which includes the performance of a medical function such as the withdrawal of blood from volunteer students . . . owes a duty to the volunteer patient or blood donor to see that the same precautions are taken for the safety and well-being of that patient as would be taken by licensed medical doctors in that locality.[217]

All schools would be advised to have only properly licensed personnel perform medical procedures, or, in the case of certain simple class experiments such as taking blood samples, ascertain the standard local safety procedures from a local medical doctor prior to the experiment.[218]

---

214 The preemption doctrine is based on the conflicts-of-law principle that state law contradicting, or interfering with the enforcement of, federal law is invalid under the supremacy clause. U.S. Const. Art. VI Sec. 2 ("This Constitution, and the laws of the United States which shall be made in pursuance thereof ... shall be the supreme law of the land....")

215 *See* Sacramento City Unified Sch. Dist. v. Rachel H., 14 F.3d 1398 (9th Cir. 1994).

216 331 So.2d 192 (La. Ct. App. 1976).

217 *Id* at 202.

218 For an example of another case where a court held that an injured football player had a cause

A final medication problem that has been a frequent source of concern among school officials has been the dispensing of over-the-counter medications, such as aspirin or antacids, by personnel in the school office.[219] Nonpublic schools have responded in one of three ways to this problem area: absolute prohibition of dispensing of any over-the-counter medications by the school; dispensing over-the-counter medications in reasonable amounts to any student who requests them; and dispensing such medications to a student only if the school has written or oral parental permission. The absence of any reported cases in this area probably reflects the low risks involved with dispensing over-the-counter medications. Nonetheless, the low risk of liability from unverified dispensing of such medications needs to be balanced against unnecessary student discomfiture because the school adamantly refuses to give him two aspirins.[220] There seems to be little reason why such medications should not be made available to students, provided that the school has first received parental permission orally or in writing.[221] A simple phone call to a parent or guardian plus a notation in a school log book, should the student desire the same medication in the future, would seem to be an adequate compromise.

On balance, nonpublic schools that do not allow students to carry their own medications would still do well to have parents sign a release excusing the school from any responsibility for administering and monitoring dosages. However, even if such a narrowly drawn advance release were to be an enforceable exculpatory clause,[222] schools may want to consider whether they have sufficient staff to administer medications and whether the

---

of action for negligence based on a medical standard of care, see Orr v. Brigham Young Univ., 960 F. Supp. 1522 (D. Utah 1994).

[219] This discussion of over-the-counter medications assumes that there is no emergency situation, in which case use of such medications, e.g., ointments and disinfectants, would probably be required under a "reasonable person" standard. *See* Mogabgab v. Orleans Parish Sch. Bd., 239 So.2d 456 (La. Ct. App. 1970).

[220] *See* S. THOMAS, HEALTH RELATED ISSUES IN EDUCATION 34 (NOLPE 1987) (author's assertion that even over-the-counter medications need written parent [and possibly physician] authorization is correct, even though author's citations referring to parental consent for surgical operations and physician incorrectly giving a prescription drug do not support that conclusion).

[221] For an excellent parental permission form to use for administration of any medications at school, see Mary Jane Rapport, *Suggested Guidelines for Dispensing and Controlling Student Medications at Your School*, LEGAL LEGISLATIVE UPDATE , 8, No. 4, p. 42 (ACSI, Spring 1998).

[222] A nonpublic school would have to decide what to do if parents insisted that their student be allowed to carry his own medications and refused to sign the release. It hardly seems worth losing a student when that prospect is weighed against the ambiguous appearance of illicit drug-taking.

possible increased risk of liability for the school is worth the rule directing medications be kept in the office.[223]

Some public schools, which operate under a "zero tolerance"[224] policy for drug abuse, may permit students to carry their own medications (prescription or nonprescription) but then punish any student who distributes any of the medications to other students. Inflexible application has created a furor and demonstrates a regressive approach to discipline by overlooking basic fairness.[225] One can question the merits of a zero tolerance policy that suspends a student for giving a pain relief tablet to another student, when the same act outside school would be viewed as an act of kindness. At the very least, officials in nonpublic schools have the opportunity to treat students as individuals and not confuse acts of kindness with illegal acts.

Defamation

Defamation, the modern-day combination of common law libel (written comments) and slander (oral statements), has become generally recognized because of the difficulty in a technology age of distinguishing between the two. Written comments were generally considered more serious at common law because of their permanency,[226] but so much of what appears in the media today as oral statements by persons being interviewed has already been recorded on tape and is broadcast from that tape, or is being recorded as the statements are being made and will be stored on tape. With general school access to the Internet and its services, as well as the ease with which persons can create their own Web pages, the tort of defamation seems better suited to the technological reality of our schools.

Defamation concerns statements of fact, as opposed to pure opinion, that disparage a person's reputation. Schools, like any

---

223 *See* Bertens v. Stewart, 453 So.2d 92 (Fla. Dist. Ct. App. 1984) (public school rule prohibiting students from personally possessing "medicine" and requiring that "medicine" be left with designated school staff member was violative of due process as applied to fifth grader who had been suspended for bringing three vitamin pills to school and giving two of them to another student).

224 Zero tolerance began as a national enforcement policy in the 1980's to interdict the flow of illegal drugs in the United States. M. Falco, The Making of a Drug Free America 6 (1992).

225 *See* Bethany Baxter, *The Intolerance of Zero Tolerance* (Intellectual Capital.com, Aug. 19, 1999).

226 Even if a state has abolished the distinction between libel and slander, some vestige of that distinction may still remain. *E.g., see* Stanley v. Taylor, 278 N.E.2d 824 (Ill. App. Ct. 1982).

social organization, contain professionals (teachers, administrators, counselors, nurses) whose function it is to make evaluative statements. Whether those statements are made orally or in writing, they may reflect negatively on someone. Probably no other tort evokes the same degree of outrage as does defamation where persons liken negative statements about them to arrows that have pierced (and damaged) their reputations. However, although school employees, including administrators, are prone to believe they have been defamed on certain occasions and may even threaten legal action, they need to realize that defamation is a very difficult cause of action to prove in court. Any person maintaining a defamation cause of action must overcome a formidable number of defenses, particularly truth, qualified privilege, consent, and in some cases, "public figure."

A person who wants to state a defamation claim must produce evidence that an untrue statement was published to a third party not privileged to receive it, and that the publication resulted in injury. However, in four areas, the law will presume that an injury has occurred without a person having to produce evidence of injury:

(1) Words that impute the commission of a criminal offense;

(2) Words that impute infection of a communicable disease of any kind that would tend to exclude from society;

(3) Words that impute inability to perform or express lack of integrity in the discharge of duties of office or employment;

(4) Words that prejudice a particular person in his profession or trade.[227]

---

[227] *See* M. Appleman, Illinois Tort Law and Practice 381. To these four categories some jurisdictions would add a fifth, unchastity to a woman. *See* Bauer v. Murphy, 530 N.W.2d 1 (Wis. Ct. App. 1995) (statement by coach that a player was a "disgrace" did not refer to assistant basketball coach with whom the player had been seen and who had been discharged because of an inappropriate relationship with plaintiff, and, therefore, did not, as plaintiff alleged, impugn her chastity by referring to some form of sexual misconduct with the assistant coach).

In the above four categories, a plaintiff must prove that a statement of fact (as opposed to opinion) is untrue and that there was a publication of the defamatory material to a nonprivileged third party, but the plaintiff need not prove special damages. To be actionable at all, allegedly defamatory remarks must be "more than unpleasant and offensive."[228] However, remarks that could be interpreted as presenting negative statements of fact about a person's reputation can be actionable. In *Kovacs v. Briarcliffe School, Inc.*,[229] an associate professor and department chair in the school, who had been discharged from his position, was entitled to go to trial on a defamation claim based on a memorandum sent to the faculty by the president of the school. The memorandum, although not mentioning plaintiff by name, stated that plaintiff had been replaced "because there was no responsible alternative" and the president "was confident that the quality of the department would improve under the new chairperson."[230] The court held that this memorandum disparaged the discharged faculty member "in his office, trade or profession" and did not constitute unactionable "pure opinion" because it "implied the existence of undisclosed detrimental facts."[231]

Employees of public institutions have some protection under the "liberty' clause of the Fourteenth Amendment, a protection that would not be available to employees of nonpublic institutions. In the seminal case of *Board of Regents v. Roth*,[232] the United States Supreme Court observed that an employee who had been stigmatized through an employment decision was entitled to a name-clearing hearing. However, alleging sufficient facts to establish a liberty interest violation is a formidable task. In *Meyer v. University of Washington*,[233] a departmental reprimand to a faculty member, which allegedly caused his estrangement from his colleagues (and thus, an alleged damage

---

[228] Howard Univ. v. Best 484 A.2d 958, 989 (D.C. App. 1984), *after remand* 547 A.2d 144 (D.C. App. 1988) (statement that dean of college was "actively opposed to the present administration" not actionable); Harris v. School Annual Publication Co., 466 So.2d 963 (Ala. 1985) (no defamation where teacher who declined to have her picture taken for yearbook found, in place where picture would have been, a cartoon of monkey sitting on a swing with caption at side "munching out" and teacher's name and grade underneath); Avins v. Moll, 774 F.2d 1150 (E.D. Pa. 1984) (former dean was "nothing" to the law school held not actionable).

[229] 228. 617 N.Y.S.2d 804 (N.Y. App. Div. 1994)

[230] *Id.* at 805.

[231] *Id.*

[232] 408 U.S. 564 (1979).

[233] 719 P.2d 98 (Wash. 1986).

to reputation), failed to state a liberty interest violation because affidavits of his colleagues indicated that the reprimand did not have the estrangement effect claimed by plaintiff. In *Harris v. Arizona Board of Regents*,[234] allegations of poor performance or inability to get along with other faculty were insufficient. In *Garvie v. Jackson*,[235] a university department head was not deprived of a liberty interest either from a rumor circulated in his department regarding his removal or from a provost's statement in the student newspaper that nonrenewal was in the department's best interest.

However, depending on the facts, a name-clearing hearing may be required. In *Kramer v. Horton*,[236] a tenured music professor whose contract included teaching and performance with a faculty quintet was entitled to a name-clearing due process hearing when he was removed as a member of the quintet. The following reasons were identified by the court as affecting his reputation: (1) while the university had not published plaintiff-faculty member's removal, the music faculty was close-knit, and rumor had circulated for two years prior to plaintiff's removal; (2) other members of the quintet had met with the dean for two years to complain about plaintiff without providing him notice; (3) a replacement oboist had been chosen and hired without giving plaintiff an opportunity to rebut charges against him; and (4) testimony from professional musicians indicated that plaintiff's employability as a performing chamber musician had been partially damaged by his removal.

Truth is always a complete defense to defamation, but open for discussion under the federal and some state constitutions is the extent to which motive of the person making the statements can be a factor in determining the truth or falsity of those statements.[237] In *Abdelsayed v. Narumanchi*,[238] a faculty

---

[234] 528 F. Supp. 987 (D. Ariz. 1981).

[235] 845 F.2d 647 (6th Cir. 1988).

[236] 371 N.W.2d 801 (Wis. Ct. App. 1985).

[237] *See, e.g.*, Delis v. Sepsis, 292 N.E.2d 138 (Ill. App. Ct. 1972); In light of New York Times Co. v. Sullivan, 376 U.S. 254 (1964) it is doubtful under the first amendment freedom of speech protections that good motivation mitigates a defense of truth. The Illinois Constitution, article I, § 4, would appear to increase a defendant's burden in libel trials: "all persons may speak, write and publish freely, being responsible for the abuse of that liberty. In trials for libel, both civil and criminal, the truth, when published with good motives and for justifiable ends, shall be a sufficient defense." In Foote v. Sarafyan, 432 So.2d 877 (La. Ct. App. 1983) false charges of "deceit of the university" and "false pretenses" were harsh but not so unfair as to create liability. However, a justifiable case of action was presented as to the good faith of a statement to a tenure committee that a faculty member being considered for tenure mismanaged funds, plagiarized research and violated professional ethics, *See* Goodman v. Gallerano, 695 S.W.2d 286 (Tex. Ct. App. 1985).

[238] 668 A.2d 378 (Conn. Ct. App. 1995).

member who had been charged with plagiarism by another professor in the same department regarding the content of a new course proposal prevailed in his defamation lawsuit. Factors which demonstrated defendant's awareness of the falsity of his charge were a history of ill will between the two men and an admission by defendant that the idea for the new course had not been his. Even where the defendant's absence of malice may be a factor in determining what is truth, a jurisdiction may undercut the requirement with a rule of innocent construction.[239]

An open question for students and school personnel is whether written or oral statements are defamatory if they do not declare the "entire" truth. Essentially two kinds of concerns appear to be raised: whether substantially correct statements are defamatory and whether statements that relate the negative but not the positive are defamatory. There appears to be some support for the proposition that statements need be only substantially correct with no requirement of word-for-word accuracy,[240] but, of course, the more summary and conclusive the statement, the greater the risk of defamation.[241] Regarding the second kind of concern, there does not appear to be a requirement that statements balance positive and negative elements in order to be true. In *Hett v. Ploetz*,[242] a school district superintendent who had given a favorable recommendation for a teacher to secure a permanent teacher's license and who had encouraged the teacher to resign because he did not want to dismiss the teacher, did not act in bad faith when he later wrote an essentially negative letter of recommendation to another school superintendent to whom the teacher had applied to teach.

---

239 For an application of the rule *see* Valentine v. North Am. Life & Health Ins., 328 N.E.2d 265 (Ill. 1974) where termination of an employee because "he was a lousy agent" was construed innocently to mean a generally unsatisfactory agency relationship existed. *See also*, McConnell v. Howard Univ., 621 F. Supp. 327 (D. D.C. 1985) (statement that faculty member's refusal to teach a class constituted neglect of professional duties was an opinion only and not actionable); Belliveau v. Rerick, 504 A.2d 1350 (R.I. 1986) (statement that only one of faculty member's listed publications was a "published" one was opinion only and not actionable).

240 Wilson v. United Press Ass'n, 98 N.E.2d 391 (Ill. 1951); Ft. S. Press Co. v. Davis, 96 S.W.2d 416 (Tex. Civ. Ct. App. 1936). *See also* Bookout v. Griffin, 639 P.2d 1190 (N.M. 1982). In Foote v. Sarafyan, 432 So.2d 877 (La. Ct. App. 1983), a false charge of payroll fraud was not actionable in defamation because the crime was insupportable by the evidence.

241 The vagaries of the use of conclusive language are illustrated by two cases where it was actionable to write of a minister, "I would not have anything to do with him or touch him with a ten foot pole," Cole. v. Millspaugh, 126 N.W. 626 (Minn. 1910) but it was not actionable to call a lawyer a "bum in a gin mill," Werdberg v. La Guardia, 10 N.Y.S.2d 445 (N.Y. Sup. Ct. 1939).

242 121 N.W.2d 270 (Wis. 1963).

A defamation complaint by a private liberal arts college[243] was dismissed against a book publisher who had published the following statement:

> Sex, drugs, and booze are the staples of life ... Sex is casual, and formal dating is unheard of; the pickup scene thrives in Ithaca ... the use of pot is a foregone conclusion, and cocaine occasionally manages to send its way into the hands of those who can afford it. Speed and downers are common ....

The court never had to address the actual question of truth of the statement because it determined that the statement was not defamatory to the reputation of the college, and the college failed to prove special damages.

Even if students or school personnel can prove that a statement is not true, they must prove that the untruth was published to a third person who was not privileged to receive it.[244] Untrue statements made directly to the party himself are not defamatory, but if the statement is overheard by a third party who would have no privilege to know the statement, then there has been a publication.[245] A publication normally occurs only if made by the defendant so that a plaintiff's republication would not meet the requirement. However, there is some indication that a republication by a minor child may constitute a publication for defamation purposes, presumably because it could be foreseen that a minor child would tell his parents or friends about any untrue statements.[246] Thus, it would be wise for nonpublic school officials to beware of making unfounded charges against minor children, especially if the charges involve one of the four categories mentioned earlier which do not require proof of special damages (e.g., sale or use of narcotics, venereal disease, theft, extortion, assault).

A publication has not occurred if statements, albeit untrue, are available only to school personnel directly involved with the student or employee who are considered qualified to have access to the information in the statements. Normally this privileged

---

243 Ithaca College v. Yale Daily News Publ'g Co., Inc., 445 N.Y.S.2d 621 (N.Y. App. Div. 1981).

244 The question of the point in time of publication is important because it begins the running of the statute of limitations.

245 Untrue statements dictated to secretaries appear to be a publication, but the cases are older. Rickbeil v. Grafton Deaconness Hosp., 23 N.W.2d 247 (N.D. 1946); Ostrowe v. Lee, 175 N.E. 505 (N.Y. 1931).

246 *See* Davis v. Askins's Retail Stores, Inc., 191 S.E. 33 (N.C. 1937).

group (hence the term "qualified privilege") for a student would include the student's classroom teacher(s), counselor, school administrator(s), and in relevant cases the school board members, school nurse, psychologist, social worker, or other learning specialists.[247] A qualified privilege has even been extended to include an oral communication to a law school to cancel an applicant's test scores.[248]

Qualified privilege also can apply to employers who reveal information about employees. Revelations of suspected wrong doing to supervisory personnel[249] or a disciplinary or evaluation committee[250] within an organization are clothed with a qualified privilege. In *Gallo v. Princeton University*,[251] a university statement and statements by university officials in alumni newsletters that three staff members had resigned after the university had started investigating them for improper use of university resources off-campus were entitled to qualified privilege. In dismissing a defamation lawsuit by one of the employees, the court reasoned that "members of the University community have a legitimate interest in being informed of any allegations of improprieties involving the diversion of University property for private gain and the University response to such allegations."[252]

Likewise, letters of recommendation as part of an employment or admissions procedure have a qualified privilege.[253] Comments regarding teachers by parents to school boards or letters to principals are generally covered by a qualified

---

247 Federal and state privacy acts appear to be broad enough to permit access by school officials with "legitimate educational interests" to information about a student and thus fall within the "qualified privilege" defense of tort liability. *See* 20 U.S.C. § 1232(g) and 45 C.F.R. § 99.30(a). *Cf.* Brown v. McConn, 138 S.E. 247 (Ga. Ct. App. 1927).

248 Johnson v. Educational Testing Serv., Inc., 615 F. Supp. 633 (D. Mass. 1984).

249 Jerolamom v. Farleigh Dickinson Univ., 448 A.2d 1064 (N.J. Super. App. Div. 1985) (security report sent to Provost held to be within privilege); Dominguez v. Babcock, 727 P.2d 362 (Colo.1986) (memo by faculty critical of department chairman sent to Vice President of Academic Affairs held to be within privilege).

250 Baker v. Lafayette College, 504 A.2d 247 (Pa. Super. Ct. 1986); Scarpelli v. Jones, 626 P.2d 1190 (N.M. 1982); Small v. McRae, 651 P.2d 982 (Mont. 1982); Colson v. Stieg, 433 N.E.2d 246 (Ill. App. Ct. 1982); McGowen v. Prentice, 341 So.2d 55 (La. Ct. App. 1976).

251 656 A.2d 1267 (N.J. Super. Ct. 1995).

252 *Id.* at 1274.

253 Manguso v. Oceanside Unified Sch. Dist., 200 Cal. Rptr. 535 (Ct. App. 1984); Hett v. Ploetz, 121 N.W.2d 270 (Wis. 1963); Burdett v. Hines, 87 So. 470 (Miss. 1921); Lattimore v. Tyler Commercial College, 24 S.W.2d 361 (Tex. Comm'n App. 1930).

privilege.[254] However, the protection of the qualified privilege is lost if plaintiff can prove the untrue statements, even though made only among a privileged group, were made with malice or reckless disregard for the truth.[255]

In *New York Times Co. v. Sullivan*[256] the United States Supreme Court declared that untrue statements about "public officials" (later extended to include "public figures"[257]) were not actionable unless there was proof of actual malice. Although the identity of public officials is relatively discernible, just who would be public depends on state law and has been extended to a wide range of school personnel in the public sector.[258] The *New York Times* privilege about public officials obviously does not apply to cases involving private citizens,[259] but a state can make the public-private distinction difficult to discern when a public official includes anyone

> carrying out a function of government or (who) is participating in acts relating to matters in which government has a substantial interest.[260]

Since the identification of a person as a "public figure" can affect a plaintiff's recovery for defamation, an important legal determination is whether the plaintiff is a public figure. A person who is a public figure must prove actual malice in order to recover damages for defamation. In an unusual case, *Estep v. Brewer*,[261] a public high school assistant principal recovered $150,000 damages for emotional distress, $50,000 for damage to

---

254 Nodar v. Galbreath, 462 So.2d 803 (Fla. 1984) (statements to school board); Swenson-Davis v. Martel, 354 N.W.2d 288 (Mich. Ct. App. 1984) (letter to principal); Zuber v. Bordier, 522 N.Y.S.2d 610 (N.Y. App. Div. 1987) (letter to principal and conference with parent, student and teacher).

255 Vinson v. Linnmar Community Sch. Dist., 360 N.W.2d 108 (Ia. 1984) (statements that bus driver had falsified time card held actionable); Welch v. Chicago Tribune Co., 340 N.E.2d 539 (Ill. App. Ct. 1975); Farrell v. Kramer, 193 A.2d 560 (Me. 1963).

256 376 U.S. 254 (1964).

257 Curtis Publ'g Co. v. Butts, 388 U.S. 130 (1967).

258 Waterson v. Cleveland State Univ., 639 N.E.2d 1236 (Ohio Ct. App. 1994) (deputy chief of university police department); State v. Defley, 395 So.2d 759 (La. 1981) (school superintendent and school supervisor); Jimenez v. United Fed'n of Teachers, 657 N.Y.S.2d 672 (N.Y. App. Div. 1997) (acting public school principal); Elstrom v. Independent Sch. Dist. No. 270, 533 N.W.2d 51 (Minn. Ct. App. 1995) (classroom teacher); Johnston v. Corinthian Television Corp., 583 P.2d 1101 (Okla. 1978) (wrestling coach); Gallman v. Carnes, 497 S.W.2d 47 (Ark. 1973) (assistant dean and professor of law); Byers v. Southeastern Newspaper Corp., Inc., 288 S.E.2d 698 (Ga. Ct. App. 1982)(dean).

259 Gertz v. Robert Welch, Inc., 418 U.S. 323 (1974).

260 Doctors Convalescent Ctr., Inc. v. East Shore Newspapers, Inc., 244 N.E.2d 373 (Ill. App. Ct. 1968) (medical personnel in a private nursing home).

261 453 S.E.2d 345 (W.Va. 1994).

reputation, and $50,000 punitive damages against the parents of a special education student in his school for statements that they had made about him. The trial court's instruction on "actual malice" was that this requirement is met if a person "is motivated by a sense of hate, ill will or revenge against the party he is making statements or writings about and communicates the false or misleading information in hopes of doing injury to the person or reputation of the subject of the comment."[262]

A person in a nonpublic setting can acquire a public figure status by injecting him or herself into the public spotlight. For example, in *Hustler Magazine v. Falwell*,[263] The U.S. Supreme Court found that because Jerry Falwell had injected himself into the public spotlight through his media and political activities, he could not recover in defamation without proof of actual malice. In *Walko v. Kean College*,[264] a New Jersey court applied the concept of limited purpose public figure in denying recovery for alleged defamation to a person serving as an assistant to the dean of education and an instructor. A limited purpose public figure is defined in terms of a particular issue, and the status limited purpose public figure applies only when the publication in controversy concerns that issue. In *Walko*, plaintiff's role with the College involved her in the controversy about the use of a hotline to answer student questions, a hotline that had been parodied by students in the campus newspaper as "whoreline." Even though plaintiff alleged that she had suffered damages as a result of the parody, she was not able to recover without proof of actual malice.

By nature of their functions, nonpublic school personnel would not be public officials, although they may become public figures if they have injected themselves into the public light or have been drawn in by virtue of the nature of a controversy. The operative term is "public," which means that controversies may arise among members of nonpublic organizations that do not raise participants to the level of public figures. If a person about whom untrue statements have been made is not a public figure, then that person need not prove malice to recover damages.

Under certain circumstances, certain kinds of revelations may enjoy an absolute privilege, which means that no cause of

---

[262] *Id.* at 348, note 3.
[263] 485 U.S. 46 (1988).
[264] 561 A.2d 680 (N.J. Super. Ct. 1988).

action will be viable, even if proof of actual malice is made. In *Rothman v. Emory University*,[265] a federal district court held that contents of a letter from a law school dean to the Illinois Board of Law Examiners was absolutely privileged because the Board served a quasi-judicial function, even though the letter made reference to the student's disability (epilepsy) and hostility to other students. Because the student's appeal concerned ADA and Section 504 issues, the Seventh Circuit commented favorably on the absolute immunity defense but did not have to address the defense on the merits.[266]

Statements that represent opinions are not actionable under defamation.[267] However, if statements offered as opinion imply facts capable of defamatory meaning, a cause of action for defamation may be stated.[268] Statements of fact do not become opinions simply because a person chooses to preface statements with the words, "in my opinion."[269]

However, statements of opinion in areas of public concern may be protected by the free speech clause of the First Amendment. In *Washington v. Smith*,[270] a statement about a women's basketball coach in a preseason publication was held to be protected by the Free Speech Clause because success in women's basketball is a matter of public concern. The comment that the coach "usually finds a way to screw things up," in order

---

265 828 F. Supp. 537 (N.D. Ill. 1993).

266 Rothman v. Emory Univ., 123 F.3d 446 (7th Cir. 1997).

267 *E.g., see* Yeagle v. Collegiate Times, 497 S.E.2d 136 (Va. 1998) (caption, "Director of Butt Licking," beneath Assistant to Vice President of Student Affairs' picture, although "disgusting, offensive, and in extremely bad taste," could not reasonably be understood as stating an actual fact about plaintiff's job title or her conduct); Albano v. Sylvester, 635 N.Y.S.2d 55 (N.Y. App. Div. 1995) (statements by school district trustee that principal's transfer of two students was "cruel" and "inhumane" act constituted "personal opinion and rhetorical hyperbole rather than objective fact"); Epstein v. Board of Trustees of Dowling College, 543 N.Y.S.2d 691 (N.Y. App. Div. 1989) (letter to editor with following student comments about faculty member not actionable as opinion: "lying, deceiving, making false promises, not advising, lost time and credits, poor treatment of students, insulting, harassing, limited office hours, long lines of students waiting for extra help, poor teaching activities, lack of organization, losing assignments"); McConnell v. Howard Univ., 621 F. Supp. 327 (D. D.C. 1985) (statement that faculty member's refusal to teach a class constituted neglect of professional duties not actionable); Belliveau v. Rerick, 504 A.2d 1360 (R.I. 1986) (statement that only one of faculty member's listed publications was a "published" one not actionable); Foote v. Sarafyan, 432 So.2d 877 (La. Ct. App. 1983) (characterization of one faculty member's requirement to refund $127 as "payroll fraud" and another faculty member's publications on his biographical data sheet as "deceit" of the university and "false pretenses" not actionable).

268 Petula v. Mellody, 588 A.2d 103 (Pa. Commw. Ct. 1991) (statements by two super-intendents to over 100 potential employers of former principal contained statements that could be understood as communicating facts).

269 *See* Washington v. Smith, 893 F. Supp. 60 (D.C. 1995).

270 *Id.*

to be actionable, required that the coach, if she were to have a cause of action, produce evidence that no reasonable person could find the statement's characterizations supportable interpretations of underlying material. Nonetheless, *Washington v. Smith* was decided against the backdrop of *Milkovich v. Lorain Journal Co.,*[271] where the Supreme Court refused to create a separate constitutional privilege for opinion statements. In *Milkovich*, the Court decided that the free speech clause provided sufficient protection to publications without creating a separate privilege. As a result, the Court permitted the State of Ohio to apply its defamation law to a reporter's comments in a column that a high school wrestling coach had perjured himself, and left the decision up to state courts to determine whether the comments were sufficiently factual to allow for damages recovery for defamation.

Although defamation is a difficult cause of action to prove, statements that affect a person's employment or academic standing offer the greatest potential for litigation. Some suggestions may make the prospect of such a lawsuit less likely:

(1) Do not send unsolicited letters of recommendation. Generally, no one can be required to write a letter of recommendation[272] but sending one that is not requested may eliminate any qualified privilege and, if statements are untrue, may suggest malice.

(2) Where possible, make comments as data based as possible. In some cases, as with timeliness in completing tasks, some specific comments may be possible, such as "he attended five of twenty faculty meetings" or "she did not turn in ten of her twenty assignments on time." However, such data based statements may be neither desirable nor possible in areas where information regarding descriptions about written and oral communication skills and respect for differences is requested. In making sum-

---

[271] 495 U.S. 1 (1990).

[272] Exception to this rule would involve licensure or employment situations where references from certain persons or offices are required. Failure to submit such a reference might be actionable under a defamation theory. *See e.g.,* Rothman v. Emory Univ., 213 F.3d 446 (7th Cir. 1997) (as part of process for admission to the bar, law school from which applicant graduates is required to submit letter regarding character and fitness to practice law).

mary comments, the guide should be accuracy and fairness. Remember that references for students and employees are opportunities to provide useful information for the future, not vehicles to punish past behaviors.

(3) If student or staff evaluation comments appear to be substantially negative, submit the statement to the student or staff member for his or her comment prior to filing or sending. This procedure is not always possible, but since consent is a defense to defamation, it may be a safeguard worth taking where possible. Always make it a practice to send a copy of the recommendation to the student or staff member prior to mailing, with a three to four day delay to provide time for possible response.

(4) Limit comments in student files or in letters of recommendation to firsthand accounts. To go beyond this into the realm of rumor and hearsay is not only speculative, but may demonstrate reckless disregard for the truth.

(5) Permit student and staff to have access to their files even though such access may not be required by federal or state statutes.[273] There is no need to have information in a file that is hopelessly out of date and no excuse to have information that is possibly untrue.

(6) School officials need to be aware that even though truth may be a defense to defamation, it is not a defense to an action for invasion of privacy.[274]

---

273 The Federal Privacy Act applies only to schools receiving funds administered by the Department of Education, 20 U.S.C. § 1232(g), 45 C.F.R. § 99.1. State privacy statutes generally apply only to public schools, *e.g.*, Ill. Ann. Stat. ch. 105 § 10/2; Va. Code Ann. § 22.1-287.

274 For a discussion of invasion of privacy in an educational setting, *see* Diaz v. Oakland Tribune, Inc., 188 Cal. Rptr. 762 (Ct. App. 1983) ($250,000 judgment).

Invasion of Privacy

In states that recognize invasion of privacy as a cause of action,[275] this tort has become increasingly popular in situations where defamation would not be a viable cause of action. Although frequently referred to as a separate tort, invasion of privacy is actually a complex of four analytically distinct causes of action: (1) intrusion upon seclusion; (2) appropriation of name or likeness; (3) publicity given to private life; and (4) publicity placing a person in false light.[276]

Generally, the standard in each of these actions is whether a disclosure "(a) would be highly offensive to a reasonable person, and (b) is not of legitimate concern to the public."[277] Thus, two newspaper articles making reference to parent-plaintiffs' son as having a learning disability were not publicity into their son's private life because the son's disability had been discussed at a school board meeting in the context of reimbursing the parents for the cost of an independent evaluation by a certified school psychologist.[278] In this case, the confidentiality normally accorded personally identifiable information under IDEA[279] was offset by the public's interest in knowing "that the school district was being asked to pay with tax dollars the cost of a privately retained psychologist...."[280]

In *Salek v. Passaic Collegiate School*,[281] a picture in a school yearbook did not give rise to a false light invasion of privacy tort. In this case, a picture with plaintiff seated next to a male teacher who had his right hand raised to his forehead was captioned, "Not tonight, Ms. Salek." In essence, the trial judge determined as a matter of law that the meaning assigned by plaintiff to this picture, namely that the male teacher was declining plaintiff's proposition to engage in a sexual relationship, was not "highly

---

275 *E.g., see* Russell v. Salve Regina College, 890 F.2d 484, 488 (1st Cir. 1989) (tort of invasion of privacy in Rhode Island is purely statutory and overweight student could not recover for unreasonable publicity concerning her obesity where the obesity was public); Anderson v. Strong Mem'l Hosp., 531 N.Y.S.2d 735, *aff'd* 542 N.Y.S.2d 96 (N.Y. App. Div. 1988) (New York does not recognize common law invasion of privacy resulting from unauthorized publication of one's picture).

276 Restatement (Second) of Torts §§ 652 B-E.

277 Culver v. Port Allegany Reporter Argus, 598 A.2d 54, 55 (Pa. Super. Ct. 1991).

278 *Id.* at 55, 56. IDEA provides that parents are entitled to an independent evaluation of a child "by a qualified examiner" at public expense. 34 C.F.R. § 300.503.

279 34 C.F.R. § 300.129.

280 *Culver*, 598 A.2d at 56.

281 605 A.2d 276 (N.J. Super. Ct. 1992).

offensive to a reasonable person."[282] As an interesting sidelight, the court held that under *Hazelwood School District v. Kuhlmeier*,[283] the school administration had no obligation "to exercise greater censorship over the content and/or style of the yearbook....; [t]he desire on the part of school officials, however laudatory, to avoid any discomfort of unpleasantness to plaintiff would not have justified suppression of student speech by preventing publication of the photograph...."[284]

In *Jarrett v. Butts*,[285] a faculty member who took pictures of a student in a classroom and in the hallway of a school building during regular school hours when other students were present, did not intrude upon the plaintiff-student seclusion or appropriate her name or likeness. The teacher had not revealed any aspect of the student "not readily visible to anyone who saw her during the day," and the teacher "received nothing of value for the photographs" nor were the photographs "sold, published or publicly displayed."[286]

However, a Colorado appeals court has held that a student had an invasion of privacy claim where he had given a blood sample to test for rubella, but his school performed an additional test for HIV. The court held that the student had a cause of action for disclosure of the test results to third parties and for intrusion upon his seclusion.[287]

An invasion of privacy claim against someone who has public figure status faces the same difficulty of recovery as for defamation. In *Walko*,[288] plaintiff who was an assistant to the dean of the school of education had a "limited purpose public figure" status. This case involved a student parody in the college newspaper of a communication help center hotline in which plaintiff was one of four persons listed as a person to call under the heading 'Whoreline.' Following the Supreme Court's decision in *Hustler Magazine v. Falwell*,[289] the New Jersey court determined that even assuming "that the 'Whoreline' ad would be highly offensive to a reasonable person,"[290] "a publication

---

282 *Id.* at 279.
283 484 U.S. 260 (1988).
284 *Salek*, 605 A.2d at 279.
285 379 S.E.2d 583 (Ga. Ct. App. 1989).
286 *Id.* at 585.
287 Doe v. High-Tech Inst., 972 P.2d 1060 (Colo. Ct. App. 1998).
288 *Supra* note 264 and accompanying text.
289 485 U.S. 46 (1988).
290 *Walko*, 561 A.2d at 687.

which no reasonable person could interpret as an allegation of fact is the equivalent of an expression of opinion that is fully protected under the First Amendment."[291] Thus, as in *Hustler Magazine*, where the tort of intentional infliction of emotional harm cannot pierce the constitutional shield protecting parodies, neither can causes of action framed in defamation or invasion of privacy pierce that shield.

Corporal Punishment, Child Abuse, and School Liability for Sexual Misconduct by Employees

Corporal Punishment

Corporal punishment and child abuse are related but not identical problems. Corporal punishment in its broadest sense includes any physical contact between school personnel and students.[292] But more generally it is understood as a disciplinary measure for allegedly unacceptable behavior.

Corporal punishment, as a means of student punishment, has not received constitutional protection. In *Ingraham v. Wright*,[293] despite an egregious set of facts, the United States Supreme Court refused to find an Eighth Amendment[294] violation for excessive physical punishment, leaving students to pursue available state civil and criminal remedies. In addition, the Supreme Court has given at least tacit assent to denial of procedural rights before a student is spanked.[295] States have varied in their approach regarding how schools should deal with

[291] *Id.* at 688.

[292] *See, e.g.*, Andreozzi v. Rubano, 141 A.2d 649 (Conn. 1958) (teacher slapping student); Thomas v. Bedford, 389 So.2d 405 (La. Ct. App. 1980) (teacher shaking student); Rodriguez v. Johnson, 504 N.Y.S.2d 379 (N.Y. Civ. Ct. 1986) (bus matron slapping student).

[293] 430 U.S. 651 (1977). *See also* Hale v. Pringle, 562 F. Supp. 598 (M.D. Ala. 1983).

[294] The Eighth Amendment prohibits "cruel and unusual punishments."

[295] Baker v. Owen, 395 F. Supp. 294 (M.D. N.C. 1975), *aff'd without opinion* 423 U.S. 970 (1975). *Compare* Goss v. Lopez, 419 U.S. 565 (1975) (before suspension for up to ten days, public school students entitled at least to an informal hearing and opportunity to present their side of the conflict).

corporal punishment, from a blanket endorsement[296] to prohibition.[297]

Civil or criminal liability for the use of corporal punishment depends upon a variety of factors such as: motive of the person inflicting the punishment; size of the student; and instrument used.[298] Where permitted by state law, school personnel's administration of corporal punishment will be subjected to a reasonableness test.[299] Nonpublic schools usually attempt to prevent litigation by including consent to use corporal punishment in admission or re-enrollment forms. Unless corporal punishment is prohibited by state statute or is excessive, such forms are generally valid defenses to a civil or criminal charge that physical contact with the child was unlawful.[300] However, civil damages[301] or a criminal conviction[302] can occur for physical contact which may not seem excessive but which leaves marks such as bruises.

Religious schools that may object to statutory limitations on, or civil or criminal penalties for, the use of corporal punishment, need to carefully consider the following: whether education of a child is a parental or institutional function; whether the biblical mandates about parental use of corporal punishment have direct

---

296 Minn. Stat. Ann. § 609.06 (reasonable force to restrain or correct by a parent guardian, teacher or other lawful custodian of a child or pupil); W. Va. Code, § 18A-5-1 (1993); Ill. Ann. Stat. Ch. 105, § 24-24; Okla. Stat. Ann. tit. 70, § 6-114; Pa. Stat. Ann. tit. 24, § 1317 (teacher stands in place of parent or guardian in exercising authority over the pupil). *See also* Streeter v. Hundley, 580 S.W.2d 283 (Mo. 1979) (result of *Baker v. Owen* accepted as state law).

297 Mass. Gen. Laws Ann. ch. 71, § 37G; Me. Rev. Stat. Ann. tit. 17-A, § 106 (2); N.J. Stat. Ann. §18A:6-1 (applies to public and private schools); Vt. Stat. Ann. tit. 16, § 1161 A (applies to public and "approved schools"). In addition, Hawaii, the District of Columbia and the City of New York are examples of jurisdictions that have prohibited corporal punishment by administrative regulation.

298 Tinkham v. Kole, 110 N.W.2d 258 (Iowa 1961) (teacher found to have acted in anger where teacher struck student on ear, bursting an eardrum, after directive given but before student had time to obey); Frank v. Orleans Parish Sch. Bd., 195 So.2d 451 (La. 1967) (6'2", 230 pound physical education teacher squeezing student standing 4'9" and weighing 101 pounds, breaking student's arm found excessive); People v. Ball, 317 N.E.2d 54 (Ill. 1974) (paddle three inches wide and twenty inches long when used excessively found to be unreasonable); Rodriguez v. Johnson, 504 N.Y.S.2d 379 (N.Y. Civ. Ct. 1986) and Landis v. West Chester Area Sch. Dist., 353 A.2d 895 (Pa. 1976) (slapping student on face with bare hand not upheld).

299 Campbell v. Gahanna-Jefferson Bd. of Educ., 717 N.E.2d 347 (Ohio Ct. App. 1998) (single swat did not cause "substantial risk of serious physical harm" under state statute and its use was reasonable in light of teacher's belief that student had referred to him as "stupid.").

300 *See* R. Mawdsley, Child Abuse Reporting: Crisis in Christian Education, Vol. II (No. 1) 56 (1981).

301 Thomas v. Bedford, 389 So.2d 405 (La. Ct. App. 1980) (shaking student left bruises). *But see Rodriguez*, *supra* note 298 ($250 damages awarded for physical contact even though the court found the slapping not to be excessive and no physical marks were left).

302 People v. Ball, 317 N.E.2d 54 (Ill. 1974).

application to institutions; whether institutions have a legitimate interest in requiring parents to delegate a parental responsibility regarding the use of corporal punishment regardless of whether parents use corporal punishment at home; whether institutions that require the delegation of corporal punishment are prepared to apply the delegation concept to all aspects of their operation; and whether an institution can perform its educative function without the use of corporal punishment.[303]

In addition, schools need to determine whether their liability insurance covers corporal punishment, and, if not, whether a rider is available. If a rider is not available or would be too expensive, the schools must consider whether they can afford to be self-insured, should a parent sue and secure a judgment.

For nonpublic educational institutions which insist on using corporal punishment, the following parameters may serve as helpful guidelines:

(1) Provide notice to students and parents of the kinds of conduct that may result in corporal punishment, as well as notice to parents when spanking is to be administered;

(2) Use corporal punishment as a last resort, and instead emphasize alternative means of changing behavior;

(3) Investigate any denial of guilt prior to administering corporal punishment;

(4) Designate only one person in the school to administer the punishment;

(5) Have a witness present;

(6) Limit punishment to no more than three swats;

---

303 The comments of Dr. Kerby Aloy, a consultant on mental health, are worth considering: "Children, who are being abused at home are more likely to have learning problems at school . . . and, therefore, they are more likely to be candidates for corporal punishment. These children do not need the school to also teach them that violence is the way to solve problems and to prepare them for adulthood. They need to see that other adults are more creative and more caring." For a helpful set of guidelines regarding corporal punishment, see *It's Time to Review Your Corporal Punishment Policy,* LEGAL LEGISLATIVE UPDATE, 9, No. 2, 22-27 (ACSI Winter 1998-99).

(7) Do not paddle students in daycare, preschool, or kindergarten programs.

Child Abuse Reporting

Child abuse differs from corporal punishment in two significant aspects. First, neither delegation of authority to spank nor consent to spank are valid defenses in a criminal prosecution for child abuse, based upon the concept that no parent can consent to child abuse.[304] Second, the emphasis in corporal punishment is upon purposes, methods, and motives, whereas in child abuse, the emphasis is solely upon the results produced.[305] Every state has a statute defining child abuse and mandating reporting of such abuse by certain categories of people with sanctions that can be imposed upon those who fail or refuse to report. The marked tendency among the states is to use an expansive definition of child abuse, such "as any nonaccidental physical injury, mental injury or sexual mistreatment inflicted on a child other than by accidental means."[306] Another similarity among the states has been a trend toward expansion of the categories of those required to report suspected child abuse,[307] although the specific designation of who is to report the abuse is as varied as the legislatures who have enacted the reporting requirements.[308] Every state appears to mandate child abuse reporting by school teachers and administrators, although the expansiveness of the statutory language varies somewhat.[309] Clearly some of the mandated school categories could include not only the principal, teacher, coach, nurse, and counselor, but also the secretary, custodial staff, and in some cases, even clergy.

Civil liability may flow from failure to report child abuse, but two factual issues are at stake in determining liability: whether a

---

304 Mawdsley, *supra* note 300 at 57. PURSUING JUSTICE FOR THE CHILD 225-246 (M. Reonheim, ed., 1976).

305 Mawdsley, *supra* note 300 at 58.

306 Ark. Code Ann. § 12-12-502.

307 Criminal sanctions are generally imposed for failure to report by those mandated to do so: Ala. Code § 26-14-13; Ill. Ann. Stat. ch. 325, para. 5/4; Minn. Stat. Ann. § 626.556 ("a professional ... who is engaged in the practice of ... education"); Nev. Rev. Stat. Ann. § 200.507; Va. Code Ann. § 63.1-248.3 (B); N.Y. Soc. Serv. Law § 420; Ark Code Ann. § 12-12-503.

308 A thorough discussion of child abuse reporting statutes can be found in R. Mawdsley and S. Permuth, *Child Abuse Reporting: A Search for an Acceptable Balancing of Interests*, 9 NOLPE SCHOOL L. J. 115 (1981).

309 Ill. Ann. Stat. ch. 325, para. 5/4 (school personnel, director or staff assistant of a nursery school or a child care center); Ala. Code § 26-14-3(a) (school teachers and officials, day care workers or employees); Neb. Rev. Stat. § 28-711 (school employee); Tex. Family Code Ann. § 34-01 ("any person having knowledge of abuse or neglect").

person is mandated to report under state law and whether a person mandated to report knew about the abuse. In *Wilson v. Darr*,[310] a student in a parochial school, who was sexually and physically abused by her father, sued the church that operated the school, the priest of the church, and the guidance counselor of the school. The theories under which plaintiff sued were that the priest and guidance counselor should be liable because they knew or should have known about the abuse and had failed to report it, and that the church should be liable under *respondeat superior*. In upholding summary judgment for all defendants, the state supreme court held that the priest, even though there was a factual issue as to whether he had been told specifically about the abuse, was not mandated to report. State statute required a "counselor" to report a reasonable belief of abuse acquired "in the scope of professional practice," but since the priest's professional practice was that of a clergyman not a counselor, he did not fall within the mandated category.[311] Regarding the guidance counselor who clearly fell within the statutory mandated category, the court held that, in the absence of evidence that the counselor had been told by the student about the abuse, she had no reasonable belief ("know or should have known") under the statute[312] for reporting abuse. Finally, the church was not liable under *respondeat superior* because it had provided training to the counselor as required by state statute regarding instruction on reporting child abuse.[313]

In addition to designating who must report and what types of suspected abuse must be reported, child abuse reporting statutes also designate to whom the suspected abuse is to be reported and what rights the alleged child abusers have. Reports are normally made to the local child welfare unit,[314] but reports to local law enforcement officials are generally acceptable since

---

310 553 N.W.2d 579 (Iowa 1996).

311 Iowa Code Ann., § 232.69 (1)(b).

312 The court uses two different standards, apparently with the inference that they have the same meaning. The statute requires mandatory reporting if a person "reasonably believes" a child has suffered abuse, while the tort standard for liability regarding an invitee (as, for example, a student in a school) is what a defendant knows or should have been known. *See* Iowa Code Ann, § 232.69 (1)(b) and *Wilson*, 533 N.W.2d at 583.

313 The state statute provides that any person required to report child abuse must have completed two hours of training relating to identification and reporting of child abuse within six months of initial employment and two hours of additional training every five years. Iowa Stat. Ann, § 232.69 (3).

314 *See, e.g.*, La. Rev. Stat. Ann. § 14:403 (D)(1).

the law enforcement officials must in turn contact the welfare agency.[315]

There are three levels of rights for the alleged child abuser:

(1) Rights prior to reporting;

(2) Rights after reporting to civil and criminal action;

(3) Rights after civil suit or criminal prosecution is commenced.

Since serious sanctions can be imposed upon an alleged abuser even after the filing of a report, such as immediate temporary removal of a child from his parents, the most basic right of a parent or other person acting *in loco parentis* is to not have his name reported. For those in the educational field, the professional humiliation and fear of prosecution created by unnecessary reports are reason enough to exercise caution, even though statutes do not provide procedural safeguards at this point. In almost all states the parent and school officials are left at the mercy of broad definitions of abuse that seem to mandate and encourage the reporting of any physical or mental injury as long as it did not occur by accidental means. The occasional temporary bruise or scratch from corporal punishment or the alleged mental trauma because of repeated verbal reprimands to a problem student are all possible areas of reporting. Some states, like Wisconsin, have attempted to remedy this problem by requiring the reporting of "severe bruising . . . or any injury constituting great bodily harm,"[316] but in fact all bruises and injuries tend to be reported regardless of severity. The problem for the person whose name is unnecessarily reported is exacerbated by the statutory immunity from criminal or civil prosecution granted to those who report alleged child abuse. Most statutes protect the reporter who acts in "good faith,"[317] but some states have gone so far as to grant total immunity.[318]

---

[315] La. Rev. Stat. Ann. § 403 (D)(3).

[316] Wis. Stat. Ann. § 940.201.

[317] Ill. Ann. Stat. ch. 325, para. 5/9; La. Rev. Stat. Ann. § 14:403(E); N.Y. Soc. Law § 419; Ohio Rev. Code Ann. § 2151.42.1; Mont. Code Ann. § 41-3-203 ("unless the person acted in bad faith or with malicious purpose"); Cal. Penal Code § 11172 ("unless it can be proven that a false report was made and the person knew or should have known that the report was false or was made with reckless disregard of the truth").

[318] Ala. Code § 26-14-9.

Because of the difficulty in proving "bad faith" or "malice," a reporter has virtual immunity from any legal sanctions. Disclosure of information related to child abuse charges to a limited number of persons who have legitimate interest is probably entitled to a qualified privilege protecting the person making the disclosure from defamation or invasion of privacy charges.[319]

The rights of an alleged child abuser after reporting and prior to civil or criminal sanctions are more clearly delineated in the statutes. At least one state authorizes investigators to talk to any child suspected of being abused "without consent of and outside the presence of his parent, guardian, legal custodian, or other person standing in loco parentis or school personnel."[320] Generally, an alleged child abuser is entitled to a copy of the investigative report of the local social service agency with an opportunity to amend or expunge the report.[321] At a hearing to amend or expunge the report, Illinois specifically requires that the person making the report must testify. At the same time, Illinois follows the pattern of most other states in prohibiting the maker of a report from invoking a privileged relationship, such as a physician-patient or pastor-penitent.[322] Needless to say, alleged abusers are entitled to employ an attorney to represent them.

The rights of a person charged with child abuse or molestation after the commencement of a civil or criminal action are the same as for any other civil or criminal defendant with one notable exception: courts will permit the tolling of statutes of limitations involving sexual offenses so that school personnel may be sued or charged with a crime years after the offense occurred.[323] The most basic right is the engaging of competent counsel. If the action is a civil suit for damages against school

---

319 Ginwright v. Unified Sch. Dist. No. 457, 756 F. Supp. 1458 (D. Kan. 1991).

320 Va. Code Ann. § 63.1-248.10.

321 Ill. Ann. Stat. ch. 325, para. 5/7.4.

322 Ill. Ann. Stat. ch. 325, para. 5/4 (Christian Science practitioner); Va. Code Ann. § 63.1-248.3 (Christian Science practitioner); Nev. Rev. Stat. Ann. § 432B.220(2)(d) (clergyman); Mont. Code Ann. § 41-3-201(2)(c) (religious healers).

323 *See* Doe v. Durtschi, 716 P.2d 1238 (Idaho 1986) (statute of limitations to file claim based on sexual abuse tolled during minority); Stoneking v. Bradford Area Sch. Dist., 667 F. Supp. 1088 (W.D. Pa. 1987) (whether statute of limitations should be tolled until three years after sexually molested student graduated from high school and became aware that cause of her emotional problems was the sexual abuse to which she had been subjected by a teacher was a question of fact to be decided by trier of fact). *But see* Doe v. First United Methodist Church, 629 N.E.2d 402 (Ohio 1994) (claims for assault and battery resulting from sexual abuse dismissed against church because minor failed to assert claims against perpetrator within one

personnel concerning alleged abuse arising out of the employment relationship, the insurer for the school will probably provide an attorney as part of the liability insurance coverage.[324] If the action is criminal prosecution—and most likely it will be—the accused abuser will have to secure and pay his own attorney, unless the school employee is indigent.

(1) Child abuse and child abuse reporting statutes apply equally to the public and private sectors. There is no exemption for nonpublic schools.

(2) Almost all child abuse reporting statutes do not permit school personnel to exercise their judgment in deciding whether marks or injuries resulting from other than accidental means constitute child abuse. Apparently only social services personnel are permitted to make such a determination.

(3) A legislative policy mandating reporting cannot be subverted by a school's internal administrative policies. It is not unusual for schools to have a written or unwritten policy that school personnel are to report cases of alleged child abuse to a designated administrative official. Subordinate school personnel, if mandated to report by state statute, need to be aware that reporting suspected child abuse to a school administrator does not excuse them from their statutory responsibility if the administrator fails or refuses to notify social services.[325]

(4) Any school personnel whose names are reported should act promptly to protect themselves and con-

---

year of reaching majority where he knew identity of the perpetrator and was fully aware that a battery had occurred).

[324] *See* Eversole v. Wasson, 398 N.E.2d 1246 (Ill. App. Ct. 1980) (duty of the school to protect students may be broader than the employment and in such a case the school district insurer is still obligated to defend the teacher); Durham City Bd. of Educ. v. National Union Fire Ins. Co., 426 S.E.2d 451 (N.C. Ct. App. 1993) (insurance company had obligation to defend school district for rape of twelve-year-old student by employee where claim was based on negligent hiring and retention rather than *respondeat superior*).

[325] *E.g., see* Ill. Ann. Stat. ch. 325, para. 5/4 ("Under no circumstances shall any person in charge of such institution, school, facility or agency, or his designated agent to whom such notification has been made, exercise any control, restraint, modification or other change in the report or the forwarding of such report to the Department [of Children and Family Services]").

tact an attorney prior to granting an interview to a social services representative. Waiting until trial to engage legal counsel may jeopardize one's case if damaging admissions have already been made.

School Liability for Sexual Abuse of Students

Acts of sexual abuse or molestation by school employees may very well result in a civil action for damages against the employee and the employer, as well as criminal charges that flow from the sexual abuse. Civil actions against employees will be grounded in torts such as assault and battery, but actions against employers will be based on theories such as *respondeat superior* and negligent hiring, supervision and/or retention. Actions against employers depend on commencing a lawsuit within the appropriate statute of limitations. In *Harrison v. Gore*,[326] a female student who had been sexually molested by her coach at a Christian school was denied her claim against the school because she had failed to file her lawsuit in a timely manner.

Nonpublic schools may find that liability insurance purchased to protect against just such lawsuits can be limited. Liability policies may have limitations that restrict the company's obligation to defend the action and/or indemnify the teacher or school in the event of a successful damages recovery. In *Horace Mann Insurance Company v. Analisa N.*,[327] the insurance company was granted a summary judgment that it was not required to indemnify a teacher who, over the period of three months, had subjected one of his third grade students to twenty separate incidents, including exhibitionism, fondling, and masturbation. The liability policy provided for payment of damages "arising out of an occurrence in the course of the insured's educational employment activities."[328] The *Horace Mann* court concluded that a "reasonable insured could [not] expect that exclusively personal pursuits would be protected by the policy."[329] But an insurance company's obligation to defend an action based on sexual abuse may depend on whether the complaint is grounded in *respondeat superior* or negligent hiring and retention.[330] To the extent that faculty handbooks or state

---

[326] 660 So.2d 563 (La. Ct. App. 1995).

[327] 263 Cal. Rptr. 61 (1989).

[328] *Id.* at 62.

[329] *Id.* at 64.

[330] *See* Durham City Bd. of Educ. v. National Union Fire Ins. Co., 426 S.E.2d 451 (N.C. Ct. App. 1993) (insurance company had obligation to defend school district against claims resulting

statutes require employers to "hold harmless" employees against whom damage awards have been granted, employers may in some cases be able to avoid the obligation where the employee's sexual abuse was considered to have been intentional or criminal in nature.[331]

School liability on the basis of *respondeat superior* requires that two elements be proved: (1) an official, job-related, hierarchical relationship exists in which the employee is given authority over a group of persons; and (2) the nexus between the exercise of the authority and the commission of the tort is such that it is reasonable to foresee that the authority might be abused to the detriment of the victim.[332] *Respondeat superior* is a difficult theory on which to base a recovery. In *Rita M. v. Roman Catholic Archbishop*,[333] seven priests had sexual relations with a sixteen-year-old girl; she became pregnant and was sent to the Philippines to have her baby. In dismissing the complaint against the Archbishop as employer on the basis of *respondeat superior*, the court found the priests' misconduct to be both outside the scope of employment and not foreseeable. Sexual relations with parishioners "are [n]either required [n]or instant to a priest's duties."[334] Foreseeability requires that some basis in fact must have existed upon which one might anticipate the misconduct. In *Rita M.*, the court observed that "[t]he foreseeable event must be characteristic of the activities of the enterprise.... It would defy every notion of logic and fairness to say that sexual activity between a priest and a parishioner is characteristic of the Archbishop of the Roman Catholic Church."[335] In another nonpublic school case, *Anonymous v. Lyman Ward Military Academy*,[336] sexual misconduct by an employee of the school was not foreseeable, in part, because the school had conducted a thorough background check of the employee before hiring him.

---

from rape of eighth-grade student by basketball coach where plaintiff's claims were based on negligent supervision rather than *respondeat superior*).

331 *See* Doe v. Durtschi, 716 P.2d 1238 (1986) (school district had no obligation to indemnify a fourth grade teacher under Idaho's Tort Claims Act where sexual assaults on students were considered to have been committed with criminal intent); Boykin v. District of Columbia, 484 A.2d 560 (D.C. App. 1984) (no obligation of school district to indemnify teacher for assault on twelve-year-old blind, deaf, mute student where teacher's actions were considered to have been for his own malicious and selfish purposes).

332 *See* John R. v. Oakland Unified Sch. Dist., 256 Cal. Rptr. 766, 772 (Cal. 1989).

333 232 Cal. Rptr. 685 (Cal. Ct. App. 1986).

334 *Id.* at 690.

335 *Id.*

336 701 So.2d 25 (Ala. Civ. App. 1997).

Negligent Hiring, Supervision, and Retention

Negligent hiring, supervision, and/or retention has increasingly become a popular cause of action to challenge employment decisions. Although the cause of action can be used in a variety of factual situations, it has most frequently become associated with sexual misconduct by school employees. This cause of action depends on the thoroughness with which an employer investigates an applicant,[337] and then after hiring, the adequacy of supervision and the employer's decision to retain an employee against whom sexual abuse charges have been sustained. Where a student has been sexually abused by an employee, this cause of action will compel examination of the thoroughness with which school officials reviewed an applicant's references and ability to perform the responsibilities of the job.

The hiring process depends on receiving accurate information from previous employers. In *Randi W. v. Muroc Joint Unified School District*,[338] the Supreme Court of California held that a former employer, in writing a letter of recommendation for a placement file, owed a duty not to misrepresent the facts in describing qualifications and the character of former employees. In *Randi W.*, a student who had been sexually assaulted by a school administrator sued the administrator's former school district (in addition to her own school district) on the grounds that the former district had made positive statements concerning the administrator's character and rapport with students but failed to disclose that disciplinary actions had been taken against him for alleged sexual harassment. In reversing a judgment for the school district, the California Supreme Court held that the plaintiff student's injuries were reasonably foreseeable and proximately caused by the former employer's misrepresentations. In addition, the court held that the student did not need to prove that she personally had relied on the negligent misrepresentations in the letter, but only that the hiring decision by officials in her school district had been made in reliance on the representations in the letter.

Although *Randi W.* could be considered of limited precendental value since it is only a state supreme court decision, it is well to remember that the case arose in California, a state that has a history of creating new tort claims which are later

---

337 *See Id.*

338 929 P. 2d 582 (Cal. 1997).

adopted by other states. Since the case involves a mispresentation tort theory, both nonpublic and public schools could be affected.

Randi W. casts doubt on the viability of permitting employees who have allegedly engaged in sexual misconduct to quietly resign rather than face discharge proceedings. Even if schools have no affirmative duty to reveal unsolicited information about a former employee's misconduct, under *Randi W.,* they have a duty to provide accurate information about a former employee if requested. Schools need to be aware that, by avoiding the present unpleasantness of an investigation of alleged sexual misconduct, the problem could return when future mispresentation claims are made by injured students at another school where information had been requested about a former employee, but was not forthcoming because the former employer had only unproved allegations to report. On the other hand, former employers face the possibility of invasion of privacy or defamation claims from former employees where representations regarding allegations of misconduct are made without the employees having had opportunities to defend themselves. The matter is especially troublesome where the former employer has negotiated a confidential, nondisclosure agreement with its former employee.[339]

Beyond the hiring decision, the school's responsibility will depend on making clear that sexual misconduct/harassment between employees and students (and other employees) is prohibited. In *Scott v. Blanchett High School,*[340] a private high school was not liable in negligent hiring and retention for a sexual relationship that developed between a new teacher and a student where the school had found references to be excellent and the school principal had expressed the school's opposition to premarital sex between faculty and students. Not only is it important to check references prior to hiring, but school personnel have an ongoing responsibility to investigate rumors after an employee has been hired and to make reference checks

339 *Cf.* Picton v. Anderson Union High Sch., 57 Cal. Rptr.2d 829 (Ct. App. 1996) (agreement between former teacher and school district whereby teacher agreed to resign after allegations of improper contact with students held to be unenforceable as against public policy; super intendent had sent information regarding allegations to state licensure board) *with* Church v. Stibler, 35 F. Supp.2d 215 (N.D. N.Y. 1999) (former superintendent had civil contempt action against school board where board had revealed information from sealed settlement agreement that could negatively affect superintendent's retirement benefits).

340 747 P.2d 1124 (Wash. Ct. App. 1987).

when a teacher is moved from a teaching position to an administrative position.[341]

In religious schools, hiring and retention of clerical personnel may encounter establishment clause issues. In *Isely v. Capuchin Province*,[342] a negligent hiring and retention claim against a religious order for hiring and retaining two priests who had sexually abused students admitted into a prenovitiate program, was dismissed under the establishment clause. The court reasoned that, even though the religious order might be liable for negligent supervision, any inquiry by a court into "who should be permitted to become or remain a priest necessarily would involve prohibited excessive entanglement with religion."[343] According to the court, negligent supervision, assuming the cause of action is recognized by a state, does not implicate First Amendment issues.

Liability by a school under a *respondeat superior* theory for negligent supervision requires that a plaintiff produce evidence regarding three factors: (1) the school had knowledge of the abuse; (2) school officials conducted an investigation immediately upon learning about the abuse; and (3) the school took appropriate action regarding the employee. In *Anonymous v. Lyman Ward Military Academy*, a state court held that an abused student had failed in his burden of proof as to all three factors: the school, upon receiving information regarding possible abuse in August, discussed the allegations with the employee, and, despite the employee's vehement denials, requested (and received) the employee's resignation in September.

In conclusion, there are general admonitions nonpublic school personnel should be advised of concerning school liability for the sexual abuse or molestation of students by employees.

(1) Check all applications for periods of employment that are accounted for.

(2) Require a reference from the most recent place of employment.

---

[341] *See* Medlin v. Bass, 398 S.E.2d 460 (N.C. 1990) (investigation conducted prior to hiring teacher and again prior to promoting teacher to position as principal).

[342] 880 F. Supp. 1138 (E.D. Mich. 1995).

[343] *Id.* at 1150.

(3) If the applicant has prior teaching/administrative experience, require a reference from each prior school.

(4) Adopt a policy prohibiting sexual conduct (including both physical contact and sexually inappropriate conversation) between students and employees.

(5) State your policy on sexual conduct to each reference, and ask whether the applicant has been involved in conduct or has been accused of conduct that would violate your policy.

(6) Where permitted by your state, conduct a criminal background check.[344]

(7) Ask the applicant to respond on the application whether he or she has been convicted of any felony or misdemeanor involving sexual conduct with minors.

(8) Come to closure on every allegation or rumor involving past or present sexual misconduct of an employee, documenting the persons contacted, the substance of each contact, and the result of the investigation.

(9) If closer supervision is the result of the investigation, identify the person to perform the supervision, the times/places to be supervised, and frequency of reviewal of supervision.

(10) Place statements pertaining to allegations or rumors and documentation pertaining to investigation in the employee's personnel file, not in a separate administrative file.

---

344 The State of Ohio provides that both public and chartered nonpublic schools can request information pertaining to applicants for convictions of felonies and mis-demeanors in the first degree. Ohio Rev. Code § 109.51 et seq.. The Bureau of Criminal Identification and Investigation performs this service after receiving the following information:
(1) The complete name, current address, and other identifying characteristics of the individual whose records are sought; "Other identifying characteristics" means birth, social security number, height, weight, sex, race, and nationality. Ohio Admin.Code § 109:5-1-01.
(2) A complete set of fingerprints of the individual whose records are sought;
(3) The signed consent of the individual whose records are sought.

(11) Reflect complaints regarding sexual misconduct in employee evaluations where the result of the investigation has involved any form of discipline or increased supervision.

(12) Publicize the school policy on sexual conduct and encourage students, parents, and employees to report violations.

Equipment and Facilities

The potential for liability involving defective equipment or facilities theoretically exists in all areas of education but is a special concern in certain high-risk areas. As will be noted in this section and the one to follow on supervision, legal problems involving defective equipment or facilities frequently overlap with problems of supervision.

Clearly, the highest risk areas involving defective equipment or facilities are the industrial arts shop, the science lab, the playground, and areas used for athletics. Persons working in these areas are expected to have the knowledge and skills to recognize those dangerous instrumentalities that contribute to an unsafe school environment.

School personnel have been found to be negligent in permitting students to use a known-defective burner in the science lab.[345] Likewise, a defective blade guard on a circular table saw in an industrial arts wood shop generated liability for the school and the manufacturer of the saw because a school has a high responsibility for programs which "frequently expose young persons to dangers which they otherwise would not encounter in the school setting."[346] School personnel have a responsibility to issue equipment which is appropriate. Thus, a teacher issuing an adult size bat to an elementary student who has never swung a bat or been taught how to do so is responsible to the catcher hit in the face with the bat.[347] Football appears to be the most dangerous athletic sport, and the helmet the most frequently litigated piece of equipment.[348]

---

[345] Station v. Travelers Ins. Co., 292 So.2d 289 (La. Ct. App. 1974).

[346] South Ripley Community Sch. Corp. v. Peters, 396 N.E.2d 144 (Ind. Ct. App. 1979).

[347] Ausmus v. Board of Educ. of Chicago, 508 N.E.2d 298 (Ill. App. Ct. 1987).

[348] Gerrity v. Beatty, 373 N.E.2d 1323 (Ill. 1978) (improperly fitted football helmet); Everett v. Bucky Warren, Inc., 380 N.E.2d 653 (Mass. 1978) (manufacturer liable for improper hockey

The absence of safety features has frequently been the subject of litigation. In *Scott v. Independent School Dist. No. 709*,[349] a Minnesota statute required that,

> Every person shall wear industrial quality eye protective devices when participating in, observing or performing any function in connection with, any courses or activities taking place in eye protection areas . . . of any school, college, university or other educational institution in the state.[350]

The defendant school district was found liable for an eye injury to a student who had temporarily removed his safety goggles, despite repeated warnings not to do so. The *Scott* court noted that the statute did not impose strict liability and hypothesized a set of facts that, despite repeated warnings, the school district would not be liable where the student continued to take off his goggles. However, it is doubtful that a court would ever find that set of facts. Similarly, courts generally find on behalf of injured students where blade guards are not present on shop equipment.[351] Shop teachers are expected to be able to anticipate safety hazards and act to minimize potential injuries. In *Edkins v. Board of Education of City of New York*,[352] student injury resulting from being drawn into a piece of equipment by a loose shirt was determined to have been preventable had the school simply issued shop aprons to students to prevent the contact of loose clothing with equipment. Similarly, failure to furnish a safety helmet or face mask to a catcher in an elementary baseball game[353] or to provide sufficient matting protection around a vaulting horse to ensure a safe landing[354] can be the basis for liability. It is expected that teachers will be familiar with the proper safety equipment to be used, and substitution of a

---

helmet construction and private school hockey coach liable for requiring student to wear helmet).

349 256 N.W.2d 485 (Minn. 1977).

350 Minn. Stat. Ann. § 126.20(1) (West 1994). The statute applies equally to both public and private schools.

351 Barbin on behalf of Barbin v. State, 506 So.2d 888 (La. Ct. App. 1987) ($185,000 judgment, eighty percent of which against the teacher for regularly using saw without a guard); Knight v. City of Philadelphia, 445 A.2d 778 (Pa. Super. Ct. 1982); Scott County Sch. Dist. No. 1 v. Asher, 312 N.E.2d 131 (Ill. App. Ct. 1974); Matteucci v. High Sch. Dist. No. 208, 281 N.E.2d 383 (Ill. App. Ct. 1972) (blade guards not on circular table saws); Severson v. City of Beloit, 167 N.W.2d 258 (Wis. 1969) (absence of guard over a grinder that exploded).

352 41 N.E.2d 75 (N.Y. 1942).

353 *Ausmus*, *supra* note 347.

354 Singer v. School Dist. of Philadelphia, 513 A.2d 1108 (Pa. Commw. Ct. 1986).

less safe piece of equipment may result in liability.[355] Generally, faculty members have the responsibility to know what the limits of safety are for any equipment to be used by students.[356]

School personnel will be expected to choose facilities appropriate to the danger represented in high-risk areas. In the case of *Bush v. Oscada Area Schools*,[357] a student was seriously burned when a ninth grade physical science lab was moved from the science laboratory to a vacant math room because repairs were being made to the laboratory. In addition to the classroom teacher's liability for failure to adequately instruct and supervise, the building principal was negligent in making the room assignment because a reasonable administrator would know that chemicals, fumes, and flames would be present. School personnel and the school itself will generally be liable if a student is injured by a defect on the premises that could have been discovered with a reasonable amount of diligence.[358]

Knowledge of dangerous conditions at a site used by school students can result in liability for a school, even though the site is not on school property. In *Drake v. Mitchell Community Schools*,[359] a high school student contracted a severe case of histoplasmosis from pigeon droppings in an old grain elevator owned by a local bank and used by the school for an annual Halloween fund raising event as a haunted house. Even though the school district was immune under the state's Tort Claims Act for inadequate or negligent inspection of the grain elevator, the school's student council advisor was aware, independent of any inspection, of the risk to students' health. Failure to communicate the risk to the students and to take precautionary measures constituted a breach of the school's duty. With appropriate warning, "students could have been forbidden to enter the building before it had been cleaned or could have been required to wear dust masks until the elevator was cleaned."[360]

The problem of defective, inadequate, or inappropriate equipment or premises ought to be a concern for all school

---

355 Kirchner v. Yale Univ., 192 A.2d 641 (Conn. 1963) (use of push stick instead of push block).

356 Miller v. Macalaster College, 115 N.W.2d 666 (Minn. 1962) (college failed to provide instructions for setting up rented scaffolding).

357 250 N.W.2d 759 (Wis. 1977).

358 Adoin v. Evangeline Parish Sch., 376 So.2d 372 (La. 1979)(large piece of concrete on base path); Sims v. Etowak County Bd. of Educ., 337 So.2d 1310 (Ala. 1976)(improperly installed spectator bleachers); Short v. Griffits, 255 S.E.2d 479 (Vt. 1979) (glass on track). *Contra* Nunez v. Isidore Newman High Sch., 306 So.2d 457 (La. 1975)(wet gym floor).

359 628 N.E.2d 1231 (Ind. Ct. App. 1994).

360 *Id.* at 1234.

officials since it is difficult to defend a lawsuit based upon such a complaint. As between students who generally must use whatever equipment or faculties they are instructed to use and a faculty member who is responsible for selection of equipment and facilities, it is virtually impossible for schools to win.[361] Even where a student increases the risk of injury through his own forgetfulness or disobedience courts are reluctant in noncomparative negligence states to allow a student's error to be the basis for dismissal of the complaint.[362] Courts will sometimes go to what would appear to be extreme limits to find school liability, as where a school was negligent in not replacing a floor to ceiling glass window prior to a student running through it while engaging in unauthorized races in a hallway. The school had earlier replaced glass at the other end of the hallway after a visiting coach had walked through it.[363]

A more troublesome area is whether premises are reasonably safe so as to protect students from outside intruders. In *Vangeli v. Schneider*,[364] a dormitory student at Cornell University had been assaulted in his dormitory room after an intruder had scaled a three story steel grating, entered the dorm from an exterior stairwell through an unlocked fire door, and broke down the student's room door which was locked with a dead bolt lock. Despite the unlocked fire door, the court found the university provided "reasonable security measures" in light of the "extraordinary and unforeseeable means" by which the intruder gained entrance.[365]

Because of the substantial likelihood of successful lawsuits where defective equipment or facilities are involved, the following steps should be taken to reduce the prospect of liability:

(1) Regularly inspect all equipment;

---

361 However, *see* Paulsen v. Unified Sch. Dist. No. 368, 717 P.2d 1051 (Kan. 1986) (school and teacher not liable to student injured on table saw, even though teacher knew students were not using guard and teacher had replaced blade just before injury leaving guard lying on floor, because student had taken beginning woodworking and had passed test on table saw).

362 *See* Matteucci v. High Sch. Dist. No. 208, 281 N.E.2d 383 (Ill. App. Ct. 1972) where the court imposed a higher duty on the teacher to offset student error. For an example of a comparative negligence state, *see* Scott v. Independent Sch. Dist. No. 709, 256 N.W.2d 485 (Minn. 1977) where a $60,000 judgment in favor of the injured plaintiff was reduced to $54,000 because of ten percent student contributory negligence.

363 Wilkinson v. Hartford Accident & Indem. Co., 411 So.2d 22 (La. 1982).

364 598 N.Y.S.2d 837 (N.Y. App. Div. 1993).

365 *Id.* at 839.

(2) Hire only properly qualified personnel so as to be reasonably assured that those personnel will be familiar with equipment/facilities defects and safety measures;

(3) Instruct students about equipment defects, and have them immediately report any indications of defects;

(4) Remove students from high-risk classes when they demonstrate disregard for safety rules;

(5) Instruct faculty to report all defects in equipment and facilities;

(6) Discontinue use of any equipment and facilities until defects or hazards are corrected;

(7) Inspect facilities prior to each use for defects or hazards.

Supervision of Students

Supervision of students is a multifaceted problem involving the interplay of a number of legal questions: whether the teacher's immediate presence could have prevented the student's injury;[366] whether the teacher adequately instructed the students regarding safety hazards;[367] whether a teacher adequately instructed subordinate or substitute employees;[368] whether a teacher made and enforced adequate safety rules;[369] whether the number of supervisory personnel was adequate for the circumstances;[370]

---

366 Hanley v. Hornbeck, 512 N.Y.S.2d 262 (N.Y. App. Div. 1987) (no liability where teacher separated fighting boys within seconds of beginning of fight); Patterson v. Orleans Parish Sch. Bd., 461 So.2d 386 (La. Ct. App. 1984) (no liability where student's leaving line occurred despite teacher's safe, orderly procedures).

367 Webber v. Yeo, 383 N.W.2d 230 (Mich. Ct. App. 1985) (failure to adequately instruct beginner swimming class); Levine v. Live Oak Masonic Hous., Inc., 491 So.2d 489 (La. Ct. App. 1986) (teacher instruction on electrical wiring adequate so no liability for school or teacher for deaths resulting from incorrect wiring).

368 Verkel v. Independent Sch. Dist. No. 709, 359 N.W.2d 579 (Minn. 1984) (failure of school to instruct cheerleader adviser on responsibilities).

369 Gathright v. Lincoln Ins. Co., 688 S.W.2d 931 (Ark. 1985) (absence of rule not cause of student hanging himself); Kingsley v. Independent Sch. Dist., Hill City, 251 N.W.2d 634 (Minn. 1977) (failure to enforce rule a cause of injury).

370 Comuntzis v. Pinellas County Sch. Bd., 508 So.2d 750 (Fla. Dist. Ct. App. 1987) (liability for failure to assign teacher to cafeteria near which a student was beaten); Collins v. Bossier

and whether dangers or risks requiring supervision were known by the school.[371]

Clearly the threshold concern in supervising students ought to be the competency of those directly responsible for supervision. Such competency may be related to formal training or to instructions by someone on the school premises. Thus, a school has been negligent in permitting a janitor to supervise noontime gym activities[372] and in permitting a student to treat an injured athlete.[373] The absence of teacher certification does not in itself appear to constitute negligence per se since presumably a certified teacher, instructing in certain subareas of a broad certification area, may have less knowledge of safety hazards than a noncertified teacher with extensive practical experience in the subareas. In high-risk areas, practical experience may be more important to successful defense of a lawsuit than formal certification. In *Green v. Orleans Parish School Board*,[374] a teacher presumably certified in physical education but with no formal training in wrestling, escaped liability largely because the student's serious injury did not result from improper instruction. The teacher in *Green* had learned some wrestling techniques from college wrestlers, books, and short clinics; however, it would seem foolhardy for a teacher to test the adequacy of his knowledge by the vagaries of the manner in which a student is injured.

The use of persons to instruct in high-risk areas without knowledge of common hazards and safety procedures is potentially dangerous. In *Brahatcek v. Millard School District No. 17*,[375] a student teacher who was assigned by the cooperating school to take the place of the absent regular physical education teacher was liable, along with the school, for the death of a

---

Parish Sch. Bd., 480 So.2d 846 (La. Ct. App. 1985) (ratio of one teacher to one hundred students not inadequate).

371 Fazzolari v. Portland Sch. Dist. No. 1J, 734 P.2d 1326 (Or. 1987) (school liable for student rape because of knowledge of prior attempted assaults); Lawrence v. Grant Parish Sch. Bd., 409 So.2d 1316 (La. Ct. App. 1982) (school liable where teacher knew table saw was stored in classroom without guard or warning sign); Carr v. Indian Lake Sch. Dist., 490 N.Y.S.2d 950 (App. Div. 1987) (no liability for thrown snowball where no prior notice); Velez v. Our Lady of Victory Church, 486 N.Y.S.2d 302 (App. Div. 1985) (no liability for toppled desk where no prior notice of problems); Rhea v. Grandview Sch. Dist. No. JT, 694 P.2d 666 (Wash. Ct. App. 1985) (no liability despite knowledge by adviser and principal that high school students on release day may have alcohol at party).

372 Garber v. Central High Sch. Dist., 251 N.Y.S. 214 (App. Div. 1937).

373 O'Brien v. Township High Sch. Dist., 392 N.E.2d 615 (Ill. App. Ct. 1979).

374 365 So.2d 834 (La. 1979).

375 372 N.W.2d 680 (Neb. 1979).

student. The liability in *Brahatcek* appeared to hinge not on the status of the student teacher but upon the alteration of procedures in the curriculum manual by the other regular physical education teacher, plus the student teacher's lack of awareness of safety hazards involving the swinging of golf clubs in a gymnasium. In *Lynch v. Board of Education of Collinsville*,[376] coaching by untrained and inexperienced classroom teachers of a "powderpuff" girls' tackle football game created liability for the school district.

If a teacher does not have practical experience in certain subareas of high-risk subjects, it would probably be better to not offer those subareas at all. In a tragic set of facts, a student was rendered a quadriplegic as a result of an injury in the gymnastics part of a physical education class. The student recovered a judgment in excess of $1,000,000,[377] ninety percent of which was against the physical education teacher who had just taken over the class a few weeks earlier after the former teacher had been drafted. The new teacher not only unwisely continued the gymnastics part of the class, but he also increased the difficulty of a basic gymnastics skill, a headspring over a rolled mat. By failing to sit on the rolled mat while the student performed a headspring, the teacher demonstrated a lack of even the most rudimentary knowledge of safety procedures. Thus, a simple gymnastics exercise that could have been performed quite safely if supervised by a teacher trained in safety procedures was rendered extremely dangerous.

Although the usual high-risk areas will probably always continue to exist in schools, new areas of risk may appear. One such area is cheerleading, which has tended to become as much a gymnastics display as leading cheers. In *Fisher v. Northwestern State University*,[378] a female cheerleader fell to the ground breaking her ankle while performing a stunt during practice. She recovered $74,448.50 against the university on the theory that the university was sixty-five percent liable in failing to provide adequate supervision. In reversing the damages award, the appeals court identified the following reasons why the university had no duty to provide adult supervision to monitor cheerleading practice:

---

[376] 390 N.E.2d 526 (Ill. App. Ct. 1979).

[377] Larson v. Independent Sch. Dist. No. 314, 289 N.W.2d 112 (Minn. 1980).

[378] 624 So.2d 1308 (La. Ct. App. 1993).

(1) No adult supervisor probably exists "who has the capability of telling cheerleaders what stunts they can safely try next."[379]

(2) There are not enough experts in the state to go around to all high schools and colleges.

(3) Cheerleaders are young adults (at least at the university level) who had been instructed in proper safety techniques at required training camps.

(4) Cheerleaders used spotters at practice.

(5) Policy choice by the university and cheerleaders that cheerleaders should gain responsibility through autonomy did not create liability.

Although much is made of the fact of certification in certain situations,[380] the courts in tort liability cases appear to largely ignore the facade of certification and examine the teacher's knowledge and implementation of safety procedures. In one interesting Title VII non-tort liability case, a federal district court actually rejected a school district's defense that it could not accommodate an industrial arts teacher's claim to be absent for religious reasons because it had no certified industrial arts substitute.[381] The federal court appeared satisfied that even though the substitute was not a certified industrial arts teacher, he had helped construct buildings and had taken three years of industrial arts in high school. What tort liability implications such accommodation in Title VII cases might have where a student is injured while the noncertified teacher is in charge is uncertain, but liability would probably hinge upon the substitute's safety procedures and not upon his or her certification status.

---

379 *Id.* at 1311.

380 Even though certification may not be required to defend successfully against a tort liability claim, states have treated certification in the past as one of the requirements to assure that students are appropriately taught. The failure of nonpublic schools to employ certified teachers has resulted in truancy convictions against parents, State v. Shaver, 294 N.W.2d 883 (N.D. 1980), State v. Moorhead, 308 N.W.2d 60 (Iowa 1981), and an injunction against operation of the school, State v. Faith Baptist Church of Louisville, 301 N.W.2d 571 (Neb. 1981).

381 Wangsness v. Watertown Sch. Dist., 541 F. Supp. 332 (D. S.D. 1982).

The supervisory responsibilities of school personnel are affected by the nature of the area to be supervised. To increase the number of team players or reduce the size of a playing area may create liability. In *Sutphen v. Benthian*,[382] a physical education teacher was negligent in increasing the number of players on a floor hockey team and at the same time reducing the playing area for each game to one-half of the gymnasium. The teacher's intention to involve as many of the students in the class is admirable, but deviations from prescribed rules or standard practice are always calculated risks in high-risk areas. It is possible to enhance a school's potential for liability by increasing the size of the area to be supervised. In *Kersey v. Harbin*,[383] an injured student alleged sufficient facts to warrant a trial on the issue of negligence where one physical education teacher, during the absence of another physical education teacher, agreed to handle both classes at the same time. The student injury occurred between the locker room and the gymnasium while the teacher was in the locker room. In *Kersey,* both teachers had assured the principal that one teacher could handle both classes. The failure of the principal to take reasonable safety measures, irrespective of the teacher's assurances, resulted in the appellate court's refusal to dismiss plaintiff's action against him.

The distance that supervisory personnel are away from the site of injury is a factor in court decisions, but there is obviously no requirement that a teacher be in close proximity to every student. There is no way to predict what is a safe distance to prevent liability because the distance must always be related to the nature of any danger. A teacher 1,000 feet from a student injured on a playground has been held to be too far away to provide adequate supervision.[384] Such a great distance probably provides inadequate supervision regardless of the apparent safety of a play area. One teacher, while supervising alone a play area the size of a football field, prevented liability for herself and her school district by positioning herself approximately thirty feet from the stump of a tree recently cut down.[385] The stump had

---

382 397 A.2d 709 (N.J. 1979).

383 591 S.W.2d 745 (Mo. Ct. App. 1979). *See also* Brahatcek v. Millard Sch. Dist. No. 17, 372 N.W.2d 680 (Neb. 1979) (deviations from a school's prescribed curriculum guide as to where student were to stand to swing golf clubs was a basis for liability).

384 Decker v. Dundee Cent. Sch. Dist., 151 N.E.2d 866 (N.Y. 1958).

385 Partin v. Vernon Parish Sch. Bd., 343 So.2d 417 (La. Ct. App. 1977).

been cut smooth on top, apparently by an observant school employee. Just how the court would have decided the case had the student been injured on an untrimmed stump with rough, jagged edges is difficult to say. Similarly, a teacher supervising 100 students on a playground was not liable because the court considered adequate her instructions to students regarding the use of playground equipment.[386] Occasionally teachers have work or storage areas that do not permit visual contact with all students at all times. Liability in such cases is never predicated solely upon the distance of the teacher from the student or the lack of visual contact, but upon whether the teacher should have reasonably anticipated certain kinds of problems, such as conflicts among students,[387] danger represented by certain kinds of equipment,[388] and the possibility of student error due to inadequate instruction for new equipment.[389]

Adequacy of teacher instruction as related to the potential danger of a school area is a legal problem that demands particular attention. The case of *Smith v. Archbishop of St. Louis*[390] is a good example of the relationship among teacher supervision, teacher instruction, and a potentially dangerous classroom situation. In *Smith*, a teacher in a Roman Catholic elementary school had placed a lighted candle on her desk as a religious exercise. The second graders in plaintiff's room were preparing for a school play, and while plaintiff and her classmates were putting on their paper costumes in the classroom, plaintiff's costume caught fire on the candle resulting in burns to twenty-two percent to forty-five percent of her upper body. The plaintiff spent twenty-six days in a hospital with much physical and psychological pain because of burns and grafting. Plaintiff's psychologist testified regarding permanent psychological harm when plaintiff reaches adolescence because of very noticeable scars. In upholding a $1,250,000 judgment against defendant

---

386 Collins v. Bossier Parish Sch. Bd., 480 So.2d 846 (La. Ct. App. 1985).

387 Hanley v. Hornbeck, 512 N.Y.S.2d 262 (N.Y. App. Div. 1987); Hammond v. Scott, 232 S.E.2d 336 (S.C. 1977); Collins v. Wilson, 331 So.2d 603 (La. 1976); Kim v. State of Hawaii, 616 P.2d 1376 (Hawaii 1980).

388 Lawrence v. Grant Parish Sch. Bd., 409 So.2d 1316 (La. Ct. App. 1982).

389 Miles v. School Dist. No. 138, 281 N.W.2d 396 (Neb. 1979) (instruction to student who had operated same machine in prior class); Potter v. North Carolina Sch. of the Arts, 245 S.E.2d 188 (N.C. 1978) (instruction to student who had never operated a fog machine); Brittan v. State, 103 N.E.2d 485 (N.Y. 1951) (instruction to students administering physical education tests); Miller v. Macalaster College, 115 N.W.2d 666 (Minn. 1962) (instruction in assembling and use of scaffolding).

390 632 S.W.2d 516 (Mo. Ct. App. 1982).

archdiocese, the appellate court relied upon the following facts in the case:

(1) The classroom teacher knew that students and lighted candles posed danger, but no special instruction had been given prior to the day of injury and none given on the day of the injury.

(2) The principal of the school acknowledged that seven- and eight-year-old children do not pay much attention to their own safety.

(3) Defendant archdiocese had no guidelines or policy regarding burning candles in a classroom.

While noting that school is not an insurer of a child's safety and that a teacher is not required to keep each member of her class within her eyesight at all times, the *Smith* court declared that ordinary care for children requires more vigilance and caution than for adults.

The responsibility to supervise includes not only dangerous items such as fire, as in *Smith*, but activities that students are performing for the first time. In *Johnson v. School District of Millard*,[391] the district was liable for injury to a first-grade student who was thrown into a wall while participating in a game of London Bridge. The students had never played the game before, and the teacher, demonstrating how two other students were to hold plaintiff and swing him back and forth, instructed them not to swing their arms too much and not to yell. While the two students swung plaintiff, the teacher turned her back to write on the board, and she did not hear plaintiff's cries for help over the noise in the room. The court observed that the teacher had breached her duty to supervise where appropriate supervision should have included direct observation of the students during the early portions of a new classroom game.

Supervision of students is obviously a critical school responsibility and one that can be costly in money and public relations where such supervision is inadequate. The higher the risk area the greater the duty to supervise and the greater the likelihood that a school may be found negligent even where it

391 573 N.W.2d 116 (Neb. 1998).

has appeared to exercise ordinary care. The chain reaction effect of liability is illustrated in *Sansonni v. Jefferson Parish School Board*[392] where an injured sixth-grade plaintiff recovered $45,000 as a result of a fall in a school lunchroom on some spilled spaghetti sauce. The *Sansonni* court noted that a school lunchroom is a high-risk area, and the defendant school's failure to adequately supervise made it responsible for all costs and damages. Normally a fall on a lunchroom floor might produce a bruise, but in the case of the plaintiff, it resulted in a broken leg because plaintiff had osteogenesis imperfecta, a congenital defect causing brittle bones. Plaintiff spent thirty-four days in traction and six weeks in a body cast, as a result of which he developed kidney stones necessitating six more days in the hospital. The prolonged hospitalization and wearing of the body cast contributed to a fracture of the vertebrae resulting in the need to wear a back brace. However, despite the correct medical care, one leg did not heal properly so that it was shorter and bowed. The bowed and shorter leg put strain on the other leg necessitating wearing a leg brace. What began as a simple fall in a high-risk area ended up as a pain-ful experience for the student and an expensive lesson for the school.

No area of supervision gets more attention from nonpublic (or public) school administrators than absence of supervision. Normally, absent supervision is approached solely as an absent teacher problem. Such an approach is unfortunate since there are really two separate and distinct problem areas—the absent student and the absent teacher. A student may be absent from adult supervision for a number of reasons. Students in hallways during classes and in restrooms are very often unsupervised. In *Larry v. Commercial Union Insurance Co.*,[393] a day care student injured in a restroom successfully sued the school because of the large number of students in the classroom, the student was able to leave the classroom for the restroom without the teacher's knowledge.

Liability in such absent student situations is based less on the absence of direct supervision than upon the presence of dangerous conditions, such as wet restroom floors, assaults in the hallways or restrooms by older students, or strangers that could have reasonably been anticipated by school personnel. The

---

[392] 344 So.2d 42 (La. Ct. App. 1977).
[393] 277 N.W.2d 821 (Wis. 1979).

critical factor is whether the danger could have been reasonably expected. In *Roe v. Catholic Diocese of Memphis, Inc.*,[394] a sexual assault by one four-year-old student upon another in an unsupervised restroom was not the kind of event the classroom teacher could have foreseen in order to provide appropriate warning and supervision. Obviously, even though a school wins in court in such a case, it still may have to deal with any residual concerns among parents regarding the safety of their children.

Students need to be frequently instructed about safety rules in hallways and restrooms, including the need to promptly report dangerous or suspicious circumstances, such as wet floors or strangers in the building. A fourth-grade girl in *District of Columbia v. Doe*[395] recovered over $250,000 in damages when she was lured from the school and raped after a teacher had left her in charge of a second-grade class while the teacher went to another area of the building for supplies.

The more that school personnel deviate from established rules or routines, the greater the likelihood of liability. To send students to restaurants, neighboring stores, or a teacher's car in the parking lot to personally secure items for teacher use or items for school use are situations that would be difficult to justify in court. Ill or injured students are frequently sent to a nurse's office or the school office, yet seldom is much thought given to problems that should be reasonably anticipated on the way to the office. Does the student know the way to the office? Is he or she so ill or injured that other students should be sent with him or her? Is there reason to expect problems in the hallways, such as other aggressive students? With elementary students it is never a bad practice to send one or two students along with a student sent to the office to assure that he or she does in fact arrive at the intended destination. Junior and senior high students would probably not want a fellow traveler unless they do not know the way or appear too ill to be sent alone. A teacher or school would normally not be liable for assaults in hallways, restrooms, or other unsupervised areas unless there was actual knowledge of specific indications of bad feeling between students[396] or of systemic school unrest, such as racial unrest.[397] A student who leaves

---

[394] 950 S.W.2d 27 (Tenn. Ct. App. 1997).
[395] 524 A.2d 30 (D.C. App. 1987).
[396] Gammon v. Edwardsville Commun. Unit Sch. Dist. No. 7, 103 N.E.2d 43 (Ill. App. Ct. 1980).
[397] School Bd. of Palm Beach v. Anderson, 411 So.2d 940 (Fla. Dist. Ct. App. 1982).

school without permission and is injured or killed normally does not generate liability for the school.[398]

The teacher who absents herself or himself from the classroom or area where students are located presents a more frequently litigated problem, but such a problem is one over which nonpublic school administrators should have more direct control. Contrary to popular myth, there is no absolute liability for a teacher or school if a teacher leaves the classroom unsupervised. Any liability in such a situation will depend upon resolution of two factual questions. First, could the teacher's presence have prevented the student injury? Such a determination will depend upon the nature of the class (e.g., English composition versus industrial arts), upon knowledge of the students in the class, e.g., personal hostilities or medical or special education problems and upon school requirements.[399] Second, what was the reason for the teacher's absence? That reason needs to be balanced against the items in the first question. Reasons for teacher absence can best be viewed on a spectrum from emergency situations at one end, as where a teacher assists an ill or injured student to the office, to solely personal concerns at the other end, as when a teacher goes to the faculty lounge during classtime for a cup of coffee.

The farther toward the emergency end of the spectrum for a teacher's absence, the more substantial the proof will have to be by an injured student that instructions left by the teacher were not adequate. In emergencies, courts are more likely to focus on the teacher's instructions, rather than on whether the teacher's presence would have prevented an injury. Instructions to an industrial arts class not to use equipment (including how to shut off the central power switch) or to a physical education class to sit along the wall and talk without engaging in activities or fighting may well be adequate. The variable factor that could offset even the best instructions is the amount of time a teacher is absent. The longer the absence, and thus, the longer the period of time a group of students do not have a teacher present, the

[398] Levandoski v. Jackson City Sch. Dist., 328 So.2d 339 (Miss. 1979) (student killed after skipping school); Oglesby v. Seminole City Bd. of Instr., 328 So.2d 515 (Fla. Dist. Ct. App. 1976) (student killed on way home from school). *Contra* Hoyem v. Manhattan Beach City Sch. Dist., 585 P.2d 851 (Cal. 1978) (student injured after skipping out of school).

[399] Rock v. Central Square Sch. Dist., 494 N.Y.S.2d 579 (N.Y. App. Div. 1985) (no liability for school or teacher when student struck in eye by thrown pencil; teacher was in classroom doorway observing hallway during passing of classes as required in Faculty Handbook).

greater the likelihood that a school may be responsible for injury to students left in the classroom.

Absence of a teacher from a classroom where one student is injured by another because the teacher is in the hallway between classes monitoring students moves substantially away from the personal end of the supervision spectrum and makes recovery for lack of supervision by a plaintiff more difficult.[400] The emergency end of the spectrum is illustrated by *Kim v. State of Hawaii*[401] where a female teacher left her classroom to go next door to get the principal and assistant principal to restrain a student who had suddenly entered her classroom to attack another student. During her brief absence, the student attacked was seriously injured. The supreme court affirmed the trial court's dismissal of the complaint, primarily because this was an emergency situation with no reasonable notice to the teacher of the probability of invasion of the classroom by another student.

In *Hammond v. Scott*,[402] an industrial arts teacher was in a storage room adjacent to the classroom supervising storage of projects when one student standing two feet from a trash barrel threw a nail toward the trash barrel and struck plaintiff in the eye. Dismissal of the complaint against the teacher and the school was sustained because the teacher consistently enforced his rule against throwing objects, and because there was no evidence of ill feeling between the two students.

The reverse of this is true when the teacher's absence moves closer to the personal end of the spectrum. In *Lawrence v. Grant Parish School Board*,[403] an industrial arts teacher who frequently left the class to get scrap metal for welding and to catch students smoking was found negligent, along with the school, when a student severed a finger on a table saw stored in one of the welding booths. The fact that the teacher told the students at the beginning of the course not to use the power equipment and that he gave them a list of over 200 rules regarding the use of equipment in class did not excuse or mitigate his absence. Industrial arts classrooms are high-risk areas, and the teacher's absence in *Lawrence* suggested poor lesson planning as well as

---

400 *See* Coyle v. Harper, 622 So.2d 303 (Ala. 1993) (teacher monitoring passage of students in hallways performing a discretionary function and entitled to immunity in suit brought by student in classroom injured by another student).

401 616 P.2d 1376 (Hawaii 1980).

402 232 S.E.2d 336 (S.C. 1977).

403 409 So.2d 1316 (La. Ct. App. 1982).

performance of unnecessary policing functions during classtime. In *Cirillo v. City of Milwaukee*,[404] forty-eight twelve- to fourteen-year-old students were instructed to shoot baskets and not engage in horseplay while the teacher left the class for some unknown reason. The teacher was absent for twenty-five minutes, and during that time, two students began engaging in a progressively rougher game of keepaway until plaintiff was injured. Whereas the teacher's positive and negative instructions to the students were commendable, and are proper procedures to follow for any teacher absence, the supreme court reversed the trial court's dismissal of the complaint. Adequate supervision is definitely the key to the avoidance of unwanted litigation. The following general suggestions may tend to increase the safety awareness of supervisory personnel:

(1) Hold at least one faculty and staff in-service day at the beginning of each school year to make school personnel aware of potential problems. Faculty and staff should have primarily a preventive function with regard to student safety rather than a reactive function.

(2) School officials should assert leadership and set safety policies that authorize teachers to take certain kinds of actions, without the fear that those actions in an emergency would not be supported by the school. For example, teachers should be encouraged, where possible, to establish partnerships with neighboring classroom teachers to watch their classes in an emergency.

(3) Faculty in high-risk equipment areas should test each student on each piece of equipment and have each student sign a set of course safety rules to acknowledge receiving and reading them.

(4) Periodic oral instructions in high-risk equipment areas are always advisable (e.g., reminding students that a guard must be on the saw before use).

---

[404] 150 N.W.2d 460 (Wis. 1967).

(5) Instruct students of specific safety hazards on school facilities that are to be reported (e.g., water on floor, broken stair treads, broken desks, glass or sharp stones on playground, malfunctioning equipment, strangers in the building).

(6) Permit faculty to supervise activities only if their qualifications are sufficient for the level of risk of the subject area being supervised.

(7) Have a set of procedures regarding class expectations when a teacher must be absent in an emergency. Publish these procedures and go over them periodically.

Chapter II

Institution, Student, and Faculty Relationships: Constitutional and Contractual Considerations

Introduction

The relationship between nonpublic educational institutions and their faculty and students is contractual in nature. Courts have consistently held that both conduct and academic matters in nonpublic schools raise contractual, as opposed to constitutional, issues. In this sense, nonpublic schools differ from public ones in that these same issues in public schools frequently have a constitutional overlay.[405] Although courts tend to grant considerable deference to public institutions in handling academic matters, a modicum of due process is still required.[406]

Courts offer several reasons for treating student and faculty conduct academic matters as similar contractual issues in nonpublic schools. First, the constitutional, substantive, and procedural constraints affecting public schools are generally not applicable to nonpublic schools.[407] Second, nonpublic school student and faculty rights alike are generally expressed in or implied from written documents such as applications, promotional literature, and handbooks.[408] Third, although

405 *See generally,* Mawdsley, Academic Misconduct: Cheating and Plagiarism 45-52 (NOLPE 1994) for a discussion regarding similarities and differences between public and nonpublic educational institutions in addressing academic and conduct violations.

406 *See* Board of Curators of Univ. of Missouri v. Horowitz, 435 U.S. 78, 84 (1978) (in upholding dismissal of a medical student in her last semester of medical school, the Court found acceptable the faculty's informal review process, with the observation that "courts are particularly ill-equipped to evaluate academic performance.")

407 *See generally* Valente, Education Law; Public and Private Vol. 2, 337-38 (1985).

408 *E.g. see* R. Mawdsley, *Litigation Involving Higher Education Employee and Student Handbooks*, 109 Ed.Law Rep. 1091 (1996).

contractual rights for faculty in nonpublic schools tend to involve greater judicial scrutiny than for students, there is nonetheless more similarity between conduct and academic matters in the nonpublic sector than in the public one.[409] Fourth, the relative dearth of reported cases involving private school rights, when compared to the multitude of cases in the public sector, makes the consideration of faculty and students together more feasible.[410]

Constitutional Constraints

Concepts of Fairness

Students and employees in nonpublic schools do not enjoy the panoply of constitutional rights that their colleagues in the public sector enjoy because the purpose of the rights ensconced within the Bill of Rights of the U.S. Constitution is to protect against government action. Nonpublic schools may come into conflict with their students' and employees' contractual,[411] statutory,[412] or regulatory rights,[413] but, without a sufficient connection to government, they cannot violate their constitutional rights. However, although nonpublic schools may

---

409 The limitation or expansion of student and faculty rights seem to go hand-in-hand in nonpublic institutions. *Cf.* Bob Jones Univ. v. U.S., 461 U.S. 574 (1983) (religious university with rigid student and faculty conformity to rules and no faculty tenure) *with* Gay Rights Coalition v. Georgetown Univ., 536 A.2d 1 (D.C. App. 1987) (religious university with faculty tenure and well-established and independent student senate recognition of student groups). However, even though both universities had quite different approaches to the nature of faculty and student rights, both ran afoul of established public policies, Bob Jones University for racial discrimination among students and Georgetown University for discrimination against students based on sexual orientation.

410 The reluctance of parents and students, especially those in religious schools, to sue their institutions is an undocumented but probably quite real constraint. *See generally*, Valente, *supra* note 407, Vol. 1 and 2, for the considerably fewer number of pages needed to discuss nonpublic school law as compared with public school law.

411 *See* Andre v. Pace Univ., 618 N.Y.S.2d 975 (N.Y. City Ct. 1994) (university liable for damages for breach of contract where professor had taught a computer course in a more advanced manner than had been advertised in the catalog).

412 *See* Axelrod v. Phillips Acad., Andover, 36 F. Supp.2d 46 (D. Mass. 1999) (ADHD student discharged from private school ordered reinstated where school had not adhered to ADA requirements); Keefe v. Youngstown Diocese of Catholic Church, 698 N.E.2d 1009 (Ohio Ct. App. 1997) (employee entitled to go to trial as to whether her discharge had violated the state Whistleblower Act); Patzka v. Viterbo College, 917 F. Supp. 654 W.D. Wis. 1996) (college violated Federal Debt Collection Practices Act and state law by attempting to collect interest on student charges not authorized in settlement agreement).

413 *See* Bob Jones Univ. v. U.S., 461 U.S. 574 (1983) (Court upheld IRS regulation revoking tax exempt status for section 501(c)(3) organizations that discriminated on the basis of race, which, in the case of Bob Jones University, amounted to internal prohibitions against interracial dating and marriage).

not be subject directly to the constitution, they cannot totally remove themselves from its shadow. Due process concepts that are so much a part of the public sector have influenced the expectations that students and employees have in their relationship with nonpublic schools.[414] Thus, litigants suing nonpublic schools, although they cannot successfully invoke constitutional due process rights, will invoke concepts of fairness that mimic due process.[415]

At the heart of due process is the expectation that persons will be treated fairly and will be subject to fair rules. In the public sector, this expectation is identified by the terms "procedural" and "substantive" due process rights, while in the nonpublic sector, the expectation is identified as rules that are clearly stated and a process for reviewing violations that is neither arbitrary nor capricious.[416] Generally in nonpublic schools, this expectation of fairness is translated into reasonable contractual notice of acceptable (or unacceptable) conduct, as well as penalties for violations. Frequently, a common dilemma is that nonpublic school applications, promotional materials, handbooks, and documents that form the basis for student and employee contracts, contain language that is incomplete, inconsistent, or inaccurate. To the extent that these documents create conflicting or ambiguous standards, students and faculty are likely to contest any discipline on the basis that they have been treated unfairly.

All nonpublic educational institutions should be committed to clearly stating their expectations for conduct and the process

---

414 The watershed of public sector student and teacher rights has usually been attributed to Tinker v. Des Moines Indep. Community Sch. Dist., 393 U.S. 503, 506 (1969) ("students, and teachers, [do not] shed their constitutional rights to freedom of speech or expression at the schoolhouse gate"). For an analysis of *Tinker* in light of the more recent Supreme Court decisions in Hazelwood Sch. Dist. v. Kuhlmeier, 484 U.S. 260 (1987), Bethel Sch. Dist. v. Fraser, 478 U.S. 675 (1986), and New Jersey v. T.L.O., 469 U.S. 809 (1985), see R. Mawdsley and A. Mawdsley Free Expression and Censorship: Public Policy and the Law (NOLPE 1988).

415 *See* Harvey v. Palmer College of Chiropractic, 363 N.W.2d 443, 444 (Iowa Ct. App. 1984) ("requirements imposed by the common law on private universities parallel those imposed by the due process clause on public universities.")

416 A good resource for examining constitutional requirements for public schools and those for nonpublic schools as well is the Yearbook of Education Law, published annually by the Education Law Association (ELA), that contains all reported law cases involving education for that year, including those cases dealing with public and nonpublic employees and students. *See, e.g.*, C. Russo (ed.), The Yearbook of Education Law 1999 3-41, 83-117, 261-293, 297-328. (ELA: Dayton OH.) *See also*, Ahlum v. Administrators of Tulane Educ. Fund, 617 So.2d 96 (La. Ct. App. 1993) (disciplinary actions in nonpublic institutions will be viewed in terms of whether they are arbitrary and capricious).

by which they will determine whether those expectations have been violated. Accomplishing this purpose requires that a school's contractual documents be regularly monitored by competent legal counsel. One source has ably expressed the nonpublic school's legal responsibility as follows:

> Critical to preventive planning is periodic review of institutional policies and practices. Many institutions develop a faculty handbook and assume the handbook contains all of the appropriate policies relating to personnel and institutional concerns. Rarely is this the case. Practices change as do federal and state statutory and regulatory requirements, all of which necessitate constant revision of faculty handbooks. Similarly student affairs policies should be reassessed periodically to ensure that they conform to institutional requirements and reflect fair process. Sometimes institutions follow practices that are inconsistent with their policies; if this is the case, then either the practice should be changed to reflect policy or the policy should be changed so that it conforms to the practice.[417]

State Action

The immunity of nonpublic schools from the constitutional rights applicable to public institutions results from the absence of state action under the Fourteenth Amendment.[418] The absence of state action means that nonpublic school litigants cannot track the constitutional rights in the Bill of Rights applicable to government-operated public schools through to nonpublic schools. Even though litigants clearly cannot make a successful claim directly under the Fourteenth Amendment, they attempt to achieve the same result using Section 1983 of the Civil Rights Act of 1964.[419] Section 1983 creates no rights on its own and is

---

417 LEGAL DESKBOOK FOR ADMINISTRATORS OF INDEPENDENT COLLEGES AND UNIVERSITIES II, 2-3 (K. Weeks, ed. 1983).

418 The Fourteenth Amendment, through which the substantive and procedural rights in the Bill of Rights are made applicable to the states, provides in part: "No State shall make or enforce any law which shall abridge the privileges or immunities of citizens of the United States; nor shall any State deprive any person of life, liberty, or property, without due process of law; nor deny to any person within its jurisdiction the equal protection of the laws." For the substantive and procedural rights applicable to public institutions, *see generally* VALENTE, EDUCATION LAW: PUBLIC AND PRIVATE, Vol. I, at 259-312.

419 42 U.S.C. § 1983 provides in part: "Every person who, under color of any statute, ordinance, regulation, custom or usage, of any State ... subjects, or causes to be subjected, any citizen of

purely a remedial statute that permits claimants to sue for violations of constitutional rights or federal law.

However, Section 1983, like the Fourteenth Amendment, applies only where there is state action.[420] To make their claim for state action under Section 1983, litigants over the years have set forth three theories[421] by which otherwise private activity might be deemed state action for federal jurisdictional and constitutional purposes:[422] the state entanglement theory;[423] the state or public function theory;[424] and the symbiotic relationship theory.[425] Under these theories, litigants have alleged a number of factual connections as creating sufficient nexus for finding state action:

---

the United States or other person within the jurisdiction thereof to the deprivation of any rights, privileges, or immunities secured by the Constitution and laws, shall be liable to the party injured .... "

420 *See* Jackson v. Strayer College, 941 F. Supp. 192 (D. D.C. 1996) (without state action, federal courts had no jurisdiction under due process to stop a private college from prohibiting students from forming a student government).

421 In order for any of the state action theories to support a finding of state action, at least one of the tests of Blum v. Yaretsky, 457 U.S. 991 (1982), must be met: (1) the extent to which the private entity is subject to state or federal regulation; (2) sufficiency of close nexus between state and private entity so that action of the latter is treated as that of the former; (3) presence of such coercive power or significant encouragement of the state that private decisions are essentially those of the state. In Milonas v. Williams, 691 F.2d 931, 940 (10th Cir. 1982), *cert denied* 460 U.S. 1069 (1983), the Supreme Court refused to hear an appeal from a case where former students in a nonpublic school for youths successfully brought a section 1983 action against the school. In finding that the state had "insinuated itself with the Provo Canyon School [so] as to be considered a joint participant in the offending actions," the court relied on the following state-school actions: involuntary placement of students by a juvenile court in the school; detailed learning contracts between the nonpublic school and public school districts; state funding for tuition; school promotion of state funding for tuition; school promotion of state funding in its literature; and a number of applicable state regulations.

422 For a discussion of the following three theories, *see* Huff v. Notre Dame High Sch., 456 F. Supp. 1145 (D. Conn. 1978).

423 *See* Howard v. Pine Forge Academy, 678 F. Supp. 1120 (E.D. Pa. 1987) (compliance with state requirement applicable to all public and private schools not state action); Vincent v. Western Technical Corp., 828 F.2d 563 (9th Cir. 1987) (reception of all funds from federal government to perform contract work according to federal standards not state action where regulations had no bearing on personnel policies).

424 *See* Hawkins v. NCAA, 652 F. Supp. 602 (N.D.Ill. 1987) (NCAA regulatory function not traditionally and exclusively a state function even though public interest may be served); Transport Careers v. National Home Study Council, 646 F. Supp. 1474 (N.D. Ind. 1986) (accreditation duties not traditionally a state function).

425 *See* Williams v. Discovery Day Sch., 924 F. Supp. 41 (E.D. Pa. 1996) (private day school using space in a federal office building not a state actor for purposes of refusing to permit parent to see child's records); Stone v. Dartmouth College, 682 F. Supp. 106 (D. N.H. 1988) (no symbiotic relationship between private college and state so that college disciplinary action against students who had torn down structures protesting investment in South Africa constituted a substitution for state criminal prosecution). *But see*, Craft v. Vanderbilt Univ., 940 F. Supp. 1185 (M.D. Tenn. 1996) (university might be liable under section 1983 where it had involved itself closely with medical research under state auspices that was later concealed).

(1) Reception of state and/or federal assistance;[426]

(2) Accreditation or state licensure;[427]

(3) Granting of a state charter;[428]

(4) Certification of teachers;[429]

(5) Tax exemption;[430]

(6) Filing of state forms;[431]

(7) Performance of a public function, viz., education;[432]

(8) Establishing policies required by government;[433]

(9) Meeting state minimum education standards;[434]

(10) State inspection and regulation;[435]

(11) Service of government officials on the governing board where the government does not have the authority to appoint a majority.[436]

---

426 Rendell-Baker v. Kohn, 457 U.S. 830 (1982); Smith v. Duquesne Univ., 612 F. Supp. 72 (W.D. Pa. 1985); Murphy v. Villanova Univ., 547 F. Supp. 512 (E.D. Pa. 1982); Grafton v. Brooklyn Law Sch., 478 F.2d 1137 (2d Cir. 1973).

427 Huff v. Notre Dame High Sch., 456 F. Supp. 1145 (D. Conn. 1978); Geraci v. St. Xavier High Sch., 13 Ohio Op. 3d 146 (Ohio 1978); Bright v. Isenbarger 314 F. Supp. 1382 (N.D. Ind. 1970).

428 Fischer v. Driscoll, 546 F. Supp. 861 (E.D. Pa. 1982); Blackburn v. Fisk University, 443 F.2d 121 (6th Cir. 1971).

429 *Geraci*, *supra* note 427.

430 *Bright*, *supra* note 427; Brown v. Mitchell, 409 F.2d 592 (10th Cir. 1969).

431 Albert v. Carovano, 851 F.2d 561 (2d Cir. 1988); *Bright*, *supra* note 427.

432 *Huff*, *supra* note 427; Berrios v. Inter-American Univ., 409 F. Supp. 769 (D. P.R. 1975), *appeal dismissed* 426 U.S. 942 (1975); Grossner v. Trustees of Columbia Univ., 287 F. Supp. 535 (S.D. N.Y. 1968).

433 Logan v. Bennington College, 72 F.3d 1017 (2d Cir. 1995) (establishing sexual harassment policy required by state law); Missert v. Trustees of Boston Univ., 73 F. Supp.2d 68 (D. Mass 1999) (creating human subjects research board required for federally funded research).

434 Nobles v. Alabama Christian Sch., 917 F. Supp. 786 (D. Ala. 1996).

435 Tavolini v. Mt. Sinai Med. Ctr., 984 F. Supp. 196 (S.D. N.Y. 1997); Moghimzadeh v. College of St. Rose, 653 N.Y.S.2d 198 (N.Y. App.Div. 1997); Gardiner v. Mercyhurst College, 942 F. Supp. 1055 (1996)

436 Hack v. President and Fellows of Yale College, 16 F. Supp.2d 183 (D. Conn. 1998).

None of these connections claimed by litigants has been successful for state action, and courts have even demonstrated creativity in using terminology to not find state action. In *Imperiale v. Hahneman University,*[437] a medical school student whose degree had been revoked by the university had no Section 1983 cause of action because the contacts between the Commonwealth of Pennsylvania and the medical school were considered to be "state-aided" rather than "state-related."

Generally, the Section 1983 status of nonpublic schools continues to be controlled by *Rendell-Baker v. Kohn.*[438] In *Rendell-Baker*, the U.S. Supreme Court refused to find state action despite the fact that the defendant, a nonpublic school for maladjusted high school students, received virtually all of its referrals from public school districts, received at least ninety percent of its operating budget from state and federal funds, and had to comply with a variety of regulations common to all public schools such as record keeping, student-teacher ratio, maintenance of job descriptions, and written statements describing personnel standards and procedures.

Since *Rendell-Baker,* federal courts have consistently refused to permit plaintiff-students or employees to drag constitutional rights into nonpublic schools via Section 1983. In *Albert v. Carovano,*[439] students who had occupied a private college's administration building for a weekend were suspended under college rules. The State of New York required every college and university in the state to submit rules adopted by the institution's governing body pertaining to maintenance of public order and providing ejections, suspension, expulsion, or other appropriate action for infractions. However, the state requirement was an insufficient nexus to support a Section 1983 claim because the state's role was "merely to keep on file rules submitted by colleges and universities," and the state "never sought to compel schools to enforce these rules and has never even inquired about enforcement."[440] In *Ben-Yonatan v. Concordia College Corporation,*[441] a federal court refused to bestow constitutional

---

437 776 F. Supp. 189 (E.D. Pa. 1991), *aff'd* 966 F.2d 125 (3d Cir. 1992).

438 457 U.S. 830 (1982).

439 851 F.2d 561 (2d Cir. 1988).

440 *Id.* at 568. However, the court did observe that inconsistent enforcement of the schools' rules to blacks and Latinos might be the basis for a claim under section 1981 of the Civil Rights Act. *Id.* at 573, citing to Bernbaum v. Trussell, 347 F.2d 86, 90 (2d Cir. 1965).

441 863 F. Supp. 983 (D. Minn. 1994).

procedural rights upon a suspended student. As the court observed, "the fact that Concordia [was] in the business of furnishing higher education [did] not establish state action."[442] In addition, the college's receiving substantial amounts of state and federal financial support did not constitute state action where it had not received "any support that was not available to other educational institutions."[443]

Contractual Due Process

The effect of finding no state action for schools is that the student and employee rights in nonpublic educational institutions will be determined by contract rather than under the federal constitution. However, constitutional concepts, especially due process, frequently find their way into litigation involving interpretation of contractual terms. One important due process constitutional standard with two different aspects is that of notice.[444] Notice can mean awareness of what kinds of punishable conduct are includable within contract language (frequently found within student or employee handbooks), or notice can refer to awareness of matters pertaining to one's defense of contract violations, such as specificity of charges, hearing dates, or presence of counsel.

Both aspects of notice were issues in *Fellheimer v. Middlebury College.*[445] In *Fellheimer*, a student was suspended for one year after having been found guilty of "disrespect of persons," language mirroring that in the student handbook requiring all students "to respect the dignity, freedom, and rights of others." The student had been notified by school officials prior to his hearing that he was charged with rape, a charge of which he was found not guilty at the hearing, but he had not been notified that his conduct was also being reviewed under the "respect" provision. In the student's challenge to the hearing committee's decision, the court addressed both aspects of notice. Regarding the first aspect of notice, the court held that "disrespect of persons," although broad enough to encompass a wide variety

---

442 *Id.*at 987.

443 *Id.*

444 *See, e.g.* Goss v. Lopez, 419 U.S. 565 (1975) (the seminal public education case involving notice, where a suspension of ten days or less for a public school student requires notice of charges, explanation of evidence against a student and an opportunity in an informal hearing for the student to present his side).

445 869 F. Supp. 238 (D. Vt. 1994).

of conduct, was not so vague as to be unenforceable. However, with regard to the second aspect of notice, because the student had not been notified of the "disrespect of persons" charge prior to the hearing, he was entitled to another hearing. The court observed that the college's contractual responsibility was "to state the nature of the charges with sufficient particularity to permit the student to defend himself."[446] In other words, the court agreed with the student that the two charges—rape and respect of persons—were different enough that the student should have been notified that he would be expected to defend himself against both conduct standards.

Fellheimer is consistent with earlier higher education case law that, although nonpublic colleges and universities may not have to meet constitutional standards of due process in dealing with students or employees, courts seem quite willing to impose upon the disciplinary options of such schools a general sense of fairness.[447] In *Aronson v. North Park College*,[448] the court upheld a student dismissal where the student had been diagnosed as a chronic paranoid and had refused to appear for treatment. Apparently because of the student's uncooperative attitude, the court found no infirmity with the school catalog provision permitting dismissal where a student is "undesirable and whose continuation in the school is detrimental to himself or his fellow students."[449] A troublesome companion catalog provision that "dismissal may be made without specific charges"[450] was not at issue under the facts of this case. Since this provision had not been litigated, one is not certain what the college meant by "specific charges," but presumably it was something different from the broad handbook language under which the student had been dismissed. The notion that colleges or universities could dismiss a student today without identifying the specific conduct that allegedly violates the handbook standard would seem to be the kind of unfairness that could result in judicial intervention.

Courts are less likely today, with judicial concern for due process, to defer to the discipline decisions of nonpublic

---

446 *Id.* at 246.

447 *See* Corso v. Creighton Univ., 731 F.2d 529 (8th Cir. 1984) where the appeals court appeared to have applied a quasi-constitutional fairness standard in interpreting the university's handbook regarding punishment of a student for cheating. For an analysis of *Corso*, *see* R. Mawdsley, Academic Misconduct: Cheating and Plagiarism 51-52 (NOLPE 1994).

448 418 N.E.2d 776 (Ill. App. Ct. 1981).

449 *Id.* at 782.

450 *Id.*

educational institutions where students (and employees) have not had reasonable notice of charges to defend themselves. In an earlier, and perhaps less enlightened, decision, a court upheld an expulsion of two university students married in a civil ceremony, as well as two students acting as witnesses, under a university regulation stating that "in conformity with ideals of Christian education and conduct the university reserved the right to dismiss a student at any time on whatever grounds the university judged advisable."[451] The case is silent as to whether the four students actually knew this civil ceremony violated school policy, but, hopefully, they knew that the civil ceremony was the conduct that the university considered to be in violation of the regulation.

The *Fellheimer* concern for due process fairness in higher education applies as well to K-12 nonpublic education. In *Geraci v. St. Xavier High School,*[452] a student's expulsion was upheld where the school catalog listed as grounds for expulsion, "conduct detrimental to the reputation of the school" and "immorality in talk or action." Although the *Geraci* court found no state action so as to invoke Section 1983 constitutional safeguards, the court did balance the general language in the rule against the nature of the student's conduct and the fair treatment accorded the student. The expelled student in *Geraci* had aided another student who threw a pie in the face of a teacher who was monitoring an exam. The student, when he was called to the office, admitted complicity in the act and was notified he was expelled. However, the expulsion did not become final until after there was a series of discussions among various school officials and between the school president and the student's father. The *Geraci* court's standard for substantive and procedural fairness in nonpublic schools is a clear and concise statement of the current status of the law:

> Although ... a nonpublic school's disciplinary proceedings are not controlled by the due process clause, and accordingly such schools have broad discretion in making rules and setting up procedures for their enforcement, nevertheless, under its broad equitable powers a court will intervene where such discretion is abused or the proceedings do not comport with fundamental fairness.[453]

451 Carr v. St. John's Univ., 187 N.E.2d 18 (N.Y. App. Div. 1962).

452 3 Ohio Op.3d 146 (Ohio 1978).

453 *Id.* at 149. *See also*, Blaine v. Savannah Country Day Sch., 491 S.E.2d 446 (Ga. Ct. App.

Some measure of fundamental fairness, in terms of what is referred to as procedural due process in the public sector, must still be provided students or employees even if they are being penalized for acts protected or not punishable in the public sector, acts protected under what is known as substantive due process. In *Rendell-Baker v. Kohn*[454] dismissal of a teacher was upheld even though she "was dismissed as a legitimate exercise of her free speech and [even though] her dismissal was not accompanied by the procedural safeguards which would be required if the action were attributable to the State."[455] In the public sector, free speech would be protectable as a substantive constitutional right under the First Amendment.[456] Rendell-Baker's summary discharge had resulted after she supported a petition from student members of a student-staff council regarding greater responsibilities for making hiring decisions. The court never had to address the question whether Rendell-Baker's conduct constituted protected free speech, nor whether her discharge satisfied procedural due process, because of the absence of state action.[457]

1997) (expulsion of student shortly before graduation for violation of honor code not a violation of fundamental fairness, but rather, a reasonable exercise of administrative discretion).

454 457 U.S. 830 (1982).

455 *Rendell-Baker* 488 F. Supp. 764, 765 (D. Mass. 1980). The evolution of public employee free expression rights can be observed in the cases of Pickering v. Board of Educ., 391 U.S. 563 (1968) (teacher has free speech right to make public statements); Mt. Healthy City Sch. Dist. Bd. of Educ. v. Doyle, 429 U.S. 274 (1977) (teacher disciplined as result of free speech must prove motivating purpose for discipline was his exercise of free speech); Connick v. Myers, 461 U.S. 138 (1983) (public employee's free speech right applies only to matters of "public concern").

456 The seminal Supreme Court decision establishing the substantive right to free speech for students and teachers in public schools in Tinker v. Des Moines Indep. Sch. Dist., 393 U.S. 503 (1969).

457 Whether conduct by a public sector employee is protected by free speech depends on if the conduct is a matter of public concern. Even if a matter of public concern, courts will uphold employee discipline where the employee's conduct interferes with workplace efficiency or the discipline would have been administered apart from the issue of free speech. *See* Harris v. Victoria Indep. Sch. Dist., 168 F.3d 216 (5th Cir. 1999) (two employees entitled to trial on issue of retaliation for exercise of free speech because their criticism of their school principal's failure to implement a site-based school improvement plan was on a matter of public concern); Dudley v. Augusta Sch. Dep't, 23 F. Supp.2d 85 (D. Maine 1998) (former administrative assistant's reporting of suspected teacher sexual abuse to police was a matter of public concern). *But see*, Wallace v. School Bd. of Orange County, 41 F. Supp. 1321 (M.D. Fla. 1998) (remarks made by a school bus driver to a state investigator about racially hostile work environment not a matter of public concern because the driver had made the comments as an employee, not a citizen, in that he had not attempted to involve the public at large). *See also*, Dewey v. Tacoma Sch. Dist. No. 110, 974 P.2d 847 (Wash. Ct. App. 1999) (maintenance coordinator's complaint that a supervisor had used school district employees to move his personal furniture was not protected free speech because the district's interest in promoting efficiency was greater than employee's free speech interest and because the district had other non-free speech reasons for terminating the coordinator).

Likewise, in *Flint v. St. Augustine High School,*[458] the expulsion of two students was upheld when they violated a school rule prohibiting smoking within two blocks of the school. The rule specifically provided for a fine after the first offense and dismissal after a subsequent violation. Despite the fact that prior student repeat offenders had always been fined, and no one had ever been dismissed for smoking, the expulsion of the student plaintiffs was upheld because the court observed:

> we cannot say that such a penalty was beyond the scope of the disciplinary powers granted to the principal and acknowledged to be clearly within his authority and discretion . . . [B]oth young men were on notice of the result which would ensue upon their next violations of the smoking rule. When the specific dismissal precipitating violations did, indeed, occur, the young men were confronted by their accusers and the record offers no indication that these specific accusals were unjustly or erroneously made.[459]

The minimal safeguards provided the plaintiffs of notice of offense, notice of punishment, and opportunity to present their side, satisfying the court's sense of fairness:

> [P]rivate institutions like St. Augustine High School have a *near* absolute right and power to control their own internal disciplinary procedure which, by its very nature, includes the right and power to dismiss students. That is not to say that due process safeguards can be cavalierly ignored or disregarded. But if their is *color of due process* that is enough.[460]

Even handbook requirements may have to be read in terms of a standard of arbitrariness. In *Ahlum v. Administrators of Tulane Educational Fund,*[461] the Louisiana Court of Appeals determined that, absent state action, a private university's adherence to its student discipline requirements was not to be decided by constitutional standard. Despite a university requirement that a tape recording of a student disciplinary hearing be made, the absence of a hearing transcript for an appeal, due to a tape recorder failure, was not fatal as long as the

458 323 So.2d 229 (La. Ct. App. 1976).
459 *Id.* at 234, 235.
460 *Id.* at 234-35 (emphasis added).
461 617 So.2d 96 (La. Ct. App. 1993).

student had an opportunity to present his version of the facts and was informed of the charges against him. A court will not "substitute its own view of appropriate standards of conduct or appropriate penalties for the breach of those standards in place of a private university's decision ... Instead the disciplinary actions of a private university may be viewed for arbitrary and capricious action."[462]

Nonpublic institutional discipline will generally not be considered improperly arbitrary or capricious as long as it conforms to published regulations.[463] However, one unusual case where constitutional and contractual standards were equated was *Franklin v. Leland Stanford, Jr. University*.[464] In *Franklin*, a tenured faculty member's dismissal for 1971 speeches, which encouraged physical damage to the university's computation center and which prolonged student disruption, was upheld, but only after applying the *Pickering* constitutional free speech balancing test[465] and the *Mt. Healthy* mixed motive test.[466] Without deciding the seminal question as to whether First Amendment free speech applies to private schools, the *Franklin* court applied constitutional due process standards to the university because the faculty members had been accorded the same constitutional protection as would have been provided by a state university, and because the university declared that the outcome would be the same whether it were viewed as a private

---

462 *Id.* at 98, 99. *Cf.* Harvey v. Palmer College of Chiropractic, 363 N.W.2d 443, 444 (Iowa Ct. App. 1984) (expelled student presented jury question as to whether college had followed its regulations; court noted that "requirements imposed by the common law on private universities parallel those imposed by the due process clause on public universities.")

463 Allen v. Casper, 622 N.E.2d 367, 371 (Ohio Ct. App. 1993) (dismissal of two elementary age children because of unacceptable parent behavior upheld by court; "Absent a clear abuse of discretion by the school in the enforcement of its policies and regulations, courts will not interfere in these matters"); Galiani v. Hofstra Univ., 499 N.Y.S.2d 182 (N.Y. App. Div. 1986) (student's due process to which he was entitled prior to suspension was institution's conformity to its disciplinary procedures.)

464 218 Cal. Rptr. 228 (1985).

465 Pickering v. Board of Educ., 391 U.S. 563 (1968) (balancing test involves consideration of the following factors: (1) whether the communication would interfere with close working relationships; (2) whether the communication would provoke conflict or otherwise undermine the employer's operations; (3) whether the communication concerned a topic of public interest; (4) whether there was an opportunity to rebut or refute any errors in the communication; (5) whether the communication shows the employee's incompetence at his position; (6) whether the communication was intentionally false).

466 Mt. Healthy City Bd. of Educ. v. Doyle, 429 U.S. 274, 276 (1977) (even if an employee meets her burden of proof in producing evidence of employer action based on employee's protected constitutional rights, the employer can still prevail if it can show by a preponderance of the evidence "that it would have reached the same decision ... even in the absence of the protected conduct.")

or public employer. This gratuitous gesture by Stanford University raises two important legal questions: whether existence of contractual due process equal to constitutional due process automatically invokes a constitutional analysis[467] or whether an institution must affirmatively assert that its contractual standards are equal to constitutional ones before a constitutional analysis will be performed.[468] A sounder approach would seem to be reflected in *Kyriakopoulos v. George Washington University*[469] where, even though a private university's status did not shield the university from First Amendment scrutiny regarding faculty promotion, it was subjected only to scrutiny necessary to ensure that the university performed its contractual duty.

The following guidelines and suggestions may be helpful in assessing a nonpublic school's limitations on enforcing its rules and policies:

(1) Substantive due process rights (e.g., speech, association, press) can be defined and limited by nonpublic schools. Courts will not inquire into the reasonableness of rules or policies unless they are contrary to an established or fundamental public policy.[470] However, where a public policy is contravened, courts will not invalidate the school's rule or policy but will deny the nonpublic school access to a benefit[471] or will require the school to confer a benefit.[472]

(2) Whatever fundamental fairness standards apply to nonpublic schools will apply equally to faculty and stu-

---

467 *But cf.* Galiani v. Hofstra Univ., 499 N.Y.S.2d 182 (N.Y. App. Div. 1986) (only due process to which student entitled prior to suspension was institution's conformity to its own disciplinary procedures).

468 *See* Life Chiropractic College v. Fuchs, 337 S.E.2d 45 (Ga. Ct. App. 1985) (college bulletin statement that "due process is followed in all disciplinary cases" had been met in a student discipline situation even though the student had been denied a request to confront witnesses).

469 866 F.2d 438 (D.C. Cir. 1989).

470 *See* discussion on *Government and Fundamental Public Policies* in chapter, "Governmental Regulation of Nonpublic Schools".

471 Bob Jones Univ. v. United States, 461 U.S. 574 (1983) (revocation of tax exempt status); Bob Jones Univ. v. Johnson, 396 F. Supp. 597 (D. S.C. 1974) (denial of student eligibility for V.A. benefits).

472 Gay Rights Coalition v. Georgetown Univ., 536 A.2d 1 (D.C. App. 1987) (homosexual groups must be provided tangible benefits). *See also* Roberts v. United States Jaycees, 468 U.S. 609 (1984) (women must be admitted to full membership in Jaycees under state law, applying a public policy argument).

dents. Courts consistently view nonpublic school faculty and student rights as controllable on a contractual theory by the school officials. As long as minimal procedural safeguards are provided with a view toward fairness, and as long as additional contractual rights accorded faculty and students in school handbooks are honored, courts do not require more rigid standards. For religious nonpublic schools, there may be the additional First Amendment protection from unnecessary intrusion into internal doctrinal matters.[473]

(3) Minimal procedural safeguards required by an equitable sense of fairness are notice of the kinds of conduct prohibited by school rules, notice of possible punishment (e.g., contract termination or expulsion) and

---

473 *See* Dlaiken v. Roodbeen, 522 N.W.2d 719 (Mich. Ct. App. 1994) (decision of parish priest not to readmit children to school not reviewable under First Amendment); Gabriel v. Immanuel Evangelical Lutheran Church, Inc., 640 N.E.2d 681 (Ill. App. Ct. 1994) (contract offered to teacher could be withdrawn with First Amendment protection where teacher's service considered a "call" and selection of ministers was a responsibility of congregation); Sabatino v. St. Aloysius Parish, 654 A.2d 1033 (N.J. Super. Ct. 1994) (judicial abstention on basis of First Amendment applied to selection of religious order person for school principal over lay person); Gaston v. Diocese of Allentown, 712 A.2d 757 (Pa. Super. Ct. 1998) (court did not have subject matter jurisdiction in tort suit brought after children expelled for violation of church doctrine). *See generally*, McClure v. Salvation Army, 460 F.2d 558, 560 (5th Cir.), *cert. denied* 409 U.S. 896, (1972) (refusal to promote female ordained minister not subject to Title VII investigation because "an investigation ... would ... cause the State to intrude upon matters of church administration and government"); Alicea v. New Brunswick Theological Seminary, 608 A.2d 218 (N.J. 1992) (inquiry into polity impermissible where discharged faculty member performed a ministerial function); Rayburn v. General Conference of Seventh-Day Adventists, 772 F.2d 1164, 1169 (4th Cir. 1985) (inquiry denied into theological belief prohibiting hiring of woman as associate pastor because "[i]n quintessentially religious matters, the free exercise clause of the First Amendment protects the act of a decision rather than the motivation behind it."); Maguire v. Marquette Univ., 627 F. Supp. 1499 (E.D. Wis. 1986), *aff'd* 814 F.2d 1213 (7th Cir. 1987) (female applicant with theological views antithetical to Catholic Church beliefs did not have to be offered theology department teaching position); Scharon v. St. Luke's Episcopal Presbyterian Hosp., 929 F.2d 360, 363 (8th Cir. 1991) (discharge of hospital chaplain not subject to ADEA and Title VII scrutiny because "to review such decisions would require the courts to determine the meaning of religious doctrine and canonical law and to impose a secular court's view of whether in the context of the particular case religious doctrine and canonical law support the decision the church authorities have made"; Walker v. First Presbyterian Church, 22 FEP 762, 763 (Cal. Super. Ct. 1980) (city ordinance prohibiting discrimination on basis of sexual orientation not applicable to church organist position where "organist in a congregation is part of the worship team"). *But see* Geary v. Visitation of the Blessed Virgin Mary Parish Sch., 7 F.3d 324, 330, 331 (3d Cir. 1993) (fifty year old teacher discharged from Catholic school after marrying divorced man had ADEA claim. "[A] court could adjudicate [plaintiff's] claim without the entanglement that would follow where employment of clergy and religious leaders involved ... [The court is not forced] to choose between parties' competing religious visions ... [where plaintiff does not] challenge the validity, existence or plausibility of a proffered religious doctrine....")

notice of opportunity for the student or faculty member to present his side of the case. Nonpublic institutions are bound by their published guidelines or rules[474] and enforcement will be upheld as long as such enforcement is not arbitrary.[475] While right to counsel, right of cross examination of witnesses, and right to an appeal would probably not be included as part of fundamental fairness imposed on nonpublic schools, those schools would most likely not survive a challenge to a hearing which did not involve an impartial person or tribunal deciding the case.[476] However, a better policy would seem to permit cross examination[477] and an appeal to someone beyond the first decision making level.

(4) School rules or procedures that conform to equitable standards of fairness will not immunize a nonpublic school from administrative judicial review under various state or federal statutes.[478]

---

474 *See* Beilis v. Albany Med. College, 525 N.Y.S.2d 932 (App.Ct. 1988).

475 *See* Rosen v. Vassar College, 525 N.Y.S.2d 399 (App. Div. 1988) (president's interpretation of "evidence of sound scholarship" could differ from department recommendations and was controlling in absence of bad faith); Levi v. University of Texas at San Antonio, 840 F.2d 277, 281 (5th Cir. 1988) (denying tenure to plaintiff for awarding too many high grades and granting tenure to another faculty member for awarding low grades did not violate equal protection; the "University's decision [may be] unwise but [it was] not irrational"); Kyriakopoulos v. George Washington Univ., 657 F. Supp. 1525 (D. D.C. 1987) (appropriate test in private educational institution where faculty member not promoted is "gross arbitrariness"). *But compare* McConnell v. Howard Univ., 818 F.2d 58 (D.C. Cir. 1987) (review of tenured professor for refusal to teach assigned class not limited to whether decision was "arbitrary, irrational or infected by improper motivation"). *See also* Bischoff v. Brothers of the Sacred Heart, 416 So.2d 348 (La. Ct. App. 1982) (cancellation of divorced Catholic lay teacher's contract prior to beginning of school year upheld because the teacher's educational background in Catholic seminary and graduate programs should have alerted him to divulge his divorced status on employment application).

476 However, in the public sector a hearing is considered impartial unless there is evidence of actual personal bias or partiality. Rouse v. Scottsdale Unified Sch. Dist., 752 P.2d 22 (Ariz. Ct. App. 1988); State Tenure Comm'n. v. Randolph County Bd. of Educ., 523 So.2d 1076 (Ala. Civ. App. 1988); Plymouth-Canton Community Sch. Dist. v. State Tenure Comm'n., 419 N.W.2d 783 (Mich. Ct. App. 1988). For a good example of a careful deliberative process in a student expulsion case, *see* Geraci v. St. Xavier High Sch., 13 Ohio Op.3d 146 (Ohio 1978).

477 *See* Life Chiropractic College v. Fuchs, 337 S.E. 2d 45 (Ga. Ct. App. 1985) (college bulletin specifying that "due process is followed in all disciplinary cases" was met even though student accused of falsifying grades was denied request to confront witnesses but only because of solid evidentiary support for college's conclusions.)

478 *E.g., see* Rothman v. Emory Univ., 828 F. Supp. 537 (N.D. Ill. 1993) (private law school subject to OCR jurisdiction under ADA); Stouch v. Brothers of Order of Hermits of St. Augustine, 836 F. Supp. 1134 (E.D. Pa. 1993) (monastery subject to EEOC jurisdiction under ADEA); EEOC v. Mississippi College, 451 F. Supp. 564 (S.D. Miss. 1978) *rev'd in part* 626

Contractual Constraints

Elements of a Contract

In nonpublic education the relationship between the institution and parents, students, or employees is generally recognized to be one of contract, although determining how much of what a school publishes is part the contract is not always easy to do. Most nonpublic educational institutions normally have numerous documents, such as application forms, brochures, handbooks, and school board policies, that define and describe relationships and programs.[479]

While one assumes that certain documents, such as faculty or student handbooks, are part of the contract, an institution may elect not to include such documents in the contract.[480] The dilemma in determining whether handbooks are part of a contract is that, since frequently they can be altered unilaterally by the administration, they may not readily fit into contract concepts of offer, acceptance, consideration, and mutuality of benefit.[481] Where contract language has been changed, students or employees may have to demonstrate that they relied on prior language to their detriment if they hope to have any contract claim at all.[482]

In determining the content of student or employee contracts, courts are influenced by the intent of the parties. In *Wall v.*

F.2d 477 (5th Cir. 1980); EEOC v. Southwestern Baptist Theological Seminary, 485 F. Supp. 255 (N.D. Tex. 1980) *rev'd in part* 651 F.2d 277 (5th Cir. 1981) (religious institutions subject to jurisdiction of EEOC under Title VII); Donovan v. Shenandoah Baptist Church, 573 F. Supp. 320 (W.D. Va. 1983) (church subject to Department of Labor jurisdiction to enforce FLSA minimum wage requirements; Christ the King Reg'l High Sch. v. Culvert, 815 F.2d 219 (2d Cir. 1987), *cert. denied* 484 U.S. 830 (1988); Catholic High Sch. Ass'n of the Archdiocese of New York v. Culvert, 753 F.2d 1161 (2d Cir. 1985) (religious schools subject to jurisdiction of state labor boards to require collective bargaining).

479 *E.g., see* Moffice v. Oglethorpe Univ., 367 S.E.2d 112 (Ga. Ct. App. 1988) (faculty handbook incorporated by reference into contract).

480 *See* Wall v. Tulane Univ., 499 So.2d 375 (La. Ct. App. 1986) (university's change in tuition waiver benefit not violative of employment contract because such benefits were in staff handbook which was not part of contract); Shannon v. Bepko, 684 F. Supp. 1465 (S.D. Ind. 1988) (handbook did not apply to hourly employee); Goodkind v. University of Minnesota, 417 N.W.2d 636 (Minn. 1988) (selection procedures set forth in dental school's statement of policy not part of faculty member's contract); Dunfey v. Roger Williams University, 824 F. Supp. 18 (D. Mass. 1993) (a personnel manual that could be altered or revoked at any time by the administration does not create any contractual rights.)

481 For a good discussion of these concepts, see G. Wong, Essentials of Amateur Sports Law (2d ed.) 63-80 (1994).

482 *See* Tuomala v. Regent Univ., 477 S.E.2d 501 (Va. 1996) (university change of three-year faculty contracts provided for in handbook to five-year contracts renewable on one-year basis not a breach of contract where faculty members could not demonstrate that they had relied to their detriment on faculty handbook provisions for three-year contract).

Tulane University,[483] a university tuition waiver policy could be changed because "Tulane's Staff Handbook, which described the benefits and conditions of employment with Tulane, was not made part of [plaintiff's] employment agreement with Tulane."[484] Even though plaintiff alleged that he had turned down more lucrative offers to attend Tulane because of the tuition waiver policy, the court, in sustaining summary judgment for the university, opined that the "Handbook appear[ed] to be primarily informational in nature and did not, in our opinion, constitute a binding promise by Tulane to continue indefinitely the benefits described therein."[485]

Contract and Student/Faculty Conduct

Contract problems in educational institutions (public or private) involve one or more of the following three kinds of issues:

(1) Whether allegedly improper student or faculty conduct is covered by published contract language;

(2) Whether the school has complied with its own contractual requirements in dealing with students or employees;

(3) Whether the school's interpretation or enforcement of contract terms exhibited good faith and fairness.

Regarding the first issue, even general contract language will support faculty or student discipline provided that the faculty member or student knew or reasonably should have known his or her conduct was included within the contract terms. In *Aronson v. North Park College*,[486] a student's dismissal was upheld under a college catalog provision allowing the college "to dismiss at any time a student who in its judgement is undesirable and whose continuation in the school is detrimental to himself or his fellow students"[487] because the student, after being diagnosed as paranoid and a serious detriment to herself and others, refused to cooperate with remediative efforts.

483 So.2d 375 (La. Ct. App. 1986).
484 *Id.* at 376.
485 *Id.*
486 418 N.E.2d 776 (Ill. App. Ct. 1981).
487 *Id.* at 781.

One of the differences between public and nonpublic schools is that contracts in public institutions will be viewed against a backdrop of constitutional rights. In the public sector, both employee and student contractual relationships with their institutions carry at least a minimal expectation of fairness under the due process clause. Handbook provisions concerning discipline of students or employees must meet due process requirements.[488] Likewise, public school students and employees cannot be retaliated against for exercising their substantive constitutional rights. While nonpublic students and employees enjoy no protection under the Constitution, their relationship to an institution may be protected under state or federal statute.[489]

To the extent that nonpublic employees do not serve under a contract of fixed duration, they may only be employees-at-will. Many states have created a presumption that employment contracts for an indefinite period of time are at-will and, not only might employees be subject to dismissal at any time,[490] but an offer of employment could be revoked at any time prior to commencement of work.[491] However, nonpublic school employers need to be aware that states often have modified the at-will doctrine to limit dismissal or discipline in situations involving public policy, implied contracts, and covenants of good and fair dealing.[492]

---

488 *See* Mueller v. Regents of Univ. of Minnesota, 855 F.2d 555 (8th Cir. 1988) (procedure used under handbook for termination of tenured faculty member not violative of due process); Newman v. Burgin, 930 F.2d 955 (1st Cir. 1991) (procedure adopted by university to review charge of faculty plagiarism, that led to censor, not violative of due process); Clifton-Davis v. State, 930 P.2d 833 (Okla. Ct. App. 1996) (denial of degree to student did not violate contract or due process); *Cf.* Hernandez v. Don Bosco Preparatory High, 730 A.2d 365 (N.J. Super. Ct. 1999) (expulsion of student upheld where school had followed its handbook procedures and those procedures were fundamentally fair).

489 *See* Gallo v. Salesian Soc'y, Inc., 676 A.2d 580 (N.J. Super. Ct. 1996) (lay teacher could sue religious school under state statute prohibiting age and sex discrimination).

490 *See* Tramontozzi v. St. Francis College, 648 N.Y.S.2d 431 (N.Y. App. Div. 1996) (athletic director an employee-at-will and could be dismissed for no cause at all); Roberts v. Wake Forest Univ., 286 S.E.2d 120 (N.C. Ct. App. 1982) (contract for indefinite period of time considered to be employment-at-will under North Carolina law). For the same analysis in the public sector, *see* Strother v. Columbia-Brazoria Indep. Sch. Dist., 839 F. Supp. 459 (S.D. Tex. 1993) (public school employee without written or oral contract identifying length of employment was employee-at-will with no property rights and thus could be terminated under state law without cause). However, the employment-at-will doctrine has important exceptions restricting dismissal or discipline in the cases of public policy, implied contract, and covenants of good and fair dealing. *See* I. Shepard, H.Olsen and R. Dustin Employment At Will: A Guide to an Eroding Doctrine (CUPA 1987).

491 *See* Heinritz v. Lawrence Univ., 535 N.W.2d 81 (Wis. Ct. App. 1995).

492 The employment-at-will doctrine has important exceptions restricting dismissal or discipline in the cases of public policy, implied contract, and covenants of good and fair dealing. *See* I. Shepard, H.Olsen and R. Dustin Employment At Will: A Guide to an Eroding Doctrine (CUPA 1987).

Termination of the contracts of nonpublic employees, either as nonrenewal at the end of the contract year or dismissal during the term of the contract, can be a traumatizing and contentious experience for both the employee and school officials. Generally, faculty members with annual contracts have no expectation of contract renewal[493] unless an expectation has been created in a handbook.[494] Courts provide nonpublic schools considerable latitude in determining what conduct warrants employee dismissal during the life of a contract. For example, dismissal of a teacher who failed to follow established policies has been upheld[495] as has dismissal of a teacher carrying on an extramarital affair.[496] In addition, the terms of an employment contract may be broad enough to permit employer reassignment without constituting a constructive discharge.[497] A teacher's knowing of a serious student violation (drunkenness) but failing to report it constituted good cause for contract termination.[498] Even if a breach of contract claim is successful, a plaintiff's remedy probably will be limited to damages as opposed to reinstatement.[499]

School officials in religious schools have an advantage in that courts may refuse to intervene in contract disputes because of religious or doctrinal issues. A principal, terminated by his bishop during the term of his contract as a result of discord and disunity

---

493 *See* DeSimone v. Sienna College, 663 N.Y.S.2d 701 (N.Y. App. Div. 1997) (probationary faculty member with contract that stated that it was for one year and nonrenewable had no breach of contract claim even if he received notice of nonrenewal two days late); Muhitch v. St. Gregory the Great Catholic Church and Sch., 659 N.Y.S.2d 679 (N.Y. App. Div. 1997) (former teacher with one-year contract could not sue for breach of contract).

494 *See* United States *ex rel.* Yesudian v. Howard Univ., 946 F. Supp. 31 (D. D.C. 1996) (conflict in employee handbook regarding rights prior to termination on employee prevented summary judgment for university).

495 Odem v. Pace Acad., 510 S.E.2d 326 (Ga. Ct. App. 1998).

496 Gosche v. Calvert High Sch., 997 F. Supp. 867 (N.D. Ohio 1998).

497 *See* Johnson v. College of Art and Design, Inc., 453 S.E.2d 80 (Ga. Ct. App. 1995) (contract with plaintiff for "teaching and/or service" permitted college to reassign plaintiff from teaching to service responsibility during school year with no reduction in pay, without breaching contract); Klinge v. Ithaca College, 663 N.Y.S.2d 735 (N.Y. App. Div. 1997) (faculty member demoted for plagiarism and granted one-year contract had no breach of contract claim).

498 Watts v. St. Mary's Hall, Inc., 662 S.W.2d 55 (Tex. Ct. App. 1983).

499 *See* Chady v. Solomon Schlechter Day Schs., 645 N.E.2d 983 (Ill. App. Ct. 1995) (court would not issue writ of specific performance to reinstate teacher who alleged breach of contract, because teaching contract is personal service contract). *Cf.* Gargano v. Diocese of Rockville Ctr., 80 F.3d 87 (2d Cir. 1996) ($83,000 breach of contract award upheld, over establishment clause objection, that the school had violated ADEA in not following its handbook criteria in not considering plaintiff for a new position).

in the diocese, had no breach of contract action for the balance of his salary because "it would infringe on ecclesiastical authority to deny the Bishop authority to dismiss the church school principal in order to end a schism in the congregation."[500] Similarly, a New Jersey court abstained from interfering in a parochial school's decision to select a person from a religious order rather than a lay person, for a school principal position.[501] Likewise, where a teacher's service in a religious school was considered a ministerial "call" by the church congregation, a contract was not binding on the school without congregation approval.[502] A state court in Ohio determined that it had no jurisdiction to inquire whether two discharged faculty members had breached their contract with a religious school by entering into canonically invalid marriage that made them unfit for the school's religious mission.[503] A Catholic seminary faculty member, discharged after she protested Pope John Paul II's refusal to ordain women priests, had no breach of contract claim, where the faculty handbook's reference to academic freedom and responsibility as "among the terms of appointment" was broad enough to include religious doctrine and ecclesiastical law, and therefore, a court determined, under the establishment clause, it had no jurisdiction to address the breach of contract claim.[504]

School Compliance with Contract Language

A second major problem area of contractual constraints concerns whether the nonpublic school has complied with its contractual requirements in dealing with students or faculty. The extent to which a written contract and its reference documents represent the fully integrated expression of the parties can present legal problems. Whether handbooks are part of an

500 Black v. St. Bernadette Congregation of Appleton, 306 N.W.2d 550, 553 (Wis. Ct. App. 1984), citing for authority to Serbian Eastern Orthodox Diocese v. Milivojevich, 426 U.S. 696, 721-22 (1976) (bishop's reason "to eliminate discord within a congregation" was ecclesiastical in nature rather than "purely secular").

501 Sabatino v. St. Aloysius Parish, 654 A.2d 1033 (N.J. Super. Ct. 1994).

502 Gabriel v. Immanuel Evangelical Lutheran Church, Inc., 640 N.E.2d 681 (Ill. App. Ct. 1994).

503 Bassinger v. Pilarczek, 707 N.E.2d 1149 (Ohio Ct. App. 1997) (however, even though the court could not inquire into the breach of contract issue, the court could determine whether the breach of contract reason for termination was a pretext for age discrimination under ADEA).

504 McEnroy v. St. Meinard Sch. of Theology, 713 N.E.2d 334 (Ind. App. Ct. 1999).

employee's contract may vary with institutions.[505] Special problems can result when one or more of the parties seeks to introduce statements or policies external to the contract, other than those found in handbooks. In *Welter v. Seton Hall University*,[506] two nuns stated a cause of action for improper discharge when the University sought to invoke several Catholic Canon Law provisions relating to the relationship between a cleric and superiors. In this case, the employment contract contained no condition that the nuns secure permission of religious superiors before seeking employment, and the contract contained no reference to Canon Law. In *Lewis v. Loyola University of Chicago*,[507] a faculty member was entitled to tenure when, among other letters, a preemployment letter from the Dean of the School of Medicine stated, "I will propose early approval of tenure for you...,"[508] and he failed to do so. In accepting the faculty member's claim that the letters were part of the contract, the court expressly rejected the idea that "a form contract for a teaching position ... embodied the complete agreement and understanding of the parties" and the school's claim that the letters were only "expressions of goodwill and [were] not an enforceable promise creating a contractual obligation."[509] Ambiguities in contract terms can lead to introduction of oral evidence regarding past custom and usage in handling similar problems.[510]

---

505 Handbook part of contract: Moffice v. Oglethorpe, 367 S.E.2d 112 (Ga.Ct. App. 1988) (faculty handbook incorporated by reference into contract); Fogel v. Trustees of Iowa College, 446 N.W.2d 451 (Ia. 1989) (college employee handbook part of contract but too ambiguous to support cause of action for breach of unilateral contract of employment); Dahlman v. Oakland Univ., 432 N.W.2d 304 (Mich. Ct. App. 1988) (failure of employee to exhaust grievance procedure in handbook prohibited breach of contract action). Handbook not part of contract: Wall v. Tulane Univ., 499 S.E.2d 375 (La. Ct. App. 1986) (university's change in tuition waiver not violative of employment contract because such benefits were in staff handbook which was not part of contract); Shannon v. Bepko, 684 F. Supp. 1465 (S.D. Ind. 1988) (handbook did not apply to hourly employee); Goodkind v. University of Minn., 417 N.W.2d 636 (Minn. 1988) (selection procedures set forth in dental school's statement of policy not part of faculty member's contract); Faur v. Jewish Theological Seminary of Am., 536 N.Y.S.2d 516 (N.Y. App. Div. 1989) (admission policies not part of faculty contract so seminary could alter policy and admit women).

506 608 A.2d 206 (N.J. 1992).

507 500 N.E.2d 47 (Ill. App. Ct. 1986).

508 *Id.* at 48.

509 *Id.* at 50.

510 *See* Holland v. Kennedy, 548 So.2d 982 (Miss. 1989) (evidence of past employment practices of college admissible to clarify ambiguous terms of express contract); Ozerol v. Howard Univ., 545 A.2d 638 (D.C. 1988) (no oral statements regarding pre-employment negotiations between faculty member and university admissible concerning tenure status where "Indefinite Status" could have been marked and it had not been so marked); Howard Univ. v. Best, 484 A.2d 958 (D.C. App. 1984), *after remand* 547 A.2d 144 (D.C. 1988) (evidence of prior

Normally, the specific facts of each situation will govern the results. In *Lindsey v. University of Arizona*,[511] a head basketball coach was entitled to a large award of damages following his contract nonrenewal after one year on the basis of "statements of [the] Athletic Director ... and some unidentified member of the search committee regarding the University's policy of giving coaches four years to prove their worth ...."[512] In *Harris v. Arizona Board of Regents*,[513] a faculty member was accorded de facto tenure on the basis of a preemployment statement by the Dean of the College of Liberal Arts that the faculty member would automatically receive tenure in his third year.

Employees who claim that they have relied on statements of school officials may not find a favorable judicial response. In *Bruner v. University of Southern Mississippi*,[514] some statements to a prospective coach by an athletic director suggesting the coach would be hired, and reliance by the coach and his wife on those statements were insufficient to create an enforceable contract. Mississippi state law provided that only the state board of trustees had the authority to authorize teaching contracts, and therefore, any preemployment representations were unenforceable. In a similar vein, the sending of letters of intent to teachers to determine whether they plan to return may be misunderstood by some as a contract for employment. In *Knipmeyer v. Diocese of Alexandria*,[515] a letter of intent in which a school expressed to employees the salary which might be expected and inquired whether they planned to return lacked a specific offer by either the employer or employee, and therefore, could not create a binding contract. Likewise, where a nonpublic school has a formal contract, a letter from the administrator to a teacher with words to the effect of "I am planning for you to be a part of our faculty next year" lacks the specificity characterized by the employment contract and is therefore unenforceable.[516]

---

practice in interpreting "previous appointment" term in Faculty Handbook not sufficient to sustain faculty member's claim to indefinite tenure based on only one example); Roberts v. Wake Forest Univ., 286 S.E.2d 120 (N.C. Ct. App. 1982) (attempt by golf coach dismissed after sixteen months unsuccessful in proving through custom and usage claim to a contract for long term based on terms of prior coaches because a person employed for indefinite period of time considered under state law to be employee-at-will).

511 754 P.2d 1152 (Ariz. Ct. App. 1987).

512 *Id.* at 1157.

513 528 F. Supp. 987 (D. Ariz. 1981).

514 501 So.2d 1113 (Miss. 1987).

515 492 So.2d 550 (La. Ct. App. 1986).

516 Braun v. Glade Valley Sch., Inc., 334 S.E.2d 404 (N.C. Ct. App. 1985).

One strategy for resolving disagreements in contract language or in differences between contract language and institutional practice is the concept of custom and usage. A faculty member may attempt to invoke custom and usage to demonstrate that contracts in a particular area are normally for a period of time longer than the employee served, but such efforts require more than comparison to other institutions.[517] In addition, custom and usage must be consistent from one set of facts to the next within the institution or the concept is inapplicable.[518]

Questions raised during contract negotiations regarding elements of the employment relationship may lead to later claims of misrepresentation when the contract is terminated. In *Conway v. Pacific University*,[519] a one-year visiting faculty member at the university, who had been offered a tenure track position at the end of that visiting year, inquired of the dean whether his poor evaluations during the spring semester would be a problem in the tenure process. The dean responded that it would not, but when plaintiff continued to receive poor student evaluations during his first tenure track year, his tenure track contract was nonrenewed at the end of that year. In reversing a negligent misrepresentation judgment for plaintiff, an Oregon appeals court held that an employer owes no duty "to further the economic interests of the employee in the negotiation of the employment contract."[520]

Confusion can result when a handbook appears to create a benefit but then the handbook also gives the institution the right to alter the handbook at any time. In *Dunfey v. Roger Williams University*,[521] a discharged admissions officer sought to enforce a personnel policy manual provision that an involuntarily discharged administrator was entitled to one month's salary for every six month's service. However, the manual provided that: "Additional policies and practices or changes may evolve and the

---

517 Roberts v. Wake Forest Univ., 286 S.E.2d 120 (N.C. App. 1982) (golf coach discharged at end of sixteen months unsuccessful in custom and usage claim of longer contract based on contracts for golf coaches at other institutions because in North Carolina contracts of indefinite duration are employment-at-will). *Contra* Toussaint v. Blue Cross & Blue Shield of Michigan, 292 N.W.2d 880 (Mich. 1980); Pine River State Bank v. Mettille, 333 N.W.2d 622 (Minn. 1983) (employment practices can change at-will contract into implied contract).

518 *See* Kakaes v. George Washington Univ., 683 A.2d 128 (D.C. Ct. App. 1996) (university's past practice of submitting tenure decisions to board of trustees where there was agreement between faculty committee and administration not applicable where there was disagreement).

519 879 P.2d 201 (Or. Ct. App. 1994).

520 *Id.* at 203.

521 824 F. Supp. 18 (D. Mass. 1993).

Personnel Policy Manual may be amended, modified, or superseded at any time. Written notice of such changes will be distributed as soon as possible." In rejecting the former employee's claim, the court held that under Rhode Island law, "the Manual does not create any contractual rights between [the university] and [plaintiff] ... because an employee cannot rely on statements in a manual if the manual can be altered or revoked at any time and for any reason ...."[522] Interestingly enough, the court chose not to treat provisions in the manual as part of the employment contract enforceable until such time as they were changed. *Dunfey* indicates that contract language permitting changes at any time means that benefits conferred on employees amount to nonnegotiated gratuities, not enforceable promises. Many, perhaps most, courts would not agree with this analysis.

In *Fairbanks v. Tulane University*,[523] a Louisiana appeals court refused the university's motion for summary judgment using this argument regarding its change in a tuition waiver policy for children of employees. In *Fairbanks*, a student sued for the $40,000 he had paid for an M.B.A. degree, claiming that the university's handbook change eliminating tuition waiver for graduate classes amounted to a breach of contract. The student's breach of contract argument was that the language of the former handbook amounted to a contract with his father, a faculty member who had died before the handbook change (eliminating the benefit), and therefore, the university was obligated to honor the tuition waiver provision in effect when his father died, not the provision in effect when the student began the M.B.A. program.

Both *Fairbanks* and *Dunfey* suggest contract problems involving handbooks. *Fairbanks* offers a caveat that changes in a handbook, even if an institution can make the changes at will, may have residual obligations that need to be honored, provided that a person can demonstrate reliance on a prior handbook provision. *Dunfey*, on the other hand, presents a glaring anomaly regarding the contract value of handbooks. Would an employer that refuses to honor a benefit under a handbook because the handbook could be changed unilaterally nonetheless be able to enforce standards of conduct expressed in the handbook through disciplinary procedures prescribed in the handbook? When

522 *Id.* at 22.

523 731 So.2d 983 (La. Ct. App. 1999).

handbook language can be enforced by one party but not by both, contract concepts of offer, acceptance, consideration, and mutuality of benefit no longer seem to apply.

To avoid misunderstandings regarding contract language, the prospective employee should be informed clearly as to which office authorizes contracts, and the contract itself should state in bold print words to the effect that the contract represents the total agreement between the parties. Nonpublic institutions that may prefer a provision in employment handbooks authorizing changes to be made at any time by the administration should either identify the handbook as not part of the contract or identify which parts of the contract will be enforceable as part of the contract, even if changes can be made at a later date. Where schools do not want to use written contracts, or oral statements have not yet been reduced to writing, the intent of the parties is left to witnesses' memories.[524] If employees are being handled on an employment-at-will basis, the rights of such employees should be clearly identified, especially where the rights of employees-at-will may differ from other employees.[525]

A unique problem can arise where an employee under contract at a nonpublic school seeks to resign after the beginning of the school year in order to accept another educational employment. In *Weisfeld v. Peterseil School Corporation*,[526] a teacher under contract to a nonpublic school signed a contract with the public school after the beginning of the school year, but then was informed by the nonpublic school administrator that he would not release her from her contract. The public school district, which had a policy not to offer a contract to a teacher under contract to another school, withdrew its offer after finding out about the existing nonpublic school contract. The teacher sued the nonpublic school and its administrator for tortious interference with contract in refusing to release her from her contract and for breach of contract for refusing to permit her to

---

524 *See* Hyde Park Union Church v. Curry, 942 F. Supp. 360 (N.D. Ill. 1996) (oral agreement to settle a contract nonrenewal dispute binding on the parties, even though not yet reduced to writing, where the intent of the parties as to the content of the agreement was clear).

525 *See* Steele v. Board of Educ. Inglewood Unified Sch. Dist., 251 Cal. Rptr. 360 (Ct. App. 1988) (director of personnel who served at pleasure of employer nonetheless entitled to minimal constitutional requirements of due process); Leikvold v. Valley View Community Hosp., 688 P.2d 170 (Ariz. 1984) (handbook which does not specifically state it is not part of employment contract creates implied obligation of employer to honor entire handbook if it selectively attempts to enforce only part of handbook against employee.)

526 623 So.2d 515 (Fla. Dist. Ct. App. 1993).

serve out her nonpublic school contract. Although the nonpublic school and its administrator were not liable for tortious interference with contract, the school and administrator were liable for breach of contract in refusing to permit the teacher to serve out her contract. In other words, the nonpublic school could not have it both ways; refusal to release the teacher was an implicit acknowledgment that an enforceable contract existed and thus the teacher was entitled to serve out her contract, even though the nonpublic school had hired someone else to replace the teacher.

The importance of nonpublic schools following existing procedures applies to students as well. In *Lyon College v. Gray*,[527] an Arkansas appeals court reversed a breach of contract award for a student who had been found guilty of an honor code violation (cheating on the final exam for a physics course), suspended for the balance of the academic year, and awarded an "F" in the course. In holding that the trial judge should have granted a directed verdict for the college and not submitted the case to a jury, the court held that "once it was shown that [the college] followed its own procedural guidelines and based its disciplinary decision on substantial evidence, judicial review of [the college's] actions should have ceased...."[528] In *Lyon College*, the college had followed the procedures specified in its handbook and, even though the evidence was conflicting as to whether the student had prior knowledge of the exam questions, the court held that a court had no reason to second guess the college's decision. In *Dinu v. President and Fellows of Harvard University*,[529] two seniors who were required to withdraw from the university and denied permission to participate in graduation lost in their breach of contract claim. A federal district court held that, even though the university's decision ordering the students to withdraw had occurred after the students had completed all course requirements for graduation, the university had the right to refuse permission for them to participate in graduation because the student handbook required that students be in "good standing" in order to graduate.

However, failure of a university substantially to follow its procedures in a student disciplinary matter can result in a triable

---

527 999 S.W.2d 213 (Ark. Ct. App. 1999).

528 *Id.* at 217.

529 56 F. Supp.2d 129 (D. Mass. 1999).

breach of contract action. In *Schaer v. Bandeis University*,[530] a Massachusetts appeals court held that a student suspended for sexual harassment was entitled to a trial as to whether the university had followed the procedures in its handbook: the student judicial system was required to make a careful evaluation of the facts; the hearing board was required to make a record of its proceedings; the board was to make its decision based on evidence and testimony introduced at the hearing without permitting irrelevant and inflammatory testimony; the board's decision was to be based on a "clear and convincing" evidence standard; and the board and its advisor were to prepare the student for the hearing process.

Problems of contract interpretation frequently arise where an educational institution misstates its commitments, seeks to alter its commitments, or refuses to honor its commitments. Displeased students have brought claims on a variety of legal theories, including breach of contract, misrepresentation, fraud, and violation of state statutes prohibiting consumer fraud or deceptive practices. In *Idrees v. American University of the Caribbean*,[531] a prospective medical student successfully sued the university on the theory of fraudulent misrepresentation. The university's medical school brochure advertised the school's library facilities, classroom microscopes and skeletons, student slides, and names of faculty, but through circumstances beyond its control, viz. delayed construction and faculty defections, the facilities were not ready when classes were scheduled to begin. The key element seemed to be that the university failed to advise incoming students of its changed circumstances. In addition, the medical school brochure contained a picture of a nearby hospital but failed to explain that no relationship existed between the school and the hospital.

Students occasionally have been successful in recovering damages where courses taught have been different from their catalog descriptions. In *Dezick v. Umpqua Community College*,[532] a student recovered $12,500 damages for promissory fraud and misrepresentation when he had received assurance from school personnel that he would receive advanced welding training as advertised in the school catalog, but during his three

---

530 716 N.E.2d 1055 (Mass. Ct. App. 1999).

531 546 F. Supp. 1342 (S.D. N.Y. 1982)

532 599 P.2d 444 (Ore. 1979).

consecutive terms, none of the courses in the program were ever taught, either because equipment was inoperable or was on order. In *Andre v. Pace University*,[533] students prevailed in recovering damages involving a computer course for breach of contract, breach of fiduciary duty, and violation of a state statute prohibiting deceptive practices. The professor who taught the course had used a more difficult book than the introductory level of the course warranted. When the students complained, the university refused to refund the students' tuition and refused to address the level of instruction because the instructor was tenured. Plaintiff-students not only recovered damages equal to the cost of tuition and the textbook, but also $1,000 each under the state deceptive practices statute.

The possibilities of contractual obligations are wide-ranging. *Britt v. Chestnut Hill College*[534] drives home the obligation of nonpublic educational institutions to honor their commitments to students. In *Britt*, a student for whom life experience credits had been granted by the college upon enrollment and later revoked had a cause of action for breach of contract. Considering the changing demographics among higher education student populations, the court's comment is worth reflection:

> The economic reality is that colleges and universities are competing to attract nontraditional age students and many of these institutions have designed programs to cater to them. Through advertising and recruitment campaigns, an increasing number of colleges and universities are promising students who wish to return to school, flexible schedules, evening and weekend classes, and academic credit for life experience. Students, in turn, attracted by these options, may seek to apply to a particular institution and inquire as to the requirements they will have to meet in order to achieve their degrees. When an individual is induced to enroll in a university or college based upon an award of certain life experience credits, the institution cannot then, after the student's enrollment, revoke those credits.[535]

---

533 618 N.Y.S.2d 975 (City Ct. 1994).
534 632 A.2d 557 (Pa. Super. Ct. 1993).
535 *Id.* at 560.

Actions for breach of contract and misrepresentation can also lie where the school uses superior knowledge about an area and abuses its fiduciary relationship with a student. In *James v. SCS Business and Technical Institute*,[536] a student who thought he was applying for $5,100 in financial aid to cover tuition and books, but in fact signed documents for a $4,000 A.L.A.S. loan, a $2,625 G.S.L. loan, and a $1,400 Pell Grant, could rescind the enrollment agreement as unconscionable. The school had returned $3,187 after the student's withdrawal in October and retained $2,400 to cover the cost of tuition prior to the student's withdrawal, but the student was being dunned by the lender for $4,928.85. The student was entitled to recover the $4,928.25 because the enrollment agreement was unconscionable, and the $2,400 for failure of consideration (many of instructors failed to show for class). The plight of this student hopefully is not typical of nonpublic school students in general, but the court's description of his predicament is worth repeating in light of the importance of financial aid to higher education:

> The relatively short duration of the enrollment interview, the sheer number of documents plaintiff was required to sign, the legal nature of those forms, plaintiff's eagerness to learn the promised skills [six month computer entry operator program], and his total reliance on the apparent expertise of [defendant's] enrollment support his testimony that he followed the school's advice to just sign the forms and trust them even though he did not understand what he was signing.[537]

Because virtually all nonpublic schools operate on a quid pro quo basis, exchanging tuition dollars for services, a failure to deliver services as promised, either orally or in writing, presents the kind of factual dispute courts are equipped to address. In *Van Loock v. Curran*,[538] parents stated a cause of action for breach of contract and fraud where they had paid a preregistration fee but were told on the last day of school, without a reason being given, that their sons would not be permitted to return the next year. Return of the preregistration fees did not

---

536 595 N.Y.S.2d 885 (N.Y. Civ. Ct. App. 1992).

537 *Id.* at 893.

538 489 So.2d 525 (Ala. 1985).

necessarily refute "an inference that upon acceptance of the Van Loocks' registration, the school impliedly contracted to educate [their sons] for the upcoming school term in exchange for the Van Loocks' payment of preregistration fees and continued compliance with the school's rules and regulations."[539] Similarly, in *Squires v. Cambridge School*,[540] parents of a child enrolled in a private school stated causes of action in both breach of contract and misrepresentation when their child's learning disabilities were not remediated as promised by the school principal. Whether in providing services or in meting out discipline, nonpublic schools will be expected to act according to the contract.[541]

As a variation on *Van Loock*, a school may be contractually obligated to refund tuition if the child does not enroll,[542] and parents may be responsible for an entire year's tuition and fees if they cancel registration for a reason not considered acceptable in the handbook.[543] Where the contract provides that no cancellation of a contract would be made and no refund made where parents unilaterally withdraw their child, the school may even have no obligation to mitigate damages.[544]

However, the presence of a liquidated damages clause in a school-parent contract may affect the obligations of both parties. In *Perez v. Aerospace Academy, Inc.*,[545] a parent whose child had been expelled from the Academy after two months sued for a partial refund of tuition and room and board charges. The Academy counterclaimed for the unpaid balance of the contract.

---

539 *Id.* at 529.

540 823 P.2d 256 (Nev. 1991).

541 *See* Jones v. Howe Military Sch., 604 F. Supp. 122 (D. Ind. 1984) (misconduct justified nonenrollment second semester). For expulsion during life of contract for student violation of rules, *see* Thomas Jefferson Sch. Inc. v. Kapros, 728 S.W.2d 315 (Mo. Ct. App. 1987); Hutcheson v. Grace Lutheran Sch., 517 N.Y.S.2d 760 (App. Div. 1987); Spell v. Bible Baptist Church, Inc., 303 S.E.2d 156 (Ga. Ct. App. 1983).

542 Brenner v. Little Red Sch. House, Ltd., 295 S.E.2d 607 (N. C. Ct. App. 1982) (school principal had made oral statement to one parent that tuition could be refunded, even though written school policy apparently would have not authorized the refund).

543 *See* Princeton Montessori Soc'y v. Leff, 591 A.2d 685 (N.J. Super. Ct. 1991); Bishop v. Westminster Schs., Inc., 397 S.E.2d 143 (Ga. Ct. App. 1990); Moyse v. Runnels Sch., Inc., 457 So.2d 767 (La. Ct. App. 1984). *See also* Dr. Perkins Sch. v. Freeman, 741 F.2d 1503 (7th Cir. 1984) (parents obligated to pay tuition to out-of-state school for disabled children based on oral statements, but parents not required to pay amount reflected by retroactive tuition increase where parents had no notice of the increase).

544 *See* Princeton Montessori Soc'y v. Leff, 591 A.2d 685, 687 (N.J.Super. Ct. 1991) ("where the contract expressly provides that no deduction or refund will be made, the entire tuition is payable despite the fact that the student withdraws from the school ... [and] [i]n these circumstances, the educational institution has no duty to mitigate damages.")

545 546 So.2d 1139 (Fla. Dist. Ct. App. 1989).

While upholding the position that a private school is entitled to the full amount of tuition and room and board if a child is expelled, the court ruled that a liquidated damages clause in the contract is unenforceable as a penalty to the extent that it fails to allow out-of-pocket savings by the Academy on board charges. If the board charge could be determined, the parent was entitled under Florida law to a credit for the school's savings on food as a result of his daughter not attending the school. Judicial reluctance to enforce a liquidated damages clause is reflected in *O'Brian v. Langley School*,[546] where the Virginia Supreme Court permitted parents to conduct discovery as to whether their breach of contract was measurable and whether the stipulated damages were grossly in excess of actual damages.

Efforts by students to rely on catalog language will not be successful if their reliance was not reasonable. In *Marquez v. University of Washington*,[547] a student claimed a special program providing "academic aid ... for students of minority ethnic groups"[548] as advertised in the AALS prelaw handbook prohibited the university from replacing a formal tutoring program with a voluntary assistance program after the student's first year of law school. In response to the student's claim that a handbook provision could not be changed, the court observed, "the concept of a binding, absolute, unchangeable contract is particularly anomalous in the context of postgraduate work."[549] In a slightly different situation, occasionally contracts will incorporate documentation external to institutions, such as the *AAUP's Principles of Academic Freedom and Tenure,* but courts will normally not find that such documents confer contractual rights.[550] Students may seek recovery under state consumer protection statutes, but recovery will be denied if the student does not satisfy the terms of the statute.[551] Likewise, students

546 507 S.E.2d 363 (Va. 1998).

547 648 P.2d 94 (Wash. Ct. App. 1982).

548 *Id.* at 96.

549 *Id.* at 97.

550 Waring v. Fordham Univ., 640 F. Supp. 42 (S.D. N.Y. 1986) (AAUP position against tenure quotas cannot form basis of contract claim); Hill v. Talladega College, 502 So.2d 735, 739 (Ala. 1987) (AAUP guideline that "probationary period should not exceed seven years" did not confer tenure on plaintiff who had taught at College for ten years); Krasek v. Duquesne Univ., 437 A.2d 1257 (Pa. Super. Ct. 1981) (employment standards determined by faculty handbook, not ABA and AALS standards).

551 *See* Finstad v. Washburn Univ. of Topeka, 845 P.2d 685 (Kan. 1993) (even though university's statement that its court reporting program was approved when it was not was a *per se* violation of the state's Consumer Protection Act, plaintiffs of the program were not "aggrieved" within the terms of the statute because there was no causal connection between the university's

who allege they have been misled after they complete an academic program but then are ineligible to take a licensing examination in another state, will be unsuccessful in their claim where the university has advised students that regulations for licensing examinations vary from state to state, and that students should seek information directly from the licensing state.[552]

A distillation of the law reflected by the cases discussed above suggests that contractual language can become susceptible to misrepresentation or breach of contract claims when:

(1) The alleged changes or inaccuracies deal with curricular or tenure matters;

(2) The student or employee has specifically relied on the changes or inaccuracies as demonstrated by prior inquiry regarding the item at issue;

(3) The changes in, or inaccuracies concerning, a curricular program affect the substance or completion of a professional or vocational program so the student's livelihood is negatively impacted;

(4) The changes or inaccuracies are so substantial as to not be reasonably reflected in a typical handbook statement permitting alteration, amendment, or abolition of rules or regulations at any time.[553]

Good Faith and Fairness in Contract Enforcement

The third major problem area of contractual constraints concerns the good faith or fairness of contract enforcement. Good

---

statement and the high percentage of the university's graduates who failed the state's licensing exam.)

552 Abraham v. New York Univ. Sch. of Dentistry, 593 N.Y.S.2d 229 (N.Y. App. Div. 1993).

553 *See* Peretti v. Montana, 464 F. Supp. 787 (D. Mont. 1979) ("an educational institution ... is a living changing thing [and cannot] reasonably be expected to remain static ... " However, damages awarded for cancellation of a six unit course in aviation without giving students enrolled in the program an opportunity to complete it); Eden v. SUNY, 374 N.Y.S.2d 686 (App. Div. 1975) (state budget office decision to postpone opening of new program in podiatric medicine after students had been admitted and had foregone opportunities to enroll elsewhere resulted in court order to open program); Behrend v. State, 379 N.E.2d 617 (Ohio Ct. App. 1977) (university decision not to pursue accreditation of its School of Architecture after statements had been made to that effect to students by faculty and administrators resulted in award of monetary damages). *But see*, Beukas v. Farleigh-Dickinson Univ., 605 A.2d 776 (N.J. Super. Ct. 1992) (in absence of bad faith, students had no cause of action for arbitrary behavior in closing dental school).

faith can be intimated from the actions of the parties as well as from verbal comments.[554] Generally, a covenant of good faith and fair dealing is implied in every contract. However, this covenant cannot be used to obliterate express contract language. For example, in *Tollefson v. Roman Catholic Bishop of San Diego*,[555] an administrator whose one-year contract was nonrenewed prior to the date for nonrenewal provided in the contract was not entitled to have superimposed on the contract an "objective standard" requiring "objective and justifiable cause" before the contract could be nonrenewed.[556] Where contract nonrenewal occurred not "by an act inconsistent with the terms of the contract but rather by the expiration of the agreed contract term," the covenant of good faith and fair dealing cannot be used "to rewrite a contract to include provisions entirely foreign to and expressly negated by the original."[557] This principle was pressed even further in *Willitts v. Roman Catholic Archbishop of Boston*[558] where a court refused to agree with a nonrenewed teacher's claim that her one-year contract should have been automatically renewed when the school allowed her contract to expire at the end of the year without providing notification suggested (but not mandated) in the faculty handbook.[559]

Educational institutions normally will have broad discretion in interpreting rules, policies, or handbooks, especially where academic standards are concerned, without being considered to have exercised bad faith. The classic statement was made in *Shields v. The School of Law, Hofstra University*[560] where a student's breach of contract against the law school for continuing to calculate a failing grade in her GPA was dismissed by the court. The student attempted to argue that her reliance upon an assistant dean's statement that, if she rewrote a brief and received

---

554 *See* McGhee v. Miller, 837 S.W.2d 596 (Tenn. 1992) (in a bizarre case that has gone three times to the Tennessee Supreme Court, a teacher who had failed a basketball player and was dismissed by school board was ordered reinstated with backpay and forward pay for lack of fairness following threats to teacher by athletic department, a shot fired through her windshield, and sale of buttons at school expressing desire she had been shot).

555 268 Cal. Rptr. 550 (Cal. Ct. App. 1990).

556 *Id.* at 555.

557 *Id.* at 556.

558 581 N.E.2d 475 (Mass. 1991).

559 The nonrenewal language in the faculty handbook was considered by the court to be advisory rather than mandatory: "The teachers *should* be formally notified of a decision prior to April 15, so that opportunities to seek other employment will not be lost." *Id.* at 478 (emphasis added).

560 431 N.Y.S.2d 60 (N.Y. Sup. Ct. 1980).

a higher grade, her failing grade would not be counted in her GPA, caused her not to appeal the failing grade. The plaintiff did in fact receive a passing grade on the second brief, but "consistent with its academic regulations as set forth in its bulletin, the school continued to count plaintiff's failing grade . . . ."[561] In dismissing the student's complaint, the court made a fairly typical and representative statement concerning the academic relationship between an institution and its students (or faculty):

> In the absence of any allegations of such a provision, there is no basis to conclude that the law school's decision with respect to those matters involved anything other than the exercise of sound academic discretion, unfettered by contract and unreviewable by courts.[562]

Courts will uphold judgment regarding academic decisions even though the penalty may appear severe. In *Napolitano v. Princeton University*,[563] a court upheld one year's delay in awarding a baccalaureate degree to a student who had plagiarized a paper. Even though the judge was troubled by the severity of the penalty and even though in twenty or more disciplinary cases no student had been penalized as severely, the court observed that such a comparison "is totally irrelevant because each penalty obviously must be viewed with regard to the offender and the community."[564] A student who was denied a Ph.D. degree after she failed her final dissertation defense was not entitled to damages for breach of contract since the university had followed the procedures in its handbook. The court observed that it was not its function "to second-guess academic decisions and judgments made in colleges and universities," and, as long as the faculty decision had a rational basis, the court would not find the decision to be arbitrary or capricious.[565] In *Susan M. v. New*

---

561 *Id.* at 61.

562 *Id.* at 63. The effect of oral statements upon institutional policies is problematic and courts are not consistent in their treatment of such statements. *Compare* Healy v. Larsson, 323 N.Y.S.2d 625 (N.Y. Sup. Ct. 1971) (oral representation made to students during "consultation with dean, director of admissions, acting president, a guidance counselor and chairman of a department of the community college" created obligation to award a degree) *with* Olsson v. Board of Higher Educ., 492 N.E. 2d 1150 (N.Y. 1980) ("representation" or "information given" by faculty member regarding number of comprehensive examinations to receive passing grade was merely professor's "unfortunate slip-of-the-tongue" and was not binding on the college.)

563 453 A.2d 263 (N.J. Super. Ct. 1982).

564 *Id.* at 278. For a discussion of *Neapolitano*, *see* R. Mawdsley, Academic Misconduct: Plagiarism and Cheating (NOLPE 1994). The leading case on institutional discretion in academic penalties is Board of Curators of Univ. of Missouri v. Horowitz, 435 U.S. 78 (1978).

565 Swartley v. Hoffner, 734 A.2d 915, 921 (Pa. Super. Ct. 1999).

York Law School,[566] a law student dismissed from the law school as the result of receiving a failing grade was denied a trial on the issue of the fairness of the faculty member's grading. In upholding the student's dismissal, the court observed that:

> As a general rule, judicial review of grading disputes would involve the courts in the very core of academic and educational decision making. Moreover, to so involve the courts in assessing the propriety of particular grades would promote litigation by countless unsuccessful students and thus undermine the credibility of the academic determinations of educational institutions.[567]

In a case involving a religious educational institution, *Bischoff v. Brothers of the Sacred Heart*,[568] a court upheld cancellation of a contract for a new religion teacher prior to the beginning of the year. On his employment application under the category "Religion," the applicant had checked off "Practicing Catholic: Yes" and under "Marital Status" had noted "married." Even though the subject of marriage and divorce had not been discussed during the interview, the school subsequently learned the applicant had a prior marriage and divorce and canceled his contract because divorced persons were not permitted to teach religion. In deciding this close case for the school, the court relied upon the applicant's background of six years in a Catholic Seminary and his assertion at trial that "he didn't divulge his marital history because he knew Brother Farrel would not have hired him under these circumstances."[569] As an addendum to sets of facts such as *Bischoff* involving employees in religious organizations, the United States Supreme Court has given greater protection to religious institutions under Title VII in enforcing religious standards on employees, even if the standards are enforced after the employee was hired and even if the employee is not performing a religious function.[570]

However, institutions do not have unfettered discretion in arbitrarily or capriciously enforcing contracts. In *Blank v. Board*

---

566 556 N.E.2d 1104 (N.Y. 1989).

567 *Id.* at 1107.

568 416 So.2d 348 (La. Ct. App. 1982).

569 *Id.* at 351.

570 Amos v. Corporation of Presiding Bishop, 107 S.Ct. 2862 (1987) (employee was janitor in a church-owned gymnasium that was open to the public). For an analysis of *Amos* see R. Mawdsley, *Religious Universities and Title VII: The Right To Discriminate on Religious Grounds*, 43 EDUC. L. REP. 1143 (1988)

of Higher Education of City of New York,[571] a court ordered Brooklyn College to confer a baccalaureate degree upon a student. This rather extraordinary judicial remedy was prompted because the college had refused to transfer credits for work done at another institution. The college had arbitrarily attempted to rely upon a newly added provision in the school catalog for the year following the one in which the student should have graduated and to rely upon only one part of the catalog when other portions of the catalog made differing statements.[572] In *Heisler v. New York Medical College*,[573] a court overturned a dismissal of a student who had failed four courses during her first year when three other students, some with more failures and weaker excuses, were not dismissed. In ordering reinstatement the court observed that,

> when a school deviates from its rules and makes exceptions thereto, it must employ some understandable, unified standards. The failure to establish and maintain such standards constitutes an impermissible abuse of discretion and a lack of good faith on the part of the educational institution.[574]

Enforcement of a rule may be arbitrary not because of contract interpretation but because a contract provision is superseded by public policy. Frequently, nonpublic schools will attempt to collect past due obligations by denying readmission to students or refusing to send official transcripts.[575] However, in *In re Parkman*,[576] a private college could not discontinue a student for refusal to accelerate a past due account after the student had arranged a Chapter 13 debtor's plan.[577] Although normally state action is required before an institution is affected by nonretaliation protection under a debtor's plan, the court

---

571 273 N.Y.S.2d 796 (N.Y. Sup. Ct. 1966).

572 Similarly, new catalog provisions cannot be applied retroactively if the catalog under which a student entered made promises that certain catalog provisions would not be subject to change. University of Texas Health Science Ctr. at Houston v. Babb, 646 S.W.2d 502 (Tex. Ct. App. 1982).

573 449 N.Y.S.2d 834 (Sup. Ct. 1982).

574 *Id.* at 837.

575 Under the Family Educational Rights and Privacy Act (FERPA) a student in an institution receiving federal assistance must be permitted access to his education records. Where the student is beyond a reasonable distance (FERPA office suggests fifty miles) from the institution, he will have been considered to have been denied access to his records if the institution refuses to mail him a transcript. However, the transcript can be stamped "Issued to student." *See* 20 U.S.C. § 1232g(a)(1)(A); 34 C.F.R. § 99.10 (d).

576 27 B.R. 460 (Bkrtcy. N.D. Ill. 1983).

577 11 U.S.C. §§ 362 (a), (b); 1301.

observed that "where the actions of a private institution such as withholding a transcript are really tools to collect a discharged debt or a debt provided for under a plan, debtors are denied the fresh start contemplated by Congress enacting the Bankruptcy Code."[578]

Since contract is the basis for defining institution-student relationships, special contractual concepts such as substantial performance can come into play. In *Russell v. Salve Regina College*,[579] although the U.S. Supreme Court set aside, on procedural grounds, a $49,903.45 judgment for a student who had been dismissed from the nursing program for failing to lose weight, the Court suggested that state law regarding substantial performance could be the basis, on remand, for affirming the judgment. In *Russell*, the issue was whether an overweight student in a nursing program who had signed an agreement to enroll in a weight loss program and lose two pounds per week had substantially performed the contract even though she did not lose the weight. Substantial performance can also work for the educational institution if a student (or employee) alleges that the institution has not complied with contractual language. In *Fraad-Wolff v. Vassar College*,[580] a student who withdrew from the college while under investigation for harassment unsuccessfully claimed that he had been constructively discharged when the college had not followed its written procedures for investigating charges of harassment. In dismissing the student's claims, the court found that the college had substantially complied with its handbook requirements concerning investigation of disciplinary offenses.[581]

Courts have not been willing to go beyond contractual rights and to permit disgruntled parents or students to sue nonpublic or public schools for educational malpractice.[582] The policy reasons for not recognizing a cause of action for educational malpractice can be summarized as follows: "(1) a lack of a

---

578 *Parkman*, 27 B.R. at 462.

579 938 F.2d 315 (1st Cir. 1991), reversed and remanded, Salve Regina College v. Russell, 499 U.S. 225 (1991) (the basis for the Supreme Court's decision was that the court of appeals should have reviewed the state law question of substantial performance de novo rather than deferring to the district court's conclusion of law).

580 932 F. Supp. 88 (S.D. N.Y. 1996).

581 The student relied on language in the 1986 faculty handbook that had been in effect while he was pursuing his undergraduate degree. The handbook had been changed in 1992 before he began his M.B.A. program in 1994.

582 *See* Livolsi v. Hicksville Union Free Sch., 693 N.Y.S.2d 617 (N.Y. App. Div. 1999).

measurable standard of care; (2) inherent uncertainties as to the cause and nature of damages; (3) the potential for a flood of litigation; and (4) the courts' overseeing the day-to-day operation of the schools."[583] The classic and frequently quoted rationale for not recognizing educational malpractice as a cause of action was stated in *Ross v. Creighton University*:[584]

> Education is an intensely collaborative process, requiring the interaction of student with teacher. A good student can learn from a poor teacher; a poor student can close his mind to a good teacher. Without effort by a student, he cannot be educated. Good teaching methods may vary with the needs of the individual student. In other professions, by contrast, client cooperation is far less important; given a modicum of cooperation, a competent professional in other fields can control the results obtained. But in education, the ultimate responsibility for success remains always with the student. Both the process and the result are subjective, and proof or disproof extremely difficult.[585]

Ross has been relied on to bar an educational malpractice claim, camouflaged as breach of contract, where a former student, unsuccessful in satisfying job requirements, alleges that he had not been properly trained.[586] Unless supported by contractual language,[587] courts have been unwilling to entertain causes of action based on "quality of education,"[588] particularly if a court

---

583 Finstad v. Washburn Univ. of Topeka, 845 P.2d 685, 694 (Kan. 1993) (Wachtler, J. concurring).

584 740 F. Supp. 1319 (N.D. Ill. 1990) (student who had been recruited by the university to play basketball and completed eligibility without accumulating sufficient credits to graduate had no cause of action in educational malpractice but did state a cause of action for breach of contract in that the university failed to provide promised remedial help).

585 *Id.* at 691.

586 Whayne v. U.S. Dep't of Educ., 915 F.Supp. 1143 (D. Kan. 1996).

587 *See* Squires v. Cambridge Sch., 823 P.2d 256 (Nev. 1991) (breach of contract and misrepresentation causes of action permitted when a student's learning disabilities not remediated as promised); Village Community Sch. v. Adler, 478 N.Y.S.2d 546 (N.Y. Civ. Ct. 1984) (breach of contract and fraud complaint upheld for school's failure to detect learning deficiencies).

588 *See* Sirohi v. Lee, 634 N.Y.S.2d 119 (N.Y. App. Div. 1995) (Columbia University not responsible in tort for its educational environment and for an atmosphere conducive to academic pursuits). Generally, in nonpublic education, *see* Houston v. Mile High Adventist Academy, 846 F. Supp. 1449 (D. Colo. 1994); Paladino v. Adelphi Univ., 454 N.Y.S.2d 868 (N.Y. Sup. Ct. 1982); Pietro v. St. Joseph's Sch., 48 U.S.L.W. 2229 (N.Y. Sup. Ct. 1979). In public education *see* Tubell v. Dade County Pub. Schs., 419 So.2d 388 (Fla. Dist. Ct. App. 1982); Hunter v. Board of Educ. of Montgomery County, 439 A.2d 582 (Md. 1982); D.S.W. v. Fairbanks N. Star Borough Sch. Dist., 628 P.2d 554 (Alas. 1981).

will be called upon to interpret whether the education provided is consistent with denominational religious tenets.[589]

However, courts have pointed out that "[i]f ... a nonpublic school were simply to accept a student's tuition and thereafter provide no educational services, an action for breach of contract might lie. Similarly if the contract with the school were to provide for certain specified services, such as for example, a designated number of hours of instruction, and the school failed to meet its obligation, then a contract with appropriate consequential damages might be viable."[590] Thus, even if a school promised that "a student would reach a certain proficiency after pursuing certain studies"[591] the cause of action is still contract and not educational malpractice.

Special Contractual Problems

Three problems which nonpublic schools most likely have dealt with, or will deal with, are search and seizure, communicable diseases (particularly AIDS/HIV), and pregnant students. In the public sector, school litigation involving these areas has been prolific under constitutional and statutory requirements.[592] Obligations for nonpublic schools are problematic since those schools may not be subject to the same set of constraints as public schools.

Search and Seizure

The expectation that a person and his or her property will not be searched or seized by government officials is grounded in the Fourth Amendment's prohibition against unreasonable searches and seizures.[593] Freedom from unreasonable searches and seizures is part of a broader right of privacy that extends far

---

589 *Houston*, *supra* note 588 (no neutral principles of law or final determination of highest ecclesiastical authority to form basis of resolving dispute).

590 *Paladino*, *supra* note 588 at 873.

591 *Pietro*, *supra* note 588 at 55.

592 A comprehensive discussion of case law on an annual basis involving these, as well as other areas or litigation, can be found in the yearbooks of Education Law published each year by the Education Law Association (ELA). *E.g.*, *see* C. Russo (ed.) THE YEARBOOK OF EDUCATION LAW 1999 (ELA 1999).

593 Amendment IV
The right of the people to be secure in their persons, houses, papers, and effects, against unreasonable searches and seizures, shall not be violated, and no warrants shall issue, but upon probable cause, supported by oath and affirmation, and particularly describing the place to be searched, and the persons or things to be seized.

beyond searches for material objects.[594] In terms of the Fourth Amendment's application of search and seizure to educational institutions, there are two judicially constructed limitations: The Amendment applies to searches and seizures by agents of the government ("state action"), not by private parties; and the amendment requires only "reasonable suspicion" (as opposed to the higher standard of "probable cause") when applied to searches by school officials in public schools.[595] However, in the absence of state action, the cornucopia of litigation in the public sector involving search and seizure does not apply to nonpublic schools.[596] Nonpublic schools are able to define their expectations of privacy in their contracts with students and employees. The caveat, of course, is that, like with other areas involving student or employee misconduct, courts will apply a quasi-due process or fairness standard.

Three issues will need to be addressed by nonpublic schools: defining contraband; explaining the inception and scope of a search; and deciding when to involve government law enforcement officials. Contraband refers to materials or objects that students or employees are prohibited from possessing and/or distributing on school premises. In religious schools, contraband may take on a more expansive definition than in other nonpublic schools and may be tied to biblical references pertaining generally to purity of life, character development, concern for others, and moral integrity. Such a general religious foundation permits broad proscriptions, including having obvious objects such as weapons and illegal drugs as well as wearing apparel and publications that present a message contrary to that of the religious school. As long as students and employees have reasonable notice through written or oral communications of what the school considers to be contraband, courts will let schools define their own environment.

Inception and scope of search and seizure are separate issues in the public sector but are easily combined in nonpublic

---

594 *See e.g.*, Cypress Media, Inc. v. Hazelton Area Sch. Dist., 798 A.2d 866 (Pa. Commw. Ct. 1998) (newspaper did not have access under state's Right to Know statute to teacher applications because, even though the applications might be public records under the statute, they contained confidential information such as home addresses, social security numbers, college transcripts, physical examination reports, and child abuse clearances).

595 *See* New Jersey v. T.L.O., 469 U.S. 325 (1985).

596 *See, e.g.*, DesRoches v. Caprio, 156 F.3d 571 (4th Cir. 1999) (search of backpack for pair of shoes held reasonable); Commonwealth v. Cass, 709 A.2d 350 (Pa. 1998) (use of drug sniffing dogs to search lockers upheld); Kennedy v. Dexter Consol. Schs., 955 P.2d 693 (N.M. Ct. App. 1998) (use of metal detectors upheld).

schools.[597] When a search should occur (inception) and how far it should go (scope) are undergirded by an expectation of privacy. Nonpublic schools can declare in handbooks that school-owned property (e.g., rooms, lockers, desks) are subject to search at any time. The inception of a search in the public sector must be tied to reasonable suspicion. Much of the litigation involving inception in the public sector focuses on two kinds of issues: whether the school had a reasonable suspicion to search a specific student, or students, for an identified object (e.g., searching a specific student's locker based on an anonymous tip that drugs are in the locker); and whether suspicionless searches are permissible (e.g., requiring all students to pass through a metal detector on entering a school).

Officials in nonpublic schools can avoid all of these problem areas because they are not required to satisfy the constitutional standard of reasonable suspicion, and thus, can set their own contractual standards. The only limitations would be whether a school has restricted its right to search under its contract (e.g., no search will be conducted without the student's or employee's consent, or searches will be conducted only for specific, identified objects) and whether the search was arbitrary and capricious. Under the arbitrary and capricious standard, the inception of searches would be upheld as long as students and employees had notice of what school officials could search (e.g., all school-owned property), when they could conduct a search (e.g., at any time), and what reason was needed (e.g., search conducted without a specific reason).

However, searching a space that belongs to the school is quite different from searching personal property that belongs to students and employees (e.g., book bags, brief cases, purses). When school officials request that students or employees open their personal property, an argument can be made that an arbitrary and capricious standard should apply to the reasonableness of the request. In other words, even though a school would not need a reason to search its own property, it should need a reason to search a student's or employee's property. The problem is determining whether the reason should apply only to the nature of the object for which the search is being

---

597 *See*, *New Jersey v. T.L.O.*, (inception for search of student's purse was student's lying about smoking in restroom asnd scope of search within the purse flowed from the nature of objects found).

conducted (the specific items of contraband) or whether the reason should identify why certain students or employees have been singled out for a search. Unfortunately, there is a dearth of case law involving searches and nonpublic schools, but fairness would suggest that, given the fact that searches of personal property are more intrusive than searches of school property, students and employees should at least know the kind of contraband at issue. Again, keeping in mind the absence of case law, nonpublic schools could probably require in handbooks that students and employees submit their personal property to searches or face disciplinary action. If students or employees do not consent to searches of their personal property and school officials still want to conduct a search, officials would probably be better served by complying with the reasonable suspicion standard used in the public schools.

The most intrusive of searches, those that involved a search of an employee's or student's person, are also the most difficult to justify. Even though reasonable suspicion does not apply to nonpublic schools under the Fourth Amendment, a court's arbitrary and capricious standard for searches of a person in a nonpublic school would probably be close to having the same definition. In other words, nonpublic school officials would need to identify object(s) that are the reason for the search and identify a reason why certain persons have been selected for a search (assuming that the search is not a general search). For example, a federal district court in Rhode Island has upheld public school officials' patting down of students' pockets in a cafeteria. The search was reasonable because the object was identified (a knife from the cafeteria), and all students were searched.[598]

A third area of concern deals with the point at which involvement of law enforcement officials makes searches subject to Fourth Amendment requirements. Although searches by private parties are not subject to the Fourth Amendment, searches by or at the direction of law enforcement officers, will require probable cause. Even in the public sector, searches conducted according to a contract by school officials will be governed by contract law, not by the Fourth Amendment.[599]

---

598 Broussea v. Town of Westerly, 11 F. Supp.2d 177 (D. R.I. 1998).

599 *See* State v. Burroughs, 926 S.W.2d 243 (Tenn. 1996) (residence hall director who searched a student's room and turned over drugs to police did so pursuant to contract and not as state agent).

Communicable Diseases

Although many diseases can be classified as communicable, AIDS has received the most attention. The AIDS/HIV crisis has been difficult for religious nonpublic schools to address because many of those infected with the HTLV-3 virus may reflect lifestyles antithetical to the religious beliefs of some schools regarding sexuality (e.g., religious views may include judgmental opinions concerning homosexuality, bisexuality, heterosexual promiscuity, and intravenous drug use). However, a significant number of AIDS carriers have contracted the disease as a result of contacts other than sexual, particularly through blood transfusions.

In public schools, students infected with the AIDS virus have been protected from automatic exclusion from the public school classroom under the Individuals with Disabilities Education Act (IDEA),[600] the Rehabilitation Act,[601] and the Americans with Disabilities Act (ADA).[602] ADA reflects the United States Supreme Court decision in *School Board of Nassau County, Florida v. Arline* under the Rehabilitation Act that communicable diseases were disabilities and a public school district had to make a "reasonable accommodation" for a teacher with tuberculosis who was "otherwise qualified."[603] However, ADA applies to nonpublic educational institutions, and thus, the body of law that has developed under the Rehabilitation Act will now be extended to a significant extent to nonpublic schools. But ADA applies only to discrimination against employees in religious nonpublic schools, while students in such schools have no ADA protection. In nonsectarian nonpublic schools, the ADA applies to both employees and students.

Legal responsibility for nonpublic schools comes from several directions. First, even though IDEA applies directly only to public schools, the Rehabilitation Act only to recipients of federal assistance, and the ADA only partially to nonpublic schools, these schools in general may be subject to state or local antidiscrimination provisions. Although religious schools may

600 *In re* Ryan White, 507 EHLR 239 (homebound program not "least restrictive environment")

601 District 27 Community Sch. Bd. v. Board of Educ., 502 N.Y.S.2d 325 (Sup. Ct. 1986) (person with AIDS is physically impaired).

602 29 U.S.C. § 706; 42 U.S.C. § 12101 *et seq.*

603 *See* School Bd. of Nassau County, Florida v. Arline, 480 U.S. 273 (1987) *on remand*, 692 F. Supp. 1286 (M.D. Fla. 1988) (teacher subject to relapses of tuberculosis was "otherwise qualified" and had to be accommodated under Rehabilitation Act).

contemplate a free exercise religious exemption, it is difficult to construct an argument that a disease like AIDS is a moral wrong. In order to make this argument, an institution would have to be prepared to declare that a student or employee who acquired AIDS through means without any connotation of moral culpability, such as a blood transfusion, has become a moral leper, an improbable leap in religious belief. Second, with the enactment of ADA, the possibility exists that nondiscrimination against those with disabilities may become another established public policy and, if such were to happen, educational institutions could face loss of institutional tax exemption.[604] Third, regardless of responsibility under the various statutes, nonpublic institutions may be subject to breach of privacy lawsuits if employee or student removal results in the unauthorized release of confidential information.[605] A preferable approach to the AIDS crisis would seem to be a deliberate policy that considers each AIDS carrier on an individual basis.[606]

Pregnancies

A second major problem area concerns the handling of pregnant students. In the public sector, pregnant students are protected from exclusion from an education under Title IX of the Education Amendments of 1972,[607] the Fourteenth Amendment's equal protection clause, or various state statutes.[608] These provisions will not apply to most nonpublic schools, which are free to determine their own policy.

For those nonpublic schools that automatically exclude pregnant students, the following legal concerns may be of interest. First, school policies cannot be enforced in an arbitrary and capricious manner. Dismissal of a pregnant girl, but not the boy who admitted paternity, would certainly raise that issue. Second, any effort to expand public school standards to religious

---

604 *See infra*, section on *Government and Fundamental Public Policy* in chapter on "Governmental Regulation of Nonpublic Schools." See also, Glover v. Williamsburg Local Sch.Dist. Bd. of Educ., 20 F. Supp.2d 1160 (S.D. Ohio 1998) (public school teacher who had been nonrenewed because of sexual orientation was entitled to traditional level of scrutiny under equal protection clause which required the school board to offer a rational basis for its decision).

605 *See* R. Mawdsley, *Privacy Rights of AIDS Victims*, 31 Ed. Law Rep. 697 (1986); F. Hartog-Rapp, *AIDS Poses Legal Risks for School Boards*, 40 Ed. Law Rep. 112 (1987).

606 For an example of such a policy *see* the one prepared by William Ball in R. Mawdsley and A. Fortosis, What Every Christian School Should Know About the Law (ACSI 1989).

607 20 U.S.C. § 1681 (applicable to institutions receiving federal assistance).

608 *See* Thomas, Health Related Legal Issues in Education at 66-72.

schools would normally be met with a free exercise defense. However, applying to female students a moral principle opposing marital sex, a claim made in every situation where a pregnant student is excluded, would seem to oppose the pregnancy rather than the premarital sex. Presumably a student who engaged in premarital sex but did not become pregnant would be treated the same way as one who did become pregnant. Treating the presence in school of a pregnant girl as an endorsement of premarital sex depends upon considering pregnancy as equally reprehensible as premarital sex. Those institutions which take a strong right-to-life position in the abortion conflict may want to consider whether it is consistent to fight strenuously to protect the fetus and prevent termination of pregnancies but then punish the fetus carrier. Third, the creation of an established public policy to eradicate gender discrimination would bring under scrutiny any school policies disciplining all pregnant students, on the theory that only females would be affected.[609]

In view of these issues, nonpublic schools may want to consider whether exclusion of pregnant student is consistent with their mission and ministry. Schools may at least want to consider alternative educational opportunities, such as homebound education.

Recommendations

In summarizing this chapter on constitutional and contractual considerations regarding institutional relationships, the following recommendations may be of assistance:

(1) Parties to an employment contract would do well to discuss general or ambiguous terms (e.g., "other assigned duties") prior to signing. Any special arrangements, such as exclusion from certain duties, need to be committed to writing.

(2) Special service obligations or conduct standards need to be clearly spelled out in faculty, staff, and student handbooks. If faculty and/or staff handbooks are to be part of the contract, they need to be incorporated by

609 For a fuller treatment of these three legal concerns *see supra* book cited in note 606.

reference in the employment contract signed by the employee. Administrative desire to maintain freedom to modify the handbooks at any time may need to be balanced with possible negative effects on employee and student morale when rights/benefits can be altered or deleted at an employer's discretion.

(3) Employment-at-will contracts should include a disclaimer statement expressly stating the employment relationship is "at-will."[610]

(4) Handbooks should state the institution's discipline policy, including punishable offenses, kinds of punishments, and the discipline procedure.

(5) Institutional materials need to be reviewed annually so that conflicts or contradictions among policies are eliminated. This review should include not only handbooks but also promotional materials.

610 For a sample, *see* I. SHEPARD, H. OLSEN AND R. DUSTIN EMPLOYMENT AT WILL: A GUIDE TO AN ERODING DOCTRINE 8 (CUPA 1987).

Chapter III

Governing Board Responsibilities and Liability

Introduction

The personal liability of members of governing boards of nonpublic educational institutions has generated relatively little litigation or literature when compared to that generated by the public sector.[611] This relative absence of case law or commentary can probably be attributed to a number of factors: less likelihood by clientele to sue nonpublic schools; the diminishing role of nonpublic school boards in actual governance; and the greater visibility of administrators as the actual source of policy as well as day-to-day decision making. Nonpublic elementary and secondary schools, especially those with religious affiliations, tend to be very hierarchal (almost monolithic) in administrative structure and operation. Governing boards of postsecondary institutions frequently have more authority in school decisions, but the geographical separation of board members often makes board meetings on anything other than an annual or semiannual basis difficult for some members to attend. It is not uncommon for postsecondary boards to delegate more frequent governance decisions to executive committees composed of board members who are able to meet more frequently. Although executive committees are generally predominantly composed of line

[611] In Wood v. Strickland, 420 U.S. 308, 322 (1975) the United States Supreme Court decided that a public school board member could be individually liable under section 1983 of the Civil Rights Act according to "a standard of conduct based not only on permissible intentions, but also on knowledge of the basic, unquestioned constitutional rights of his charges." The absence of sufficient involvement between a nonpublic educational institution and a state immunizes nonpublic schools from section 1983, Rice v. President and Fellows of Harvard College, 663 F.2d 336, *cert. denied*, 456 U.S. 928 (1982). However, private schools can be as equally unsusceptible to mandamus actions as public institutions. Carr v. St. John's Univ., 198 N.E.2d 18 (N.Y. 1962); Harris v. Trustees of Columbia Univ., 470 N.Y.S.2d 368 (N.Y. App.Div. 1983).

administrators, there are usually several board members who are not administrators.

The trend among educational institutions with endowments is to hire professional money managers to manage endowments, but the governing board has a duty to oversee the money managers. In *Bache Halsey Stuart v. University of Houston,*[612] the university's board of regents sought unsuccessfully to keep from having to reimburse a brokerage firm for a half-million dollars in losses when the firm liquidated securities at the direction of the university. The university's claim, rejected by the court, was that the university employee dealing with the firm was not authorized to permit buying and selling of securities. In essence, the court recognized that the board of regents of this university could delegate the management of investment funds, but the board was required to retain control over the investment program and to review the status of investments. Since *Bache Halsey Stuart* was decided on the basis of contract law, the principle in this case would seem to apply equally to nonpublic educational institutions.

Notwithstanding the relative infrequency of lawsuits against nonpublic universities, the *Bache Halsey Stuart* case suggests that board members in all educational institutions should not permit themselves to be anesthetized as to their legal responsibilities. The minimum responsibilities for board members are:

(1) To attend meetings of the board and committees;

(2) To examine financial statements of the institutions;

(3) To acquire working knowledge of institutional policies;

(4) To make inquiries;

(5) To discharge responsibilities in a reasonable, prudent, and informed manner.[613]

---

[612] 638 S.W.2d 920 (Tex. Ct. App. 1982).

[613] Legal Deskbook for Administrators of Independent Colleges and Universities (K. Weeks, ed. 1982) at III-7. *See also*, Association of Governing Boards of Universities and Colleges, Trustee Responsibility for Academic Affairs (1984); Dominguez, *To Reign or To Rule: A Choice For University Boards of Trustees,* 3 Conn. L. Rev. 375 (1971).

Ascending Liability

Governing boards of nonprofit organizations may be responsible for the action of other organized and separately incorporated units that can be viewed as part of a hierarchal unit.[614] Structural separation, frequently and successfully sought among for-profit corporations to separate legal entities and yet remain in control, is not as successful among nonprofit corporations. Existing judicial attitudes make structural separation an unreliable device to separate legal responsibilities, partly because of the differences between members of nonprofit corporations and stockholders of for-profit corporations, and partly because a similarity in a common enterprise or mission among several related nonprofit (especially religious) entities tends to be viewed as a principal-agent relationship.[615]

In *Barr v. United Methodist Church*,[616] the church, an unincorporated association, was held financially responsible following the bankruptcy of a California nonprofit corporation that operated fourteen retirement homes. When the corporation, which had contracted to furnish convalescent care, accommodations, and food service in exchange for full prepayments or monthly payments, was unable to meet its commitments, the residents sued the Methodist denomination. Brushing aside First Amendment religious issues,[617] the court determined that the church denomination should be responsible for denominational subunits which "share a common purpose" and "function under a common name."[618] In hierarchal organizations where various subunits function in a manner that equates with a corporate organization, board members and officers of the parent denomination which enjoy "the benefits, both economic and spiritual of [the subunit's] projects"[619] and which oversee a system that "does not provide any method of redress for . . . [a] class of plaintiffs who have alleged fraud, breach of contract and statutory violations,"[620] can be required to respond to plaintiff's claims.

---

[614] For a definitive work on this subject see, E. Gaffney, Jr. and P. Sorenson, Ascending Liability in Religious and Other Nonprofit Organizations (1984).

[615] *Id.* at 75-82. P. Moots, Ascending Liability: Planning Memorandum 5-6 (1987).

[616] 153 Cal. Rptr. 322 (Cal. Ct. App. 1979).

[617] *Id.* at 332-33.

[618] *Id.* at 328.

[619] *Id.* at 331.

[620] *Id.* at 333.

The lesson from *Barr* would seem to be that church board members and officers may not be immune from liabilities in a church's educational institutions. In fact, immunity may not be desirable because the governance in a separate subunit (the school) necessary to achieve that immunity may well be incompatible with the church's religious tenets or inconsistent with the church's goal of religious homogeneity in all units of the organization.

Fiduciary Relationship

Board membership is a fiduciary relationship, and any business dealings between a board member and his institution will be examined with the greatest scrutiny. The allegations from plaintiff's complaint in *Gilbert v. McLeod Infirmary*[621] illustrate the type of dealings between a board member and his or her institution that can result in such dealings being rendered voidable at the option of the institution's officers, minority board members in the transaction, or even the institution's employees. In *Gilbert,* the actions that resulted in a sale of institutional property to a board member being set aside were:

(1) The attendance and activity of the purchasing board member at the meeting where the transaction was considered;

(2) Profit to the board member and potential or actual present or future loss to the institution;

(3) Consideration of less than two-thirds of the fair market value;

(4) Authorization of the transaction at an irregular board meeting with ratification at a subsequent board meeting advocated by the purchasing board member;

(5) Failure to satisfy the notice requirement imposed by the corporation's constitution.[622]

---

[621] 64 S.E.2d 524 (S.C. 1951).
[622] *Id.* at 527, 531.

Even though the *Gilbert* court found no "actual fraud or fraudulent intent,"[623] the court set aside the board member's purchase because "his conduct failed to measure up to the high standard required by the law of one in his fiduciary relation . . . ."[624] Although a board member is not prevented from dealing with his own nonprofit institution, he bears the burden of proof that he made full disclosure regarding his purchase, paid full value, and imposed no burden upon the institution. The *Gilbert* court concluded that the doctrine is firmly established that "a person occupying a place of trust should not put himself in a position in which self-interest conflicts with any duty he owes to those for whom he acts."[625]

In *Jarvis Christian College v. National Union Fire Insurance Company*[626], the Fifth Circuit Court of Appeals demonstrated the financial harm that can occur where a member of a nonpublic college's board of trustees has breached his fiduciary duty. A member of the college's board, who also had a forty-nine percent interest in an investment company, persuaded the entire board, without divulging his interest,[627] to transfer $2,000,000 of the college's endowment to his company. The company invested the money in accounts receivable from hospitals and health care providers, and then lost all the money when these institutions went bankrupt. The college was awarded judgments of $1,800,000 against the former trustee[628] and $2,000,000 against the investment company, but collected nothing. At that point, the college filed a claim against its liability insurer for the maximum $1,000,000 coverage under a provision insuring against "wrongful acts" of directors and officers. However, the insurance policy had an exclusion as to "any claim arising out of the gaining of any personal profit or advantage." The federal district court denied recovery to the college on the basis of this exclusion and the Fifth Circuit upheld that decision. The Fifth

[623] *Id.* at 531.

[624] *Id.*

[625] *Id.* at 530. *See also, In re* Beychok, 495 So.2d 1278 (La. 1986) (setting aside board contract for advertisement space where contract was on behalf of company owned by a board member); Smith v. Dorsey, 530 So.2d 5 (Miss. 1988) (declaring null and void teaching contracts entered into between school board and spouses of board members under state statute prohibiting public officers from having any direct interest in a contract).

[626] 197 F.3d 742 742 (5th Cir. 1999).

[627] *Id.* at 744 (the trustee was co-owner, director, and employee of the investment company.)

[628] The trustee resigned at the insistence of the college board when it discovered his interest in the investment company.

Circuit found that, even though the investment company lost the $2,000,000, the former board member gained a personal profit or advantage from the money because the money could have caused the company (concerning which the former trustee was a co-owner, director, and employee) to become successful and "business success clearly qualifies as personal advantage."[629] The court agreed that the former trustee breached his fiduciary duty by "wrongfully [giving] *himself* the personal advantage in transferring $2,000,000 of Jarvis's money to a small, highly risky business."[630] In defining the fiduciary duty that a board member owes to his college, the court observed that "a fiduciary is not legally entitled to any profit or advantage he gains as a result of a breach of duty or trust."[631] As the college learned, its liability protection depended on the integrity of its board members. The fiduciary duty expected of board members, as reflected in one of the jury instructions is that "the director must act in good faith and must not allow his personal interests to prevail over the interests of his corporation."[632]

In 1996, Congress addressed excess benefits that accrue to certain persons having dealings with Section 501(c)(3) organizations.[633] Any person "in a position to exercise substantial influence over the affairs of the organization" (including a member of the person's family)[634] can be subject to an excess benefit tax that will be either twenty-five percent or 200 percent of the excess benefit, depending on whether the transaction has been corrected during the taxable period. An excess benefit transaction is one in which:

> an economic benefit is provided by an applicable tax-exempt organization directly or indirectly to or for the use of any person if the value of the economic benefit exceeds the value of the consideration (including the performance of services) received for providing such benefit .... [A]n economic benefit will not be treated as consideration for the performance of services unless such organization clearly indicated its intent to so treat such benefit.[635]

[629] *Id.* at 747.
[630] *Id.* (emphasis in original).
[631] *Id.* at 749.
[632] *Id.*
[633] 26 U.S.C. § 4958.
[634] 26 U.S.C. § 4958(f)(1)(A) (any person who fits within this category is referred to as a "disqualified person").
[635] 26 U.S.C. § 4958(c)(1)(A).

Any organization manager, defined as "any officer, director, or trustee" who willfully participates in an excess benefit transaction, is subject to a tax equal to ten percent of the excess benefit, not to exceed $10,000.[636]

Business Dealings with Institutions

The responsibility of board members to exhibit fair dealing and loyalty in transactions with their nonpublic institutions was stated very well in *Stern v. Lucy Webb Hayes National Training School for Deaconesses and Missionaries*.[637] Because *Stern* represents the all-too-common situation in nonprofit institutions where there is a dominant administration and relatively passive board members, the facts as well as the law of this case are especially important. In *Stern,* a hospital board of twenty-five to thirty-five members was required by their bylaws to meet at least twice a year; between meetings the board was to be represented by an executive committee. In addition, the board created a finance committee to review the budget and report on the cash available for investment. However, for approximately twenty years the board and its committees were dominated by two trustee officers, the hospital administrator, and the treasurer. Not until the deaths of both men did the other trustees appear to have assumed an identifiable supervisory role over investment policy and hospital fiscal management in general.

Plaintiffs in *Stern* were patients of the hospital who brought a class action challenging various aspects of the hospital's fiscal management. Plaintiffs essentially alleged two causes of action: (1) hospital board members who were also board members of banks or investment firms conspired to enrich themselves and their financial businesses by favoring those businesses in financial dealing with the hospital; (2) hospital board members breached their fiduciary duties of care and loyalty in the management of hospital funds.

Plaintiffs sought to substantiate their claims with the following facts:

(1) The hospital maintained much of its liquid assets in savings and checking accounts rather than in treasury bonds or investment securities;

---

[636] 26 U.S.C. § 4958(a))2((d)(2).
[637] 381 F. Supp. 1003 (D.S.C. 1974).

(2) Most investment funds were deposited in the financial institutions with which the hospital board members were involved;

(3) A yearly audit was prepared for the board members, but they rarely, if ever, read the details and approved the treasurer's investment recommendations as a matter of course;

(4) None of the board members attempted to force their views upon the treasurer, who considered their suggestions as interference;

(5) Renegotiation of a mortgage with board members' financial institutions;

(6) Signing an investment advisory agreement with one of the board member's investment firms.

The court found no evidence to support plaintiff's conspiracy claim. Although, as the court observed, "defendants were able to offer no adequate justification for utilization of the hospital's assets,"[638] there was no evidence of board members' directions or encouragement of the treasurer's favoritism for defendant's financial institutions; there was no evidence that mortgage terms or investment fees were unreasonable; there was no evidence that the financial institutions had any contact among themselves relating to the handling of the hospital's business; and there was no evidence that any of the board members solicited business for his own financial institution.

Standard of Care

The general rule for standard of care seems to be that governing boards of religious institutions will be held to corporate rather than charitable trust principles. In *Corporation of Mercer University v. Smith*,[639] the Georgia Supreme Court determined that decisions by the Tift College Board of Directors, flowing from the merger of two institutions affiliated with the

---

[638] *Id.* at 1010.
[639] 371 S.E.2d 858 (Ga. 1988).

Georgia Baptist Convention, Tift College and Mercer University, were to be based on corporate principles. Because of Tift College's declining enrollment, this women's college entered into a merger agreement with Mercer in 1986, with Mercer agreeing to "make a good faith effort to operate Tift College of Mercer University on Tift's present Forsyth, Georgia campus,[but to hold as paramount] the preservation of an entity bearing the Tift name for the education of women in a Christian context...."[640] When the Mercer University board of directors voted in 1986 to close the Tift campus, the Tift College plaintiffs sought to vacate the merger on the ground that the Tift Board of Directors had failed to exercise a standard of care compatible with trust principles. In upholding the merger, the state supreme court found on behalf of the Tift Board of Directors.

> The formalities of trust law are inappropriate to the administration of colleges and universities which, in this era, operate as businesses. These institutions hold a variety of assets, and those persons responsible for the operation of the institutions need the administrative flexibility to make the many day-to-day decisions affecting the operation of the institutions, including those decisions involving the acquisition and sale of assets.[641]

Moreover, in *Stern v. Webb Hays National Training School for Deaconesses and Missionaries*,[642] the court, in responding to plaintiff's breach of duty claims of mismanagement and self-dealing, made a more detailed analysis as to what the legal standard of care ought to be for board members. The court distinguished between trustees who manage charitable trusts and directors who manage charitable corporations:[643]

> Both trustees and corporate directors are liable for losses occasioned by their negligent mismanagement of investments. However, the degree of care required appears to differ in many jurisdictions. A trustee is uniformly held to a high standard of care and will be

---

640 *Id.* at 860.

641 *Id.* at 860-61.

642 *Supra* note 629.

643 For a discussion of the difference between charitable trusts and corporations see G.G. Bogart and G.T. Bogart, Handbook of the Law of Trusts (5th ed. 1973) at 245-46. *See also*, Corcoran v. Rockewell, 410 A.2d 202, 205 (D.C.Cir. 1979).

> held liable for simple negligence,[644] while a director must often have committed 'gross negligence' or otherwise be guilty of more than mere mistakes of judgment.[645]

Where funds are managed by a charitable corporation or where funds are left to a charitable corporation, "by the better view, no trust in the strict sense is created."[646]

But even if nonprofit institution board members are "held to the less stringent corporate standard of care" and "are required to exercise ordinary and reasonable care in the performance of their duties, exhibiting honesty and good faith,"[647] the court in *Stern* made the following statements of law regarding the responsibilities of corporate board members:

(1) Corporate board members can delegate investment decisions to committees "so long as all directors assume the responsibility for supervising such committees by periodically scrutinizing their work;"[648]

(2) A corporate board member who fails to supervise or even attend board meetings "has violated his fiduciary duty to the corporation;"[649]

(3) While a corporate board member may rely upon the expertise of corporate officers, such reliance is no excuse for dispensing with or ignoring officer reports;

(4) A corporate board member who permits negligent mismanagement by others to go unchecked "has committed an independent wrong against the corporation; he is not merely an accessory under an attenuated

---

644 Attempts by the settlor to reduce the amount of skill and prudence required of the trustee through appropriate exculpatory language often meets with judicial hostility. *See* G. G. Bogart and G. T. Bogart, Handbook of the Law of Trusts (5th ed. 1973) at 330-343.

645 *See* Stern, 381 F. Supp. at 1013.

646 Midatlantic Nat'l Bank v. Frank G. Thompson Found., 405 A.2d 866 (Pa. Super. Ct. 1979). Lefkowitz v. Cornell Univ., 271 N.E.2d 552 (N.Y. 1971) (gift of wind tunnel to Cornell was a corporate asset rather than trust, and therefore university could sell asset if it chose). *See generally* J. Beach, *The Management and Governance of Academic Institutions*, 12 J.C.U.L. 301, 320-21 (1985).

647 *Stern*, 381 F. Supp. at 1013.

648 *Id*

649 *Id.* at 1014.

theory of *respondeat superior* or constructive notice;"[650]

(5) A corporate board member "should not only disclose his interlocking responsibilities but also refrain from voting on or otherwise influencing a corporate decision to transact business with a company in which he has a significant interest or control."[651]

Although the court in *Stern* dismissed the complaint against defendant financial institutions, rejected all claims of conspiracy, and refused to cancel the disputed mortgage, the court found the defendant board members to have breached their duties of care and loyalty to the hospital and ordered the board to enact and implement certain policies to prevent future conflicts.[652]

Donors and Gifts

Nonpublic schools rely on private contributions to cover operating costs. Issues can arise regarding use of funds and enforcement of promises. In *Russell v. Yale University*,[653] heirs of the settlor of a charitable trust, alumni donors, and students at the University's Divinity School sued to stop the university from reorganizing the Divinity School, including demolishing large portions of the Sterling Divinity Quadrangle that had been erected with funds left in trust by John W. Sterling. In upholding the trial court's dismissal of plaintiffs' complaint, a state appeals court applied the common law rule that a donor (and thus, his heirs and successors) has no standing to challenge the use of a gift where no right was reserved under the gift or trust to enforce its use. Where unrestricted funds have allegedly been used in a manner inconsistent with their purpose, the remedy is a suit by the Attorney General, rather than the donor's heirs or representatives, to compel the property to be held for the charitable purpose of the donor.[654] In another case, *Virginia School of the Arts, Inc. v. Eichelbaum*,[655] a pledge to donate

---

650 For a thorough discussion of corporate board member or director liability for acts of a codirector or officer see W. Fletcher, Cyclopedia of the Law of Private Corporations § 1065 (1975).

651 *See Stern*, 381 F. Supp. 1014; *see also* case and accompanying text at notes 626-632.

652 An enumerated summary of the courts declaratory order can be found at W. Porth, *Personal Liability of Trustees of Educational Institutions*, 2 J.C.U.L. 143, 152-53 (1974-75).

653 737 A.2d 941 (Conn. Ct. App. 1999).

654 *See* A. Scott, Trusts (4th ed. 1989) , sec. 348.1.

655 493 S.E.2d 510 (Va. 1997).

$100,000 was unenforceable where it had been made as a matching gift, and the school had failed to raise the matching $100,000. In *Phillips Exeter Academy v. Howard Phillips Fund, Inc.*[656] a New Hampshire private school, charging a Florida company with tort and breach of contract claims in disbursing interest payments from a bequest, could not bring its lawsuit in New Hampshire. The Florida company's contacts with New Hampshire were not sufficent to meet jurisdictional requirements.

Areas of Vicarious Liability

Board members have occasionally been found personally liable in cases other than financial dealings. In *Gamble v. Vanderbilt University*,[657] members of the executive committee of a private university charged with supervision of an office building owned and operated by the university were liable to a person injured in the fall of an elevator in the building for their misfeasance in permitting the elevator to be operated when they knew it was unsafe. In *Love v. Nashville Agricultural and Normal Institute*,[658] the manager of a private, normal school that committed a nuisance by polluting an adjoining landowner's water supply was held personally liable even though he did not purposely commit the wrong and merely acted as an agent of the school. In *Jones v. Jones*,[659] the owner and director of a day care facility was found personally and solely liable when one of her employees left on the serving tray a container of hot food which spilled on two-year-old plaintiff, despite defendant's explicit instruction to her employees that to leave food on a serving tray from which food was to be served would be in violation of the rules. Occasionally board members of educational institutions have been sued where they have refused to ratify or have altered employment contracts negotiated by the school's administrator. Such lawsuits are generally unsuccessful because persons negotiating employment arrangements with a school

---

[656] 196 F.3d 284 (1st Cir. 1999).

[657] 200 S.W. 510 (Tenn. 1918).

[658] 243 S.W. 304 (Tenn. 1922).

[659] 168 S.E.2d 883 (Ga. Ct. App. 1969). The standard of care for the director's vicarious liability appeared to be the same as if she had been personally involved. "Children of tender years are entitled to that degree of care proportioned to their ability to foresee and avoid perils that may be encountered." (*Id.* at 885).

administrator are presumed to know that such arrangements are not final until approved by the governing board.[660]

Governing boards of churches increasingly have been sued by disciplined church members for invasion of privacy or intentional infliction of emotional distress[661] Although technically not vicarious board liability because the board members themselves were responsible for the discipline, these lawsuits do highlight the vulnerability of board members to litigation for unpopular or unwarranted decisions.

Indemnification

Since most board members of nonprofit educational institutions generally consider their duties to be a charitable service and serve without compensation, it is not unreasonable that many such institutions may want to indemnify board members against any liabilities incurred by reason of their service. However, such indemnification will be limited by the charter or bylaws of the corporation or separate agreement with the board members, subject in all cases to whatever further limitations the statutes or decisions of the jurisdiction of incorporation may impose. The Model Business Corporation Act, which has been adopted in at least half the states, permits indemnification for a board member if:

(1) He conducted himself in good faith;

(2) He reasonably believed (a) in the case of conduct in his official capacity with the corporation, that his conduct was in its best interests, and (b) in all other cases, that his conduct was at least not opposed to its best interests;

(3) In the case of any criminal proceeding, he had no reasonable cause to believe his conduct was unlawful.[662]

---

[660] *See* Bruner v. University of S. Mississippi, 501 So.2d 1113 (Miss. 1987); Pelotte v. Simmons, 152 S.E. 310 (Ga. Ct. App. 1930).

[661] See cases discussed in L. BUZZARD AND T. BRANDON, JR. CHURCH DISCIPLINE AND THE COURTS (1986).

[662] Model. Bus. Corp. Act section 5(a)(6).

The Model Act prohibits indemnification in situations where a board member "shall have been adjudged to be liable on the basis that personal benefit was improperly received by him,"[663] where limited by the articles of incorporation[664] or where rejected by a court of appropriate jurisdiction.[665] Board members need to carefully check statutes regulating nonprofit corporations in their own states because some states have limited the right of nonprofit corporations to indemnify board members beyond the limitations in the Model Act.[666]

Liability Insurance

It can probably be assumed that all nonprofit educational corporations have purchased liability insurance to protect board members against personal liability, and that the coverage is as broad as is necessary in dollar amount and activity coverage to be commensurate with the scope of the corporation's functions. However, insurance protection would not apply to situations where state law prohibits indemnification, and generally, an umbrella liability policy of a nonprofit institution would not provide insurance protection beyond those areas that the school has authorized to indemnify.[667] In some states nonprofit corporations are permitted to purchase insurance coverage beyond the indemnification allowed by statute.[668] However, some states have legislated that uncompensated directors of nonprofit organizations are immune from lawsuits.[669] Obviously

---

663 *Id.* at § 5(c).

664 *Id.* at § 5(d).

665 *Id.*

666 *E.g.*, New York prohibits indemnification where an "officer or director is adjudged to have breached his duty to the corporation" by failing to discharge his duties "in good faith and with that degree of diligence, care and skill which ordinarily prudent men would exercise under similar circumstances in like positions." N.Y. Not-For-Profit Corp. Law §§ 717, 722. The New York statute is exclusive in that it specifically declares invalid any bylaw or other provision for indemnification of officers and directors which is not consistent with the statute. *Id.* at § 721).

667 Porth, *Personal Liability of Trustees of Educational Institutions*, 2 J.C.U.L. 90 (1974-1975). *But see*, Alexander v. CNA Ins. Co., 657 A.2d 1282 (Pa. Commw. Ct. 1995) (board members covered by board of education liability policy for breach of duty).

668 *See e.g.*, N.Y. Not-For-Profit Corp. Law § 727.

669 *E.g.* Del. Code Ann. tit. 10, § 8133 (uncompensated trustees, directors, officers, agents or workers not subject to suits for civil damages); Ohio Rev. Code Ann. § 2305.38 (uncompensated officers, trustees or other persons not liable for civil damages); Va. Code Ann. § 13.1-870. 1 (B) ("An officer or director who serves [a corporation exempt from income taxation under sec. 501 (c) of the Internal Revenue Code] without compensation shall not be liable for damages [arising out of a single transaction, occurrence or course of conduct].")

each nonprofit educational institution needs to carefully review its own insurance coverage in light of applicable state law.

Closing a School

A board decision to close a religious school can raise a variety of legal issues for board members. Obviously, such a decision can be devastating to parents and students, if an alternative school is not readily available, and to employees, if similar employment in the area is unlikely.

The interests of parents and students were raised in the case of *Save Immaculata/Dunblane, Inc. v. Immaculata Preparatory School, Inc.*[670] In *Immaculata*, legal title to the property of elementary and secondary schools separately incorporated was retained by a religious order. In 1972, the order decided to eventually sell the property because of declining enrollment and decreasing income and because deficits were being made up by borrowing from the order's retirement fund. After unsuccessfully attempting to sell the property to the Archdiocese of Washington, the order entered into a noncontractual letter of intent in July 1983 to sell the property to American University. Parties to the letter of interest agreed to maintain confidentiality of its contents. The Holy See at Rome granted permission to sell the property in July 1984 (a necessary condition for this sale), but in the meantime, freshman high school students were admitted for the fall of 1983 and 1984. Not until October 1984, after the school year had begun, did the order announce the schools would be closed in 1986. Unable to effect a change, parents and students brought suit against the order and the schools, alleging violation of express and implied trusts, as well as breach of contract, fraud, and unlawful trade practices.

Before resolving the legal theories, the court declared that a determination regarding disposition of church property involved "familiar corporate and trust principles of law,"[671] and therefore, did not run afoul of the First Amendment religion clauses.[672] In rejecting the breach of trust argument, the court refused to accept

[670] 514 A.2d 1152 (D.C. App. 1986).

[671] *Id.* at 1156.

[672] For discussions of application of neutral principles of law to religious institutions, see Presbyterian Church in the United States v. Mary Elizabeth Blue Hull Mem'l Presbyterian Church, 393 U.S. 440 (1969); Jones v. Wolf, 443 U.S. 595 (1979); Serbian E. Orthodox Diocese v. Milivojevich, 426 U.S. 696 (1976).

that the parents and children had an equitable interest, even though the order had legal title. The court refused to construct a trust where the school corporation's articles of incorporation provided that all assets would revert to the order in case of dissolution. Students did not have a four-year contract for education once they were admitted as freshman because "as a matter of law the term of the individual contracts was for a single year."[673] There was no evidence of misrepresentation or fraud because final approval to sell was not received until several months after students had been accepted in April and May 1984. But even if the order had known about the closure prior to April and not disclosed it, there would have been no fraud because the parents received the year's education for which they had paid. Finally the order was not subject to the District of Columbia Consumer Protection Procedures Act because a nonprofit educational institution is not a merchant under the Act.

Immaculata makes good sense as to equitable trust and breach of contract claims, but in today's consumer age, courts in many states may be likely to find a remedy under consumer protection legislation. For example, in *Andre v. Pace University*,[674] a New York court awarded $1,000 each, under the state's Deceptive Practices Act, to students where the university had failed to teach a class as advertised. Although not a school-closing case, as was *Immaculata*, *Andre* nonetheless indicates that nonpublic educational institutions may be liable under legal theories that would not have been viable in the past.[675]

Access to Tax Exempt Bonds and Other Public Funds

One of the more popular strategies by governing boards of nonpublic educational institutions is to access public funds for

[673] *Immaculata*, 514 A.2d at 1158.

[674] 618 N.Y.S.2d 975 (N.Y. City Ct. 1994).

[675] *See* Alsides v. Brown Inst., Ltd., 592 N.W.2d 468 (Minn. Ct. App. 1999) (school that had failed to deliver a curriculum as set forth in the catalog could not be sued in educational practice, but could be sued for statutory fraud); Hamilton Chapter of Alpha Delta Phi, Inc. v. Hamilton College, 28 F.3d 59 (2d Cir. 1997) (college's new requirement that all students had to live on-campus in dorms was subject to challenge by off-campus fraternities under monopoly provision of Sherman Antitrust Act).

expansion, restoration, or covering short-term indebtedness. Tax exempt bonds have an advantage because interest rates are low and because, for the investor, interest is not taxable by the state. But not all educational institutions qualify for tax exempt bonds. For example, in *State v. Palm Beach County*,[676] an elementary and secondary school that had been converted from for-profit to not-for-profit status was not eligible to receive $3,214,000 in industrial revenue bonds that had been issued for its use to refinance a capital improvement loan ($2,050,000), to construct a gymnasium ($600,000), and to cover the cost of issuing the bonds ($64,000). The court, having determined that the school had been improperly incorporated under the wrong not-for-profit statute, decided that the correct statute did not permit reception of tax exempt bond revenues. Obviously, this kind of decision could have devastating effects on a school with high indebtedness and numerous creditors.

In another case, Liberty University lost in its claim to $60,000,000 in tax exempt revenue bonds to be used to finance an indebtedness in excess of that amount.[677] However, rejection of access to tax exempt bonds in this case was because the Virginia Supreme Court determined that, despite the university's effort to dilute church control and religious influence, the university continued to be pervasively sectarian.[678] Similarly, in *Columbia Union College v. Clark*,[679] the Fourth Circuit Court of Appeals reversed a district court's denial of state funds to a religious college, but only for the purpose of determining whether the college's practices were pervasively religious, which if true, would mean that funds could not be made available. As suggested in both *Palm Beach County* and *Liberty University*, rejection of access to tax exempt funds can present considerable financial problems to the boards of directors and administrators of cash-strapped institutions in dealing with persistent and angry creditors.

---

[676] 575 So.2d 652 (Fla. 1991).

[677] Habel v. Industrial Dev. Auth. of the City of Lynchburg, Va., 400 S.E.2d 516 (Va. 1991). For a discussion of this case, see Mawdsley, *Access to Tax Exempt Bonds by Religious Higher Education Institutions*, 65 Ed. Law Rep. 289 (1991).

[678] *See also*, Beth McMurtrie, *Va. Backing Opposed for Regent U. Bonds*, Chronicle of Higher Ed., July 2, 1999 at A29 (relying on the precedent in Liberty University case, Americans United for Separation of Church and State opposed Regent University's request for $54.5 million in tax exempt bonds for construction projects).

[679] 159 F.3d 151 (4th Cir. 1998).

Access by religious institutions to tax exempt bond revenues is not impossible. The United States Supreme Court has, over establishment clause objections, upheld the issuance of tax exempt bonds to a religious higher education institution to construct, finance, and refinance projects.[680] However, under state law, the bond proceeds could not be used to finance a facility used for religious purposes, and even after repayment of the bonds, the facilities could not be used for such purposes. This decision involving tax exempt bonds is compatible with an earlier Supreme Court decision in *Tilton v. Richardson*[681] that federal construction grants are available to church-related colleges and universities, provided that buildings financed with these funds are never used for sectarian instruction or for religious worship.

Access to other forms of public funding tends to depend on the level of instruction and who is considered to be the recipient of the aid. The child benefit theory, popularized by the Supreme Court thirty years ago as a legal fiction to justify state aid to religious elementary and secondary schools,[682] has experienced a recent resurgence.[683] Although most state aid is made available to the nonpublic school, some state assistance may go directly to parents who have children in nonpublic schools.[684] However,

---

[680] Hunt v. McNair, 413 U.S. 734 (1974).

[681] 403 U.S. 672 (1971).

[682] *See* Everson v. Board of Educ., 330 U.S. 1 (1947) (public school district provision of transportation to religious school students not violation of establishment clause); Board of Educ. of Cent. Sch. Dist. v. Allen, 392 U.S. 236 (1968) (public school district loaning textbooks to religious schools not violation of establishment clause). For a more recent interpretation, see, Kelly v. Forest Hills Local Sch. Dist. Bd. of Educ., 19 F. Supp.2d 797 (S.D. Ohio 1998) (loaning of text-books not violation of establishment clause).

[683] *E.g., see* Agostini v. Felton, 117 S. Ct. 1997 (1997) (public school employees providing chapter I services in religious schools not establishment clause violation); Zobrest v. Catalina Foothills Sch. Dist., 509 U.S. 1 (1993) (sign interpreter for deaf student in religious school paid for by public school district considered as benefit to student and not the school, so no establishment clause violation); Minnesota Fed'n of Teachers v. Mammenga, 500 N.W.2d 136 (Minn. Ct. App. 1993) (high school students permitted to enroll in pervasively religious college as part of state's Post-Secondary Enrollment Options Act where state paid tuition held not to violate state or federal religion clauses); Barnes v. Cavazos, 966 F.2d 1056 (6th Cir. 1992); Pulido v. Cavazos, 934 F.2d 912 (8th Cir. 1991) (method of calculating distribution of Title I funds for services to religious schools not violative of establishment clause where students considered to be direct beneficiaries); Witters v. Washington Dep't of Servs. for the Blind 474 U.S. 481 748 (1986) (state vocational assistance to blind student at Bible college not violative of federal establishment clause where student, not college, considered to be direct beneficiary).

[684] *See* Zobrest v. Catalina Foothills Sch. Dist., 509 U.S. 1 (1993)., parents entitled to school district reimbursement under IDEA for monies expended to provide sign interpreter in religious school); Florence County Sch. Dist. Four v. Carter, 510 U.S. 7 (1993) (parents entitled to reimbursement from public school district under IDEA for unilateral placement of child in private school where school district had failed to provide free appropriate public education). *See also*, Jackson v. Benson, 578 N.W.2d 602 (1998) (checks under state voucher system payable to parent as co-payee with private school).

access to any form of public funding is a fragile balance between the nature of the institution and the nature of the aid.

All of these Supreme Court precedents were cited in upholding the use of tax exempt bonds to make improvements in a parochial school in Bloomfield Hills, Michigan. In *Johnson v. Economic Development Corporation*[685], a federal district court upheld the use of Economic Development Corporation (EDC) bonds for new construction and renovation of Academy of the Sacred Heart School. These changes to classrooms did not include the school's chapel. In upholding the use of EDC tax exempt bonds in this case, the court noted that 100 percent of the funds came from private investors and that "not a single penny of the funds came from any state, county, or municipal source, and no public entity has any obligation whatsoever in connection with the sale or purchase of these *limited obligation* bonds."[686] With regard to plaintiff's objection that tax exemption for interest earned from the bonds amounted "to a direct subsidy of the academy,"[687] the court observed that such "indirect costs" occurring when a general benefit is provided to a broad class of recipients does not violate the establishment clause.

Defining the Mission of a Religious School

Special problems of access to financial benefits have given focus to the responsibility of governing boards of religious schools to define and maintain the institution's religious mission. Although maintenance of an institution's religious identity may carry loss of some financial benefit,[688] the issues are really more systemic than just eligibility for public funds. For educational institutions with church affiliation, boards of trustees must determine what degree of church control will best serve the overall interests of the institution. Whereas church-controlled schools may have difficulty in accessing many forms of public funds, church control may nonetheless offer benefits that might

---

685 64 F. Supp.2d 657 (E.D. Mich. 1999).

686 *Id.* at 667 (emphasis in original).

687 *Id.*

688 *See* Bob Jones Univ. v. United States, 461 U.S. 574 (1983) (loss of tax exempt status for refusal to eliminate religion-based rules prohibiting interracial dating and marriage); Bob Jones Univ. v. Johnson, 396 F. Supp. 597 (D. S.C. 1974) (loss of veterans benefits because of racially discriminatory rules).

be attractive to some schools or their employees. For example, church-controlled organizations are generally exempt from participation under state unemployment compensation statutes[689] and can be exempt from Social Security[690] and ERISA requirements.[691] A church that maintains control over school property may be able to limit liability. For example, in *Morris v. State Farm Insurance*,[692] a worker at a religious school in Louisiana who was injured in the school's gymnasium was prohibited from suing in negligence the church that owned the gymnasium. The court reasoned that, even though the school and church were incorporated separately, the church maintained control over the school: the school administrator's name appeared on the church bulletin as a member of the pastoral staff; school board members had to be members of, and be elected by, the church; and all of the property used by the school was under the control of church trustees. In Louisiana, employees are prohibited from suing their employers in negligence; the only remedy is under worker's compensation. Since the school worker in *Morris* was really a church employee, because of the church's control over the school, the employee's only remedy was under worker's compensation.

However, the pressure today seems to be in the direction of severing, or at least diluting, church control, either to distance the institution from political denominational dissension[693] or

[689] *E.g.*, Ohio Rev. Code Ann. § 4141.01(B)(3)(h)(I) (exempt from unemployment compensation are employees "in the employ of a church or convention or association of churches, or an organization which is operated primarily for religious purposes and which is operated, supervised, controlled, primarily supported by a church, convention, or association of churches.") *See*, Miller v. Sts. Peter and Paul Sch., 711 N.W.2d 311 (Ohio Ct. App. 1998) (this exemption interpreted to exclude religious school employees from eligibility for unemployment compensation).

[690] 42 U.S.C. § 410(a)(8)(B) ("Service performed in the employ of a church or qualified church-controlled organization," provided an exemption has been filed by the IRS, is exempt from coverage under the Social Security Act).

[691] 29 U.S.C. §§ 1002(33)(A); 1321(b)(3);26 U.S.C. § 414(e)(3)(B) (church benefit plans exempt from reporting and disclosure requirements of Employee Retirement Income Security Program for "a church or ... a convention or association of churches [and] an employee of an organization ... which is controlled by or associated with a church or a convention or association of churches." Under § 414(e), a church of convention or association of churches is one "which is exempt from tax under section 501.")

[692] 649 So.2d 58 (La. Ct. App. 1994).

[693] *See Georgia Baptists Reject Fundamentalist Plan to Control Mercer University*, Chronicle of Higher Education, Nov. 18, 1987, at A1; *Trustees Limit Baptist Control Over University*, New York Times, Oct. 21, 1990, at 47; *Baptist Board OKs New Governing Plan for Baylor University*, Houston Post, Sept. 11, 1991, at A1; *Fundamentalist Lose Bid To control Baylor*, Washington Post, Nov. 12, 1991, at A3.

to gain access to financial benefits.[694] Nonetheless, the alternative to these concerns may be more troublesome for religious schools. Absence of church control may mean an increased likelihood that the NLRB or state labor relations boards could assert jurisdiction over the educational institution.[695] For institutions that announce their religious values and then act consistently with them, they can expect to become a gazing stock for the media.[696]

In certain situations, dilution of religious distinctives could lead to loss of protection under the religious exemptions in Title VII. In a recent case, *EEOC v. Kamehameha Schools/Bishop Estate*,[697] the Court of Appeals for the Ninth Circuit determined that lack of church control denied the schools protection under Title VII religious exemptions. In *Kamehameha*, the schools had been established in 1896 pursuant to a bequest that required teachers to be "Protestant." When a non-Protestant was refused a teaching position, the applicant filed suit under Title VII and the schools defended under the same statute, claiming that they were entitled to discriminate on the basis of religion. The Court of Appeals denied a Title VII religious exemption to the schools on the basis of the factual pattern of the case: no religious organization supported or controlled their schools, and the schools were not affiliated with "any denomination of Protestants or with any organization or with any association of religious schools;"[698] the schools were part of the Bishop Estate, "a large and overwhelmingly secular business" that made no mention of religion in its annual reports;[699] the faculty, while nominally

---

[694] *Cf. Falwell Tells 2,000 Employees To Join His Church or Lose Job*, ATLANTIC JOURNAL CONSTITUTION, March 11, 1989, at A4 (effort to require church membership of all employees of several organizations considered to be controlled by the church) *with Falwell's College Alters Mission to Keep Alive*, NEW YORK TIMES, Aug. 19, 1992, at B7 (later decision to reduce church control over university, including church membership requirement for faculty and students, to attempt qualification for tax exempt bonds and to satisfy creditors).

[695] *E.g., see* NLRB v. Hanna Boys Ctr., 940 F.2d 1295 (9th Cir. 1991) (NLRB election required for non-teaching employees in Catholic school); Catholic High Sch. Ass'n of Archdiocese of New York v. Culvert, 753 F.2d 1161 (2d Cir. 1985) (state labor relations board had jurisdiction over lay teachers).

[696] See K. Landy, *Brigham Young Denies Tenure to Scholar for Contradicting Mormon Views*, CHRONICLE OF HIGHER ED., June 21, 1996, at p. A15 (tenure denied to faculty member who advocated, contrary to Mormon doctrine, that prayers be made to Heavenly Mother and that women be ordained as priests).

[697] 780 F. Supp. 1317 (D. Hawaii 1991), *rev'd* 990 F.2d 458 (9th Cir. 1993), *cert. denied* EEOC v. Kamehameha Schs./Bishop Estate, 510 U.S. 963 (1993).

[698] *Kamehameha*, 990 F.2d at 461 (the Court of Appeals considered important the fact that the Bishop Memorial Church, which was controlled by the Schools, was a member of the Hawaii Conference of the United Church of Christ, but the Schools themselves were not).

[699] *Id.*

Protestant, were not required to maintain membership in a church and did not have to subscribe to a set of beliefs, and the Chaplain, who taught religious education and was pastor of the Bishop Memorial Church, had no authority over the curriculum;[700] religious affiliation was not taken into consideration for the 3,000 boarding and day students and the more than 36,000 other students reached through off-campus and outreach programs;[701] the wide variety of student activities did not differ appreciably from public and private schools across the nation;[702] and the curriculum, while incorporating some religious songs, prayer, and religious courses, lacked any "effort to instruct students in Protestant doctrine ...[and] disavowed any effort to convert non-Protestant students."[703]

Kamehemeha does not seem to have spawned a progeny of similar cases scrutinizing the religious nature of non-church-controlled schools, but, if nothing else, the case is a benchmark worth noting. There is wide variation among religious non-church-controlled schools as to the religious requirements imposed on students and employees. Elaborate religious requirements that at one time might have included attendance at and participation in religious services on-campus by employees, as well as requirements concerning church attendance off-campus, may well have over the years been made voluntary and finally eliminated. *Kamehameha* suggests that non-church-controlled schools may find that a court will scrutinize not only the nature of religious influence in the schools, but also the extent to which the religious influence has increased or decreased. In *Kamehameha,* the court examined school publications that revealed "the purpose and emphasis of the Schools had shifted over the years from providing religious instruction to equipping students with ethical principles that will enable them to make their own moral judgments."[704] Diminution in religious influence was indicated by such changes as: a decrease in the number of students from the schools participating in

---

[700] *Id.* at 462.

[701] *Id.* (less than one-third of the on-campus students were Protestant).

[702] *Id.* (the court noted that some of the activities such as Bible studies and prayer before athletics can be found in public schools; in addition, major events such as Founder's Day and Baccalaureate incorporated celebrations of both religion and Hawaiian culture).

[703] *Id.* at 463 (the court seemed to consider important a curricular change that no longer made a religious course mandatory).

[704] *Id.* at 462.

religious deputation services;[705] a revision of the requirement that all students take a religious course each year to state that only freshmen need take it;[706] and a change of course content from an emphasis on the religious faith of the school (Protestantism, in this case) to a comparative study of religion and the local culture (in this case, the Hawaiian culture).[707] Thus, non-church-controlled educational institutions could face judicial examination in two linear directions: the nature of religious requirements imposed on faculty, students, and the curriculum; and the extent to which current religious requirements have been diluted over the years.

Kamehameha appears limited on its facts to non-church-controlled schools. The court found "no case holding the [Title VII] exemption to be applicable where the [educational] institution was not wholly or partially owned by a church."[708] As further support for its interpretation, the court referenced a statement of a member of Congress that the Title VII exemptions were "limited to church affiliated colleges and universities, part of whose mission ... is to propagate the belief of the denomination that is supporting the educational institution."[709]

For governing boards, the difficult balancing task will be to determine whether any advantages that come to the school from church control are offset by political dissension and lack of access to financial resources. The factors on both sides need to be carefully weighed, because once a school diminishes church control and dilutes religious influence, it is doubtful that the school can ever go back.

---

[705] *Id.* at 462-63.
[706] *Id.*, note 10.
[707] *Id.* at 464, 465.
[708] *Id.* at 461, note 7.
[709] *Id.* at 464, quoting from Representative Purcell, 110 Cong. Rec. 2585-86 (Feb. 8, 1964).

Chapter IV

Governmental Regulation of Nonpublic Schools

Basis for State Regulation

The range of nonpublic schools in the United States is considerable and includes home instruction, religious K-12, and higher education institutions, as well as private schools with no religious affiliation.[710] The continuing growth in nonpublic education[711] can hardly be tracked simply to disenchantment with, or antipathy toward, public schools.[712] The central common denominator is a basic concern that parents should be able to determine the forum of education.[713]

Determining a single cause for removal of children from the public schools is generally not possible since parents may state their decisions in terms of factors such as religious beliefs that may camouflage problems with the public schools. However, parent decisions to fund their children's education in nonpublic

---

710 For numerical data on growth among nonpublic schools, see Cooper, *The Changing Universe of U.S. Private Schools*, in Comparing Public and Private Schools (T. James and H. Levin, eds.) Vol. I, 18-45 (1988). For a general history of nonpublic schools, see O. Kraushaar, American Nonpublic Schools (1972) and Hunt and Carper (eds.), Religious Schools in America: A Selected Bibliography (1986).

711 For representative figures on two large Christian day school organizations, see Cooper, *supra* note 710 at 33 (627 percent increase in enrollment in evangelical schools from 1965-1983). The number of children in home schools in 1996-97 has been estimated at 1.23 million with a growth rate since 1990 of fifteen percent per year. *See* Ray, Home Instruction Across the States (1997).

712 Public education has not been without its detractors in the past. For example, see Rushdoony, The Messianic Character of American Education (1963) and Towns, Have The Public Schools Had It? (1974). More recently, criticism of public education has focused on state choice initiatives where parents could receive public funds to enroll children in nonpublic schools. For a comprehensive discussion of the school choice debate, including vouchers, see S. Sugerman and F. Kemerer (eds.), School Choice and Social Controversy: Policy, Politics and Law (1999).

713 For the role of parents, as representing community values, in seeking to effect curricular change, see R. Mawdsley and D. Drake, *Involving Parents in Public Schools*, 76 Ed. Law Rep. 299 (1992).

schools may reflect frustration with their inability to effect changes in public school programs or curricula.[714] The single greatest deterrent to parent placement of children in nonpublic schools is finances. Parents with limited resources[715] frequently find that they have no real option but to continue in a public system that does not satisfactorily address their children's needs.[716] Before making a nonpublic school decision, parents often attempt to seek changes in public schools where they disagree with curricula or programs.[717] However, those who cannot afford the cost of nonpublic education often find their children captive within the government's schools.[718] Those parents, fortunate enough to have located resources to fund nonpublic education, generally find programs designed to meet the needs of their children, as well as compatibility between their philosophical beliefs and those of the school.[719]

The emerging debate concerning state vouchers, tax credits, and tax deductions for parents with children in sectarian and

---

714 For a discussion of related problem areas, see R. Mawdsley, and A. Mawdsley, *Diminished Status of Religious Liberty in Public Education: Interpreting Mozert and Smith*, 46 ED. LAW REP. 897 (1988) (inability of parents for religious reasons to effect curricu lar changes in public schools).

715 Mueller v. Allen, 463 U.S. 388 (1983) (state tax deductions permitted for tuition, textbooks and transportation but that offers nothing in the way of financial resources for those who cannot afford the initial dollar investment in public education). However, *see* Zobrest v. Catalina Foothills Sch. Dist., 509 U.S. 7 (1993) (under IDEA, public school district not prohibited by Establishment Clause from providing sign language interpreter for a deaf student in a Catholic school); Florence County Sch. Dist. v. Carter, 510 U.S. 1 (1993) (parents entitled to reimbursement under IDEA for unilateral placement of child in out-of-state private school not on state's approved list where school district had not provided "free appropriate public education.")

716 *See* Triplett v. Livingston County Bd.of Educ., 967 S.W.2d 25 (Kent. Ct. App. 1997) (parents unsuccessfully argued that board requirement that their children in public schools take state assessment exam violated free exercise and establishment clauses, and Hatch Amendment).

717 The philosophical differences divide themselves essentially into three categories. A first group would argue against all formal schooling outside the home. *See* State v. Bowman, 653 P..2d 254 (Or. Ct. App. 1982). A second group would consider a nonpublic school only if it were philosophically consistent with the parent's views. *See* State v. Riddle, 285 S.E.2d 359 (W.Va. 1981). A third group would oppose all attempts to remove children from public schools and would seek to reform the public schools, by litigation if necessary. *See* Smith v. Ricci, 446 A.2d 501 (N.J. 1982).

718 For information regarding the relative cost of public and nonpublic education, *see* J. WHITEHEAD AND W. BIRD, HOME EDUCATION AND CONSTITUTIONAL LIBERTIES (1984). The most significant detraction from such a selection of nonpublic education is finances. The two most direct proposed solutions are some form of government tax assistance to parents of nonpublic school pupils or a nonpublic school scholarship program especially directed at the disadvantaged. On the former, see E. WEST (ed.), NONPUBLIC SCHOOL AID (1976), and on the latter, see Crain and Rossell, *Catholic Schools and Racial Segregation*, in PUBLIC VALUES, PRIVATE SCHOOLS (N. Devins, ed.) 184-214 (1989).

719 For a philosophical model for religious schools, see J. CUNNINGHAM AND A. FORTOSIS, EDUCATION IN CHRISTIAN SCHOOLS: A PERSPECTIVE AND TRAINING MODEL (1987); P. KIENEL, CHRISTIAN

nonsectarian schools has focused attention on the role of government in education.[720] At the core of the debate are two questions: Who is responsible for making educational choices for children—government or the parents? Why should parents be required to support a public school system that does not meet the needs of their children?

Complicating the debate regarding state funding of parent choice in education has been the fear that the public educational system might collapse if it does not receive its full infusion of state foundational aid. Lost in the debate are the important issues of efficiency and effectiveness in providing educational services, issues that involve market factors of free enterprise, and supply and demand.[721] Generally, nonpublic schools provide education at a considerably lower per-student cost than their public school counterparts,[722] yet the monopoly position of the massive public education system in the United States requires ever larger inputs of local property taxes and state funds. Political pressure to increase the public school's funding base continues. Even with limited legislative approval of financial assistance to nonpublic schools and creation of charter schools, both of which take students from regular public school classrooms, do public schools have any incentive to improve if state legislatures continue to increase public school funding but do not require improvements in efficiency and instructional effectiveness?

To suggest that public funds should follow the students has met with two reactions. The most obvious reaction is the challenge under state and federal (establishment clause) law to

---

Day Schools, An Introduction To Biblical Christian Education (Graendorf, ed.) (1981). The interrelationship of Christian education and secularization is discussed in K. Gangel and W. Benson, Christian Education: Its History and Philosophy (1983). For a discussion of the role of nonpublic schools in general in today's society, see E. McGlynn Gaffney, Private Schools and The Public Good: Policy Alternatives for the Eighties (1981).

720 *See* R. Mawdsley, *State Tax Credits for Private Education: The Arizona Experience in Kotterman v. Killian*, 136 Ed. Law Rptr. 647 (1999).

721 *See* Levin, *Education as a Public and Private Good* in Public Values, Private Schools (D. Nevins, ed.) 215-232 (1989). An excellent discussion of the desirability and feasibility of administering education on a free enterprise model is found in E. West (ed.), Nonpublic School Aid (1976). A pointed question by E. West, "Are we more egalitarian than libertarian?" reflects the economic tensions between the state supported public educational system and the largely privately financed nonpublic system. *Id.* at 53.

722 In the most recent year for which statistics are available (1993-94), the average per student cost for nonpublic schools was $3084, compared to $5513 for public schools. National Center for Education Statistics in the United States, Private Schools in the United States: A Statistical Profile (1997).

use public funds in nonpublic (particularly religious) schools.[723] The second reaction is to impose statutory or regulatory requirements on nonpublic schools with students using public funds. Generally, aggressive state efforts prior to the 1980s to force nonpublic schools to follow state curriculum and teacher certification regulations on nonpublic schools have dissipated in the face of sympathetic judicial decisions and legislative enactments.[724] The newest regulatory efforts, however, may seek enforcement of state or federal regulations where nonpublic schools receive government funds, either directly or through assistance to students.[725]

The extent to which states can regulate nonpublic schools was the subject of two early U.S. Supreme Court cases. In *Meyer v. Nebraska*,[726] the Court struck down a state statute that prohibited teaching in any language other than English, even though the teaching in this case involved instruction from the German bible in a religious schools. In *Pierce v. Society of Sisters*,[727] the Court struck down a state statute that required attendance at public schools. Although frequently cited as establishing the legal right of parents to direct the education of their children, the Court subsequently stressed in *Runyon v. McCrary*[728] that *Pierce* was "simply affirm[ing] the right of private schools to exist and to operate."[729] More recently, the Supreme Court has endorsed quality education as that which is not racially discriminatory[730] and has suggested that such

---

[723] *Cf.* Strout v. Abanese, 178 F.3d 57 (1st Cir. 1999) (Maine did not violate establishment clause in excluding sectarian nonpublic schools from direct state grants).

[724] For a sample of early state regulation, see D. Erickson, Public Controls for Nonpublic Schools (1969). *See also*, State of Ohio v. Whisner, 351 N.E.2d 750 (Ohio 1976) (comprehensive set of state regulations abrogated parental liberty interest right to direct education of their children). For examples of state statutes that have liberalized student taught at home or nonpublic schools, see Minn. Stat. Ann. § 120A.22; Va. Code Ann. § 22.1-254; N.C. Gen.Stat. § 115C-563; Wash. Rev. Code Ann. § 28A.225.10; Conn. Gen. Stat. Ann. § 10.184.

[725] For an example of state control tied to reception of funds, *see* Jackson v. Benson, 578 N.W.2d 602 (Wis. 1998) (state supreme court upheld constitutionality of statute permitting vouchers for religious schools, but with an opt-out provision that students did not have to participate in religious activities or classes).

[726] 262 U.S. 390 (1923) (state prohibition of teaching of German in public or private schools interfered with right of parents with children in religious school to direct children's education).

[727] 268 U.S. 510 (1925) (state statute requiring attendance at public schools "unreasonably interfere[d] with the liberty of parents ... to direct the upbringing and education of children.")

[728] 427 U.S. 177 (1976).

[729] *Id.* at 177 (1976) (successful section 1981 claim against racially discriminatory nonsectarian private school).

[730] Bob Jones Univ. v. U.S., 461 U.S. 574 (1983). (revocation of tax exempt status upheld because of racially segregative dating and marriage rules).

education must be free of gender discrimination.[731]

No court has ever declared that nonpublic schools are immune from government regulation. Very early in *Pierce* the Supreme Court stated that "no question is raised concerning the power of the State, reasonably to regulate all schools, to inspect, supervise and examine them, their teachers and pupils."[732] Subsequent courts have had to wrestle with determining the reasonableness of government's regulatory efforts. Indeed, from the nonpublic school's perspective, the issue may more properly be stated whether a state agency, which cannot prohibit outright the operation of nonpublic schools,[733] may nonetheless regulate them out of existence by imposing statutory or regulatory requirements that nonpublic schools cannot meet.

Schools With a Religious Nexus

The application to states of the religion clause in 1940[734] meant that state regulation of religious conduct must have something other than merely a rational purpose.[735] For the first time, in *Wisconsin v. Yoder*,[736] the United States Supreme Court had occasion to determine the validity of a state's enforcement of its compulsory attendance statute against the protective standards of the free exercise clause. In that case, the Court developed a threefold test to determine the constitutionality of state attempts to regulate religious education: (1) whether or not the activity objected to by the state is motivated by and rooted in legitimate and sincerely-held religious beliefs;[737] (2) whether or not the parties free exercise of religion has been burdened by the state's action and the extent of or impact on their religious

---

[731] *See* Dayton Christian Schs. v. Ohio Civil Rights Comm'n., 578 F. Supp. 1004 (S.D. Ohio 1984), *rev'd* 766 F.2d 932 (6th Cir. 1985), remanded to state commission, 477 U.S. 619 (1986) (gender based discrimination grounded on religious doctrine requiring female employees to quit for purpose of staying home with baby may be protected by free exercise of religion but "elimination of prohibited sex discrimination is sufficiently important state interest").

[732] *Pierce*, 268 U.S. at 534.

[733] The U.S. Supreme Court in *Pierce* invalidated under the due process clause an Oregon statute which would have required attendance only at public schools. Successful plaintiffs were a Catholic and a private military school.

[734] Cantwell v. Conneticut, 310 U.S. 296 (1940).

[735] *See Pierce*, 268 U.S. at 535 (in *Pierce*, under the due process clause, decided prior to 1940, the Oregon statute had "no reasonable relation to some purpose within the competency of the state").

[736] 406 U.S. 205 (1972).

[737] *Id.* at 216-16.

activity;[738] and (3) whether the state has a compelling interest for its action justifying the burden imposed on the parties' religious activity.[739] However, the viability of the compelling interest was placed in doubt by *Employment Division v. Smith*,[740] where the Supreme Court disallowed use of the *Yoder* compelling interest test when a "neutral, generally applicable law"[741] was being applied. The only exception to the *Smith* alteration of *Yoder* was where a free exercise claim was linked with another constitutional right, such as parental direction of children's education.[742]

The *Yoder* compelling interest test enjoyed a brief resurgence under the Religious Freedom Restoration Act (RFRA)[743] before the Act was declared unconstitutional by the Supreme Court in *Flores v. City of Boerne*.[744] Notwithstanding the advent of *Smith* and the demise of RFRA, courts can still act to prevent religious organizations from being treated in an arbitrary manner in violation of other constitutional rights. In *Fairfax Covenant Church v. Fairfax County School Board*,[745] the Fourth Circuit relied on four Supreme Court decisions favoring religion[746] to find that a school board lacked a compelling interest in setting

---

[738] *Id.* at 217-19.

[739] *Id.* at 219-34.

[740] 494 U.S. 872 (1990).

[741] *Id.* at 880-881.

[742] For a discussion of the aftermath of the *Smith* case on claims under the free exercise clause, see R. Mawdsley, *Employment Division v. Smith Revisited: The Constriction of Free Exercise Rights Under the U.S. Constitution*, 76 Ed. Law Rep. 1 (1992).

[743] 42 U.S.C. §§ 2000bb-2000bb-4 (the Religious Freedom Restoration Act had as one of its purposes, "to restore the compelling interest test as set forth in *Sherbert v. Verner* and *Wisconsin v. Yoder....*" In Sherbert v. Verner, 374 U.S. 398 (1963), the Supreme Court required the government to prove that its regulation was the least restrictive means of accomplishing its interest). *See* Porth v. Roman Catholic Diocese of Kalamazoo, 532 N.W.2d 195 (Mich. Ct. App. 1995) (RFRA prohibited state religious discrimination claim by nonrenewed protestant teacher in Roman Catholic school).

[744] 521 U.S. 507 (1997) (Court upheld local ordinance, neutral on its face, establishing historic landmarks, when applied to a church designated as a historic landmark, even though the application of the ordinance had the effect of preventing the church of altering its building in the desired manner).

[745] 17 F.3d 703 (4th Cir. 1994).

[746] Widmar v. Vincent, 454 U.S. 263 (1981) (public university having designated its campus as a public forum could not restrict religious student meetings); Board of Educ. of Westside Community Sch. Dist. v. Mergens, 496 U.S. 226 (1990) (Equal Access Act permitting student-initiated religious meetings at public high schools not violative of Establishment Clause); Lamb's Chapel v. Center Moriches Union Free Sch. Dist., 508 U.S. 384 (1993) (school district refusal to permit religious group to use school facilities during non-school hours an impermissible content-based free speech violation); Church of the Lukumi Babalu Aye, Inc. v. City of Hialeah, 508 U.S. 520 (1993) (city ordinance directed at Santeria religion practice of animal sacrifices violative of free exercise).

differential rental rates for school property so that churches paid more than nonreligious groups.[747] The school board's rationale that extended use of public school facilities could be interpreted as "domination"[748] prohibited by the establishment clause was held by the Fourth Circuit to be an "unfounded ... view of the First Amendment." The *Fairfax* court found the ordinance to have violated the churches' free speech, which meant that, by using the free speech clause, the court could skirt free exercise problems under *Smith* and invoke compelling interest analysis.

Beyond the free exercise clause, the United States Supreme Court has suggested that governmental regulatory efforts may also run afoul of the establishment clause as interpreted in *Lemon v. Kurtzman*.[749] The *Lemon* test, formulated as it was in the context of government aid to religious schools,[750] might offer limited protection to religious educational institutions.[751] Despite vocal opposition in the Supreme Court [752], the *Lemon* test, with its three parts, is still the standard measure for interpreting the

---

[747] The ordinance read as follows: "Churches/religious organizations servicing Fairfax County citizens may be granted use of a school for as many as five years.... Church/religious groups may be authorized usage after five years of use at increasing rental rates until the full commercial rates become effective in the ninth year of use." *Fairfax*, 17 F.3d at 705.

[748] *See Widmar*, 454 U.S. at 275 (the Supreme Court implied that even in a public forum setting an Establishment Clause violation could occur if a religious group dominated the open forum). In *Fairfax*, the school board's argument was that a combination of low rents and extended use by churches could amount to such domination, but the court of appeals found no facts to support that speculation and the rents charged (at least for the first five years before rental charges escalated significantly for churches) were the same for both religious and nonreligious organizations). *Fairfax*, 17 F.3d at 708-709.

[749] 411 U.S. 192 (1973) (all three tests stated for the first time in this case, although the first two tests originated in Abingdon Sch. Dist. v. Schempp, 374 U.S. 203 (1963)).

[750] *See* School Dist. of Grand Rapids v. Ball, 473 U.S. 371 (1985) (Share Time and Community Education classes taught in religious schools by teachers paid by public school district a violation of *Lemon* test); Aguilar v. Felton, 473 U.S. 402 (1985) (teaching of Title I programs in religious schools by teachers paid by public school district violation of *Lemon* test).

[751] *Cf.* Alicea v. New Brunswick Theological Seminary, 608 A.2d 218 (N.J. 1992) (judicial intervention into terms of employment for those who perform ministerial functions would constitute excessive entanglement under *Lemon* test) *with* Welter v. Seton Hall Univ., 608 A.2d 206 (N.J. 1992) (judicial intervention as to whether two nuns had been improperly dismissed not excessive entanglement where employment contracts had not incorporated Canon Law or religious requirements).

[752] *See* Lamb's Chapel v. Center Moriches Sch. Dist., 508 U.S. 384 (1993) (Scalia, J., concurring) ("Like some ghoul in a late-night horror movie that repeatedly sits up in its grave and shuffles abroad, after repeatedly being killed and buried, *Lemon* talks our Establishment Clause jurisprudence once again, frightening the little children and school attorneys of Center Moriches Union Free School District .... The secret of the *Lemon* test's survival, I think, is it is so easy to kill.")

establishment clause:[753] (1) whether the statute or regulation has a secular purpose; (2) whether the statute or regulation has the primary effect of advancing or inhibiting religion; and (3) whether the statute or regulation will result in excessive entanglement between the state and the religious school.

In *National Labor Relations Board (NLRB) v. Catholic Bishop of Chicago*,[754] the United States Supreme Court had occasion to determine under the *Lemon* test whether Roman Catholic schools could be required by the National Labor Relations Board to permit representation elections for lay teachers in diocesan schools. In discussing the NLRB interest in promoting and protecting labor peace and the school's interest in protecting and promoting its religious doctrine, the Court observed that negotiation of terms and conditions of employment would involve the NLRB in "nearly everything that goes on in the schools."[755] *Catholic Bishop* announced a three-step level of analysis for resolving the conflict between statutory language and constitutional infringement. The first step is to determine whether government action represents a "substantial risk" of constitutional infringement.[756] A court need not decide that an infringement has occurred, only that an infringement might occur.[757] If a "substantial risk" of infringement exists, the second step is to determine whether the legislative intent was to apply the statute to the religious institution. The general legal principle is that a case will not be resolved on constitutional grounds if it

---

[753] Two alternate tests have been proposed by the Supreme Court for analyzing the establishment clause: endorsement and psychological coercion. See Board of Educ. of Westside Community Sch. Dist. v. Mergens, 496 U.S. 226 (1990) (plurality opinion) (Justice O'Connor used endorsement test to uphold constitutionality of Equal Access Act); Lee v. Weisman, 505 U.S. 577 (1992) (Court struck down school-organized graduation prayers using a psychological coercion test). Not surprisingly, lower courts have felt constrained to analyze establishment clause issues using multiple tests. See Doe v. Madison Sch. Dist. No. 321, 147 F.3d 832 (9th Cir. 1998) (court upheld under both *Lemon* and endorsement tests student graduation speech selection system based on class rank that would allow for religious content).

[754] 440 U.S. 490 (1979).

[755] *Id.* at 502-03.

[756] *Id.* at 506.

[757] *See* NLRB v. St. Louis Christian Home, 663 F.2d 60, 65 (8th Cir. 1981) (in response to allegation by the Home that it might have to disclose source and destination of contributions from affiliated Christian Church if collective bargaining required for its employees, the court observed that "[t]he Home has not demonstrated that such impairment will likely occur"); Volunteers of America-Minnesota-Bar None Boys Ranch v. NLRB, 752 F.2d 345, 249 (8th Cir. 1985) (Ranch's claim that NLRB might intervene if staff were to be disciplined for not carrying out duties related to Ranch's religious tenets held to be insufficient to deprive NLRB of jurisdiction over maintenance, laundry, housekeeping and child care workers).

can be resolved on statutory grounds.[758] If the court determines that the legislative intent was to exclude the religious institution, the *Catholic Bishop* analysis is at end and the court will find in favor of the religious institution.[759] However, if the religious institution cannot be excluded by examining legislative intent, the court must move to the third step and address the merits of the constitutional objections under the Religion Clauses. An example of application of the *Catholic Bishop* test to the merits of a case is reflected in *New Life Baptist Church Academy v. East Longmeadow*.[760] In *New Life*, the court held that a state nonpublic school approval process that included on-site visits to evaluate classes not taught by college graduates did not represent, under the *Lemon* excessive entanglement interpretation of the establishment clause, "the overarching control of the school's possibly religiously motivated choices that was struck down in *NLRB v. Catholic Bishop of Chicago....*"[761]

Although the Court resolved *Catholic Bishop* on other than constitutional grounds, it suggested that inquiries into the practices of religious schools that did not "go beyond resolving factual issues" might be permissible.[762] But where the inquiry would involve conclusions to be drawn regarding "the good faith of the position asserted by the clergy-administrators and its relationship to the school's religious mission," the process of inquiry as well as the conclusions drawn "may impinge on rights guaranteed by the Religion Clause."[763] *Catholic Bishop* has come to be interpreted to mean that the NLRB does not have

---

[758] *Catholic Bishop*, 440 U.S. at 500 ("An Act of Congress ought not to be construed to violate the Constitution if any other possible construction remains," citing to Murray v. The Charming Betsy, 2 Cranch 118 (1804). *But see* Zobrest v. Catalina Foothills School Dist., 509 U.S. 1, (1993) (four dissenting justices argued that this case involving publicly paid sign language interpreter assigned to parochial should have been remanded to a lower court for consideration of statutory and regulatory issues; "[i]f there is one doctrine more deeply rooted than any other in the process of constitutional adjudication, it is that we ought not to pass on questions of constitutionality ... unless such adjudication is unavoidable.")

[759] *E.g., see* Cochran v. St. Louis Preparatory Seminary, 717 F. Supp. 1413 (E.D. Mo. 1989) (ADEA did not apply to Seminary where there was no language in statute or in legislative history suggesting that Congress intended to include church operated schools under ADEA). *See also* St. Martin Evangelical Church v. South Dakota, 451 U.S. 772 (1981) (state's unemployment system not applicable to church controlled schools where Congress had not expressed an intent to include them).

[760] 885 F.2d 940 (1st Cir. 1989).

[761] *Id.* at 953.

[762] *Catholic Bishop*, 440 U.S. at 502.

[763] *Id.*

jurisdiction over church-operated schools,[764] but that state labor relation boards may have jurisdiction.[765]

Where a religious school alleges that application of a state statute may constitute a constitutional violation, the school may be required under the abstention doctrine[766] to adjudicate its religious claims before the state administrative tribunal before a federal court will review the case. To suggest that a state administrative agency, although enforcing its enabling statute and own regulations, can resolve constitutional claims requires religious schools to cling to the rather tenuous hope that the agency can and will correctly interpret federal constitutional law. The right of appeal from an adverse administrative decision may not present an opportunity for a *de novo* hearing to raise constitutional claims.[767] The U.S. Supreme Court has held that federal courts must give the fact finding of a state agency, acting in a judicial capacity while resolving disputed issues of fact properly before the court which parties have had adequate

---

[764] NLRB v. Bishop Ford Cent. Catholic High Sch., 623 F.2d 818 (2d Cir. 1980), *cert. denied* 450 U.S. 996 (1981) (NLR not applicable to lay teachers in church controlled schools). *But see* NLRB v. Hanna Boys Ctr., 940 F.2d 1295 (9th Cir. 1991) (NLRB representation election required for non-teaching employees in Catholic school).

[765] *See* New York State Employ. Relations v. Christian Brothers Acad., 668 N.Y.S.2d 407 (N.Y. App. Div. 1998) (state employment board jurisdiction over lay teachers did not violate free exercise); N.Y. State Employ. Relations Bd. v. Christ the King Reg'l High Sch., 660 N.Y.S.2d 359 (N.Y. 1997) (requiring school to bargain with teachers' union not violation of free exercise or establishment clause). See also, South Jersey Catholic Sch. Teachers' Org. v. St. Theresa of Infant Jesus Church Elem. Sch., 696 A.2d 709 (N.J. 1997) (requiring church-controlled school to bargain with teachers' organization would not impair free exercise because the state has a compelling interest). *But see* Central Catholic Educ. Ass'n v. Archdiocese of Portland, 891 P.2d 1318 (Or. Ct. App. 1995) (in a somewhat convoluted decision, the court held that since the school was subject to NLRB jurisdiction, it was exempt from state employment relations statute); Hill-Murray Fed'n of Teachers v. Hill-Murray High Sch., Maplewood, 471 N.W.2d 372 (Minn. Ct. App. 1991) (application of state labor relations statute to religious school violated state and federal religion clauses).

[766] Basically, the abstention doctrine states that federal courts will abstain from asserting jurisdiction over a case involving constitutional claims as long as there is an ongoing state proceeding where the party has an adequate opportunity to present his constitutional claim. The doctrine was the key issue in the U.S. Supreme Court's disposition of Dayton Christian Schools v. Ohio Civil Rights Comm'n, 766 F.2d 932 (6th Cir. 1985). For a discussion of the doctrine, see R. Mawdsley *Challenges to Religious Liberties: Procedural Traps*, 37 Ed. Law Rep. 1 (1987).

[767] Appeals from administrative decisions generally must overcome an inference that the administrative ruling be given "considerable weight" or be supported by the facts [Florian v. Highland Local Sch. Dist., 493 N.E.2d 249 (Ohio Ct. App. 1983)] or must find support on a rational basis in the evidence [Leiphart v. North Carolina Sch. of the Arts, 342 S.E.2d 914 (N.C. Ct. App. 1986). A reviewing state court may be bound by an administrative agency's findings if supported by evidence on the record and applicable law. [Ashbourne Educ. Servs., Inc. v. Commonwealth, Dep't of Educ., 499 A.2d 698 (Pa. Commw. Ct. 1985)]. Generally, great deference is given to administrative interpretation of statutes which the courts are also asked to interpret, Western Reserve Academy v. U.S., 619 F. Supp. 394 (D.C. Ohio 1985).

opportunity to litigate, the same preclusive effect which such fact finding would have in the state's courts.[768]

Beyond the establishment clause concern as to whether government will become excessively intrusive in the operations of nonpublic schools, religious schools can also raise a defense under the free exercise clause. Free exercise claims meet with mixed response by courts. In *New Life Baptist Church Academy v. East Longmeadow*,[769] a federal court of appeals overturned a district court decision that a state's approval process requiring on-site visits was not the least restrictive means of accomplishing the state's interest in education. The court of appeals rejected the district court's determination that "standardized testing combined with individual follow-up when indicated"[770] was the least restrictive means. The appeals court reasoned that:

> the 'testing' plan risked exposing still greater burdens upon individual parents, or children, insofar as it foresees the School Committee enforcing testing or remedial or alternative schooling obligations upon individual families, potentially through the use of the courts and potentially under circumstances where the Academy itself retains the state's approval .... Given the fact that the Academy has expressed a preference for standardized testing and the fact that the Academy is the best judge of its own religious needs and interests, we cannot say that standardized testing is *no* less burdensome than the School Committee's proposal, but neither can we see how it *substantially* alleviates the burden upon the free exercise of religion, nor how it can represent a *major* improvement.[771]

Similarly, in *People v. DeJonge*,[772] the Michigan Supreme Court held that the state's teacher certification requirement was not the least restrictive means of protecting the state's interest in education, and thus, application of the requirement to parents

---

[768] University of Tennessee v. Elliott, 478 U.S. 788 (1986) (preclusive effect of state administrative civil hearings on Title VII actions depends on preclusive effect granted by such hearings by state courts).

[769] 885 F.2d 940 (1st Cir. 1989).

[770] *New Life*, 666 F. Supp. 293, 320 (D. Mass. 1987). Some states use mandatory student testing as the method of evaluating student progress in nonpublic schools. *E.g.*, *see* Alaska Stat. § 14.45.120; N.C. Gen. Stat. § 115C-549, 115C-550; S.D. Codified Laws Ann. 13-27-3; W. Va. Code § 18-28-3.

[771] *New Life*, 885 F.2d at 950 (emphasis in original).

[772] 501 N.W.2d 127 (Mich. 1993).

who home schooled their children violated the parents' free exercise rights. In this case, the court found that the state had "failed to provide evidence or testimony that supports the argument that the certification process is essential to the preservation of its asserted interest."[773]

An analysis very similar to free exercise can be used in determining exemptions under state laws. Religious schools that are integral parts of churches generally enjoy exemption from state unemployment compensation statutes. In *Miller v. Saints Peter and Paul School*,[774] an Ohio appeals court held that a teacher in a diocesan school could not recover benefits after her contract was nonrenewed. Ohio law provides that an unemployment compensation claimant is not eligible for benefits if she worked "[i]n the employ of a church or convention or association of churches, or in an organization which is operated primarily for religious purposes and which is operated, supervised, controlled, or principally supported by a church or convention or association of churches."[775] The court held that the school had been organized to teach the Byzantine Rite and Catholic doctrine, and the reasonable inference was that the school was affiliated "with a religious denomination to offer a learning experience dominated by a religious environment."[776] The school was supervised, controlled, or principally supported by a church because the pastor of the church "exercised substantial control over the operations and spending of the school, as his consent was required to hire new teachers and to purchase supplies."[777]

Miller, as helpful as it is for religious schools in not requiring them to fund unemployment compensation, does not test the question whether such schools are entitled an exemption under the free exercise clause. Should the question arise, courts are not likely to create a religious exemption if past Supreme Court precedent in dealing with social legislation is any indication.[778]

---

773 *Id.* at 140.

774 711 N.W.2d 311 (Ohio Ct. App. 1998).

775 Ohio Rev. Code Ann. § 4141.01(B)(3)(h)(i).

776 *Miller*, 711 N.E.2d at 314.

777 *Id.* at 315.

778 *See* U.S. v. Lee, 455 U.S. 252 (1982) (in this post-*Yoder* decision, the Court held that Amish employers were not entitled to an exemption from making contributions to social security for their Amish employees, even though none of them, according to their religious beliefs, would apply for social security benefits).

Schools Without a Religious Nexus

Educational institutions that have no religious nexus obviously can make no constitutional claim under either of the First Amendment religion clauses.[779] However, a substantive due process constitutional claim might be appropriate under a parents' liberty right to direct their children's education. The amount of protection that this liberty right provides depends on whether courts consider it to be a fundamental right subject to a strict scrutiny test. If a fundamental right is not affected, government actions need be justified only by a rational purpose.

In *People v. Bennett*,[780] the Michigan Supreme Court refused to apply a strict scrutiny analysis to parent direction of children's education where no free exercise claim was also involved. In the absence of a religious claim, the court determined that parents do not have a "fundamental right to direct all of their children's education."[781] Similarly, in *Ohio Association of Independent Schools v. Goff*,[782] the Sixth Circuit Court of Appeals refused to invoke strict scrutiny to strike down an Ohio statutory requirement that chartered private schools had to participate in the state proficiency testing program. The court observed that "no federal court has ... suggested that wholly secular limitations on private school education implicate a fundamental right warranting strict scrutiny."[783] In *Herndon v. Chapel Hill-Carrboro City Board of Education*,[784] a federal district court applied a rational purpose test in upholding a public school district's mandatory community service program over a claim that the program was contrary to a parent's direction of a child's education. The court found that the district had a legitimate state interest "in transmitting community values and instilling skills and habits of good citizenship to [its] students."[785]

The leading case regarding constitutional rights for nonsectarian, private schools and the rational purpose test is *Runyon v. McCrary*.[786] In *Runyon*, the Supreme Court used a

---

779 *See* State of Hawaii v. Andrews, 651 P.2d 473 (Hawaii 1982) (*Yoder* analysis not applicable where no religious claim).

780 501 N.W.2d 106 (Mich. 1993).

781 *Id.* at 112.

782 92 F.3d 419 (6th Cir. 1996).

783 *Id.* at 423.

784 899 F. Supp. 1443 (M.D.N.C. 1995).

785 *Id.* at 1452.

786 427 U.S. 160 (1976).

rational purpose test to conclude that Section 1981 of the Civil Rights Act,[787] prohibiting discrimination on the basis of race in the making of contracts, applied to "private, commercially operated nonsectarian schools."[788] However, as the Court was later to note in *Bob Jones University v. United States,*[789] even fundamental constitutional rights under free exercise and the attendant strict scrutiny test, would not survive an established public policy to eradicate racial discrimination.[790]

The absence of religion clause defense does not mean that nonsectarian educational institutions can be regulated in an arbitrary manner, a defense that applies equally well to sectarian schools. An Oregon court of appeals struck down a state statute providing that Oregon school and college members of the Northwest Association of Schools and Colleges did not have to meet certification requirements while non-Oregon schools and colleges had to satisfy the requirements regardless of whether they were members of the Association.[791] In finding that this statute violated the interstate commerce clause of the U.S. Constitution, the court determined that Oregon had failed to bear its burden of proving that its purpose of protecting state consumers from "the effects of substandard, transient, unethical, deceptive or fraudulent practices by out-of-state educational institutions ... [could not be accomplished] by available nondiscriminatory means."[792] In *Philip Crosby Associates v.*

---

[787] Title 42 U.S.C. § 1981 provides in part that "all persons within the jurisdiction of the United States shall have the same rights in every State ... to make and enforce contracts ... as enjoyed by white citizens ... "

[788] *Runyon*, 427 U.S. at 168. The Court swept aside constitutional arguments based on freedom of association, parental rights and right of privacy because "while parents have a constitutional right to send their children to private schools and a constitutional right to select private schools that offer specialized instruction, they have no constitutional right to provide their children with private school education unfettered by reasonable government regulation." *Id.* at 166.

[789] 461 U.S. 574 (1983).

[790] *See* Albert v. Carovano, 851 F.2d 561 (2d Cir. 1988) (Section 1983 cause of action dismissed but section 1981 available to black and Latino students; Parker v. Trinity High Sch., 823 F. Supp. 511 (N.D. Ill. 1993) (Section 1981 applies to dismissal of Afro-American students from Catholic school, but students had no claim where no intent to discriminate on basis of race was proved); Holland v. Board of Trustees of Univ. of District Columbia, 794 F. Supp. 420 (D. D.C. 1992) (Section 1981 available to white persons). Section 1981 is available also for claims of discrimination based on ethnicity. *See* St. Francis College v. Al-Kazraji, 107 S. Ct. 2022 (1987). *But see* Bisciglia v. Kenosha Unified Sch. Dist. No. 1, 149 F.R.D. 588 (E.D. Wis. 1993) (Section 1981 not available to person alleging discrimination on basis of Italian ethnicity and/or Italian national origin).

[791] City Univ. v. State Office of Educ. Policy and Planning, 870 P.2d 222 (Or. Ct. App. 1994).

[792] *Id.* at 225.

State Board of Independent Colleges,[793] a plaintiff that maintained classroom facilities to present management seminars could not be prevented from using the word "college" since it did not offer degrees or offer courses which led to a degree. The Florida state appeals court determined that the State Board did not have statutory jurisdiction over non-degree granting institutions. Similarly, a Florida federal district court held that a state statute prohibiting use of "Ph.D." or "Dr.," unless from an accredited university, violated free speech and lacked a compelling interest.[794]

However, in *Nova University v. Educational Institution Licensure Commission*,[795] denial of a license for a nonresident university to offer a doctoral program in the District of Columbia was upheld on the basis of the reasonableness of the criteria pertaining to library resources and the number of full-time faculty. On the other hand, in *Nova University v. Board of Governors*,[796] the North Carolina Supreme Court rejected a claim by the Board of Governors of the University of North Carolina that it could establish minimum criteria for private schools that were outside of the state. In *State v. Williams*[797] the North Carolina Supreme Court held that state's regulation of certain kinds of private schools outside the state that solicited students within the state was an unwarranted delegation of power. But in *McMinn v. City of Little Rock*,[798] a local zoning commission was upheld in refusing to grant a zoning variance to a proposed Montessori school because there was no evidence that the commission acted "arbitrarily, capriciously and unreasonably."[799] However, in *Kirsch v. Prince George's County*,[800] a mini-dormitory zoning ordinance to prevent residential homeowners from renting to large numbers of university students was struck down under the Equal Protection Clause as not "rationally related to a legitimate governmental purpose."[801]

---

[793] 506 So.2d 490 (Fla. Dist. Ct. App. 1987).
[794] Strang v. Satz, 884 F. Supp. 504 (S.D. Fla. 1995).
[795] 483 A.2d 1172 (D.C. App. 1984).
[796] 287 S.E.2d 872 (N.C. 1982).
[797] 117 S.E.2d 444 (N.C. 1960).
[798] 631 S.W.2d 288 (Ark. 1982).
[799] *Id.* at 291.
[800] 626 A.2d 372 (Md. 1993).
[801] *Id.* at 379.

Generally, regulation of private schools will be left to the state's educational agencies. The normal deference paid to those agencies is reflected in *Paladino v. Adelphi University*:[802]

> The regulatory scheme requires that the quality of education provided by private institutions be closely monitored by the State Department of Education. If the school is not meeting its obligations, then the matter is capable of resolution within the educational system.[803]

Home Instruction

Home instruction has become generally accepted among the states and is now currently permitted in all fifty states, either by express statutory language or by statutory interpretation.[804] Exact statistics on the number of children in home schools are difficult to gather, but one study has estimated that 1.23 million children were home-schooled in 1996-1997 with a growth rate of increase of fifteen percent per year.[805] The popularity of home schooling has undoubtedly enhanced a more favorable legislative and legal climate, but it is, nonetheless, a climate that has not been free from litigation.

One of the more frequently litigated issues has been whether home instruction qualifies as a "private school" under state statutes limiting or exempting such schools from state regulation.[806] To assist their case, home instruction parents may in fact give their instruction program the name of a school.[807] States vary on whether home instruction constitutes a private school, with some choosing not to define them as such,[808] while

---

802 454 N.Y.S 2d 868 (App. Div. 1982) (actually an educational malpractice and breach of contract action against an elementary school operated by the university).

803 *Id.* at 872.

804 *See generally*, DECKARD, HOME SCHOOL LAWS IN ALL FIFTY STATES (1997-98).

805 RAY, HOME INSTRUCTION ACROSS THE STATES (1997).

806 *E.g., see* Wis. Stat. Ann. § 118.15(1)(a) ("public or private school"); N.C. Gen. Stat. § 115 C-378 (approved "public schools" or non-public schools); Ark. Code Ann. §§ 6-15-502 (home school separate category from other kinds of schools).

807 State v. Popanz, 332 N.W.2d 750(Wis. 1983) (Free Thinker School); Delconte v. State, 329 S.E.2d 636 (N.C. 1985) (Hallelujah School); *In Interest of* Sawyer, 672 P.2d 1093 (Kan. 1983) (Longview school, Inc.); Strosnider v. Strosnider, 686 P.2d 981 (N.M. Ct. App. 1984) (Holy Innocents School).

808 *Cf.* Clonclara, Inc. v. State Bd. of Educ., 501 N.W.2d 88 (Mich. 1993) (home schools are schools "other than a public school"); People v. Levisen, 90 N.E.2d 213 (Ill. 1950), State v. Edgington, 663 P.2d 376 (N.M. Ct. App. 1983), and Strosnider v. Strosnider 686 P.2d 981 (N.M. Ct. App. 1984) (home instruction a private school) *with* State v. Superior Ct., 346 P.2d 999 (Wash. 1960), State v. Lowry, 383 P.2d 962 (Kan. 1963), State v. M.M., 407 So.2d 987

others consider them as private schools.[809] Where a state compulsory attendance statute requires only "equivalent instruction," there is a difference of opinion whether home instruction is equivalent to public education.[810] Generally, the burden is on the parent to prove equivalency, but at least two states place the burden on the state.[811] In some cases equivalency statutes have been discussed as possibly flawed on vagueness grounds, while in others, courts have upheld the statutes easily.[812] Special statutes dealing specifically with home instruction have minimized ambiguity and confusion regarding what regulation, if any, is permissible by the state for home schools.[813]

Two Michigan Supreme Court decisions involving home schooling, one based on religious reasons, reflect the different policy issues at stake when religion is a factor. These two cases decided on the same day reached opposite conclusions. In *People v. DeJonge*,[814] Michigan's teacher certification requirement for home schools under the compulsory attendance law violated the free exercise rights of parents whose religious convictions prohibited use of certified instructors. The *DeJonge* court applied a strict scrutiny test to find that the state needed a

(Fla. Dist. Ct. App. 1982), State v. Bigelow, 334 N.W.2d 444 (Neb. 1983), Delconte v. State, 329 S.E.2d 636 (N.C. 1985) (home instruction not a private school).

809 *See* Texas Educ. Agency v. Leeper, 893 S.W.2d 432 (Tex. 1995) (Supreme Court of Texas held that home instruction was a private school under state law and upheld award of attorney fees in excess of $400,000 to attorneys for home schools).

810 *Cf. In re* H., 357 N.Y.S.2d 348 (N.Y. 1974) (equivalency rejected) *with* State v. Massa, 231 A.2d 252 (N.J. Super. Ct. 1976) (equivalency upheld).

811 *See* Wright v. State, 209 P. 179 (Okla. 1922); State v. Cheney, 305 S.W.2d 892 (Mo. 1957); State v. Pilkinton, 310 S.W.2d 304 (Mo. 1958); State v. Davies, 589 S.W.2d 189 (Mo. 1980); *In re* Monnig, 638 S.W.2d 782 (Mo. Ct. App. 1982).

812 *See* Fellowship Baptist Church v. Benton, 815 F.2d 485 (8th Cir. 1987); Matter of Kilroy, 467 N.Y.S.2d 318 (N.Y. Fam. Ct. 1983); Bangor Baptist Church v. State, 576 F. Supp. 1299 (Me. 1983).

813 *E.g., see* Va. Code Ann. § 22.1-254 where parents have minimal reporting requirements, no home visits are provided for and in some cases a local public school superintendent is expressly denied evaluative judgment. This statute was in direct response to Griggs v. Commonwealth, 297 S.E.2d 799 (Va. 1982) where home instruction did not constitute attendance at a private school and the parents were not approved tutors or teachers under the state's separate provision for home instruction. *See also* N.C. Gen Stat. 115C-564 (state regulation limited to two requirements: home instructors must have a high school diploma or equivalent, and home school students must take an annual achievement test); Neb. Rev. Stat. § 79-1701 (parents who find existing state regulation to conflict with their religious beliefs can substitute an informational statement which declares that children attend school 175 days per year and are instructed in core curriculum subjects); La. Rev. Stat. Ann. § 17:236.1(D) (curriculum equal to that offered in public schools); Minn. Stat. Ann. § 120.101(8); Colo. Rev. Stat. Ann. § 22-33-104.5 (home school students take standardized tests). *In addition, see* Miss. Code Ann. § 37-13-91 (home schools appear not to be regulated at all).

814 501 N.W.2d 127 (Mich. 1993).

compelling interest that was "truly compelling, threatening the safety or welfare of the state in a clear and present manner."[815] However, in *People v. Bennett*,[816] the court ruled that the teacher certification requirement applied to parents whose objection was grounded only in the Fourteenth Amendment liberty interest to direct the education of their children. The *Bennett* court found that the constitutional right of directing children's education without an attendant religious claim was entitled to only a minimum scrutiny test demanding a burden of proof that the state need only produce evidence teacher certification is reasonably related to its interest in education.[817] Under the minimum scrutiny test, the court found the teacher certification to be "at least reasonably related to the state's legitimate interest," and the burden rested on the parents "to show the unreasonableness of the certificate requirement."[818] However, in *DeJonge*, where strict scrutiny was the standard, the state had the burden "to prove that the certificate requirement was essential to [its] interest."[819] The *DeJonge* court further held that the burden was not on the parents to prove that alternatives less intrusive than teacher certification exist. As a result of the court's reasoning in the two cases, the parents in *DeJonge* were exempt from the teacher certification requirement, while the parents in *Bennett* were subject to the same requirement.

Recent cases have addressed the question of whether home schooled students should be permitted to participate in public school activities. In *Swanson v. Guthrie Independent School District*,[820] parents of a home-schooled student sought unsuccessfully to have their child take foreign language, vocal music, and science courses in the local public junior high school. The Tenth Circuit Court of Appeals upheld a school district policy that only full-time students would be permitted to take courses in the public schools because only full-time students were counted by the State Board of Education for state aid purposes.

---

[815] *Id.* at 138.

[816] 501 N.W.2d 106 (Mich. 1993).

[817] *But see* Alfonso v. Fernandez, 606 N.Y.S.2d 259, 265 (N.Y. App. Div. 1993) (parental liberty interest in rearing and educating their children resulted in New York City public schools' policy of condom distribution in the schools being declared unconstitutional because the school board had not shown "an overriding necessity" for its policy.)

[818] *Bennett*, 501 N.W.2d at 117.

[819] *DeJonge*, 501 N.W.2d at 141.

[820] 135 F.3d 694 (10th Cir. 1998) (the child was home-schooled in order for her parents "to teach her Christian principles that [were] excluded from the public school curriculum.") *Id.* at 696.

In *Bradstreet v. Sobol*,[821] a New York appeals court upheld summary judgment for a school district that had refused to permit a home schooled student to participate in extracurricular activities. The appeals court upheld the constitutionality of a New York statute that required students' enrollment in a public school before they could participate in extracurricular activities.

One can ask whether parental desire to selectively involve their children in public schools contradicts the underlying purpose of home schooling.[822] To what extent does a request for such participation by parents represent a tacit admission that an inherent weakness exists in the home instruction process, namely that home instruction cannot meet all of the educational needs of a child? But, on the other hand, one could ask to what extent public schools should have a responsibility to meet the needs of all students who live in their school districts, even to those parents of home-schooled students who pay property taxes to support the public schools. Should general tax support of public education through property and income taxes create a right of access to public school programs for all students? If the barrier to home school student accessibility is the state funding formula, would not public policy be better served by assuring that public school classrooms are fully utilized, even if it means redesigning the funding formula to allow for part-time students? To press this argument to its conclusion, to what extent should public schools be considered instructional cafeterias where students, whether enrolled full-time or part-time, can selectively choose from a curricular and extracurricular menu?

More troublesome are issues representing government intrusion into home schools. In *Battles v. Anne Arundel County Board of Education*,[823] the Fourth Circuit Court of Appeals upheld a state monitoring process for home schools that included parent maintenance of a portfolio in established curriculum areas

---

[821] 659 N.Y.S.2d 402 (N.Y. App. Div. 1996).

[822] *See, e.g.*, State v. Bowman, 653 P.2d 254 (Or. Ct. App. 1982) (parent convicted for truancy for teaching child at home because of dissatisfaction with public schools); State v. Riddle, 285 S.E.2d 359 (W.Va. 1981) (parents convicted for truancy for home schooling children because of desire to instruct in religious beliefs); Delconte v. State, 329 S.E.2d 636 (N.C. 1985) (parents convicted of violating compulsory attendance law had chosen home schooling to teach religious values, to keep children from being exposed to evolution, and to keep them from being subjected to undesirable influences in public schools); *In Interest of* Sawyer, 672 P.2d 1093 (Kan. 1983) (parents home schooled children because of dissatisfaction with public school instruction of one of their children that had resulted in the child being recommended to repeat a grade).

[823] 904 F. Supp. 471, (D. Md. 1995), aff'd 95 F.3d 41 (4th Cir. 1995).

and a requirement that a state representative observe home teaching on-site. The Fourth Circuit dispatched, with parental direction of education and free exercise, constitutional claims by noting that the state law was neutral and did not alter the parents' religious beliefs. However, in *Brunelle v. Lynn Public Schools*,[824] the Supreme Judicial Court of Massachusetts held that a state statute requiring that local public schools oversee home schooling curriculum and parent teaching qualifications did not include the right of the superintendent to conduct on-site visits. More troublesome is *J.B. v. Washington County*,[825] where the Tenth Circuit Court of Appeals upheld the right of the State Division of Family Services to remove a child from the home for seventeen and one-half hours to investigate an anonymous report of sexual abuse. In rejecting a number of parent procedural and substantive constitutional rights, the Tenth Circuit deferred to the judgment of those responsible for investigating child abuse and noted that the state had a legitimate interest in conducting the interview of the child in an "out-of-home ... influence-free environment."[826]

The State and Compelling Interests

The United States Supreme Court has never clarified the limits of government regulatory intrusiveness into the operation of nonpublic schools. While the Supreme Court in *Pierce* acknowledged the state's regulatory interests,[827] the *Yoder* Court provided only the broadest outline for a governmental compelling interest where the fundamental constitutional right of free exercise of religion is at stake. The *Yoder* Court defined a government's compelling interest in compulsory education to be a "degree of education ... necessary to prepare citizens to participate effectively and intelligently in our open political

---

[824] 702 N.E.2d 1182 (Mass. 1998).

[825] 127 F.3d 919 (10th Cir. 1997) (child was returned to parents at end of 17 1/2 hours without evidence of abuse).

[826] *Id.* at 926. For cases involving deferment to state discretion, see Doe v. Hennepin County, 858 F.2d 1325 (8th Cir. 1988) (court of appeals upheld summary judgment for County, noting that even though sixteen day removal of children from home without appropriate notice to parents violated state statute, no constitutional rights of parents had been violated; Van Emrik v. Chemung Dep't of Social Services, 911 F.2d 863 (2d Cir. 1990) (court of appeals upheld grant of qualified immunity to officials who had deprived parents of custody of two-year-old child in foster care and in hospital pending a child abuse investigation that eventually resulted in the child being returned to parents).

[827] *Pierce*, 268 U.S. at 534.

system" and education "which prepares individuals to be self-reliant and self-sufficient participants in society."[828] The *Yoder* Court determined that Wisconsin's interest in literacy and marketable vocational skills for students could not override the Amish community's religious-based academic and vocational program.[829] However, the 300 years of Amish tradition and the religious homogeneity of the Amish community have allowed subsequent courts to limit the precedent value of Yoder.[830] Perhaps one prominent writer's pessimistic assessment is correct that "society is giving way to the state, and communities exist now only as created and developed by minorities against the current."[831]

The absence of clear direction by the United States Supreme Court has been translated into a tendency for state courts to define compelling interests in a very expansive manner. With very few exceptions,[832] state regulatory efforts have collided with the religious beliefs of private schools on key issues of attendance reporting[833] and teacher certification.[834]

Supreme Court guidance on the subject of compelling interests has been undercut by *Employment Division v. Smith*,[835] where the Court held that the free exercise clause would not be a defense against neutral, generally applicable government requirements. This neutral, generally applicable test has manifested itself in a variety of ways. For example, in *Hubbard v. Buffalo Independent School District*,[836] a federal district court

---

[828] *Yoder*, 406 U.S. at 221.

[829] The authority of government to regulate religious practices can be traced back to United States v. Reynolds, 98 U.S. 145 (1879) where a constitutionally protected right to believe in polygamy as a religious belief did not extend to a protected right to practice such polygamy.

[830] *See generally*, Valente, Education Law: Public and Private, Vol. 2, 357-53 (1985). *See also Fellowship Baptist Church v. Benton*, 815 F.2d 485, 496-498 (8th Cir. 1987).

[831] R. Rushdoony, Intellectual Schizophrenia 96 (1973).

[832] *See* State of Ohio v. Whisner, 351 N.E.2d 750 (Ohio 1976) (application of some 400 public school regulations, many of which were not even followed by the public schools, to religious schools would have suffocated the schools' religious distinctiveness).

[833] *See* Attorney General v. Bailey, 436 N.E.2d 139 (Mass. 1982); Fellowship Baptist Church v. Benton, 815 F.2d 485 (8th Cir. 1987) (church school reporting names, ages and attendance claimed to violate "Headship of Christ" as pertaining to church-school relationship and information should be secured directly from parents).

[834] *Fellowship Baptist Church*, 815 F.2d 485; Sheridan Rd. Baptist Church v. Department of Educ., 396 N.W.2d 220 (N.D. 1982); State v. Faith Baptist Church of Louisville, 301 N.W.2d 571 (Neb. 1981); State v. Moorhead, 308 N.W.2d 60 (1981) (all cases upheld the application of teacher certification to religious schools).

[835] 494 U.S. 872 (1990).

[836] 20 F. Supp.2d 1012 (W.D. Tex. 1998) (the student in this case was a sixteen-year-old transferring from Upper Room Christian Academy, a non-accredited school under Texas law).

in Texas held that the free exercise clause did not prohibit a school district's policy of requiring students transferring from non-accredited or home schools to pass proficiency exams at their own expense in order to receive credit toward graduation.

The effect of the *Smith* test seems to be that courts will accept government regulation as long as it has a rational basis. In *Kaptein v. Conrad School District*,[837] the Supreme Court of Montana found a school district's denial of a Christian Day School student to participate in public school sports to be reasonable. Using a classification argument reminiscent of the equal protection rational purpose test, the court held that a participation policy based on public school enrollment furthered the state's creation of its educational system in the state constitution. In *Archbishop Walsh High School v. Section VI of the New York State Public High School Athletic Association*,[838] a New York appeals court used a rational purpose argument in rejecting the school's claim that the basis for selecting membership for nonpublic schools in the state athletic association violated equal protection. The court reasoned that requiring a referendum for nonpublic schools to join but no referendum for public schools appeared to be a genuine classification with a "rational relationship to a legitimate state purpose."

One can argue that even before *Smith*'s neutral, generally applicable test, state courts had been reducing the *Yoder* compelling interest to a bland reasonableness test. In *State v. Faith Baptist Church of Louisville*,[839] the Nebraska Supreme Court declared, with reference to a requirement of teacher certification for nonpublic schools, that "the state has a compelling interest in the quality and ability of those who are to teach its young people" because "such requirement is neither arbitrary nor unreasonable" and because "reasonable government regulations as to the quality of education furnished appear to be very minimal in nature."[840] Similarly in *Sheridan Road Baptist Church v. Department of Education*,[841] the court upheld application of teacher certification with the assessment

---

[837] 931 P.2d 1311 (Mont. 1997).

[838] 629 N.Y.S.2d 346 (N.Y. App. Div. 1995).

[839] 3012 N.W.2d 571 (Neb. 1981).

[840] *Id.* at 579.

[841] 348 N.W.2d 263 (Mich. Ct. App. 1984).

that the individual state regulations at issue "[were] reasonable means to give effect to a broader, compelling state interest—in this case the provision of education to all children,"[842] which does not seem to be defining a compelling interest in the same way the *Yoder* Court did. The *Yoder* Court viewed compelling interests from the perspective of the final product or outcome of the educational process which would leave open optional methods.[843] Such inflexibility does not appear to accord free exercise of religion the full force of its fundamental constitutional right status by requiring that the government accomplish its interests by the least restrictive means.[844]

However, state inflexibility in examining state interests does not always lead to a denial of nonpublic student interests. In *People v. DeJonge*,[845] the Michigan Supreme Court, in holding that application of the state's teacher certification requirement to home schooling violated parents' free exercise of religion, distinguished between the state's interest in education and the state's interest in enforcement of teacher certification:

> The state has focused upon the incorrect governmental interest. The state's interest is not ensuring that the goals of compulsory education are met, because the state does not contest that the DeJonges are succeeding at fulfilling such aims. Rather, the state's interest is simply the certification requirement of the

---

[842] *Id.* at 274. *See also* Donovan v. Shenandoah Baptist Church, 573 F. Supp. 320 (W.D. Va. 1983) (application of FLSA minimum wage provisions to church employees upheld); EEOC v. Fremont Christian Sch., 609 F. Supp. 344 (N.D. Cal. 1984), *aff'd* 781 F.2d 1362 (9th Cir. 1986); Dolter v. Wahlert High Sch., 483 F. Supp. 266 (N.D. Ia. 1980) (application of Title VII to religious schools upheld); Christ the King Reg'l High Sch. v. Culvert, 815 F.2d 219 (2d Cir. 1987); Kelley v. The Day Care Ctr., Inc. 451 A.2d 1106 (Vt. 1982) (application of state labor relations acts to nonpublic schools upheld); Braintree Baptist Temple v. Holbrook Pub. Schs., 616 F. Supp. 81 (D. Mass 1984); State v. Andrews, 651 P.2d 473 (Hawaii 1982) (application of licensing or approval requirements to religious schools upheld); Damascus Community Church v. Clockamas County, 610 P.2d 273 (Ore. Ct. App. 1980) (application of zoning ordinance to church school upheld); Hough v. North Star Baptist Church, 312 N.W.2d 158 (Mich. Ct. App. 1981) (application of fire code to church school upheld).

[843] For example, alternative methods to teacher certification have been unpersuasive to courts. *See* Johnson v. Charles City Community Schs., 368 N.W.2d 74, 79 (Ia. 1985); Fellowship Baptist Church v. Benton, 815 F.2d at 494; Sheridan Rd. Baptist Church v. Department of Educ., 348 N.W.2d at 263; State v. Faith Baptist Church, 301 N.W.2d at 579 (student testing not satisfactory alternative to certification). *See also Fellowship Baptist Church*, 620 F. Supp. 308, 316 (D. Ia. 1985) (federal district court was unswayed by evidence that teacher certification is not an accurate predictor of teacher competency).

[844] *See* Thomas v. Review Bd. of Indiana Employment Sec. Div., 450 U.S. 707 (1981); Sherbert v. Verner, 374 U.S. 398 (1963).

[845] 501 N.W.2d 127 (Mich. 1993).

> private school act, not the general objectives of compulsory education. The interest the state pursues is the manner of education, not its goals.[846]

Similarly, in *Snyder v. Charlotte Public School District*,[847] parents of a nonpublic school student successfully compelled the school district to enroll their child in band. Under Michigan's shared time statute, the state supreme court held that nonessential classes had to be offered to both public and nonpublic students. In reversing the school board's decision to exclude the nonpublic student, the court found that the board's concern that part-time participation would be detrimental to the public school had not been proved.

The *Employment Division v. Smith* decision, although it permits states to impose neutral, generally applicable requirements on religious nonpublic schools without violating free exercise, nonetheless, does not prohibit states from relaxing requirements for such schools. *Smith* probably does not affect the confusing array of decisions among several states concerning application of state requirements to nonpublic schools. A brief review of past decisions indicates the variety of state interpretations.

Compulsory attendance and teacher certification requirements have generated considerable litigation. In *State* ex rel. *Nagle v. Olin*,[848] a state compulsory attendance requirement that students attend a school with a certified teacher was unreasonable as applied to a non-Amish child in an Amish school, whereas in *Fellowship Baptist Church v. Benton*,[849] a state statute exempting Amish schools from teacher certification requirements did not apply to a Baptist school. In *Bangor Baptist Church v. State of Maine*,[850] the Department of Education did not have express statutory authority in the compulsory attendance statute to impose direct sanctions against unapproved private schools, whereas in *State v. Faith Baptist Church of Louisville*,[851] the enforcement of compulsory attendance statutes

---

[846] *Id.* at 137.

[847] 365 N.W.2d 151 (Mich. 1984).

[848] 415 N.E.2d 279 (Ohio 1980).

[849] 815 F.2d 485, 496-98 (8th Cir. 1987).

[850] 576 F. Supp. 1299 (D. Me. 1983). *See also* Vermont v. La Barge, 375 A.2d 121 (Vt. 1976) (state department of education exceeded legislative authority in requiring Holiness Methodist school to be approved).

[851] 301 N.W.2d 571 (Neb. 1981).

included authority to enjoin operation of the school and to incarcerate the pastor.[852]

Curricular issues have also been litigated. In *State of Ohio v. Whisner*,[853] curriculum requirements regulating not only the courses to be offered but also the amount of instructional time to be allocated to the subjects offered were held to be unreasonable, whereas in *State v. Shaver*,[854] state department of education regulations specifying the courses to be offered were held to be reasonable. Finally, in *Kentucky State Board v. Rudasill*,[855] a Kentucky constitutional provision providing that no man shall "be compelled to send his child to any school to which he may be conscientiously opposed" prohibited Kentucky from requiring that any teacher in a nonpublic school be certified as well as prohibiting determining basic texts to be used in private or parochial schools; but in *Care and Protection of Charles*,[856] a statutory provision whereby a Massachusetts school committee "shall not withhold such approval [to operate nonpublic school] an account of religious teaching"[857] did not exempt home instruction parents from the obligation to furnish outlined curriculum, materials to be used, and qualifications of instructors.

Division among courts applies to zoning requirements, although cases can involve statutory language without free exercise issues.[858] In *Ramona Convent of the Holy Names v. City of Alhambra*,[859] the city had no obligation under the free exercise clause to rezone a portion of the convent's property so that the convent could lease the property and acquire funds to repair its school, which was damaged by an earthquake. "The City has no First Amendment obligation to rezone a portion of Ramona's property inorder to ensure Ramona's solvency."[860] However, in *Alpine Christian Fellowship v. Pitkin County*,[861] a

---

[852] Sileven v. Tesch, 326 N.W.2d 850 (Neb. 1982). *See also* State *ex rel.* Kandt v. North Platte Baptist Church, 365 N.W.2d 813 (Neb. 1985) (both church and pastor found guilty of contempt for refusal to cease operating a nonaccredited parochial school).

[853] 351 N.E.2d 750 (Ohio 1976).

[854] 294 N.W.2d 883 (N.D. 1980).

[855] 589 S.W.2d 877 (Ky. 1979).

[856] 504 N.E.2d 592 (Mass. 1987).

[857] *Id.* at 597.

[858] *See* Bradley v. City of Manchester, 682 A.2d 1194 (N.H. 1996) (local ordinance permitting religious schools attached to churches to expand took precedence over provision for special use permit, and, therefore, church did not need to meet notice requirements for such a permit).

[859] 26 Cal. Rptr. 140 (Cal. Ct. App. 1993).

[860] *Id.* at 148.

[861] 870 F. Supp. 991 (D. Colo. 1994).

federal district court in Colorado granted injunctive relief to a church prohibiting the county from interfering with the church's operation of a school on its premises. In rejecting the county's denial of a special use permit to operate a school in a existing church building, the court found a violation of free exercise on the grounds that "religious education is an integral part of the religious beliefs of the church's membership."[862] The court observed that "the restriction on the educational use of the building is not different, in principle, from a govern-mental restriction on the religious ceremonial practices in the church."[863]

Government and Fundamental Public Policy

Ever since the United States Supreme Court came forth with the concept of a fundamental or established public policy in *Bob Jones University v. United States*,[864] the definition of what is meant by such a policy has been elusive. Part of the elusiveness is determining how a fundamental or established public policy overlaps with the concept of a compelling interest. One way to view the overlay of the two concepts may be that a fundamental or established public policy will always be a compelling interest, but all compelling interests will not necessarily rise to the level of a fundamental public policy.

In interpreting the free exercise or establishment clauses, courts frequently rule against a religious claimant without creating a fundamental or established public policy. Thus, courts can overrule religious claimants to protect government interests in a wide range of areas without needing to invoke or create a fundamental or established public policy.[865] Nor do courts need

---

[862] *Id.* at 994.

[863] *Id.* at 995.

[864] 461 U.S. 574 (1983).

[865] *E.g.*, see Hernandez v. Commissioner, 490 U.S. 680 (1989) (disallowance of contribution as charitable deduction for auditing and training services to Church of Scientology not violative of free exercise because even a substantial burden is justified by broad public interest in maintaining a sound tax system); Lyng v. Northwest Indian Cemetery Protective Ass'n, 485 U.S. 439 (1988) (Indian objection to road building on government land for traditional Indian religious practices cannot prevail against government use of its own land); Bowen v. Roy, 476 U.S. 693, 707-708 (1986) (state termination of AFDC payments and food stamps on behalf of child for whom parents would not, on religious grounds, secure a social security number upheld as "reasonable means of promoting a legitimate public interest"); Goldman v. Weinberger, 475 U.S. 503 (1986) (military rules prohibiting headgear indoors not viola-

to raise the issue of fundamental public policy when ruling against religious educational institutions in matters of contract interpretation[866] or in application of statutes to religious organizations where legislative intent indicates that the organizations were to be covered.[867] The term "fundamental or established public policy" seems best reserved to indicate a government interest for which no exceptions can be permitted. *Bob Jones University* has become the paradigm for such an interest in eradicating race discrimination, but the important question is whether any other interest enjoys fundamental or established public policy status.

In *Bob Jones University*,[868] the Supreme Court upheld the IRS's revocation of the University's tax exempt status due to University rules prohibiting interracial dating and marriage. In so ruling, the Court identified a long list of court decisions, executive orders, and legislative acts prohibiting racial discrimination,[869] quantitatively amounting to what the Court referred to as a "fundamental public policy."[870] Although the Court identified its interest as "eradicating racial discrimination in education,"[871] a better statement of the government's interest would seem to be elimination of all legal support for racial discrimination, since Bob Jones University continues to operate with its rules and without tax exempt status. To date, no other

---

tive of free exercise as applied to yarmulke); United States v. Lee, 455 U.S. 252 (1982) (Amish employer's free exercise objection to payment of social security tax for work done by Amish employees on the ground that religion prohibits acceptance of government social payments offset by government interest in soundness of social security system).

866 *E.g., see* Welter v. Seton Hall Univ., 608 A.2d 206 (N.J. 1992) (jury award of $45,000 on behalf of two nuns against university upheld as result of contract termination, despite university's free exercise claim, where contracts had none of Canon Law or religious requirements alleged by university to have been the reasons for termination).

867 *E.g., see* Soriano v. Xavier Univ., 687 F. Supp. 1188 (S.D. Ohio 1988) (ADEA applicable to Jesuit university over free exercise and entanglement claims because no evidence in statute that Congress intended to exclude religious educational institutions); DeMarco v. Holy Cross High Sch., 4 F.3d 166 (2d Cir. 1993) (ADEA applicable to religious high school because legislative intent was to make statute applicable on same basis as Title VII).

868 461 U.S. 574 (1983) This case was actually a joinder of two separate cases from the Fourth U.S. Court of Appeals involving Bob Jones University and Goldsboro Christian Schools. Bob Jones University is a four-year, co-educational, fundamentalist religious institution that has also an elementary and secondary school on its campus. Goldsboro Christian Schools operates elementary and secondary schools. Bob Jones University admitted blacks but barred interracial dating or marriage; Goldsboro refused to admit blacks. Both schools claimed biblical reasons for their discriminatory practices. Since the Supreme Court decision, Goldsboro has dropped its discriminatory policy.

869 For the list, *see Id.* at 594.

870 *Id.* at 596, n. 21.

871 *Id.* at 604.

government interest has presented the same pervasive legal effort to address a form of discrimination, but post-*Bob Jones University* courts have flirted with the suggestion that elimination of discrimination on the basis of gender and sexual orientation might be candidates for fundamental public policy status.

In *Dayton Christian Schools v. Ohio Civil Rights Commission*,[872] a conflicting series of federal court decisions[873] left unclear whether the schools' religion-based policy requiring nonrenewal of a pregnant teacher's contract, because mothers were expected to stay at home with their preschool children, violated the state's Equal Employment Opportunity statute. Since the Ohio statute contained no religious exemption, the issue became whether an exemption was required by the free exercise and/or establishment clauses. Eventually, after remand by the Supreme Court to the Ohio Civil Rights Commission, the teacher-plaintiff withdrew her complaint and the charge of discrimination was dismissed for want of prosecution.[874] However, the district court decision, although vacated by the Supreme Court, nonetheless offers insight into how a fundamental public policy might be structured:

> The age and concomitant impressionability of the children attending [Dayton Christian Schools] probably render them more vulnerable to the influence of their environment than might be older students attending college. Exposure to an educational atmosphere wherein any form of unlawful discrimination is practiced would have a substantial impact on the values these children eventually carry out into the world when they leave school. Furthermore, the cumulative impact on the state's goal of ending discrimination could be significant if comparable religiously oriented schools and places of business likewise sought and

---

[872] 578 F. Supp. 1004 (S.D. Ohio 1094), *rev'd* 766 F.2d 932 (6th Cir. 1985), *remanded to state commission* 477 U.S. 619 (1986).

[873] The district court found for plaintiff-nonrenewed pregnant teacher on the basis of the state's interest in eradicating gender discrimination and the court of appeals for the school because the state's intrusion into the religious practices of the school violated both the free exercise and establishment clauses. The Supreme Court invoked the abstention doctrine and declared that the district court should not have assumed jurisdiction while the Ohio Civil Rights Commission was investigating the alleged discriminatory contract nonrenewal.

[874] Remarks by Dr. Clause E. Schindler, Superintendent of Dayton Christian Schools (October, 1986.)

> were to receive exemptions from the prohibitions in [the Ohio statute].[875]

More recently, a federal district court determined in *Vigars v. Valley Christian Center of Dublin, California*[876] that dismissal of a teacher for out-of-wedlock pregnancy was not permitted under Title VII, although the school would have a First Amendment protected right to discharge the teacher for adultery. Because this case was remanded for trial regarding the reason for discharge, the court did not have to address the issue of a fundamental policy, but the court's discussion of the school's claims for exemption under Title VII's religious exemptions make interesting reading:

> That this case could involve sex discrimination is made even more clear when one realizes that *only* women can *ever* be fired for being pregnant without benefit of marriage. Thus, women would be subject to something that men would not be, and that is sex discrimination, regardless of the justification put forth for the reason for the disparity. The fact that [the school's] dislike of pregnancy outside of marriage stems from a religious belief may be relevant to the Court's *First Amendment* analysis, but it does not automatically exempt the termination decision from Title VII scrutiny.[877]

Cases such as *Dayton Christian Schools* and *Vigars* need to be read against the backdrop of *United States v. Commonwealth of Virginia*,[878] where the Supreme Court addressed the Virginia Military Institute's (VMI) exclusion of women. Although the Court struck down VMI's exclusion policy, using an intermediate equal protection test of "exceedingly persuasive justification,"[879] the Court stopped short of equating gender-based discrimination with race discrimination. However, the Court iterated that any classification based on gender under equal protection must serve "important governmental objectives and the discriminatory means employed [must be] substantially related to the achievement of those goals."[880] The VMI case has no direct

875 *Dayton Christian*, 578 F. Supp. at 1036.
876 805 F. Supp. 802 (N.D. Cal. 1992).
877 *Id.* at 808 (emphasis in original).
878 518 U.S. 515 (1996).
879 *Id.* at 534.
880 *Id.* at 533.

application to nonpublic schools as long as they are not engaged in state action, but the case can be read as suggesting judicial reluctance to expand the concept of fundamental public policy to areas other than race.

As tantalizing as some cases may seem to be in suggesting a fundamental public policy for gender discrimination, courts have not hesitated to provide First Amendment protection when employment decisions have involved ministerial functions.[881] Apart from cases involving religious ministers, employment decisions of religious educational institutions are likely to come under close judicial scrutiny, but courts appear prepared to protect religious beliefs as long as they apply equally to both sexes.[882]

The same kind of judicial scrutiny suggested above for gender discrimination has also been reflected in the area of sexual orientation[883] in *Gay Rights Coalition v. Georgetown University*.[884] In this case, student gay/lesbian groups brought suit against a Jesuit University under a District of Columbia ordinance prohibiting discrimination in the use of or access to facilities and services based wholly or partially on the basis of sexual orientation.[885] Despite the University's religious belief opposing homosexuality, the federal appeals court determined that providing facilities and services to gay/lesbian students would not require the University to change its beliefs,[886] but would meet the District of Columbia's interest in "the eradication of sexual orientation discrimination."[887] Citing to both *Bob Jones*

---

881 *E.g., see* Maguire v. Marquette Univ., 627 F. Supp. 1499, 1503 (E.D. Wis. 1986) (court could not inquire into hiring practices of Jesuit university as to whether female applicant's views on abortion were consistent with the university because "such an inquiry would require the university to immerse itself not only into the procedures and hiring practices of the theology department of a Catholic University but, further, into definitions of what it is to be a Catholic"). *See generally*, Rayburn v. General Conference of Seventh-Day Adventists, 772 F.2d 1164, 1168 (4th Cir. 1985) (sex discrimination charge in failure to hire female pastors barred by Title VII and free exercise clause because "the job of associate in pastoral care is so significant in the expression and realization of Seventh-Day Adventist beliefs.")

882 *See* Boyd v. Harding Acad. of Memphis, Inc., 88 F.3d 410 (6th Cir. 1996) (discharge of out-of-wedlock pregnant teacher upheld where school had enforced its religious belief against extramarital sex against both males and females).

883 For public sector cases, see Gay and Lesbian Students Ass'n v. Gohn, 850 F.2d 361 (8th Cir. 1988); Gay and Lesbian Student Servs. v. Texas A & M Univ., 737 F.2d 1317 (5th Cir. 1984) (recognition of gay/lesbian groups on public campuses required).

884 536 A.2d 1 (D.C. Cir. 1987).

885 Ordinance is cited at *Id.* at 4, n.1.

886 *Id.* at 25.

887 *Id.* at 33.

University and *Roberts v. United States Jaycees*[888] as support for the principle that "government has a compelling interest in the eradication of other forms of discrimination,"[889] the appeals court concluded that "discrimination based on sexual orientation is a grave evil that damages society as well as its immediate victims."[890]

The emergence of sexual orientation issues in the political arena suggests that even if homosexuality, like gender, does not rise to the level of a fundamental public policy, nonpublic educational institutions with religious beliefs regarding homosexual conduct may reasonably expect pressure to accommodate those who engage in such conduct.[891] *Evans v. Romer*[892] is an example of the litigation flowing from political decisions. In *Evans*, the Supreme Court of Colorado struck down a voter-initiated state constitutional amendment that provided that homosexual, lesbian, or bisexual orientation could not act as the basis for protected class status. In permanently enjoining enforcement of the amendment, the court held that it was not narrowly tailored to meet any compelling governmental interest.

Religious Belief and Practice

The distinction between faith and practice is never an easy one to make. Over a century ago in *United States v. Reynolds*,[893] the Supreme Court, in addressing the authority of government to deal with religions, recognized a distinction between religious belief and religious practice by declaring that government could regulate the latter, but not the former. The notion, however, that government cannot interfere with religious beliefs but can regulate and/or punish religious practice is really a false dichotomy. To suggest that the government has conferred some benefit by not probing into persons' minds to change their beliefs, but only seeks to affect how one carries out one's beliefs, is the

---

[888] 468 U.S. 609 (1984) (nonadmission of women as full members Jaycees violated Minnesota's public accommodation statute).

[889] *Georgetown University*, 536 A.2d at 38

[890] *Id.*

[891] *See*, e.g., Legal Legislative Update 9, Number 4 (ACSI, Summer 1999) (U.S. Department of Agriculture nondiscrimination inclusion of sexual orientation as a basis for participating in school lunch program was deleted, but only after active investigation by ACSI revealing that no federal statute or regulation required the inclusion and after active intercession by members of Congress).

[892] 882 P.2d 1335 (Colo. 1994).

[893] 98 U.S. 145 (1879) (Court upheld penalty of Mormon practice of polygamy).

archetypal strawman argument. By stating government's role in the context of a dichotomy—belief and practice—one is left with the illusory conclusion that government is not being unreasonable by affecting only one side of the equation.

What makes religion unique among protected rights is that the definition of the importance of a religious belief will always be subjective. The centrality and criticality of religious beliefs are not susceptible to an objective test. For example, despite the *Georgetown University* appeals court assertion that "nothing can penetrate the constitutional shield protecting against official coercion to remove a religious belief or to endorse a principle opposed to that belief,"[894] there is no assurance that recognition of the student groups would not eventually lead to the silencing of the expression of religious beliefs. For example, could Georgetown University, after the court's decision, openly preach and teach its opposition to homosexuality? Could the university include its belief on homosexuality as part of its doctrinal statement required to be signed by all faculty members? If so, could a faculty member be discharged for espousing views contrary to the doctrinal statement?[895] Similarly, in the *Bob Jones University* case, even assuming that the university had eliminated its written policies against interracial dating and marriage, could it have required all students to attend chapel services where this conduct was presented as sinful, resulting in some measure of spiritual judgment?

In *Bob Jones University*, the Court relied on a long list of judicial, legislative, and administrative pronouncements to support its established public policy, which comes dangerously close to declaring that the manner in which persons practice their religious beliefs is subject to democratic processes. When the government uses the changing views of society to define its regulatory power over religion, no religion can feel safe from the reach of government.

In *Georgetown University,* one finds little comfort regarding the authorities cited by the court to support the inviolability of a person's beliefs.[896] The citations are inapposite either because

---

[894] *Id.* at 25.

[895] *Cf.* National Gay Task Force v. Board of Educ. of City of Oklahoma City, 729 F.2d 1270 (10th Cir. 1984), *aff'd per curiam* 470 U.S. 903 (1985) (portion of state statute providing for punishment for mere advocacy of homosexual activities was unconstitutionally broad).

[896] 536 A.2d at 22-23.

they deal with the government's denial of a benefit based on belief[897] or because the authority, if taken at face value, would seem to contradict the conclusions in *Bob Jones University* and *Georgetown University.*[898]

What courts appear to overlook is that a statement of belief is of little effect if the religious organization cannot enforce those beliefs among those within the organization.[899] The enforcement function which a religious organization must have to protect the verity and purity of its belief system is the very function undercut by government policies mandating uniformity of practice (or, at the very least, penalizing the refusal to conform to a uniform practice). To penalize a religious organization's practice of its belief system, however much a court may disagree with it, is to threaten the very purpose and vitality of that organization. The balance between religious belief and practice is fragile, and, unless courts are vigilant, those with the most distinctive and different religious beliefs can find those beliefs subjected to a reasonableness test that offers little more protection than the very minimal constitutional rights of association available to any voluntary organization.[900] When militancy of religious beliefs are reduced to an egalitarian common denominator, those who believe the most will have to accommodate themselves to those who believe the least.

---

897 *E.g.*, West Virginia State Bd. of Educ. v. Barnette, 319 U.S. 624 (1943) (expulsion of Jehovah's Witnesses for refusal to salute flag); Wisconsin v. Yoder 406 U.S. 205 (1972) (truancy charges against Amish parents for refusal to send children past eighth grade); Wooley v. Maynard, 430 U.S. 705 (1977) (state refusal to issue license plate without words, "Live Free or Die").

898 *E.g.*, Sherbert v. Verner, 374 U.S. 398, 403 (1963) ("The door of the First Amendment stands tightly closed against any government regulation of religious *beliefs* as such ... Government may neither compel affirmance of a repugnant belief ... nor penalize or discriminate against individuals or groups because they hold views abhorrent to the authorities") (emphasis in original).

899 *See* L. Buzzard and T. Brandon, Jr. Church Discipline and the Courts (1986) where churches have been increasingly subjected to litigation as a result of trying to enforce their belief systems.

900 For a discussion of the rights of association apart from any religious beliefs, see *Roberts*, 468 U.S. at 618-23 (in holding that Jaycees' refusal to admit women to full membership violated state public accommodation statute, the Court distinguished among different kinds of associations in terms of the degree of constitutional protection).

Chapter V

FEDERAL ANTI-DISCRIMINATION LEGISLATION

Introduction

Federal anti-discrimination legislation can basically be divided into three categories: that which imposes requirements only if the nonpublic school receives federal assistance; that which applies simply because the nonpublic school is an employer; and that which provides targeted public funds which may be available to private or parochial school students. The major anti-discrimination statutes in the first category are the Rehabilitation Act of 1973, as amended in 1974,[901] Titles VI[902] and IX[903] of the Civil Rights Act, and the Age Discrimination Act of 1975.[904] The second category includes Title VII[905] of the Civil Rights Act, the Age Discrimination in Employment Act of 1967,[906] the Equal Pay Act of 1963,[907] the Americans With Disabilities Act of 1990,[908] and the Family and Medical Leave Act.[909] The third category is best represented by the Individuals with Disabilities Education Act (IDEA, formerly EHA),[910]

---

901 20 U.S.C. § 794.
902 42 U.S.C. § 2000d.
903 20 U.S.C. § 1681-86.
904 42 U.S.C. § 6101.
905 42 U.S.C. § 2000e.
906 29 U.S.C. § 621.34.
907 29 U.S.C. § 206.
908 29 U.S.C. § 706; 42 U.S.C. §§ 12101 *et seq.*
909 29 U.S.C. §§ 2601-2654.
910 The Individuals with Disabilities Education Act (IDEA), 20 U.S.C. § 602 applies only to recipients of federal assistance operating a public elementary or secondary education program. However, IDEA provides benefits to all children in a public school district, including those enrolled in private or parochial schools.

although other state[911] and federal[912] acts may also provide assistance or services in nonpublic schools. State statutes are not discussed in this section, but those making employment decisions in nonpublic schools need to be aware that state non-discrimination laws may be applicable to factual patterns which could also arise at the federal level[913] as well as apply to areas of discrimination not covered at the federal level.[914]

Under the Civil Rights Restoration Act of 1987,[915] nondiscrimination statutes based on reception of federal assistance apply if a nonpublic school receives federal assistance in any part of the institution. Thus, for example, participation in Title IV student financial aid programs opens an entire college or university to scrutiny. Although federal regulations state that nonpublic elementary and secondary schools do not become recipients of federal assistance solely by nature of the fact that their students participate in federally funded programs,[916] at least one court has held that a religious school that received Title I and National Lunch and Breakfast Programs funds was subject to Section 504.[917]

Statutes Based on Federal Assistance

Rehabilitation Act of 1973 (Section 504)

Section 504 of the Rehabilitation Act, as amended, provides that:

---

[911] *See* Witters v. Washington Dep't of Servs. for the Blind, 474 U.S. 481 (1986) (Court upheld, against establishment clause challenge, state provision of assistance to blind student in religious college; however, on remand, the state supreme court invalidated assistance under state constitution.) *See* Witters v. Dep't of Services for the Blind, 771 P.2d 1119 (Wash. 1989).

[912] *See* Agostini v. Felton, 521 U.S. 203 (1997) (Title I remedial services under the Elementary and Secondary Act of 1965 can be provided on site at religious schools without violating the establishment clause).

[913] *E.g., see* University of Maryland at Baltimore v. Boyd, 612 A.2d 305 (Md. Ct. App. 1992) (university police officer's skin condition, pseudofolliculitis barbae (PFB), was a handicap under state human relations statute with severely scarred face creating externally visible disfigurement, which unless the officer wore a beard impaired his ability to socialize. In part because the skin condition affected primarily Afro-American males, as well as meeting definition of disability, university's policy of having officers be clean shaven was outweighed by policy's discriminatory impact).

[914] *See* River Bend Community Unit Sch. Dist. v. Human Rights Comm'n,597 N.E.2d 842 (Ill. App. Ct. 1992) (state statute prohibited discrimination on basis of marital status); Gay Rights Coalition v. Georgetown Univ., 536 A.2d 1 (D.C. App. 1987) (district ordinance prohibiting discrimination in providing services on basis of sexual orientation applied to religious university).

[915] 20 U.S.C. § 1687.

[916] 42 C.F.R. § 84.3(f) and commentary at 45 C.F.R., Part A, Appendix A, Subpart A.

[917] Hunt v. St. Peter Sch., 963 F. Supp. 843 (W.D. Mo. 1997).

> no otherwise qualified individual ... shall, solely by reason of his handicap, be excluded from the participation in, be denied the benefits of, or be subjected to discrimination under any program or activity receiving federal financial assistance.[917]

The meaning of the word "solely" in the statute is somewhat ambiguous as to whether a mixed motive by a decision-maker (nondiscriminatory reason in addition to a reason alleged to be based on disability) would constitute a violation of Section 504.[918]

Section 504 protects a person with a handicap (hereafter referred to as "disability"), which is a "person who (i) has a physical or mental impairment which substantially limits one or more of such person's major life activities, (ii) has a record of such an impairment, (iii) is regarded as having such an impairment."[919] Included among the disabilities covered by the Act are "any physiological disorder or condition, cosmetic disfigurement or anatomical loss" as well as "any mental or psychological disorder."[920] Also included within the Act's protection are "alcoholism and drug abusers who are reformed or rehabilitated" but not "individuals whose current use of alcohol or drugs prevents them from performing their job or who are a direct threat to the safety of persons or property ...."[921]

Prior to passage of the Americans With Disabilities Act (ADA), Section 504 was the only remedy available to nonpublic students and employees with disabilities since IDEA applies only to public elementary and secondary schools.[922] With the passage of Title I of ADA, which prohibits discrimination in employment, Section 504 has become largely a remedy for students. To the extent, though, that Section 504 can be used for employment

---

917 20 U.S.C. § 794

918 *See* Wood v. President and Trustees of Spring Hill College of City of Mobile, 978 F.2d 1214 (11th Cir. 1992) (without resolving the issue of mixed motive, the court suggests that "solely" cannot be changed to mean "a significant factor").

919 29 U.S.C. § 706(8)(B). *See* Byrne v. Board of Educ., School of West Allis-West Milwaukee, 979 F.2d 560 (7th Cir. 1992) (single hospital stay for allergy tests did not create "record of impairment" for purpose of bringing person within statute).

920 34 C.F.R. § 104.3(j).

921 34 C.F.R. § 104.3 (l)(A) and (B).

922 In Smith v. Robinson, 468 U.S. 992 (1984), the U.S. Supreme Court determined in public schools that EHA [IDEA] is an exclusive remedy as compared to Section 504. But to the extent that IDEA rights or remedies are inadequate, (or unavailable as in nonpublic schools) section 504 is apparently still available. *See* New York State Ass'n for Retarded Children v. Carey, 612 F.2d 644 (2d Cir. 1979); Community H.S. Dist. v. Denz, 463 N.E.2d 998 (Ill. 1984). The Supreme Court in *Smith* had also ruled that attorney fees were not available under EHA [IDEA] but the Handicapped Children's Protection Act (HCPA) was enacted as an amendment to EHA to overrule *Smith*. 20 U.S.C. §§ 1415(e)(4)(B)-(F).

disability discrimination, the overwhelming weight of authority suggests that only employers, not individuals, can be sued.[923]

For nonpublic educational institutions receiving federal financial assistance, exclusion of students from programs or discipline of students can be significantly affected. However, as in employment cases, an academic institution is not responsible for accommodation of a disability under Section 504 unless it either knew or had reason to know that a student had a disability.[924] Under Section 504 (or ADA), which requires accommodation of disabilities, no court to date has adopted the standard of IDEA that a school must continue to provide educational services to expelled students where the misconduct is a manifestation of their disability.[925]

For a student with disabilities, educational institutions must make reasonable accommodations to academic requirements. However, reasonable accommodation will not be an issue if the student has not made a demand for such accommodation.[926]

While Section 504 prohibits discrimination on the basis of disability, it does not require affirmative obligations.[927] Thus, an "otherwise qualified" person cannot be excluded from benefits solely by reasons of his or her disability, but while a school is not required to devote extra resources to bring those with disabilities up to normal,[928] it may have to provide services to enable students to participate in educational programs. In *Barnes v. Converse College*,[929] the college was required to furnish an interpreter at the school's expense after a hearing impaired teacher was admitted as a student to its summer program. Given

---

[923] *See* Coddington v. Adelphi Univ., 45 F. Supp.2d 211 (E.D. N.Y. 1999) and cases cited therein.

[924] *See* Gill v. Franklin Pierce Law Ctr., 899 F. Supp. 850 (D. N.H. 1995) (academic dismissal); Bercovitch v. Baldwin Sch., Inc., 133 F.3d 141 (1st Cir. 1998) (disciplinary misconduct).

[925] *See* S-1 v. Turlington, 635 F.2d 342 (5th Cir. 1981); Kaelin v. Grubbs, 682 F.2d 595 (6th Cir. 1982) (expulsion constituted a change of placement under IDEA). For the IDEA standard *see* Honig v. Doe, 108 S. Ct. 592 (1988) (student whose disruptive behavior included stealing, extorting money from fellow students and making sexual comments to female classmates could not be expelled where conduct was manifestation of disability). Under the 1997 amendments, the IDEA permits forty-five day expulsion, but requires manifestation hearing and, even if removal from school is allowable, school district is responsible for providing educational services to student during time of expulsion. See 34 C.F.R. §§ 300.519-300.529.

[926] *See* Wood v. President and Trustees of Spring Hill College of City of Mobile, 978 F.2d 1214 (11th Cir. 1992).

[927] *See* Lyons v. Smith, 829 F. Supp. 414 (D. D.C. 1993) (hearing officer may award special education to an "otherwise qualified handicapped" child under Section 504, but only if declining to do so would be discriminatory).

[928] *See* Parks v. Pavkovic, 753 F.2d 1397, 1409 (7th Cir. 1985).

[929] 436 F. Supp. 635 (D. S.C. 1977).

the large number of students entering colleges and universities who have had Section 504 accommodation plans in K-12 schools, postsecondary institutions will be pressed to provide the same level of services.

Whether academic program requirements can be enforced where they deny access to persons with disabilities has become an area of litigation. The leading case continues to be *Southeastern Community College v. Davis*,[930] where the United States Supreme Court upheld the denial of admission of a student with a serious hearing disability into a nursing program and ruled that an otherwise qualified applicant is one who can meet the requirements of the job represented by the training in spite of her disability. The regulations reinforce this principle by not requiring schools to modify academic programs where academic requirements "are essential to the program of instruction being pursued ... or to any directly related licensing requirement ...."[931]

Case law reinforces judicial deference to academic requirements. In *GuckenBerger v. Boston University*,[932] a federal district court upheld a faculty decision not to permit course substitutions for foreign language requirements over the objections of students with learning disabilities. The court observed that as long as the faculty had considered alternative means of accommodating the students it would not override the professional judgment of the faculty. An across-the-board faculty decision not to permit course substitutions for foreign languages was rationally justifiable even if a majority of other universities permitted such substitutions.

Courts have also supported individualized decisions by educational institutions that have resulted in denial of services for persons with disabilities. In *Doe v. New York University*,[933]

---

[930] 442 U.S. 397 (1979).

[931] 34 C.F.R. § 104.12. *See* Wynne v. Tufts Univ. Sch. of Med., 976 F.2d 791 (1st. Cir. 1992), (medical school that had weighed request of student with cognitive deficits to have alternative form of multiple choice test for biochemistry exam did not have to provide alternative exam where any alternative would result in substantial program alterations, result in lowering academic standards, and devalue school's end product). See also, Murphy v. Franklin Pierce Law Ctr., 882 F. Supp. 1176 (D. N.H. 1994) (a law student, dismissed for poor academic performance where she had received all of the accommodations requested by her physician, was not "otherwise qualified.")

[932] 8 F. Supp.2d 82 (D. Mass. 1998).

[933] 666 F.2d 761 (2d Cir. 1981). *See also* Doherty v. Southern College of Optometry, 659 F. Supp. 662 (W.D. Tenn. 1987) (refusal of college to waive clinical proficiency requirements for student with visual and neurological condition held reasonable).

the university did not have to grant readmission to a woman with a long history of recurring borderline disorders. Two students, each with vision in only one eye, could be denied participation in contact sports based upon medical testimony that they were not "otherwise qualified."[934]

Schools receiving federal assistance are not prohibited from operating separate, comparable classes for those with disabilities but cannot require the disabled to attend those classes unless education in a traditional setting cannot be accomplished satisfactorily.[935] Institutions are not required to make each facility available to the disabled as long as "the program or activity, when viewed in its entirety, is readily accessible to persons with disabilities."[936]

Nonpublic elementary and secondary schools are prohibited from charging more for providing an appropriate education to the disabled "except to the extent that any additional charge is justified by a substantial increase in cost to the recipient."[937] Services that are considered to increase costs are other than supplementary aids and services provided in the regular school environment.[938]

The Rehabilitation Act prohibits discrimination at all phases of employment including recruiting, screening, hiring, classification, working conditions, promotions, and discharge.[939] Employers are required to make "reasonable accommodation"[940] to the disability unless the accommodation would constitute an "undue hardship."[941] Although "reasonable accommodation" does not require employers to undertake affirmative action, the line of distinction can be blurred and uncertain.[942]

---

[934] Kampmeir v. Nyquist, 553 F.2d 296 (2d Cir. 1977).

[935] 34 C.F.R. § 104.4 (b) (3).

[936] 34 C.F.R. § 104.22 (a).

[937] 34 C.F.R. § 104.39 (b).

[938] 34 C.F.R. § 104.34a.

[939] 34 C.F.R. § 22 104.11(b).

[940] Reasonable accommodation may require such actions as acquiring or modifying equipment, making necessary facilities accessible or usable (e.g., use of ramps or adjusting height of work areas), restructuring work schedules or providing readers or interpreters. 34 C.F.R. § 104.12 (b).

[941] Undue hardship requires evaluation of a number of factors such as nature and cost of accommodation, size of budget, size of the program, number of employees, and type of facilities and operation. 34 C.F.R. § 104.12 (c). *See* Wood v. Omaha Sch. Dist., 985 D.2d 437 (8th Cir. 1993) (burden is on employer to prove that accommodation is not reasonable).

[942] *Compare* Southeastern Community College v. Davis, 442 U.S. 397 (1979) (provision of lip-reader not required by Section 504) *with* Strathie v. Department of Transp., 716 F.2d 227 (3d Cir. 1983) (hearing aid may have to be provided for applicant for school bus driver's license).

Section 504 treats as suspect any presumptive or automatic disqualification of any particular class of disability.[943] What is required is some evidence that the disability cannot be accommodated to perform the job function.[944] In *Cain v. Archdiocese of Kansas City*,[945] a parochial school teacher had a private cause of action under Section 504 when her contract was terminated prior to the beginning of the school year because of mild epilepsy which the teacher said could be easily controlled by Dilantin. In *Pushkin v. Regents of the University of Colorado*,[946] a medical doctor with multiple sclerosis had been wrongly denied admission to the university's psychiatric residency program. A teacher discharged from her teaching job because she had failed to meet the minimum state-imposed NTE score for a teaching license was entitled to a jury trial as to whether the failure of the state to make adequate accommodations for her disability had a disparate discriminatory impact.[947]

In light of the prior discussion, a student or employee's *prima facie* case under Section 504 requires a showing that he or she is an otherwise qualified person apart from the handicap as well as an offering of proof from which it can be inferred that the rejection was based solely on handicap. The institution must then present evidence that the student or employee was not an otherwise qualified person—that is, someone qualified in spite of the handicap. The employee or student then must present evidence that the institution's reasons are based on misconceptions or are pretextual. Damages are available to a plaintiff for both intentional[948] or disparate[949] discrimination.

---

943 *See* Gurmakin v. Constanzo, 556 F.2d 184 (3d Cir. 1977) (court disapproval of presumptive disqualification of blind person from consideration as a teacher); Jackson v. State, 544 A.2d291 (Me. 1988) (Court overturned automatic revocation of bus driver's license because he had diabetes).

944 *See* Upshur v. Love, 474 F. Supp. 332 (N.D. Cal. 1979) (court upheld refusal to hire blind administrator who lacked qualifications to supervise others).

945 508 F. Supp. 1021 (D. Kan. 1981).

946 658 F.2d 1372 (10th Cir. 1981)

947 Pandazides v. Virginia Bd. of Educ., 13 F.3d 823 (4th Cir. 1994).

948 *See* Wood v. President and Trustees of Spring Hill College of City of Mobile, 978 F.2d 1214 (11th Cir. 1992) (damages not available to schizophrenic student who withdrew from college where student was not able to prove intentional discrimination).

949 *See* Pandazides v. Virginia Bd. of Educ., 13 F.3d 823 (4th Cir. 1994).

Title VI

Title VI provides that,

> no person in the United States shall, on the ground of race, color or national origin, be excluded from participation in, be denied the benefits of, or be subjected to discrimination under any program or activity receiving Federal financial assistance.[950]

Title VI contains no exemption for religious practices and, indeed, after *Bob Jones University v. United States*,[951] it is clear that any form of racial discrimination, even if for religious reasons, will disqualify an institution from any form of government support. Federal financial assistance under Title VI includes any source of assistance, not just from the Department of Education.[952] Although the right of individuals to pursue a private cause of action under Title VI was confusing in the past,[953] the most recent case law suggests that a private cause of action has been accepted.[954] Title VI applies to national origin minority students. Although proof of discriminatory impact was all that was required in *Lau v. Nichols*,[955] the current interpretation appears to require a discriminatory purpose.[956]

Title VI has been most prominently featured recently in reverse discrimination cases. In *Hopwood v. State of Texas*,[957] nonminority applicants to the University of Texas law school challenged the school's affirmative action admission system. The school's argument that it had adopted a separate admissions process for black and Mexican-American applicants to comply with Title VI was rejected by the Fifth Circuit Court of Appeals, which struck down the process under the Equal Protection Clause

---

[950] 42 U.S.C. § 2000d. "Race, color, or national origin" does not include Appalachian and low income persons, Bronson v. Board of Educ., 550 F. Supp. 941 (D. Ohio 1982).

[951] 461 U.S. 574 (1983).

[952] Bob Jones Univ. v. Johnson, 396 F. Supp. 597 (D. S.C. 1974) (V.A. benefits).

[953] Private cause of action exists. Adams v. Bell, 711 F.2d 161 (D.C. Cir. 1983); Lyjan v. Franklin County Bd. of Educ., 766 F.2d 917 (6th Cir. 1985); University of California Regents v. Bakke, 438 U.S. 265 (1978). Private cause of action does not exist. Guardians Ass'n v. Civil Serv. Comm'n., 463 U.S. 582 (1983); Chowdburg v. Reading Hosp. and Med. Ctr., 677 F.2d 317 (3d Cir. 1982).

[954] Powell v. Ridge, 189 F.3d 387 (3d Cir. 1999).

[955] 414 U.S. 563 (1974) (Chinese students had claim under Title VI to require instruction that included the teaching of English).

[956] University of California Regents v. Bakke, 438 U.S. 265 (1978) (Title VI coextensive with equal protection); Washington v. Davis, 426 U.S. 229 (1976) (discriminatory purpose required for equal protection).

[957] 78 F.3d 932 (5th Cir. 1996), *cert denied*, 518 U.S. 1033 (1966), on remand, 999 F.Supp. 872 (W.D.Tex. 1998).

of the Fourteenth Amendment as serving no compelling state interest. However, on remand, the district court determined that even with a narrowly tailored admissions process the applicants would still not have been qualified for admission, but one of them was nonetheless entitled to $6,000 damages for mental anguish and all applicants were entitled to $761,000 attorneys' fees. In *Reynolds v. School District No. 1, Denver, Colorado*,[958] a white bilingual education teacher lost in her Title VI race discrimination claim because she had failed to prove that her employer had received federal funds for the primary objective of providing employment.

Title VI has also become a vehicle for challenging public school curriculum and conduct exposing students to racially charged language. In *Monteiro v. Tempe Union School District*,[959] the Ninth Circuit Court of Appeals held that black parents had a Title VI claim for a pattern of egregious racial harassment in school that included the use of a particularly offensive racial epithet by white students. However, the court denied the parents an injunction to prohibit the use of *Huckleberry Finn* and *A Rose for Emily*, both of which contained racial epithets, as part of the required freshman English reading assignment.

Title IX

Title IX provides that,

> no person in the United States shall, on the basis of sex, be denied the benefits of, or be subjected to discrimination under any education program or activity receiving Federal assistance.[960]

Title IX applies to "any public or private preschool, elementary, or secondary school, or any vocational, professional or higher education."[961]

A recipient of federal assistance includes schools that receive federal funds administered indirectly through states, suggesting that nonpublic schools might bring themselves within Title IX by participating in assistance (such as Title I remedial programs) that is administered by states but funded by the U.S. Department

[958] 69 F.3d 1523 (10th Cir. 1995).

[959] 158 F.3d 1022 (9th Cir. 1998).

[960] 20 U.S.C. §§ 1681-86.

[961] 20 U.S.C. § 1681(c).

of Education.[962] However, in *Buckley v. Archdiocese of Rockville Centre*,[963] a federal district court decided that a school psychologist paid by a public school district and working at a parochial school was not sufficient to invoke jurisdiction under Title IX in a damages action for alleged sexual harassment by parochial school employees. The court suggested that in order for Title IX to apply, some form of formal institutional affiliations or agreements would have to exist between a public school district and a nonpublic school.

Title IX exempts "an educational institution which is controlled by a religious organization if the application of this subsection would not be consistent with the tenets of such organization."[964] Title IX regulations provide that a religious organization must apply for the exemption, identifying which parts of the regulations conflict "with a specific tenet of the religious organization."[965] Whether a religious school would lose the benefit of the exemption if it had not applied for the exemption seems doubtful. At least one federal district court has suggested that a religious school need do nothing more than wait until sued and then raise the exemption.[966]

Beyond the issue of compliance with Title IX or its regulations, however, is the question of how religious tenets impact discipline of students or employees. In *Hall v. Lee College, Inc.*,[967] a religiously affiliated college's suspension of a female student for violating a school policy against engaging in premarital sex was not unlawful gender discrimination where the student had produced no evidence that a male student would not have been suspended under the same circumstances.

Title IX purports to bar sex discrimination in a broad range of services and activities.[968] However, the regulations do permit certain kinds of discrimination within schools such as separate but comparable toilet, locker room, and shower facilities,[969]

---

[962] 34 C.F.R. § 106.2(h).

[963] 992 F. Supp. 586 (E.D. N.Y. 1998).

[964] 20 U.S.C. § 1681(a)(3).

[965] 45 C.F.R. § 86.12 (b).

[966] Hall v. Lee College, Inc., 932 F. Supp. 1027 (E.D. Tenn. 1996).

[967] *Id.*

[968] 45 C.F.R. § 86.41 (among the areas where equal opportunity is required in athletics are equipment and supplies, game scheduling and practice time, travel and per diem allowances, coaching and academic tutor assignments, provision of housing, competitive and practice facilities and services, dining and medical services, and publicity); 45 C.F.R. § 86.21 (no discrimination in admissions to programs); 86.37 (no discrimination in financial assistance).

[969] 45 C.F.R. § 86.33.

separation by sex within physical education classes involving bodily contact sports,[970] and separation by sex in class sessions that deal exclusively with human sexuality.[971]

Early confusion as to whether Title IX permitted a private cause of action for damages by students[972] has been resolved in *Franklin v. Gwinnett County Public Schools*,[973] where a private cause of action was upheld by the Supreme Court. Courts, in interpreting Title IX, appear to follow Title VI and require proof of discriminatory intent in order to state a cause of action for damages[974] but permit a lesser standard of proof for disparate impact where plaintiffs are seeking an equitable remedy (such as reinstatement of athletic programs).[975]

Although Title IX permits a private cause of action for damages by students, it does not appear to do so for employees. In *Lakoski v. James*,[976] the Fifth Circuit Court of Appeals held that Title VII is the exclusive remedy for sex discrimination claims for damages by employees. In reversing a jury award of damages under Title IX to a faculty member denied tenure, the Fifth Circuit also held that an employee cannot use Section 1983 as a vehicle to pursue damages for sex discrimination under Title IX.

Gender discrimination under Title IX has become prominently associated with two issues: athletic programs and sexual harassment. Decisions by educational institutions to

---

[970] 45 C.F.R. § 86.34. The definition of a contact sport is unclear. *Compare* Morris v. Michigan State Bd. of Educ., 472 F.2d 1207 (6th Cir. 1973) (sex segregation in tennis upheld) *with* Brendon v. Minnesota State High Sch. League, 477 F.2d 1292 (8th Cir. 1973) (sex segregation in tennis, cross-country skiing and running rejected).

[971] 45 C.F.R. § 86.34(e).

[972] Cannon v. University of Chicago, 441 U.S. 677 (1979) (private remedy exists); Leake v. University of Cincinnati, 605 F.2d 255 (6th Cir. 1979) (no private cause of action).

[973] 503 U.S. 60 (1992).

[974] Hall v. Lee College, Inc., 932 F. Supp. 1027 (E.D. Tenn. 1996).

[975] Roberts v. Colorado State Univ. Bd. of Agric., 998 F.2d 824 (10th Cir. 1993), *cert. denied* 114 S.Ct. 580 (1993) (discriminatory intent not required equitable remedy of reinstatement of women's softball program ordered by court); Sharif v. New York State Educ. Dep't, 709 F. Supp. 345 (S.D. N.Y. 1989) (disparate impact rather than intentional discrimination was sufficient basis for injunction ordering state to cease using of SAT test as only criterion to determine eligibility for state scholarships). However, Title IX applies only to intentional violations and cannot be used where a violation appears to be grounded in negligence, Houston v. Mile High Adventist Academy, 846 F. Supp. 1449 (D. Colo. 1994)

[976] 66 F.3d 751 (5th Cir. 1995).

eliminate athletic teams[977] or to prohibit members of one sex from participating on the sports teams of the other sex have generated litigation.[978]

The leading case litigating the meaning of accommodation in athletic programs under Title IX has been *Cohen v. Brown University*.[979] Whether educational institutions subject to Title IX have adequately accommodated the athletic needs of all students will be reviewed by courts under one of three benchmarks.

(1) Whether intercollegiate level participation opportunities for male and female students are provided in numbers substantially proportionate to their respective enrollments; or

(2) Where the members of one sex have been and are underrepresented among intercollegiate athletes, whether the institution can show a history and continuing practice of program expansion which is demonstrably responsive to the developing interest and abilities of the members of that sex; or

(3) Where the members of one sex are under-represented among the intercollegiate athletes, and the institution cannot show a continuing practice of program expan-

---

977 Cohen v. Brown Univ., 991 F.2d 888 (1st Cir. 1993) (preliminary injunction ordering university to reinstate women gymnastic and volleyball teams to team status upheld; women were able to prove that disparity between gender composition of student body and its athletic program created an underrepresented gender and that the underrepresented gender had not been fully and effectively accommodated by the present program; Favia v. Indiana Univ. of Pa., 7 F.3d 332 (3d Cir. 1993) (preliminary injunction ordering reinstatement of women's field hockey and gymnastics would not be lifted even though university had replaced gymnastics with soccer in order to increase the proportion of female athletes). *See* Gonyo v. Drake Univ., 879 F. Supp. 1000 (S.D. Iowa 1995) (eliminating men's wrestling program not violation of Title IX because number of male athletes in athletic program was disproportionately high). *See also*, Roberts v. Colorado State Univ. Bd. of Agric., 998 F.2d 824 (10th Cir. 1993) (in discontinuance of women's fast pitch softball, plaintiffs had to produce evidence that termination of program was not only not substantially proportionate to relationship between female enrollment and athletic participation, but also that institution did not fully and effectively accommodate interests and abilities of women athletes).

978 *See* Williams v. School Dist. of Bethlehem, Pa., 998 F.2d 168 (3d Cir. 1993 (denial of male to participate on female hockey team may violate Title IX if field hockey is not a contact sport and if male athletic opportunities had been previously limited; in this university, female students were permitted to try out for all twenty-two high school athletic teams while male students were permitted to try out only for two).

979 101 F.3d 155 (1st Cir. 1996).

> sion such as that cited above, whether it can be demonstrated that the interests and abilities of the members of that sex have been fully and effectively accommodated by the present program.[980]

Cohen, which involved an effort by Brown University to demote two men's (golf and water polo) and two women's (volleyball and gymnastics) athletic sports from varsity to club status, resulted in a preliminary injunction ordering reinstatement of the two women's sports to varsity status. Most of the financial savings realized by the demotion in status came from the women's sports and the proportion of men to women in the university (fifty-two percent to forty-eight percent), both before and after the demotion, was substantially different from the proportion of men to women in varsity sports (63.3 percent to 36.7 percent). In a broad sense, *Cohen* stands for the principle that treating women's and men's teams equally in reducing teams can still violate Title IX if the two programs did not have parity in the beginning.

Other cases have resulted in similar results with courts utilizing their equity power to order changes in what educational institutions had proposed. In *Cook v. Colgate University*,[981] the university's refusal to grant varsity status to the women's ice hockey team was considered to be pretextual, and even though the university had legitimate financial concerns regarding the elevation in status of women's hockey, such concerns did not overcome its responsibility to satisfy the benchmarks under Title IX. In *Daniels v. School Board of Brevard County, Florida*,[982] a federal district court ordered the following changes to the girls' softball field to make it comparable to the boys' baseball field: construction of an electronic scoreboard and a batting cage; addition of comparable bleachers, signs, bathroom facilities for the players, and concession stand/press box/announcer's booth; and addition of lighting to permit night games.

Sexual harassment claims under Title IX have become a major source of litigation. In the wake of *Franklin v. Gwinnett County Public Schools*, Title IX has become a significant vehicle to address sexual harassment in schools against students by both

---

[980] 44 Fed. Reg. at 71,418. *See* Cohen v. Brown Univ., 991 F.2d 888, 897 (1st Cir. 1993).

[981] 802 F. Supp. 737 (N.D. N.Y. 1992), *vacated* 992 F.2d 17 (2d Cir. 1992).

[982] 985 F. Supp. 1458 (M.D. Fla. 1997).

employees and other students. The Supreme Court's decision in *Davis v. Monroe County Board of Education*[983] that school boards can be liable under Title IX for deliberate indifference to student-on-student sexual harassment will unquestionably increase school responsibility to respond to student complaints.

Whether Title IX can be pursued against individuals who perpetrate harassment, as well as their employers, is a matter of some disagreement among the courts. Since a cause of action under Title IX can be pursued only against recipients of federal assistance, the better position would seem to be that Title IX damage claims cannot be pursued against individual defendants.[984] Realistically, however, litigation has revolved around school liability for the acts of employees or students, since the individual perpetrators of harassment may be languishing in jail[985] and/or be judgment proof.[986]

Although a student may experience much the same harassment as an employee, the Supreme Court has made an important distinction between Title VII employee claims and Title IX student claims. While the Court held in *Faragher v. City of Boca Raton*[987] that an employer can be liable for the acts of employees based on agency principles, the Court held in *Davis v. Monroe County Board of Education* that a school district can be liable under Title IX only if it has been deliberately indifferent to student complaints of harassment. As the Court observed in *Davis*, the liability of a recipient of Title IX assistance is limited "to circumstances wherein the recipient exercises substantial control over both the harasser and the context in which the known harassment occurs."[988] The deliberately indifferent standard is less than the intentional discrimination one that an earlier federal district court had indicated was appropriate for peer-on-peer harassment.[989]

---

[983] 526 U.S. 629 (1999).

[984] *See* Niles v. Nelson, 72 F. Supp.2d 13 (N.D. N.Y. 1999); Morlock v. West Cent. Educ. Dist., 46 F. Supp.2d 892 (D. Minn. 1999); Buckley v. Archdiocese of Rockville Ctr., 992 F. Supp. 586 (E.D. N.Y. 1998); Smith v. Metropolitan Sch. Dist., 128 F.3d 1014 (7th Cir. 1997); Nelson v. Temple Univ., 920 F. Supp. 633 (E.D. Pa. 1996).

[985] *See* Kelli v. Galway Cent. Sch. Dist., 660 N.Y.S.2d 228 (N.Y. App.div. 1997).

[986] Presumably, this would be the situation with students where normally they would probably not have the resources to pay a judgment. However, an open question exists as to whether parents might be liable under state Parent Responsibility Acts for the intentional acts of their children. *See, e.g.*, Brooks v. St. Tammany Parish Sch. Bd., 510 So.2d 51 (La. Ct. App. 1987) where a school district, sued for the actions of two students in injuring a special education student, brought the parents of the two students in as third party defendants.

[987] 524 U.S. 775 (1998).

[988] *Davis*, 119 S.Ct. at 1673.

[989] *See* Doe v. Petaluma City Sch. Dist., 830 F. Supp. 1560 (N.D. Cal. 1993).

The quid pro quo and hostile environment distinctions that exist in Title VII employment cases carry over to Title IX but most Title IX litigation will involve hostile environment. Quid pro quo, as the term denotes, involves the exchange of sexual favors for some form of benefit or alternatively, the suffering of some economic loss as a result of refusing the sexual advances[990] and in the context of Title VII can be supported by one or more acts.[991] Although quid pro quo may be applicable to some student situations (such as exchange of sexual favors for grades or awarding a lower grade for refusal to accede to request for sex),[992] student sexual harassment by employees has fallen into the hostile environment category.

A hostile environment will depend on: whether the conduct was unwelcome; whether the conduct was severe or pervasive; and whether the complaining person, based on her or his own conduct, dress, and language, could reasonably have been offended by the harassing conduct. In *Patricia H. v. Berkeley Unified High School*,[993] a jury was left to decide whether a student had stated a claim of sexual harassment where a teacher who had sexually molested her was retained in the school district and where complaints and requests for assistance from the school district had gone unheeded. Whether students can recover against a school district or its administrators depends on how much school administrators knew or should have known about the harassment.[994] A school administrator who has investigated complaints about sexual harassment by meeting with a complainant and her parents as well as talking with other students and teachers about alleged misconduct will be entitled to qualified immunity.[995]

Claims for sexual harassment, whether pursued under Title IX or Section 1983 have not, thus far, been predicated on a special relationship between the harassed or molested student and the

---

[990] *See* Kariban v. Columbia Univ., 812 F. Supp. 413 (S.D. N.Y. 1993) (plaintiff failed to state quid pro quo charge where she had been promoted and her salary increased).

[991] *See* Comeau v. Board of Educ. of Ballston Spa, 554 N.Y.S.2d 359 (App. Div. 1990) (patting female employee on buttocks on almost daily basis warranted dismissal).

[992] *See* Kracunas v. Iowa College, 119 F.3d 80 (2d Cir. 1997) (a faculty member raised a student's final course grade after subjecting the student to sexually explicit comments in his office).

[993] 830 F. Supp. 1288 (N.D. Cal. 1993).

[994] *See* Stoneking v. Bradford Area Sch. Dist., 856 F.2d 594 (3rd Cir. 1988) (school officials who had discouraged female student from complaining about sexual conduct of band director not entitled to qualified immunity).

[995] Seneway v. Canon McMillan Sch. Dist., 969 F. Supp. 325 (W.D. Pa. 1997).

school.[996] Under the current status of the law, Title IX and Section 1983 are not applicable to all educational institutions. Title IX will be applicable only to nonpublic educational institutions that receive assistance administered by the U.S. Department of Education[997] and Section 1983 would be applicable to nonpublic schools only where there has been "state action."

Age Discrimination Act of 1975

This Act prohibits "unreasonable discrimination on the basis of age in programs or activities receiving Federal financial assistance."[998] Specifically excluded from coverage is "differentiation ... based upon reasonable factors other than age."[999] This Act applies to persons forty and older, but there is conflicting authority as to whether the act creates a private cause of action.[1000] This Act has very little litigation history and the Civil Rights Restoration Act of 1987 does not seem to have increased its use.[1001] The regulations indicate that any age limit on admissions of students which favors younger over older applicants and would not be necessary to the institution's normal operations would violate the Act.[1002] However, a practice that benefits older persons over younger persons may also violate the Act on a reverse discrimination theory.[1003] A student age

---

[996] *See* C.M. v. Southeast Delco Sch. Dist., 828 F. Supp. 1179 (E.D. Pa. 1993) (harassment by other students); Elliott v. New Miami Bd. of Educ., 799 F. Supp. 818 (S.D. Ohio 1992) (alleged sexual, physical and verbal abuse by teacher).

[997] *E.g., see* Houston v. Mile High Adventist Academy, 846 F. Supp. 1449 (D. Colo. 1994) (Title IX did not apply to religious school where no proof school received federal financial assistance).

[998] 42 U.S.C. § 6102.

[999] 42 U.S.C. § 6103(b)(1)(B).

[1000] Rannels v. Hargrove, 731 F. Supp. 1214 (E.D. Pa. 1990) (private cause of action exists); Mittelstaedt v. Board of Trustees of Univ. of Arkansas, 487 F. Supp. 960 (D. Ark. 1980) (no private cause of action). *See also*, Heckman v. State Univ. of New York College at Brockport 737 F. Supp 177 (N.D. N.Y. 1990) (court does not address directly whether private cause of action exists because program under which student was pursuing doctoral work did not receive federal funds).

[1001] *See* Stephanidis v. Yale Univ., 652 F. Supp. 110 (D. Conn. 1986), *aff'd* 814 F.2d 654 (2d Cir. 1987) (student's application of admission not covered by act because university English Department was not recipient of federal assistance).

[1002] 45 C.F.R. § 90.15 ("An action may be based on a factor other than age [which has a disproportionate effect on persons of different ages] only if the factor bears a direct and substantial relationship to the normal operation of the program or activity or to the achievement of a statutory objective.").

[1003] *See* Rannels v. Hargrove, 731 F. Supp. 1214 (E.D. Pa. 1990) (bank practice of granting additional 1/4 percent interest on CDs to depositors over age fifty stated age discrimination claim).

discrimination claim concerning student academic discipline must have a rational basis, and inferences as to age discrimination will not be drawn where facts indicate that the discipline was not arbitrary or capricious.[1004]

Even though seldom litigated, the Act does raise interesting questions concerning reentry of persons (particularly women) into academic institutions, especially higher education, after a lapse of years (very frequently to raise children).[1005] The connection to the Act is that very often the reentry person will be forty or older. Most of the reentry problems faced would not be cognizable under the 1975 Act because institutional rules tend to be facially neutral and they lack an intent to discriminate against persons over forty. Some of the problems somewhat unique to reentry persons are:

(1) Letters of recommendation required from schools not attended for years or which may no longer exist;

(2) Changes in prerequisite courses, which tend to increase the number of hours needed for program completions;

(3) Grade inflation in comparing acceptable G.P.A.'s from time of first admission to reentry;

(4) G.R.E. scores considered valid for only limited number of years (frequently five-ten years);

(5) Limitations on available financial aid because of spouses's higher income, as compared to younger, independent students;

(6) Part-time student problems such as financial aid limited to full-time students, class schedules where few

---

[1004] *See* Frederick v. Northwestern Univ. Dental Sch., 617 N.E.2d 382 (Ill. App. Ct. 1993) (forty-year-old dental school student dismissed for poor academic performance failed to establish that a younger student's grade was too high or that Australian professors had formed a conspiracy to fail him in his clinical courses).

[1005] Excellent materials regarding the reentry of women are available from Project on the Status and Education of Women, Association of American Colleges, 1818 R. St. N.W., Washington, D.C. 20009. The basic publication is entitled *Barriers to Reentry Women - College Transfer Policies, Residency and Graduation Requirements.*

> required courses are available evenings or weekends, faculty advisors not available evenings or weekends, and absence of child care.[1006]

Some religious institutions may choose to exclude members of one sex (usually women) from certain programs (e.g., M.Div. degrees) that are considered preparation for pastoral ministries. Where completion of the ministry preparation program is required for admission to pastoral ministry and, based on religious beliefs, only male ministers are recognized, a cognizable argument can be made for exclusion from the academic program based on gender. But exclusion from an academic program (M.Div.) may be problematic where the degree is not necessary as an entry-level requirement for entrance into a pastoral ministry. However, although a female could argue that, where an academic degree is not a requirement for a ministry, refusal to admit women to the academic degree program is discrimination, courts are unlikely to give cognizance to a claim which would seem to strike, under the free exercise clause, at the very heart of a religious organization's definition of ministry.[1007]

Regardless of how one answers the question about ministry preparation, in a competitive marketplace for students, especially in higher education, all nonpublic colleges may want to reevaluate rules, policies, or practices which discourage reentry students, including lack of auxiliary support childcare services.

Statutes Not Based on Federal Assistance

Title VII

Title VII, unquestionably the workhorse of federal employment antidiscrimination legislation, prohibits employment practices that discriminate in hiring, discharge, or classification based on race, color, religion, sex, or national

---

[1006] A decision by a college not to fund a child care service for women attending classes was held to support a Title IX cause of action. De La Cruz v. Tormey, 582 F.2d 45 (9th Cir. 1975).

[1007] *Cf.* Jocz v. Labor and Industry Rev. Comm'n, 538 N.W.2d 588 (Wis. Ct. App. 1995) (gender discrimination claim of female director of field education at seminary whose contract had not been renewed was precluded from consideration by court under the free exercise clause because the position was ministerial).

origin.[1008] Sex discrimination applies only to biological gender, not sexual orientation.[1009] Title VII can apply in a very expansive sense to the employment relationship so that discrimination can be found where a school chooses an insurance company that discriminates under Title VII to handle its annuity program.[1010] In addition, a Title VII cause of action is viable where "the [work] environment would reasonably be perceived, and is perceived, as hostile and injurious [with] no need that for it also to be psychologically injurious."[1011] A Title VII complaint must be filed within 300 days of the alleged discriminatory act or, if continuing violations are alleged, the complaint must be filed within 300 days of the last of "a number of discriminatory acts emanating from the same discriminatory animus, each act constituting a separate wrong."[1012]

Whenever religious educational institutions are involved, Title VII must be interpreted in light of the religion clauses in the First Amendment. Courts have long recognized that they cannot intrude into a religious organization's selection of its religious leaders and have fashioned a ministerial exemption under the free exercise clause.[1013] *EEOC v. Catholic University of America*[1014] represents a good study of the interaction between Title VII and the free exercise and establishment clauses. In *Catholic University*, the court upheld dismissal of a nun's sex discrimination complaint following her denial of tenure in the Canon Law Department. The court reasoned that the Canon Law Department, since it played a significant role in the graduate education of priests, was important to the spiritual mission of the Catholic Church and, therefore, those teaching in that department qualified for the ministerial exemption. The court

---

[1008] 42 U.S.C. § 2000e-2(a).

[1009] Smith v. Liberty Mutual Life Ins. Co., 569 F.2d 325 (5th Cir. 1978) (effeminate male not protected); Rowland v. Mad River Local Sch. Dist., 730 F.2d 444 (6th Cir. 1984) (self-announced lesbian not protected).

[1010] Peters v. Wayne State Univ., 691 F.2d 235 (6th Cir. 1982).

[1011] Harris v. Forklift Sys., Inc., 510 U.S. 17, 22 (1993) (although decided under a gender discrimination set of facts, presumably all areas under Title VII would be protected from abusive treatment, e.g., hostile or abusive treatment of an employee based on religion).

[1012] Kassaye v. Bryant College, 999 F.2d 603, 606 (1st Cir. 1993) (dismissal of complaint of faculty member denied tenure upheld where Title VII complaint not filed within 300 days; only act within the 300 days was college's request that plaintiff vacate his office thirty days early for a new faculty member, but that request was not discriminatory so did not become part of plaintiff's alleged serial violation).

[1013] *See* Gonzalez v. Roman Catholic Archbishop of Manila, 280 U.S. 1 (1929); Serbian E. Orthodox Diocese v. Milivojevich, 426 U.S. 696 (1976).

[1014] 83 F.3d 455 (D.C.Cir. 1996).

further noted that the ministerial exemption had survived the limitation placed on application of the free exercise clause in *Employment Division v. Smith*.[1015] Finally, the court concluded that EEOC's attempt to investigate plaintiff's sex discrimination claim not only burdened free exercise but also excessively entangled the Government with religion.

Title VII has a number of important exemptions that may affect religious nonpublic schools:

(1) The Act does not apply to employers with fewer than fifteen employees.[1016] Churches are not excluded as employers and whether church and school employees will be counted together for the Title VII jurisdictional requirement of fifteen employees depends on the "single employer doctrine." This doctrine uses a four-part test in determining whether employees of different parts of a ministry should be counted toward the fifteen employee requirement: interrelation of operations; common management; centralized control of labor relations; and common ownership or financial control.[1017]

(2) The Act exempts hiring, discharge, or classification based on religion, sex, or national origin where "religion, sex or national origin is a bona fide occupational qualification [BFOQ] reasonably necessary to the operations of that particular business or enterprise."[1018] The burden is on the employer to prove the necessity of the BFOQ. The BFOQ must be of the nature that the essence of the business would be undermined if the BFOQ exemption were not granted,[1019] but the

---

1015 494 U.S. 872 (1990).

1016 42 U.S.C. § 2000e(b).

1017 *See* EEOC v. St. Francis Xavier Parochial Sch., 20 F. Supp.2d 66 (D. D.C. 1998) (although an ADA case, the court notes that ADA incorporates jurisdictional requirements of Title VII; whether church and school employees should be counted together is a fact question)., rev'd on other grounds, 117 F.3d 621 (D.C. Cir. 1999), on remand, 77 F. Supp.2d 71 (D. D.C. 1999) (parish and school were unincorporated entities of archdiocese and could not be sued separately).

1018 42 U.S.C. § 2000e-2(e)(1).

1019 Fernandez v. Wynn Oil Co., 653 F.2d 273 (9th Cir. 1981) (undermining not proved by allegation that South American clients would refuse to deal with female director of international operations).

BFOQ cannot be based on stereotyping.[1020] In *Vigars v. Valley Christian Center of Dublin, California*,[1021] where discharge of a librarian on the basis of an out-of-wedlock pregnancy was considered to be in violation of Title VII, a BFOQ in terms of being a role model in a religious school could not be determined by the preferences of fellow employees or customers. The Equal Employment Opportunity Commission (EEOC) narrowly interprets BFOQ, especially as it relates to job qualifications. Qualifications such as educational background, practical training, and physical and mental health will be examined closely in a lawsuit,[1022] but particularly suspect will be minimum test scores based on tests which are culturally biased on job qualifications unrelated to the job.[1023] Religious qualifications tend to receive favorable judicial treatment as they apply to hiring or discharge,[1024] but courts look less favorably on claims of religious qualifications that

---

1020 *See* Hernandez v. St. Thomas Univ., 793 F. Supp. 214 (D. Minn. 1992) (university had burden of proving a factual basis of privacy considerations of BFOQ for hiring only female custodians for female dorms); Capaci v. Katz and Besthoff, Ind., 720 F.2d 1291 (5th Cir. 1983) (advertising for manager trainee in male wanted columns on sincere belief that women would not be interested violates Title VII). *See also*, 29 C.F.R. § 1625.4 which prohibits use of such terms in help wanted ads as "boy" or "girl".

1021 805 F. Supp. 802 (N.D. Cal. 1992).

1022 Shenefield v. Sheridan County Sch. Dist. 1, 544 P.2d 870 (Wyo. 1976) (hiring male without master's degree upheld over hiring female without master's degree because the male could be hired for less and in addition could coach); Covington v. Southern Ill. Univ., 816 F.2d 317 (7th Cir. 1987) (salary disparity for male professor explained by occupational experience prior to being hired); Kenneweg v. Hampton Township Sch. Dist., 438 F. Supp. 575 (D. Pa. 1977); School Dist., Township of Millercreek v. Commonwealth Human Relations Comm'n., 368 A.2d 901 (Pa. 1977) (higher pay for boys' team coach who had heavier schedule and greater coaching burdens upheld); Oates v. Dist. of Columbia 824 F.2d 87 (D.C. Cir. 1987) (honoring commitment to previous football coach legitimate reason for not hiring female football coach). *Contra* Chang v. University of Rhode Island, 606 F. Supp. 1161 (D. R.I. 1985)(quality of scholarship as reason for denying tenure to female instructor was pretextual when four males with no better scholarship records were granted tenure); Wynn v. Columbus Mun. Separate Sch. Dist., 692 F. Supp. 672 (N.D. Miss. 1988) (school district combining athletic director position with football coach, on theory that it was "dominant sport," established discriminatory treatment of female applicant who had extensive experience, over twenty years with all sports in the school but who would presumably not be qualified to be hired as football coach).

1023 *See* Griggs v. Duke Power Co., 401 U.S. 424 (1971) (high school diploma for manual labor jobs had racially discriminatory impact).

1024 Maguire v. Marquette Univ., 627 F. Supp. 1499 (E.D. Wis. 1986) (white female Catholic with pro-abortion moral views lost in her alleged discrimination claim in not being hired for theology position); Pime v. Loyola Univ. of Chicago, 585 F. Supp. 435 (N.D. Ill. 1984) (hiring Jesuit for philosophy department was reasonably necessary to operation of university and fixing number of Jesuits at seven in thirty-one faculty member department was reasonable.).

appear to treat women on a different basis from men,[1025] have no application to the facts of the case[1026] or are inconsistently applied.[1027] Physical tests must be job-related[1028] and all physical and mental qualifications must pass muster under the "otherwise qualified" and "reasonable accommodation" standards of the Rehabilitation Act.[1029] Qualifications which relate to marital status or anti-nepotism policies are suspect under Title VII[1030] and, in fact, may violate state law.[1031] In general, an employer in a Title VII law suit will have to rebut any plaintiff's *prima facie* case by proving job-relatedness of the relevant qualification.[1032]

(3) The Act also exempts employment of persons of a particular religion if the institution is "in whole or in substantial part, owned, supported, controlled or managed by a particular religious corporation, association, or society, or if the curriculum of such school, college, university, or other educational institution or institution of learning is directed toward the propagation of a particular religion."[1033]

In a legal contest the burden is on the religious institution to prove its religious preference. However, an educational institution can be a "religious corpo-

---

1025 *See* Vigars v. Valley Christian Ctr. of Dublin, Cal., 805 F. Supp. 802 (N.D. Cal. 1992) (discharge of librarian on basis of out-of-wedlock pregnancy considered violation of Title VII's prohibition of discrimination based on pregnancy, even though school could discharge on basis of adultery); EEOC v. Fremont Christian Sch., 609 F. Supp 344 (N.D. Cal. 1984), *aff'd* 781 F.2d 1362 (9th Cir. 1986) (health insurance benefits paid only to "head of household" employees interpreted by school to mean single persons and married men not an exempt BFOQ since exemption does not apply to discriminatory provision of benefits).

1026 Ritter v. Mount St. Mary's College, 495 F. Supp. 724 (D. Md. 1980) (Catholic lay female teacher in a Catholic school had Title VII cause of action when denied tenure because denial of tenure had nothing to do with religious exemption).

1027 Dolter v. Wahlert High Sch., 483 F. Supp. 266 (N.D. Iowa 1980) (unmarried pregnant Catholic high school teacher had Title VII cause of action because, despite Catholic moral views on premarital sex, male employees were allegedly not discharged for engaging in premarital sex).

1028 Berkman v. City of New York, 705 F.2d 584 (2d Cir. 1983).

1029 *See supra*, notes 918-938 and accompanying text.

1030 *See* Stuckey v. U.S. Air Force, 790 F. Supp. 165 (S.D. Ohio 1992) (questions about marital status and child care considered to be per se violations of Title VII); LEGAL DESKBOOK FOR ADMINISTRATORS OF INDEPENDENT COLLEGES AND UNIVERSITIES (K. WEEKS, ed.) IV-39.

1031 *E.g. see* Va. Code Ann., § 2.1-715 (prohibits discrimination on basis of "marital status.").

1032 *See* Personnel Admn'r of Mass. v. Feeney, 442 U.S. 256 (1979); Dothard v. Rawlinson, 433 U.S. 321 (1977); Peters v. Middlebury College, 409 F. Supp. 857 (Vt. 1976).

1033 42 U.S.C. § 20003-2(e)(1).

ration" for purposes of a Title VII exemption without espousing a particular religion. In *Wirth v. College of the Ozarks*,[1034] a nondenominational "Christian-based college" could terminate a Catholic faculty member under Title VII because his views were different from those of the college. "[T]he [Title VII] exemptions allow religious institutions to employ only those persons whose religious beliefs are consistent with the views of the religious organization."[1035]

Although a religious educational institution "supported," "controlled," and/or "managed" by a religion will be free to prefer and/or limit its employees to that religion, courts will scrutinize both the nature of control and the reason for the employment decision. An educational institution that is not controlled by a church and does not propagate a particular religion may not be able to claim this exemption. In *EEOC v. Kamehameha Schools/Bishop Estate*,[1036] the schools with a Protestant-only hiring requirement were denied Title VII exemption because the schools controlled a church, rather than vice versa, and because Protestantism had become more of a general tradition than part of its mission.

Control does not have to be formalized in order for an institution to be entitled to claim a Title VII exemption. In *Killinger v. Samford University*,[1037] this university with a Baptist emphasis was permitted to limit a faculty member's teaching assignments to its undergraduate program and deny him assignments in its Divinity School on the basis of differences of religious views between the Divinity School Dean and plaintiff. Although the university had discontinued control by the Alabama Baptist Convention in terms of appointment of its board of trustees, the Court held that because the university received $4,000,000 annually from the Baptist Convention, even though amounting to only seven percent of its annual budget,

---

1034 26 F. Supp. 2d 1185 (W.D. Mo. 1998).

1035 *Id.* at 1188.

1036 990 F.2d 458 (9th Cir. 1993), *cert. denied* 510 U.S. 963 (1993).

1037 113 F.3d 196 (11th Cir. 1997).

the university could be considered substantially supported by a religion for purposes of Title VII. Similarly, in *Hall v. Baptist Memorial Health Care Corporation*,[1038] the Baptist Memorial College of Health Sciences, which was controlled by the Corporation, was entitled to a Title VII exemption when it discharged an employee who had been ordained by a church with a large homosexual congregation. The College, which had been started by the Mississippi, Arkansas, and Tennessee Baptist State Conventions and hosted a number of religious functions, was a religious educational institution within Title VII that could discharge an employee whose views differed from the College's religious beliefs. The Court observed that the College's requirement of only one three-hour course in religion did not deprive it of its exemption. In dismissing the employee's complaint, the Court opined that "the College does not have to hire only Baptists or follow a strict policy of religious discrimination to be eligible for the Title VII exemption."[1039]

When complaints concern claims of discrimination other than religion, courts scrutinize the facts more carefully. In *EEOC v. Mississippi College*,[1040] a white Presbyterian female part-time instructor who had not been hired for a full-time teaching position subsequently filled by a white Baptist male was entitled to an evidentiary hearing in order for the college to present evidence of its preference to hire Baptists. However, the Court limited the scrutiny of EEOC, and once the college presented such proof, EEOC could not inquire further to determine whether the religious discrimination was a pretext for some other kind of discrimination.

This Title VII exemption limits but does not prohibit all government record-keeping related to protected categories of employees. In *EEOC v. Southwestern Baptist Theological Seminary*,[1041] an EEOC

1038 27 F. Supp.2d 1029 (W.D. Tenn. 1998).

1039 *Id.* at 1037.

1040 626 F.2d 477 (5th Cir. 1980).

1041 485 F. Supp. 255 (N.D. Tex. 1980), *rev'd in part* 651 F.2d 277 (5th Cir. 1981).

request for record-keeping information did not have to be honored as to employees "at the Seminary [that] fit the definition of 'ministers' ...": all faculty, "[t]he President and Executive Vice President of the Seminary, the Chaplain, the deans of men and women, the academic deans, and those other personnel who equate to or supervise faculty."[1042] The request had to be granted as to the several hundred full and part-time support personnel and "those administrators whose functions relate exclusively to the Seminary's finance, maintenance, and other nonacademic departments."[1043]

(4) Title VII exempts "a religious corporation, association, educational institution, or society with respect to the employment of individuals of a particular religion to perform work connected with the carrying on by such corporation, association, educational institution, or society of its activities."[1044]

In *Killinger*, the university fit within this exemption because of a collection of factors identifying its Baptist religious preference: ninety-five percent of the faculty and eighty-eight percent of the students were Baptist; its trustees were Baptists; seven percent of its budget was received from the Alabama Baptist Convention; it submitted financial reports to, and was audited by, the Convention; it belonged to the Association of Baptist Colleges and Schools; and its faculty handbook and contracts contained affirmations and commitments to advancing Christianity. The Court expressly rejected plaintiff's arguments that this Title VII exemption requires a "rigid sectarianism" and that the university had to engage "in a strict policy of religious discrimination--such as always preferring Baptists."[1045]

When plaintiffs at religious institutions raise discrimination claims that invoke Title VII protected categories other than religion, courts must follow the

---

[1042] 651 F.2d at 284-85.
[1043] *Id.* at 285.
[1044] 42 U.S.C. § 2000e-1.
[1045] *Killinger*, 113 F.3d at 199, 200.

normal burden of proof sequence: plaintiff states a *prima facie* case for employment discrimination based on a protected category; defendant alleges a nondiscriminatory reason for its employment decision; and plaintiff produces evidence that defendant's reason is pretextual. In *Boyd v. Harding Academy of Memphis, Inc.*,[1046] a religiously affiliated school successfully rebuffed the sex discrimination claim of a former preschool teacher discharged because she was pregnant out-of-wedlock. The court held that plaintiff had failed to prove that the school's reason for discharging her, its religious beliefs against extramarital sex, was a pretext for her claim that she had been discharged because of her pregnancy, a protected category under Title VII.[1047]

The permissible limits of this provision were explored in the context of an establishment clause challenge in *Amos v. Corporation of the Presiding Bishop.*[1048] In *Amos*, five employees of organizations wholly owned by the Mormon Church were discharged for failing to satisfy the church's worthiness requirements for a temple recommend.[1049] Four of the employees, whose complaints were dismissed by the federal district court, made clothing for temple use[1050] while the fifth, whose case went to the U.S. Supreme Court, was a building engineer in a gymnasium open to the public. *Amos* involved a serious Establishment Clause challenge that the Title VII exemption's apparent inclusion of all "activities,"[1051] nonreligious as well

---

1046 88 F.3d 410 (6th Cir. 1996).

1047 42 U.S.C. § 2000e(k). However, nonrenewing pregnant, out-of-wedlock female teachers can be problematic. *See* Cline v. Catholic Diocese of Toledo, 199 F.3d 853 (6th Cir. 1999) (court refused to uphold summary judgment for Diocese because question of fact existed as to whether school enforced its policy against pre-marital sex solely by observing pregnancy of female teachers).

1048 483 U.S. 327 (1987).

1049 *Amos* 594 F. Supp. 791, 796 (D. Utah, 1984) (temple recommend includes tithing, church attendance, and abstinence from alcohol and coffee).

1050 618 F. Supp. 1013, 1018-20 (D. Utah 1985) (religious nature of function of making temple garments not defeated by employment of nonchurch member in the past, nonenforcement of religious criteria on commercial companies manufacturing temple clothing under a license, and enforcement of more stringent standards on employees after they were hired).

1051 Prior to 1972 only "religious activities had been exempted but in 1972 after a lengthy debate "religious" was deleted. *See* 1972 U.S. CODE AND CONG. ADM. NEWS, pp. 2137, 1280. See discussion in *Amos*, 594 F. Supp. at 806-12.

as religious, violated the *Lemon* tripartite test: whether the statute has a secular purpose; whether the effect of the statute's enforcement neither advanced nor inhibited religion; and whether the statute fostered an excessive entanglement with religion.[1052] The constitutional issue was framed because of the initial trial court's determination that the building engineer was involved in nonreligious activity.[1053] The Supreme Court found a secular legislative purpose in Congress relieving religious organizations of trying "to predict which of its activities a secular court will consider religious."[1054] The second "effects" test was passed because "[a] law is not unconstitutional simply because it allows churches to advance religion, which is their very purpose."[1055] Finally, the third test was passed because "the statute effectuates a more complete separation of [church and state] and avoids the kind of intrusive inquiry into the religious belief that the District Court engaged in this case."[1056] Despite the religious victory in *Amos*, two questions were left unresolved: whether the breadth of coverage under the current exemption is required by the free exercise

---

1052 Lemon v. Kurtzman, 403 U.S. 602, 612-13, 91 S.Ct. 2015, 2111 (1971) (all three tests must be passed).

1053 *Amos*, 594 F. Supp. 15 802, 803. Legal precedence is fairly clear that a religious function is not only exempt under Title VII but is probably protected under the free exercise of religion clause. McClure v. Salvation Army, 460 F.2d 553 (5th Cir.), *cert. denied* 409 U.S. 896 (1972) (failure to promote female ordained minister not subject to Title VII); Rayburn v. General Conference of Seventh-Day Adventists, 772 F.2d 1164, 1168 (4th Cir. 1985) (discrimination charge for failure to hire female pastor barred by Title VII and free exercise clause because "the job of associate in pastoral care is so significant in the expression and realization of Seventh-Day Adventist beliefs.").

1054 *Amos*, 483 U.S. at 336.

1055 *Id.* at 337. In her concurring opinion, Justice O'Connor observed: "[t]he church had the power to put [the Gymnasium employee] to a choice of qualifying for a temple recommend or losing his job because the *Government* had lifted from religious organizations the general regulatory burden imposed by [Title VII]." *Id.* at 347 (emphasis in original).

1056 *Id.* at 339. The district court had found excessive entanglement because the gymnasium was not an integral religious part of the Mormon church and the statutory exemption benefitted religion by not creating restrictions against advancing religion through employments practices. *Amos*, 594 F. Supp. at 826-28. The *Lemon* test for excessive entanglement requires that a court "must examine the character and purpose of the institutions that are benefitted, the nature of the aid that the state provides, and the resulting relationship between the government and the religious authority." *Lemon*, 403 U.S. at 615. The *Amos* district court found the Title VII exemption violated the first two criteria but not the third.

> clause or establishment clauses;[1057] and whether application of religious standards to newly acquired businesses exceeds the statutory exemption. The first question relates to the extent of the protection for a religious organization to enforce religious homogeneity.[1058] The second question may depend on whether the business is nonprofit,[1059] on one hand, or whether it is commercial or subject to government regulation, on the other.[1060]

Title VII has become a popular vehicle for prosecuting discrimination complaints for several reasons. First, under Title VII, proof of disproportionate or disparate impact does not require proof of intent to discriminate[1061] (although disparate treatment requires proof of discriminatory intent), whereas Section 1983, Title VI, and Title IX normally require proof of discriminatory intent.[1062] A *prima facie* case is established by alleging that plaintiff:

(1) is a member of a Title VII protected class;

[1057] *See* Welter v. Seton Hall Univ., 608 A.2d 206 (N.J. 1992) (exemption from Title VII scrutiny applies only where employee passes ministerial function test, such as teaching, spreading faith, church governance, supervision of religious order, or supervision of religious ritual and worship.)

[1058] *See* EEOC v. Kamehameha Schs./Bishop Estate, 990 F.2d 458 (9th Cir. 1993), *cert. denied* 114 S.Ct. 439 (1993) (despite religious schools' program that consisted of comparative religious studies, scheduled prayers and services, quotation of Bible verses in school publications, and employment of nominally Protestant teachers, schools were essentially secular in nature and thus not entitled to Title VII exemption.)

[1059] Three concurring justices in *Amos* drew the broad conclusion that exemption of any nonprofit activity of a religious organization was constitutionally permissible. *Amos*, 483 U.S. at 345 (Brennan concurring), 346 (Blackmum concurring), 346-48 (O'Connor concurring).

[1060] *See* United States v. Lee, 455 U.S. 252 (1982) (Social Security tax withholding applicable to employees of Amish employer); NLRB v. World Evangelism, Inc., 656 F.2d 1349 (9th Cir. 1981) (union representation of building engineers not violative of religious beliefs where religious organization's building used for commercial activities); King's Garden, Inc. v. FCC, 498 F.2d 51, 54 (D.C. Cir. 1974) (religious radio station's employment of only evangelicals held violative of FCC anti-bias rules "where a job position has no substantial connection with program content, or where the connection itself is with a program having no religious dimension").

[1061] *See* Frazier v. Garrison I.S.D., 980 F.2d 1514 (5th Cir. 1993) (neutral employment practice can be violation of Title VII).

[1062] *Compare* Sable v. University of Maryland, 778 F.2d 164 (4th Cir. 1985) (no Title VII remedy for associate professor denied promotion because no proof of discriminatory intent by President) *with* Craik v. Minnesota State Univ. Bd., 731 F.2d 465 (8th Cir. 1984) (statistical methodology demonstrated disparate impact on females regarding salaries and promotions).

(2) has made application for an available position or benefit for which she is qualified;

(3) was rejected under circumstances which give rise to an influence of unlawful discrimination.[1063]

However, once defendant-employer proffers evidence of a nondiscriminatory reason for the employment decision, plaintiff must prove discriminatory intent[1064] or that the reason given was pretextual.[1065] A second advantage is that Title VII permits use of statistics to prove a disparate impact based on relationship to the population at large,[1066] a pool of applicants,[1067] or a relevant geographical area.[1068] Finally, Title VII offers a broad range of remedies: back pay up to two years, injunctive including reinstatement relief, and attorney's fees.[1069] In addition to these remedies, 1991 amendments to Title VII permit plaintiffs to recover money damages and to have the right to a jury trial.[1070]

Conclusions and Recommendations for Title VII

(1) Title VII permits discrimination based on religious beliefs, although it does not require that employers follow a narrow sectarianism in their religious practices. Sex discrimination would be permissible in elementary, secondary or post-secondary physical education programs or dormitory assignments where religious tenets of moral propriety are at stake. Like-

---

1063 Texas Dep't of Community Affairs v. Burdine, 450 U.S. 248, 253 (1981).

1064 Hatton v. Hunt, 780 F. Supp. 1157 (W.D. Tenn. 1991); Lewis v. Central Piedmont Community College, 689 F.2d 1207 (4th Cir. 1982).

1065 Chang v. University of Rhode Island, 606 F. Supp. 1161 (D.R.I. 1985) (rejection of female for faculty promotion was pretextual where four males with no better scholarship record were promoted).

1066 Dothard v. Rawlinson, 493 U.S. 321 (1977).

1067 Craik v. Minnesota State Univ. Bd., 731 F.2d 465 (8th Cir. 1984); Blake v. City of Los Angeles, 595 F.2d 1367 (9th Cir. 1979)

1068 Hazelwood Sch. Dist. v. United States, 433 U.S. 299 (1977); Kaplan v. International Alliance of Theatrical and Stage Employees, 525 F.2d 1354 (9th Cir. 1975); Schaeffer v. Tannian, 394 F. Supp. 1136 (E.D. Mich. 1975).

1069 42 U.S.C. § 20003-5(g). *See* Wangsness v. Watertown Sch. Dist., 541 F. Supp. 332 (D. S.D. 1982) where all three remedies are discussed.

1070 42 U.S.C. § 2000e. *See* Nigrelli v. Catholic Bishop of Chicago, 794 F. Supp. 246 (N.D. Ill. 1992) (however, in claim for damages, 1991 amendments would not be applied retroactively to permit discharged principal from pursuing claim for damages because of sexual misconduct of priest).

wise, religious schools whose tenets prohibit religious instruction of men by women should be able to employ only men to teach religion courses.

(2) On the other hand, Title VII protects only as far as the religious tenet. Thus, if a religious school has no religious tenet opposing female administrators (e.g. a religious belief that school administration is a pastoral function and, therefore, administrators performing that function must be male) then every female applicant who agrees with the school's doctrinal statement must be given equal consideration for a position or benefit.

(3) Any religious BFOQ is overridden by a national established public policy (e.g. an employment decision on the basis of race can never be a BFOQ).[1071]

(4) Recruiting processes, as well as processes pertaining to institutional benefits, should be formalized. A job description, applicant qualifications, and a legitimate advertised search should be made for each position. Religious institutions may tend to use informal recruiting procedures among friends and colleagues that result in all high-level administrative positions occupied by a homogeneous population, a process which may call into question whether protected Title VII categories of potential applicants have been disparately impacted.

(5) The interviewing process needs to be standardized so that the same questions are asked of each candidate. Questions directed to female candidates concerning marital status, traveling with members of the opposite sex, or child care arrangements will be considered to be *per se* violations of Title VII.[1072]

(6) Denial of promotions (or discharge) based on labeling (e.g., "troublemaker"), or inaccurate letters of rec-

---

1071 *See infra Government and Fundamental Public Policy* in chapter on "Governmental Regulation of Nonpublic Schools."

1072 *See* Stuckey v. U.S. Air force, 790 F. Supp. 165 (S.D. Ohio 1992).

ommendation, or retaliation for filing a discrimination charge constitute separate Title VII offenses.[1073]

(7) Institutional inconsistencies, coverups, and subterfuges will usually be brought to light through discovery from such questions as: "Has the educational requirement for any job ever been waived?" "Has the state regulated license requirement for any job ever been waived?" "Has the requirement of mastery of an occupational skill for any job ever been waived?" In addition, comprehensive interrogatories would discover whether a job description and applicant qualifications had been prepared and whether the position had been advertised.[1074]

(8) An important religious organization benefit, the housing allowance, should not be negatively affected by Title VII even though women could never be eligible for the benefit in many religious organizations. Since the Internal Revenue Code applies the benefit only to licensed, commissioned or ordained ministers performing ministerial functions,[1075] a religious belief regarding the gender of ministers would seem to bring this matter within *Amos*.

Age Discrimination in Employment Act of 1967 (ADEA)

ADEA prohibits hiring, discharge, classification, or wage rate discrimination of employees based on age.[1076] An ADEA *prima facie* case requires a complainant to allege:

(1) an employment decision unfavorable to complainant;

(2) an age of at least forty;

(3) favorable treatment of a person or persons younger than plaintiff;

[1073] Legal Deskbook for Administrators of Independent Colleges and Universities at IV-28-30. *See also* Indiana Civil Rights Comm'n. v. Culver Educ. Found., 510 .E.2d 206 (Ind. Ct. App. 1987) (retaliation for filing sex discrimination charge).

[1074] *See* D. Danner, Pattern Discovery: Employment Discrimination 33-45 (1981).

[1075] 26 U.S.C. § 1402 (c) (4).

[1076] 29 U.S.C. § 623.

(4) allegations indicating evidence from which the inference can be drawn that the reason for the employer's decision was complainant's age.

A *prima facie* case under ADEA can be established even though the person given favorable employment treatment is forty or older, as long as that person is younger than plaintiff.[1077]

Effective January 1, 1987, the seventy-year-old ceiling for protection under ADEA was eliminated.[1078] The Act retained an exception permitting higher education institutions to permit retirement of faculty "serving under a contract of unlimited tenure,"[1079] but this exception expired December 31, 1993.

ADEA has four important exemptions or affirmative defenses:

(1) treatment "based on reasonable factors other than age";[1080]

(2) discharge or discipline "for good cause";[1081]

(3) treatment based on "a bona fide occupational qualification reasonably necessary to the normal operation of the particular business;"[1082]

(4) observance of the terms of a bona fide seniority or employee benefit plan.[1083]

Unfavorable employment results may be the effect of a number of education decisions: reduction in force;[1084] removal from an administrative position;[1085] termination of

---

[1077] Ware v. Howard Univ., 816 F. Supp. 737 (D. D.C. 1993).

[1078] 29 U.S.C. § 631 (a). *See generally* R. Mawdsley, *Age Discrimination in Education: A New Amendment and New Problems*, 38 EDUC. L. RPTR. 387 (1987).

[1079] 29 U.S.C. § 631 (d). *See* Pollis v. New Sch. for Soc. Research, 825 F. Supp. 584 (S.D. N.Y. 1993) (graduate school could require tenured faculty member to retire at age seventy even though seventy-year-old limit would be repealed at end of 1993).

[1080] 29 U.S.C. § 623 (f) (1).

[1081] 29 U.S.C. § 623 (f) (3).

[1082] 29 U.S.C. § 623 (f) (1).

[1083] 29 U.S.C. § 623 (f) (2).

[1084] Greaves v. Jefferson State Junior College, 494 So.2d 409 (Ala. 1986).

[1085] EEOC v. Community Unit Sch. Dist. No. 9, 642 F. Supp. 902 (S.D. Ill. 1986); McLaurin v. Fischer, 595 F. Supp. 318 (S.D. Ohio 1983).

employment;[1086] nonrenewal of contract;[1087] failure to hire;[1088] denial of promotion;[1089] and changes in the manner of awarding compensation or benefits.[1090] Effecting cost-savings based on the size of employee salaries may raise ADEA questions if highest paid employees are those forty and older.[1091]

Burden of proof issues are similar to other nondiscrimination statutes. Although the minimum age of forty for a complainant is a jurisdictional requirement, he or she need not allege that the person who received the position or benefit is under forty, only that the person is "substantially" younger.[1092] A complainant can meet his or her burden of producing evidence of age discrimination by a preponderance of the evidence through several different means: statements by supervisors;[1093] direct treatment;[1094] or disparate impact.[1095]

Safety and budgetary concerns are always employment concerns. At least one court has upheld a mandatory sixty-five-year-old retirement age for school bus drivers because "safe transportation of infants to school and school-related activities is a paramount concern."[1096] A school can hire within its budget, but a school that hires under a policy to hire only less experienced

[1086] Dodge v. Susquehanna Univ., 796 F. Supp. 829 (M.D. Pa. 1992); Johnson v. University of Wisconsin-Milwaukee, 783 F.2d 59 (7th Cir. 1986); McCroan v. Bailey, 543 F. Supp. 1201 (S.D. Ga. 1982).

[1087] Palmer v. District Bd. of Trustees, 748 F.2d 595 (11th Cir.1984).

[1088] Froneberger v. Yadkin County Schs., 630 F. Supp. 291 (D. N.C. 1986).

[1089] Kauffman v. Kent State Univ., 815 F. Supp. 1077 (N.D. Ohio 1993); Anderson v. University of N. Iowa, 779 F.2d 441 (8th Cir. 1985).

[1090] Smith v. Alum Rock Union Elementary Sch. Dist., 8 Cal.Rptr.2d 399 (Cal. Ct. App. 1992) (state Education Code precluding State Retirement System members aged sixty or older from eligibility for disability benefits conflicted with ADEA); EEOC v. Governor Mifflin Sch. Dist., 623 F. Supp. 734 (E.D. Pa. 1985) (reduction of salary steps from 28 to 6).

[1091] Metz v. Transit Mix, Inc., 828 F.2d 1202 (7th Cir. 1987); EEOC v. Chrysler Corp., 733 F.2d 1183 (6th Cir. 1984).

[1092] Chipollini v. Spencer Gifts, Inc., 613 F. Supp. 1156 (D.C.N.J. 1985); Di Benedetto v. Commonwealth, 497 N.E.2d 266 (Mass. 1986).

[1093] *Di Benedetto*, 497 N.E.2d at 267 (statement by department chairman that the department was "looking for some younger people"); *McLaurin*, 595 F. Supp. at 321 (statements on several instances by division chairman that he was interested in attracting younger doctors).

[1094] EEOC v. Community Unit Sch. Dist., 642 F. Supp. at 904-05 (two administrators who had given notice of retirement more than one year in advance were demoted from administration to teachers for what would have been their last year).

[1095] Moore v. Board of Educ. for Talbott County, 63 F. Supp.2d 667 (D. Md. 1999) (alleged conspiracy by board to force early retirement of older teachers and replace with younger teachers); Leftwick v. Harris-Stowe State College, 702 F.2d 686 (8th Cir. 1983) (in staffing a new state college defendant's plan reserving certain positions on "new" state college faculty for nontenured staff had disparate impact on tenured faculty from "old" city college). *See also* Anderson v. University of N. Iowa, 779 F.2d at 443 (use of statistical evidence in Title VII case to suggest race discrimination acceptable under ADEA).

[1096] Sposata v. Ambach, 453 N.Y.S.2d 149 (Sup. Ct. 1982).

teachers may run the risk of creating a disparate impact on those forty and older.[1097] On the other hand, a school can limit the number of years of experience that it is willing to compensate on its salary scale. Similarly, a school could probably hire only graduates with baccalaureate degrees because the connection between age and graduate degrees is far more tenuous than the connection between age and years of experience.[1098] While there are a number of good reasons for not promoting or retaining an employee, such as documented poor performance, refusal to cooperate with a supervisor, or antagonism toward other employees,[1099] failure to consider a person for a promotion simply because he is two years from mandatory retirement violates ADEA.[1100]

If a school demonstrates a nondiscriminatory reason for its employment decision, the burden shifts to plaintiff/employee to establish by "clear and convincing evidence"[1101] that the employer's reason is a discriminatory pretext. Thus, the burden of proof to prove pretext is higher than the burden of proof to establish a *prima facie* case.

Religious organizations are not exempt from ADEA[1102] except probably as to employees whose obligation is to perform ministerial functions.[1103] Apart from this narrow exception, all other employees in religious organizations, including teachers, will be covered by ADEA.[1104] In religious organizations where

---

1097 Markham v. Geller, 635 F.2d 1027 (2d Cir. 1980) (policy of hiring less experienced teachers violated ADEA).

1098 However, use of such terms in advertising as "young" or "recent college graduate" are considered to be violations of ADEA. 29 C.F.R. § 1625.4 (a).

1099 *See* Legal Deskbook for Administrators of Independent Colleges and Universities at IV-49.

1100 Marshall v. Board of Educ., 15 FEP Cases (BNA) 368 (D. Utah 1977).

1101 Graham v. Renbrook Sch., 692 F. Supp. 102 (D. Conn. 1988).

1102 Soriano v. Xavier Univ. Corp., 687 F. Supp. 1188 (S.D. Ohio 1988); Ritter v. Mt. St. Mary's College, 814 F2d 986 (4th Cir. 1987).

1103 *See* Cochran v. St. Louis Preparatory Seminary, 717 F. Supp. 1413 (E.D. Mo. 1989) (ADEA not applicable to Seminary where faculty member performing ministerial functions discharged because no legislative intent to include religious institutions); Scharon v. St. Luke's Episcopal Presbyterian Hosp., 929 F.2d 360, 363 (8th Cir. 1991) (discharge of hospital chaplain not subject to ADEA or Title VII scrutiny because "to review such decisions would require the courts to determine the meaning of religious doctrine and canonical law and to impose a secular court's view of whether in the context of the particular case religious doctrine and canonical law support the decision the church authorities have made").

1104 Gallo v. Salesian Soc'y, Inc., 676 A.2d 580 (N.J. Super. Ct. 1996) (prohibition on age discrimination a simple one and not entangling under establishment clause, nor is discovery so pervasive so as to be entangling); DeMarco v. Holy Cross High Sch., 4 F.3d 166 (2d Cir. 1993) (math teacher in Catholic school covered by ADEA even though part of duties were religious in nature); Stouch v. Brothers of Order of Hermits of St. Augustine, 836 F. Supp. 1134 (E.D. Pa. 1993) (head chef in monastery covered by ADEA).

plaintiff's pretext argument suggests a mixed motive in the employment decision (one based on age and the other on a religious requirement), a court can look to church doctrine to determine whether the employer did, in fact, have a religious reason to support its decision.[1105]

The handling of employee benefits can be a problem under ADEA since the 1986 amendments protect group health coverage for employees sixty-five and older[1106] and prevent cessation or reduction in employee pension benefit plans.[1107] However, the amendments do not appear to affect life and disability insurance premiums which are related to age and which can be altered for older faculty and staff if the alterations are justified by cost consideration. The EEOC regulations make the following explanation:

> Benefit levels for older workers may be reduced to the extent necessary to achieve approximate equivalency in cost for older and younger workers. A benefit plan will be considered in compliance with the statute where the actual amount of payment made, or cost incurred, in behalf of an older worker is equal to that made or incurred in behalf of a younger worker, even though the older worker may thereby receive a lesser amount of benefits or insurance coverage.[1108]

Equal Pay Act of 1964 (EPA)

The EPA, an amendment to the Fair Labor Standards Act (FLSA) provision on minimum wage,[1109] prohibits employers from discriminating:

> by paying wages to employees ... at a rate less than the rate at which he pays wages to employees of the opposite sex ... for equal work on jobs the performance of which required equal skill, effort and responsibility,

---

[1105] *See* Geary v. Visitation of the Blessed Virgin Mary Parish Sch., 7 F.3d 324 (3rd Cir. 1993) (court upheld dismissal of fifty-year-old parochial school teacher who had married a divorced man in violation of church doctrine by determining that the reason for dismissal was religious rather than age).

[1106] 29 U.S.C. § 623(g).

[1107] 29 U.S.C. § 623(j). However, employer contributions to pension plans are not "benefits" under ERISA and for purposes of ADEA, compliance with ERISA which permits cessation of employer contributions at age sixty-five satisfies ADEA. Kadane v. Hofstra Univ., 682 F. Supp. 155 (E.D. N.Y. 1988).

[1108] 29 C.F.R. § 1625.10 (a)(1).

[1109] 29 U.S.C. § 206(d).

and which are performed under similar working conditions.[1110]

EPA exempts differential wage payments made pursuant to "(1) a seniority system; (2) a merit system; (3) a system which measures earnings by quantity or quality of production; or (4) a differential based on any other factor other than sex."[1111] However, there is no exemption for religious institutions that, because of a religious belief concerning the relative positions of men and women, choose to pay women less than men.[1112]

While teachers and administrators at all levels of education are excluded from FLSA,[1113] they are not excluded from EPA.[1114] An employer against whom a female employee has stated a *prima facie* Equal Pay Act violation cannot correct the violation by reducing the pay of the similarly situated male employees.[1115]

EPA has not been a particularly successful instrument for correcting alleged wage disparities because a *prima facie* case must demonstrate equal work, equal skills, equal effort, equal responsibility, and similar working condition.[1116] In assessing applicability of EPA, courts "look to the actual job requirements and performance, not on-job classification or titles."[1117]

EPA requires that jobs being compared be substantially equal, not just comparable.[1118] Thus, jobs performed by the university's female director of nursing services, who was also an associate professor and associate administrator at the university hospital, were not substantially equal to jobs held by two male associate hospital administrators.[1119] Comparison between the

---

1110 29 U.S.C. § 206 (d) (1).

1111 *Id.*

1112 EEOC v. Tree of Life Christian Schs., 751 F. Supp. 700 (S.D. Ohio 1990 (EPA had minimal impact on religious educational institution's beliefs regarding familial roles of men and women to extent head of household allowance paid to married male faculty members with dependents but not to female faculty members; institution free to practice religious beliefs that did not unlawfully discriminate in wage scale on basis of gender). *See* Donovan v. Shenandoah Baptist Church, 573 F. Supp. 320 (W.D. Va. 1983) (less than minimum wage paid to female employees violated EPA). *See also* EEOC v. Fremont Christian Sch., 609 F. Supp. 344 (D. Cal. 1984), *aff'd* 781 F.2d 1362 (9th Cir. 1986) (religious school's limitations of health insurance benefits to "head of household" employees which school believed could only be performed by husband violated EPA).

1113 29 U.S.C. § 213 (a) (1).

1114 Russell v. Belmont College, 554 F. Supp. 667 (M.D. Tenn. 1982).

1115 EEOC v. Romeo Community Schs., 976 F.2d 985 (6th Cir. 1992).

1116 *See* Schwartz v. Florida Bd. of Regents, 807 F.2d 901 (11th Cir. 1987).

1117 Orahood v. Board of Trustees of Univ. of Ark., 645 F.2d 651, 654 (8th cir. 1981). *See also* Goodrich v. International Bhd. of Elec. Workers, AFL-CIO, 815 F.2d 1519 (D.C. Cir. 1987) (only skills actually required for job are relevant, not abilities of those currently in job)

1118 EEOC v. Kenosha Unified Sch. Dist. No. 1, 620 F.2d 1220 (7th Cir. 1980).

1119 Spaulding v. University of Washington, 740 F.2d 686 (9th Cir. 1984).

salaries of faculty members in higher education can be especially difficult where legitimate factors such as scholarly work and teaching performance are at issue.[1120]

The requirement of equality is especially problematic in athletics. A female teacher who spent 100 percent of her time teaching lecture classes was not substantially equal to a men's varsity basketball coach who spent three-quarters of his time teaching and one-quarter coaching.[1121] Likewise, a Division I male basketball coach with a twelve month contract and extensive travel and communications responsibilities was not substantially equal to an AIAW female women's basketball coach with a nine month contract and with coaching duties that were generally limited to three days per week.[1122] In *Stanley v. University of Southern California*,[1123] the Ninth Circuit Court of Appeals quantified the dissimilarities between a women's and men's head basketball coaches that justified the university not providing a comparable compensation package for the women's coach. The men's coach was required to: spend substantial amounts of time on public relations and promotional activities that resulted in generating revenue more than ninety times that of the women's team; conduct twelve speaking engagements a year to be accessible to the media for interviews; and participate in activities designed to produce donations and endorsements.

In nonathletic situations, appropriateness of comparison is just as important. An institution's male controller who supervised more employees and whose position required knowledge and experience in financial and accounting matters was not substantially equal to a female acting director of the Office of Institutional Studies who dealt with statistics and supplied materials to the university and governmental agencies as requested.[1124] In general, positions which carry added responsibilities, such as curriculum development, and carry a heavier measure of accountability by reporting higher in the administration will justify higher compensation.[1125] Failure of

---

1120 *See* Brousard-Norcross v. Augustana College Ass'n, 935 F.2d 974 (8th Cir. 1991) (female assistant professor denied tenure had no EPA claim).

1121 Hein v. Oregon College of Educ., 718 F.2d 910 (9th Cir. 1983).

1122 Jacobs v. College of William and Mary, 517 F. Supp. 791 (E.D. Va. 1980).

1123 13 F.3d 1313 (9th Cir. 1994).

1124 Orahood v. Board of Trustees of Univ. of Arkansas, 645 F.2d 651 (8th Cir. 1981).

1125 Horner v. Mary Inst., 613 F.2d 706 (8th Cir. 1980) (Both teachers were hired for the 1974-75 school year with the male receiving $9,000 and the female $7,500. The salary increases for the male teacher for the years exceeded his female counterpart from $200-$800 each year).

an EPA plaintiff to select an appropriate office to compare herself with will be fatal.[1126]

Institutions can reply on factors other than sex to justify wage differentials such as a salary retention policy of maintaining employee's salary upon change of assignment within the institution[1127] and qualifications such as a doctoral degree and publications.[1128] Market conditions based on particular experience or skills is a factor other than sex, provided that the institution has investigated market rates.[1129] However, once an institution becomes aware that a female employee is receiving less pay for equivalent work, the institution has a responsibility within a reasonable period of time to evaluate the position.[1130]

Title VII has become an alternative to EPA in attempting to prove wage disparity under a less onerous "comparable worth" theory. The 1976 amendment to Title VII which authorized employers to "differentiate upon the basis of sex in determining the amount of wages or compensation paid or to be paid to employees if such differentiation is authorized by provisions of [EPA]"[1131] has basically had the effect of transferring the four EPA exemptions to Title VII.[1132] In the leading case, *Gunther v. County of Washington*,[1133] the Supreme Court did not find pay disparity to violate EPA because of differences in responsibilities, but the Court did leave open a Title VII lawsuit where plaintiffs might prove their wages were depressed because of intentional sex discrimination consisting of setting the wage scale for female guards, but not for male guards, at a level lower than its own survey of outside markets and the worth of the jobs warranted.[1134] However, the Court specifically noted that because of the

---

1126 *Jacobs v. College of William and Mary* (comparison to baseball coach not appropriate because coach taught full time while plaintiff did not), *Hein v. Oregon College of Educ.* (comparison only to highest paid male employee and ignoring lower paid male employee presented flawed *prima facie* case).

1127 Covington v. Southern Ill. Univ., 816 F.2d 317 (7th Cir. 1987).

1128 Ritter v. Mount St. Mary's College, 814 F.2d 986 (4th Cir. 1987). *See also Brousard-Norcross*, 935 F.2d at 979, note 10 (court appears to suggest that qualifications of faculty members can be distinguished even as to whether they received an Ed.D. rather than a Ph.D.).

1129 Brock v. Georgia Southwestern College, 765 F.2d 1026 (11th Cir. 1985) (college failed to inform itself of market rates); Chang v. University of Rhode Island, 606 F. Supp. 1161 (D. R.I. 1985) (university failed to demonstrate validity of outside offer to higher paid male faculty member).

1130 EEOC v. Maricopa County Community College, 736 F.2d 510 (9th Cir. 1984).

1131 42 U.S.C. § 2000e-2(h).

1132 Melani v. Board Higher Educ. of City of New York, 561 F. Supp. 767 (D.C. N.Y. 1983).

1133 452 U.S. 161 (1981).

1134 *Id.* at 165.

uniqueness of the *Gunther* facts, plaintiff's claims were not based "on the controversial concept of comparable worth."[1135] The concept of comparable worth does not seem to have made significant headway. Perhaps the reason can be explained by the EPA overlay of Title VII:

> [W]hen the issue of salary differentials can be brought under both statutes (Title VII and Equal Pay), the legal standards established under the Equal Pay Act controls ... Title VII ... refers specifically to the Equal Pay Act and states that a sex-predicated wage differential is immune from attack under Title VII only if it comes within one of the four enumerated exceptions to the Equal Pay Act .... It simply cannot be asserted that Title VII's standard supplants or undermines the standards established under the Equal Pay Act.[1136]

Nonetheless, school administrators do have a responsibility to set fair wage structures. While market rates may in fact justify lower comparable wages for office clerks, food service workers, librarians, nurses, and teachers aides, most of whom are female, schools should not be mere slaves to market conditions.

Americans with Disabilities Act (ADA)[1137]

The ADA deals with employees under Title I and students under the public accommodations title (Title III). Title I of ADA prohibits private employers with fifteen or more employees from discriminating against individuals with disabilities in "job application procedures, hiring, firing, advancement, compensation, job training, and other terms, conditions, and privileges of employment."[1138] The requirement of fifteen or more employees is jurisdictional. For religious schools that are part of churches, whether church employees can be combined with the school's to reach fifteen depends on the amount of control the church exerts over the school.[1139]

Concomitant with the liability of employers is the notion that individual employees cannot be held liable under ADA. Courts

---

1135 *Id.* at 166.

1136 Melanson v. Rantoul, 536 F. Supp. 271, 286 (D. R.I. 1982).

1137 42 U.S.C. § 12101 *et seq.*

1138 42 U.S.C. § 12112.

1139 *See* EEOC v. St. Francis Xavier Parochial Sch., 20 F. Supp.2d 66 (D.D.C. 1998), rev'd on other grounds, 117 F.3d 621 (D.C. Cir. 1999), on remand, 77 F. Supp.2d 71 (D. D.C. 1999) (parish and school board, which were unincorporated entities within the Diocese as a corporation, could not be sued separately).

addressing claims litigated under ADA have followed Title VII and have dismissed claims of employment discrimination seeking to hold individuals personally liable under ADA.[1140]

Section 504 of the Rehabilitation Act has become the major source for interpretation of ADA. The singular notable exception between the two acts is that ADA does not, like Section 504, require that an institution be the recipient of federal financial assistance. However, all private employers with fifteen or more employees are covered by ADA whether or not federal financial assistance is received. The definition of disability under ADA is similar to the Rehabilitation Act and prohibits discrimination against "a qualified individual with a disability because of the disability."[1141] The nature of a disability under ADA is identical to Section 504 and applies to both employees and students:

(A) a physical or mental impairment that substantially limits one or more of the major life activities of such individual;[1142]

(B) a record of such impairment;

(C) being regarded as having such impairment.[1143]

Unless "undue hardship" can be demonstrated (generally tied to financial resources of the employer),[1144] employers must make "reasonable accommodation" to an individual's disability. "Reasonable accommodation" may include:

(A) making existing facilities used by employees readily accessible to and useable by individuals with disabilities; and

(B) job restructuring, part-time or modified work schedules, reassignment to a vacant position, acquisition or

---

[1140] *See* Coddington v. Adelphi Univ., 45 F. Supp.2d 211 (E.D. N.Y. 1999), and cases cited therein.

[1141] 42 U.S.C. § 12112.

[1142] Employee alleging discrimination has burden of proving that an impairment affects a major life activity. *See* Kelly v. Drexel Univ., 94 F.3d 102 (3d Cir. 1996) (discharged employee who limped because of degenerative hip condition failed to prove that it substantially impaired his ability to walk.)

[1143] 42 U.S.C. § 12102. *See* Nedder v. Rivier College, 972 F. Supp. 81 (D. N.H. 1997) (morbid obesity considered to be a condition perceived to be a disability for which discharged faculty member could recover damages).

[1144] 42 U.S.C. § 12111(10).

> modification of equipment or devices, appropriate adjustment or modifications of examinations, training materials or policies, the provision of qualified readers or interpreters, and other similar accommodations for individuals with disabilities.[1145]

However, even with reasonable accommodations, disabled employees must still be able to perform the essential functions of the job.[1146] One of the challenges for employers is how to find out about a disability in order to determine what reasonable accommodation is possible. In the hiring process, preemployment medical inquiries and examinations are prohibited, although a medical examination can be required after an offer has been made. A job can be conditioned on the examination results, provided that "all entering employees are subjected to such an examination regardless of disability."[1147] Because disabilities can occur after employment, employers must make reasonable accommodations at that time.[1148]

Disciplining employees with disabilities where misconduct is related to a disability can occur where a job function is required by business necessity and cannot be reasonably accommodated or the employee poses a direct threat to the safety or health of other employees. In a case involving a mental disability, the Tenth Circuit Court of Appeals has observed in dictum that "the employer must tolerate eccentric or unusual conduct caused by the employee's mental disability as long as the employee can satisfactorily perform the essential functions of his job."[1149] As an additional note, employees who are subject to adverse employment decisions resulting from the disabilities of their children are protected by ADA.[1150]

1145 42 U.S.C. § 12111((9)

1146 *Cf.* Davis v. Frank, 711 F. Supp. 447 (N.D. Ill. 1989) (answering phone not essential function of attendance clerk position) *with* Salman v. Dade County Sch. Bd., 4 F. Supp.2d 1157 (S.D. Fla. 1998) (school counselor being at work at 8:15 a.m. an essential function of job); Motzkin v. Trustees of Boston Univ., 938 F. Supp. 938 (D. Mass. 1996) (teaching an essential function of instructor's job and request by instructor that he be removed from classroom to accommodate his disability was unacceptable).

1147 42 U.S.C. §§ 12112 (c)(2) and (3).

1148 *See* Susie v. Apple Tree Preschool Child Care Ctr., 866 F. Supp. 390 (N.D. Ill. 1994).

1149 Den Hartog v. Wasatch Acad., 129 F.3d 1076, 1088 (10th Cir. 1997) (school's discharge of employee justified under ADA where child's conduct was threat to physical safety of other employees). See 42 U.S.C. §§ 12113, 12114 for bases to address employee discipline decisions.

1150 *See* McGrehaghn v. St. Denis Sch., 979 F. Supp. 323 (E.D. Pa. 1997; *Den Hartog v. Wasatch Acad.*

Determining what job functions are essential is obviously critical and courts will scrutinize carefully the nature of the disability, the nature of the accommodations sought by the employee, and the nature of the accommodations provided by the employer. In a somewhat extreme set of facts, a parochial school could discharge a teacher who had missed eighteen months of work due to a number of ailments because regular attendance was an essential function of the teaching job and the teacher was thus not "a qualified individual with a disability."[1151]

The ADA does not protect "any employee or applicant who is currently engaging in the illegal use of drugs,"[1152] but the Act does protect an individual who has completed a supervised drug rehabilitation and is no longer engaging in the illegal use of drugs as well as an individual who is currently participating in a supervised rehabilitation program and is not engaging in the use of illegal drugs.[1153] Individuals with communicable diseases are expressly protected by the statute, except that if an employer has an employee with a communicable disease handling food and cannot make a reasonable accommodation, the employer "may refuse to assign or continue to assign such individual to a job involving food handling."[1154]

Religious employers are exempted from the ADA only as to "giving preference in employment to individuals of a particular religion to perform work connected with the carrying on by such [religious employer]."[1155] Thus, a person who otherwise meets the employer's religious requirements must be given the same consideration that any other job applicant (or current employee, if the employment decision involves a promotion or other job benefit). Presumably, religious employers will not be permitted to circumvent the ADA by creating and emphasizing religious requirements that might exclude persons with certain disabilities, such as AIDS.

Title III of ADA prohibits discrimination in "public accommodations" which include "a nursery, elementary, secondary, undergraduate, or postgraduate private school, or other place of education."[1156] The obvious effect of Title III is to

---

1151 Nowak v. St. Rita High Sch., 142 F.3d 999 (7th Cir. 1998).
1152 42 U.S.C. § 12114(a).
1153 42 U.S.C. § 12114(b).
1154 42 U.S.C. § 12113(d)(2)
1155 42 U.S.C. § 12113(c).
1156 42 U.S.C. § 12181(7).

protect students. Generally, Title III prohibits unequal or separate benefits for students with disabilities and specifically requires that "[g]oods, services, facilities, privileges, advantages, and accommodations shall be afforded to an individual with a disability in the most integrated setting appropriate to the needs of the individual."[1157] In *Rothman v. Emory University*,[1158] although a law school dean's letter to the Illinois Board of Law Examiners referencing a student's epilepsy and his efforts to overcome troubles in law school fell within the statutory language of "services" or "privileges," the student failed to state an ADA claim because the letter had not suggested rejection of the student, the letter's contents were forthright and candid, and the student was eventually admitted to the practice of law. Changes in buses and facilities to accommodate those with disabilities is required where "readily achievable" which, similar to "undue hardship" under Title I, means adjustments must be made unless there is "much difficulty or expense."[1159]

Discipline of students may be subject to judicial constraints under ADA. In *Bercovitch v. Baldwin School, Inc.*,[1160] the First Circuit Court of Appeals observed that a court had the authority to use a preliminary injunction to keep a disruptive student who had been diagnosed with Attention Deficit Hyperactivity Disorder in a private school.[1161] Where the school's parent contract required that disputes were subject to arbitration, the First Circuit found that this provision was consistent with ADA[1162] and was enforceable under the Federal Arbitration Act.[1163] The First Circuit's decision in *Bercovitch* made two important observations, however, regarding the relationship between student misconduct and private school accommodations: a school is not required to waive its disciplinary code to accommodate a disruptive student; and a school is not required to construct an accommodation plan comparable to the Individualized Education Plan (IEP) required by IDEA for public schools.[1164]

[1157] 42 U.S.C. § 12182(b)(1)(A) and (B).

[1158] 123 F.3d 446 (7th Cir. 1997).

[1159] 42 U.S.C. § 12181(9).

[1160] 133 F.3d 141 (1st Cir. 1998).

[1161] *See* Axelrod v. Phillips Acad., Andover, 36 F. Supp.2d 46 (D. Mass. 1999) where court used preliminary injunction to order readmission of student with ADHD dismissed for unsatisfactory academic work.

[1162] 42 U.S.C. § 12212 ("where appropriate and to the extent authorized by law, the use of alternative means of dispute resolution, including ... arbitration, is encouraged to resolve disputes under this chapter.")

[1163] 9 U.S.C. §§ 1-14.

[1164] *Bercovitch*, 133 F.3d at 152, 153.

Although ADA requires that a private school accommodate a disability, it does not require that the school forego its academic expectations. One of the more frequent disabilities that schools encounter is ADHD. In *Axelrod v. Phillips Academy, Andover*,[1165] a student diagnosed with ADHD who was required by the school to withdraw in December of his senior year, claimed that the school had failed to accommodate his disability. The student's academic struggles had extended over a period of three years and during that time the school had implemented many of the recommendations of the student's evaluating psychologist.[1166] In upholding the academic dismissal, the court found that the student was not "otherwise qualified" under ADA. The court noted that because "courts have neither the authority nor the expertise to prescribe academic standards, academic institutions have traditionally been given great latitude in establishing curriculum, grading procedures, and academic standards."[1167] In concluding that the student's ADHD would make it harder for the student to succeed and that the school, indeed, had made reasonable accommodations, the court noted that "the student will have to work harder to overcome his weakness in planning and organization. The ADA requires [the school] to make reasonable accommodations to assist students to perform, but, ultimately, a student is responsible for doing his own work."[1168]

At the present, ADA distinguishes between religious and private schools in terms of compliance with the public accommodations part of the statute. ADA exempts "any religious entity"[1169] from being a public accommodation, which it defines as "a religious organization, including a place of worship."[1170]

[1165] 46 F. Supp.2d 72 (D. Mass. 1999).

[1166] *Id.* at 77 (among the recommendations were: review of the student's medication, which the parent assumed responsibility for administering; one-on-one instruction; regularly scheduled study time; distraction-free study environment; flexible goals; immediate feedback on school assignments; unlimited tests; waiver of foreign language requirement).

[1167] *Id.* at 83.

[1168] *Id.* (the court noted that, because the school's efforts to accommodate the student demonstrated the lack of intent to discriminate, the court refused to substitute its judgment for that of the school's faculty "as to whether a given grade is appropriate or whether a student's academic record warrants his dismissal.")

[1169] 28 C.F.R. § 36.102(e).

[1170] 28 C.F.R. § 36.104.

This definition seems broad enough to exclude higher education as well as K-12.[1171] Thus, religious schools are free under ADA to refuse admission to students with some or all disabilities and are free to select disabilities (if any) that they wish to accommodate. However, exemption from ADA does not mean that religious schools would not be subject to state laws including local ordinances that might require changes in facilities to accommodate disabilities.

Family and Medical Leave Act of 1993 (FMLA)[1172]

This Act was passed by Congress to accommodate working parents who may be forced to choose between job security and the caretaking or medical needs of children, a spouse, or parents. A special section of the Act applies to "any private elementary or secondary school and an eligible employee of the school."[1173] The Act contains no exemption for religious schools.

An employer is generally defined as any person engaging in commerce with fifty or more employees,[1174] although there is no clear indication that this fifty employee limit applies also to schools. An employee is eligible for the medical and family leave benefits if he or she has performed at least 1250 hours[1175] of service during the previous twelve months for the employer.[1176] The leave entitlement is twelve workweeks during any twelve month period and can be used for the following:

(A) ...the birth of a son or daughter of the employee and ... to care for such son or daughter.

(B) ... the placement of a son or daughter with the employee for adoption or foster care.

1171 Even if religious higher education institutions are exempt from ADA, they would be subject to Section 504 if they receive funds (such as Title IV student aid) administered by the De partment of Education.

1172 29 U.S.C. §§ 2601-2654.

1173 29 U.S.C. § 2618 (a)1)(B).

1174 29 U.S.C. § 2611 (3)(A).

1175 Paid vacation and sick time are not "hours of service" within meaning of Family and Medical Leave Act because Act provides that hours of service must be determined by same principles used in Fair Labor Standards Act (29 USCS §§ 201 et seq.), and paid leave time is not considered "hours of work" under 29 USCS § 207(e)(2) of Fair Labor Standards Act. Robbins v. Bureau of Nat'l Affairs, 896 F. Supp. 18 (D.D.C. 1995).

1176 29 U.S.C. § 2611(2)(A)(i). (time employee worked for school system could not be aggregated with time she worked for county government for establishing eligibility where two employing entities were created by different state acts, they performed differing governmental functions, they were administered separately, and terms of her employment changed when she began working for county). Rollins v. Wilson County Gov't, 967 F. Supp. 990 (M.D. Tenn. 1997).

(C) ...care for the spouse, or a son, daughter, or parent of the employee if such spouse, son, daughter, or parent has a serious health medical condition.[1177]

(D) ... a serious health condition that makes the employee unable to perform the functions of the position of such employee.[1178]

The leave can be taken as unpaid leave if the employer "provides paid leave for fewer than twelve workweeks..."[1179] Where leave for medical treatment, birth, or adoption is "foreseeable" according to standards in the Act, "the employee shall provide the employer with not less than thirty days' notice."[1180] However, where medical treatment, birth or adoption must occur in fewer than thirty days, the employee is required to provide only such "notice as is practicable."[1181] Under certain conditions, an employer may require "certification issued by the health care provider of the eligible employee or of the son, daughter, spouse, or parent of the employee, as appropriate."[1182]

On return from the leave, except for certain highly compensated employees,[1183] the employee is to be restored "to the position of employment held by the employee when the leave commenced ... or ... to an equivalent position with equivalent employment benefits, pay, and other terms and conditions of employment."[1184] Restoration rights depend on complying with

---

1177 What qualifies as a "serious health condition" under FMLA for dependents is fact specific. *Cf.* Seidle v. Provident Mut. Life Ins. Co., 871 F. Supp. 238 (E.D. Pa. 1994) (employee missing four days of work to care for four-year-old with ear infection where child had mild fever, had never complained of pain, and was cleared for day school under standard medical protocol after three days not protected by FMLA because "no serious health condition") *with* Bryant v. Delbar Products, Inc., 18 F. Supp.2d 799 (M.D. Tenn. 1998) (care of physically disabled son over eighteen years of age qualified under FMLA as "serious health condition" where son was "incapable of self-care").

1178 29 U.S.C. § 2612(a)(2). What constitutes a "serious health condition" for employees is fact specific. *Cf.* Hodgens v. General Dynamics Corp., 963 F. Supp. 102 (D. R.I. 1997) (employee's hypertension and heart arrhythmia not "serious health condition" where doctor had determined the employee could continue work and employee could have obtained medical treatment without missing work) *with* George v. Associated Stationers, 932 F. Supp. 1012 (N.D. Ohio 1996) (termination of employee who stayed home with chicken pox violated FMLA because the disease was a "serious health condition.")

1179 29 U.S.C. § 2612(d)(1).

1180 29 U.S.C. § 2612(e)(1).

1181 29 U.S.C. § 2612(e)(1) and (2)(B).

1182 29 U.S.C. § 2613(a).

1183 29 U.S.C. § 2614(b).

1184 29 U.S.C. § 2614(a).

FMLS. Thus, an employee who had a twelve-week leave to care for an ailing father lost his FMLA right of restoration when the father died a month before the twelve weeks ended and the employee did not return to work until the end of the twelve weeks. In deciding for the employer, the court reasoned that the "serious health condition" that had been the basis for the leave ended with the father's death.[1185] However, the employee's FMLA rights are not forfeited if the employer has failed to notify the employee that he is required to return to work on the death of the father.[1186] Decisions concerning restoration of an employee of a private elementary or secondary school can be made "on the basis of established school board policies and practices, private school policies and practices, and collective bargaining agreements."[1187]

In addition to FMLA, schools may be subject to state Medical Leave Acts. There is no indication in the FMLA that it was intended to preempt state medical leave statutes.[1188]

Enforcement of the Act can be either by the Secretary of Labor or by the aggrieved employee.[1189] In addition to appropriate equitable relief such as employment, reinstatement, and promotion, the employee can recover compensatory damages and in certain cases an additional amount as liquidated damages[1190] when the employer has not acted in good faith. However, punitive damages are not available under FMLA.[1191]

Individuals With Disabilities in Education Act (IDEA)

IDEA represents a different approach by the federal government to addressing the needs of persons with disabilities than the other disability statutes in this chapter. ADA and Section 504 require employers and places of public accommodation to

---

[1185] Brown v. J.C.Penney Corp. 924 F. Supp. 1158,(S.D. Fla. 1996).

[1186] Sherry v. Protection, Inc. 981 F. Supp. 1133 (N.D. Ill. 1997).

[1187] 29 U.S.C. § 2618(e).

[1188] *See,* Richland Sch. Dist. v. DIHLR, 498 N.W.2d 826 (Wis. 1993) (where state medical leave statute provided greater benefit than collective bargaining agreement, the statute prevails; in this case, a teacher was able to substitute five days of reimbursable leave under the collective bargaining agreement for unpaid adoption leave under Wisconsin's Family Medical Leave Act. The collective bargaining agreement did not provide for paid leave when a child was to be adopted).

[1189] 29 U.S.C. § 2617.

[1190] *See* Rhoads v FDIC, 956 F. Supp. 1239 (D. Md. 1997).

[1191] McKiernan v. Smith-Edwards-Dunlap Co. 3 BNA WH Cas 2d 272 (E.D. Pa. 1995).

respond with reasonable accommodations only as they are made aware of disabilities and then only to the extent accommodations do not represent an undue hardship. IDEA takes on more of the flavor of an affirmative action statute in that public school districts must actively seek out school-age persons in need of related and support services[1192] and then act affirmatively to provide those services necessary for students to participate in education.

IDEA has redefined the relationship between public schools and parents by mandating that parents be part of the individualized education program (IEP) team preparing their child's IEP. Parents of students with disabilities and in need of special education services are treated as equals in the determination of those services.[1193]

Federal regulations place the burden on the state educational agency on behalf of every nonpublic school student receiving special education or related services from a public agency to "[i]nitiate and conduct meetings to develop, review, and revise an individualized education program [IEP] for the child."[1194] For children in nonpublic schools, a representative of the school must attend each meeting, and if he or she cannot, the district must use other means "to assure participation by the private school, including individual or conference telephone calls."[1195] Theoretically, the IEP could include special education or related services at the nonpublic school as well as the public school.[1196] Responsibility for appropriate implementation of the IEP always remains with the public school district even if a private school chooses to implement some or all of the IEP.[1197] Remedies for

[1192] 34 C.F.R. § 300.125(a) (local educational agency must have in place a process to identify, locate, and evaluate all children with disabilities beginning at age three, including those in private schools, "who are in need of special education and related services.") 34 C.F.R. § 300.451 (district must locate and evaluate school children with disabilities in private, including religious, schools).

[1193] For example, an IEP is a "written statement of each handicapped child developed in any meeting by a representative of the local educational agency ... the teacher, the parents or guardians of each child ...." 20 U.S.C. § 1401 (19). Parents have the procedural right "to examine all relevant records with respect to the identification, evaluation, and educational placement of the child, and to obtain an independent educational evaluation of the child ...." 20 U.S.C. § 1415 (b) (1).

[1194] 42 U.S.C. § 1413 (a)(4)(A).

[1195] 34 C.F.R. § 300.454(c)(2).

[1196] 34 C.F.R. § 300.456(a). ("Services provided to private school children with disabilities may be provided on-site at a child's private school, including a religious school, to the extent consistent with law.")

[1197] 34 C.F.R. § 300.349(c).

violation of IDEA can include injunctive relief, reimbursement, and damages under Section 1983.[1198]

In determining the relationship between placement and services in an IEP[1199], the key statutory and regulatory terms are "free appropriate public education" (FAPE)[1200] and "the least restrictive environment" (LRE).[1201] The assumption under IDEA is that FAPE will require that children with disabilities be placed with those who are nondisabled. Removal of a disabled child under an IEP to special classes or separate schooling is permissible only where the district can document that "the nature and severity of the disability is such that education in regular classes with the use of supplementary services cannot be achieved."[1202]

Parents may not want their disabled child to attend a public school and would prefer a nonpublic one. Students with disabilities can be placed in nonpublic schools in two ways: placement by a local educational agency (LEA - public school district) according to a student's IEP; and placement directly by a parent. Placement of a student by a public school district in a nonpublic school would require that the child be provided services with regard to FAPE and LRE as if he or she were in the public school including, if necessary, providing services on-site at the nonpublic school. Where school districts have agreed to nonpublic school placements, legal issues between districts and parents tend to focus on the nature of the school (e.g., residential vs. day school)[1203] and cost.[1204] When parents unilaterally choose to place their children in nonpublic schools, the litigation picture is quite different.

A considerable number of lawsuits have been filed by parents who have unilaterally placed their children in nonpublic schools

---

1198 *See* L.C. v. Utah State Bd.of Educ., 57 F. Supp.2d 1214 (D. Utah 1999) (damages permissible for procedural statutory rights under IDEA). *But see*, Parent v. Osceola County Sch. Bd., 59 F. Supp.2d 1243 (M.D. Fla. 1999) (violations of procedural requirements not basis for damages claim unless student has been harmed).

1199 20 U.S.C. § 1401 (19).

1200 20 U.S.C. § 1401 (18).

1201 20 U.S.C. § 1412 (5)(B); 34 C.F.R. §§ 300.550 - 300.554.00

1202 34 C.F.R. § 300.550(b)(2).

1203 *See* Board of Educ. of Community Consolidated Sch. Dist. v. Illinois State Bd. of Educ., 938 F.2d 712 (7th Cir. 1991) (dispute as to whether child should be placed in residential facility [school's choice] or day school thirty minutes drive from parents' home [parents' choice]).

1204 *See* Clevenger v. Oak Ridge Sch. Bd., 744 F.2d 514 (6th Cir. 1984) (dispute as to whether residential placement should be school's choice [$55,000 per year] or parents' choice [$88,000 per year]).

and then demanded either that school districts provide services on-site at the nonpublic school or that the district reimburse them for expenses attendant to their nonpublic school placement (e.g., tuition, transportation). To further complicate the issue, the nonpublic schools may not have appropriate services to address the child's special education needs.

The debate as to the responsibility of public school districts to satisfy the parents' financial demands and the child's services needs has focused on two issues. The first is permissive in nature and the second involves mandatory responsibilities. First, are districts permitted under the establishment clause to provide reimbursement and/or services at religious schools? Second, are districts required to provide reimbursement and/or services at the nonpublic school if they can provide the child FAPE at the public school?

The first issue is the easier of the two to address because the Supreme Court in *Zobrest v. Catalina Foothills School District*[1205] and *Agostini v. Felton*[1206] now permits public school personnel to provide educational services on-site in religious schools. However, neither *Zobrest* nor *Agostini* requires districts to provide services on-site and neither would prohibit states from striking down such on-site services under their own state constitutions.

The second issue is more complex. Failure of districts to provide FAPE exposes them to liability. In *Florence County School District Four v. Carter*,[1207] the Supreme Court held that parents, after the public school district had not povided FAPE, were entitled to reimbursement for the unilateral placement of their daughter in an out-of-state private school. *Florence County* is a remarkable decision because the parents had chosen a school not approved by their state. However, the Court observed that the parents' actions did not diminish the district's responsibility to meet its requirement to provide FAPE. In other words, the district could not object to the parents' decision where it had not complied with IDEA.

[1205] 509 U.S. 1 (1993) (school district provision of sign language interpreter on-site at religious school not an establishment clause violation where the presence of the child in the school was the result of parental choice).

[1206] 521 U.S. 203 (1997) (public school employees providing chapter one remedial services at religious school not violation of establishment clause where parents had made choice for private school and public teachers will not be assumed to inculcate in religious instruction).

[1207] 510 U.S. 7 (1993).

The 1997 statutory amendments and accompanying regulations to IDEA have attempted to stabilize unilateral parent placements by establishing some ground rules. School districts are not required to reimburse parents who have elected to place their child in a private school if the district has provided FAPE.[1208] However, a district can be required to reimburse parents if FAPE had not been provided in a timely manner and if the parents' placement is "appropriate."[1209] However, the reference to an "appropriate" placement by parents is an invitation to differences of opinion. The term "appropriate" does not necessarily have the same meaning as FAPE, and courts and hearing officers have discretion to provide reimbursement for parent placements that do not meet FAPE requirements applicable to school districts.[1210] Regulations adopted pursuant to the 1997 amendments, though, did add an important provision, namely that parents are required to give at least ten business days written notice to the district saying that they intend to place their child in a private school and expressing their concerns about the IEP. Failure to provide this notice permits courts or hearing officers to reduce or deny reimbursement.[1211] Prior to the 1997 amendments, parents who chose unilaterally to place their children in nonpublic schools took the risk that reimbursement might be denied for private placement.[1212] However, the reimbursement issue in the pre-1997 cases focused on the public school district's provision of FAPE as reflected in the services and placement provided by the IEP. While the 1997 amendments and regulations focus as well on the public school's IEP, they provide a measure of protection for public school districts in that courts or hearing officers are explicitly authorized to deny

---

[1208] 34 C.F.R. § 300.403(a).

[1209] 34 C.F.R. § 300.403(c).

[1210] *Id. See* Mathew J. v. Massachussetts Dep't of Educ., 989 F. Supp. 380 (D. Mass. 1998) (in requiring reimbursement for a parent's unilateral placement in a religious school, "appropriate" was defined broadly to mean services responsive to the student's educational needs, even though the religious school did not have a designated special education program).

[1211] 34 C.F.R. § 300.403(d)(ii).

[1212] Hiller v. Board of Educ. of Brunswick Cent. Sch. Dist., 687 F. Supp. 735 (N.D. N.Y. 1988) (no tuition reimbursement where nonpublic school not state-approved for handicapped); Antokowiak v. Ambach, 838 F.2d 635 (2d Cir. 1988) (tuition reimbursement denied where placement occurred in nonapproved school). *Contra* Aaron S. v. Westford Pub. Schs., 1987-88 EHLR Dec. 509:122 (school district responsible for tuition and transportation as result of inadequate IEP); Rouse v. Wilson, 1987-88 EHLR Dec. 559:214 (tuition reimbursement ordered where public school IEP had been unsuccessful in the past).

reimbursement where the districts are complying with IDEA. In addition, the 1997 amendments permit denial of, or reduction in, tuition reimbursement where parents have acted unreasonably in making demands of the public school district.[1213]

The 1997 amendments and regulations also attempt to limit on-site provision of services in private schools. "No private school child has an individual right to receive some or all of the special education and related services that the child would receive if enrolled in the public school."[1214] The regulations leave local school districts with the authority to determine "how and where services will be provided."[1215] Although the IDEA statute permits districts to limit services to private school students to a proportionality factor based on the number of disabled students being served,[1216] the regulations provide that "state and local educational agencies are not prohibited from providing services to private school children with disabilities in excess if those required by this part...."[1217] Whether school districts will choose to provide on-site services at nonpublic schools when services are available at public schools is doubtful. The Eighth Circuit Court of Appeals, in one of the first cases to interpret the 1997 amendments and regulations, held that a child voluntarily placed in a private school where a public school district would have provided IEP services at a public school had no private right to have the services delivered on-site in the private school.[1218]

Many nonpublic schools may not have staff or facilities to accommodate special education students, but they may have constituencies who have children with disabilities. Whether these schools want to enter into their own special education programs may be influenced by state requirements that they would have to meet: inability to dispute salary ceilings for teachers of

---

[1213] 20 U.S.C. § 1412(a)(10)(c)(iii)(III). *See* Warren G. v. Cumberland County Sch. Dist., 190 F.3d 80 (3d Cir. 1999) (this provision might apply where parents have provided inaccurate information, contradicted themselves, and made false accu-sations, but will not apply retro-actively to pre-1997 claims for reimbursement).

[1214] 34 C.F.R. § 300.454(a).

[1215] 34 C.F.R. § 300.454(b)(iv).

[1216] 20 U.S.C. § 1412(a)(10)(A)(i)(1).

[1217] 34 C.F.R. § 300.453(d).

[1218] Foley v. Special Sch. Dist. of St. Louis County, 153 F.3d 863 (8th Cir. 1998). *See also*, Barnett v. Fairfax County Sch. Bd., 721 F. Supp. 757 (E.D. Va. 1989), *aff'd* 927 F.2d 146 (4th Cir. 1991), cert. denied 112 S.Ct. 175 (1991) (public school district not required to provide sign-language interpreter in student's home school when one was available in a centralized location).

handicapped children;[1219] limitations on changing the student's program;[1220] and restrictions on the profits for private schools.[1221]

For nonpublic schools who currently have or would like to admit student with disabilities, the policy implications of the 1997 amendments are challenging. Although the amendments do not prohibit on-site services in nonpublic schools and/or reimbursement for parents, they have removed ambiguity regarding the public school districts' obligations. As long as the districts provide FAPE they have control over special education resources and can determine where they will be invested. For parents who want their children with disabilities in a nonpublic (especially religious) school, the choice is a hard one. Unless the public school services under the IEP are inappropriate to provide FAPE, parents will either have to fund the nonpublic cost on their own or leave the child in the public school. For parents who do not have the resources to make the up-front investment to place their child in the nonpublic school and then wait to see if a court or hearing officer will order reimbursement, nonpublic education is precluded.

Unfortunately for parents who would like to place their child in a religious school but who do not have the resources to do so, denial of on-site services under IDEA does not translate well into a denial of free exercise. IDEA clearly permits public school districts to limit use of resources to their own schools. An argument that denial of on-site services at religious schools amounts to a parent's inability to make a choice of educational forum for their child has enough plausibility to suggest a constitutional claim but probably not enough vitality to survive summary judgment.

IDEA would seem to be the kind of neutral, generally applicable government enactment that falls within the meaning of *Employment Division v. Smith.* However, even if a fundamental constitutional claim under free exercise and direction of the education of a child can be articulated, the government would seem to have a significant interest in providing

---

[1219] Organization to Assure Servs. v. Ambach, 434 N.E. 2d 1329 (N.Y. 1982).

[1220] Woods Schs. v. Comm'r, Dep't of Educ., 514 A.2d 686 (Pa. Commw. Ct. 1986).

[1221] Council of Private Schs. for Children with Special Needs, Inc. v. Cooperman, 501 A.2d575 (N.J. Super. Ct. 1985).

funds in a cost-effective manner. Even though IDEA funds flow to students with disabilities, the funds are channeled through the public school districts that are responsible for their disbursement.

CHAPTER VI

SPECIAL PROBLEMS

Copyright

The cornerstone of the use of copyrighted materials is the statutory and judicial concept of "fair use." The fair use section of the Copyright Act[1222] provides that reproduction of copyrighted material for "criticism, comment, news reporting, teaching (including multiple copies for classroom use), scholarship or research, is not an infringement of copyright."

Notwithstanding these exceptions, the Act assesses fair use according to four factors:

(1) the purpose and character of the use,[1223] including whether such use is of a commercial nature or is for nonprofit educational purposes;[1224]

(2) the nature of the copyrighted work;[1225]

1222 17 U.S.C. § 107

1223 *See* Wright v. Warner Books, 953 F.2d 731, 736 (2d Cir. 1991) (in finding that use of material from letters and journals in a biography were fair use, the court observed that analytical research in a biography "furthers the goals of the copyright laws by adding value to prior intellectual labor"); Ringgold v. Black Entertainment Television, Inc., 126 F.3d 70 (2d Cir.1997) (where TV producer's use of poster depicting plaintiff's artwork in TV set was for same decorative purpose for which original artwork [story quilt] was sold, the purpose does favor fair use).

1224 *See* Educational Testing Serv. v. Katzman, 793 F.2d 533 (3d Cir. 1986) (defendant's use of plaintiff's testing materials in a business to assist students to score higher on the SAT violated the Copyright Act because defendant operated a commercial business, and the exemption favors noncommercial use. The court also determined that whether or not such review service was educational teaching was irrelevant).

1225 *See* Association of Am. Med. Colleges v. Cuomo, 928 F.2d 519 (2d Cir. 1991) (in state effort to require publication of MCAT questions and answers, court determined that the MCAT was unpublished for fair use purposes and greater protection is given to unpublished material); Wright v. Warner Books, 953 F.2d 731 (2d Cir. 1991) (unpublished letters and journals entitled to greater protection over claim that they were subjects of fair use); Princeton Univ. Press v. Michigan Document Servs., Inc., 99 F.3d 1381 (6th Cir. 1996) (preparation of coursepacks without paying royalties created competitive advantage for copy service and placed burden that multiple copying was fair use).

(3) the amount and substantiality of the portion used;[1226]

(4) the effect of the use upon the potential market for or value of the copyrighted work.[1227]

In an important multiple photocopying case, the Sixth Circuit Court of Appeals in *Princeton University Press v. Michigan Document Services, Inc.*,[1228] held that a copy shop's preparation and sale of coursepacks to university students,without payment of royalties or seeking permission, was not fair use. The court found that the copy service had violated all four fair use factors. The purpose for not seeking permission and paying royalties was to give the copy shop an advantage over others who paid permission fees. Use of the coursepacks was not a defense where the copying was undertaken "on a profit-making basis by a commercial enterprise."[1229] Regarding the second factor, the coursepacks clearly were in violation because the copied material was creative. The copy shop failed to justify its copying under the third factor because the amount of material copied varied

---

1226 For cases where use was found to be insubstantial with no copyright violation, *see* New Era Publications v. Carol Publ'ing, 904 F.2d 152, 158 (2d Cir. 1990) (five to six percent of twelve works and eight percent of eleven works with "each of the eleven being only a few pages in length"); MaxTone-Graham v. Burtchaell, 803 F.2d 1253 (2d Cir. 1987) (4.3 percent of work); Wright v. Warner Books, 953 F.2d 73 (2d Cir. 1991) (one percent of total letters and journals). For cases where use was considered to be substantial, and thus a violation of fair use, see Ringgold v. Black Entertainment Television, Inc., 126 F.3d 70 (2d Cir. 1997) (use of poster depicting plaintiff's copyrighted "story quilt" for 26-27 seconds in TV program was not *de minimis*); Harper & Row, Publishers v. Nation Enterprises, 471 U.S. 539 (1985) (300 words copied considered to be copyright violation because the "heart" of the book had been used); Salinger v. Random House, 811 F.2d 90 (2d Cir. 1987) (quotations and paraphrasing totalling two-thirds of seventeen letters and ten percent of seventeen other letters); Basic Books v. Kinko's Graphics Corp., 758 F.Supp. 1522 (S.D.N.Y. 1991) (passages copied ranged from fourteen to 110 pages, representing 5.2 percent to 15.1 percent of the works); Iowa State Univ. Research Fund v. American Broadcasting Corp., 621 F.2d 57 (2d Cir. 1980) (eight percent of videotape used that had never been broadcast). *See also*, College Entrance Examination Bd. v. Pataki, 889 F. Supp. 554 (N.D. N.Y. 1995), as amended 893 F. Supp. 152 (N.D. N.Y. 1995) (providing copies of GRE and TOEFL test questions to state, pursuant to state statute, violated this factor; however, court permitted limited disclosure to go forward pursuant to separate agreement).

1227 Value of copyrighted material can be determined not only by the amount of material actually used, but also by the necessity to cease using copyrighted material as result of infringement. *See* Educational Testing Serv. v. Katzman, 793 F.2d 533 (3d Cir. 1985) (copyright violation where use of SAT test questions by a review course meant that Testing Service had to retire at least 289 questions).

1228 99 F.3d 1381 (6th Cir. 1996).

1229 *Id.* at 1389. As a caveat, the court observed that, "as to the proposition that it would be fair use for the students or professors to make their own copies, the issue is by no means free from doubt." *Id.*

from five percent to thirty percent of various works, percentages the court found to be "not insubstantial."[1230] The value of the amount copied was attested to by "the fact that the professors thought the excerpts sufficiently important to make them required reading."[1231] The fourth factor was violated because a for-profit copy shop had chosen to "maximize its profits—and give itself a competitive edge over the other copy shops—by declining to pay the royalties requested by the holders of the copyrights."[1232]

A leading classroom case interpreting fair use continues to be *Marcus v. Rowley*.[1233] In *Marcus*, plaintiff Marcus had written a thirty-five page booklet on cake decorating, twenty-nine of which were her original creation. Plaintiff had registered her booklet with the Register of Copyrights and all copies of the booklet contained an encircled "c" followed by her name. Plaintiff sold her booklet to students for $2 each, one dollar of which was profit. Defendant subsequently prepared a twenty-four page cake decorating learning activity package, fifteen pages of which were from plaintiff's booklet. Defendant sold none of her packages but instead placed them on file for students who wanted to do further work. Ironically, defendant's use of plaintiff's materials came to light when one of plaintiff's students, after comparing plaintiff's booklet and defendant's package, accused plaintiff of plagiarizing defendant's work.

In ruling for plaintiff the court addressed each of the fair use factors. Regarding the first factor, the court noted that defendant's purpose was nonprofit educational rather than commercial. However, the court added that there "is strong indication of no fair use" when "the alleged infringers copied the material to use it for the same intrinsic purpose for which the copyright owner intended it to be used."[1234] The absence of fair use was aided by defendant's failure to secure permission or furnish attribution to plaintiff. The second factor requires consideration of whether the work is informational or creative. Plaintiff's booklet had elements of both: information available in other books as well as creative hints and creativity in assembling the booklet. Because of lack of certainty regarding

1230 *Id.*
1231 *Id.*
1232 *Id.* at 1386.
1233 695 F.2d 1171 (9th Cir. 1983).
1234 *Id.* at 1175.

the amount of creativity, the court felt the consideration of the second factor made no contribution to a consideration of fair use. The third factor concerned "both the quantity and quality of the alleged infringement."[1235] Defendant Rowley's package contained fifty percent of material from plaintiff's booklet, most of it copied verbatim and that fifty percent constituted the substance of defendant's book. The court rebutted defendant's argument that facts in the material copied were in the public domain by noting that "defendant engaged in virtually verbatim copying."[1236] Thus, there was clear evidence of substantial quantitative and qualitative copying. Concerning the fourth factor the court found for the defendant because, despite a student's refusal to purchase plaintiff's booklet (he accused plaintiff of plagiarizing), there was not sufficient evidence to conclude that "defendant's copying had any effect on the market for the plaintiff's booklet."[1237] However, weighing all four factors, the court concluded that they "weigh decisively in favor of the conclusion of no fair use"[1238] and remanded the case for a determination of damages.

In another copyright case involving education but without the substantive merit a federal court denied a copyright remedy to students and their teacher. In *Dodd v. Fort Smith Special School Dist. No. 100*,[1239] a teacher and her students who had raised funds to publish a book on a local hero and had written a manuscript after lengthy research, sued when the book was published identifying the school principal as author and failing to give credit to the teacher and students. Plaintiffs were denied remedies under both the Copyright Act and Section 1983, the Copyright Act because registration of a copyright is a prerequisite to an infringement action[1240] and Section 1983 because the Copyright Act preempts all other remedies.[1241]

Fair use does not rely totally on judicial interpretation of Section 107 since there are a number of statutory provisions affecting educational use. The Copyright Act does not exempt

---

1235 *Id.* at 1176.

1236 *Id.* at 1177.

1237 *Id.*

1238 *Id.*

1239 666 F. Supp. 1278 (W.D. Ark. 1987).

1240 17 U.S.C. §§ 408(a), 411. However, copyright protection begins as soon as "original works of authorship [are] fixed in any tangible means of expression." 17 U.S.C. § 102.

1241 17 U.S.C. § 301(a).

nonprofit or educational uses as was the case prior to the 1976 Copyright Act; therefore, all educational institutions are subject to the Act's terms.

An important distinction in the Copyright Act is the difference between copying and performance. For example, permission to make copies of a copyrighted work does not in itself include permission to perform those works. For the benefit of religious schools the Act does exempt "performance of a nondramatic literary or musical work or of a dramatic musical work of a religious nature, or display of a work, in the course of services at a place of worship or other religious assembly."[1242] Dramatic literary or musical works are those with sequential material with a plot and sequential story line (e.g., opera, cantata, musical comedy, play, motion picture, filmstrips). Nondramatic work would presumably be permissible under this exemption without securing the copyright owner's permission unless the selection is "dramatic in its very nature and purpose."[1243] The exemption for performances in religious settings recognized the reality of constitutional conflict if courts attempted to intervene and assess the nature and extent of acceptable worship under the Copyright Act.[1244]

Dramatic and nondramatic works can also be distinguished as to any direct or indirect commercial advantage. Nondramatic literary or musical works are exempt for performance if (1) there is no direct or indirect admission charge; or (2) if there is a charge, any proceeds after reasonable costs go exclusively for educational, religious, or charitable purposes and not for private financial gain. Fees or percentages cannot be paid to performers, producers, promoters, or organizers; however, payment of a salary to an employee, such as a band or choir director, whose function includes performance does not constitute a violation.[1245]

The Copyright Act also exempts:

> performance or display of a work by instructors or pupils in the course of face-to-face teaching activities of a nonprofit educational institution, in a classroom or similar place devoted to instruction, unless, in the case of a motion picture or other audiovisual work,

---

1242 17 U.S.C. § 110 (3).

1243 H. Howell, The Copyright Law 52-53 (BNA 1979).

1244 *See* M. Nimmer, Nimmer on Copyright, § 110 (A) (1978) (the copyright act "may not be read as independent of and uncontrolled by the First Amendment.").

1245 17 U.S.C. § 110 (4)(A)(B).

> the performance, or the display of individual images, is given by means of a copy that was not lawfully made under this title, and the person responsible for the performance knew or had reason to believe was not lawfully made.[1246]

The key features of this exemption are:

(1) "face-to-face teaching activities" which exclude "large assemblies or mass meetings and which are not for the purpose of instruction." Inclusion of persons who are not students would seem to place the activity outside the exemption.

(2) limitation of the performance or display to "instruction." Thus,use of a rented videotape or film sold for entertainment purposes for the classroom or school exceeds the exemption but may be permissible according to the terms of the rental agreement.

(3) "lawfully made" audiovisual works, especially videotapes. Teachers who rent, lease, or loan videotapes can use them in face-to-face teaching for instructional purposes under Section 110 even though such use would otherwise be prohibited under Section 109 unless the teacher had acquired ownership of the tape.[1247] If the teacher had reason to believe the rented, leased, or loaned videotape was not a unlawfully made copy, then the teacher would have exceeded the Section 110 exemption. For example, an unauthorized home copy made from a rental tape is clearly not "lawfully made," but an off-the-air copy of commercial programming would now seem to be lawful made under *Sony Corporation v. Universal City Studio*.[1248] However, off-the-air videotapes from noncommercial educational broadcasts may be used in teaching "for a

1246 17 U.S.C. § 110 (1).

1247 17 U.S.C. § 109(c).

1248 464 U.S. 417 (1984) (Court upheld home use of video recorders for time shifting viewing). *See generally* R. Mawdsley, *Use of Videocassettes in the Classroom*, 32 Educ. L. Rptr. 1163 (1986).

period of no more than seven days from the date of the transmission . . . [if they] are destroyed before or at the end of such period."[1249] Courts have taken a dim view toward development of libraries of off-the-air videotape copies and video copies of rental films, even if used only for teaching purposes.[1250] Just what kind of evidence should cause a teacher to believe a videotape has not been "lawfully made" is difficult to predict. To be on the safe side, teachers could make inquiry regarding how a copy came to be made for every blank videotape without a copyright owner's label.

Libraries come into the copyright picture because they are permitted under the Copyright Act to make a copy of a work from their own collections or from the collection of another library acquired at the request of a library user through interlibrary loan, if the following conditions are met:

(1) The library must determine through "reasonable investigation that a copy ... of the copyrighted work cannot be obtained at a fair price."[1251]

(2) "The copy ... becomes the property of the user."[1252]

(3) "[T]he library ... had no notice that the copy ... would be used for any purpose other than private study, scholarship or research."[1253]

(4) "[T]he library ... displays prominently, at the place where orders are accepted, and includes on its order form, a warning of copyright in accordance with

---

1249 17 U.S.C. § 109 (c).

1250 Encyclopedia Britannica's Educ. Corp. v. Crooks, 542 F. Supp. 1156 (W.D. N.Y. 982) (copyright infringement found where county educational services organizations videotaped without permission copyrighted films and made available on request copies of its videotape masters to schools). *See also* Sony Corp. v. Universal City Studio (Court considered home videotaping to be fair use as "time shifting for private home use" and concluded for lack of evidence that such videotaping was not for library building).

1251 17 U.S.C. § 108(e).

1252 17 U.S.C. § 108 (e)(1).

1253 *Id.*

> requirements that the Register of Copyrights shall prescribe by regulation."[1254]

Libraries unable or unwilling to perform this fair price investigation regarding all forms of copies may nonetheless loan video recorders to users without fear of liability provided "that such equipment displays a notice that the making of a copy may be subject to the copyright law."[1255] However, nothing "excuses a person who uses such reproducing equipment or who requests a copy ... from liability for copyright infringement for any such act, or for later use of such copy ..., if it exceeds fair use as provided in Section 107."[1256]

The most persistent educational problem concerns the making and classroom distribution of multiple photocopies. Despite Section 107, which indicates that multiple photocopying for teaching purposes is fair use,[1257] multiple photocopying is controlled by a separate Agreement[1258] which was included in the congressional history of the text and which is far from clear.[1259] Teachers need to be certain they understand the following features of the Agreement reproduced at the end of this section:

(1) The Guidelines are minimum, not maximum, standards of fair use and therefore fair use could be more broadly defined than is suggested in these Guidelines.

1254 17 U.S.C. § 108 (e)(2). *A Notice Warning Concerning Copyright Restrictions* can be found at 37 C.F.R. § 201.14 (b).
The copyright law of the United States (Title 17, United States code) governs the making of photocopies or other reproduction. One of these specific conditions is that the photocopy or reproduction is not to be "used for any purpose other than private study, scholarship, or research." If a user makes a request for, or later uses, a photocopy or reproduction for purpose in excess of 'fair use' that user may be liable for copyright infringement.
This institution reserves the right to refuse to accept a copying order if, in its judgement, fulfillment of the order would involve violation of copyright law.

1255 17 U.S.C. § 108(f)(1).

1256 17 U.S.C. § 108 (f)(2). Intent to infringe is not a necessary precedent to a finding of copyright infringement. However, in the case of copyright violations where the "infringer was not aware and had no reason to believe that his or her acts constituted an infringement of copyright, the court in its discretion may reduce the award of statutory damages to a sum of not less than $100." 17 U.S.C. § 504 (c)(2). But for employees of nonprofit educational institutions who "believed and had reasonable grounds for believing that his or her use of the copyrighted work was a fair use" the court "shall remit statutory damages." *Id.*

1257 See preceeding discussion on "fair use."

1258 For a copy of this Agreement, see end of this section

1259 *See* R. Mawdsley and S. Permuth, *Multiple Photocopying in Educational Institutions,* 10 NOLPE School L.J. 18 (1981).

(2) Since the Copyright Act does not declare teachers' fair use to be more extensive than students, the "Single Copying for Teachers" guidelines should apply to students, provided the copy is used for the same purpose as teachers.

(3) Compliance with the Guidelines requires meeting all three tests: brevity, spontaneity, and cumulative effect.

(4) Poetry, prose, and "special" works have separate requirements which have to be harmonized with regard to the item(s) being photocopied.

(5) The amount of time between "inspiration and decision" under "Spontaneity" could well be as little as twenty-three weeks if the teacher knows from whom to request permission, or even longer if the teacher does not know, or has no address for, the copyright owner.

(6) Simply because spontaneity is met for one course does not mean the test would not be failed if multiple copies of the same item were to be distributed the next time the course was taught.

(7) While somewhat cumbersomely stated, "cumulative effect" focuses on what can be used for one course and what can be used from one source.

The Agreement is silent regarding teacher assignments that require each student to make a photocopy of an article rather than have the teacher make multiple photocopies, but a court would probably evaluate such an assignment as if the teacher herself had made the copies.

Copyright Act infringement suits can involve actions for injunctive relief and/or damages. A copyright owner can elect to prove actual damages or can use the measure of statutory damages provided in the statute. However, once the copyright owner elects a measure of damages (either actual or statutory) that remedy is usually exclusive.[1260] Actual damages can be recovered for lost profits and lost royalties.[1261] The range of statutory damages depends on the willfulness of the violation. Damages for infringements that are not willful range from a minimum of $500 to a maximum of $20,000 for each violation.[1262] Awards for willful violations can be as high as $100,000 for each violation.[1263] However, in the case of copyright violations where the "infringer was not aware and had no reason to believe that his or her acts constituted an infringement of copyright," the court in its discretion may reduce the award of statutory damages to a sum not less than $200 for each violation.[1264] But for an agent or employee of an educational institution acting in the scope of his or her employment who "believed and had reasonable grounds for believing that his or her use of copyrighted work was fair use" the court "shall remit statutory damages."[1265]

To address copyright and technology, Congress enacted the Digital Millennium Copyright Act in 1998.[1266] This act was passed in order to set criteria regarding the copyright liability of online service providers (OSP), logical access providers, and users. The Act responded to earlier case law that had suggested that an OSP might be vicariously liable for a user's copyright infringement.[1267] In addition to providing safe havens for transitory communication,[1268] system caching,[1269] information residing on a system or networks at the direction of users,[1270] and

---

1260 *Basic Books, Inc.*, 758 F. Supp. at 1543.

1261 *See* Applied Innovations v. Regents of Univ. of Minn., 876 F.2d 626, 637 (8th Cir.1989) (damages of $226,598 awarded to licensee for lost profits and $162,161 to copyright owner for lost royalties).

1262 17 U.S.C. § 504(c)(1). See *Princeton Univ. Press*, 99 F.3d at 1381 where the Sixth Circuit remanded a fine of $5,000 per work where the copy service's preparation of coursepacks was so unreasonable as to be willful.

1263 17 U.S.C. § 504(c)(2). *See Basic Books*, 758 F. Supp. at 1543-45 (statutory damages set at $510,000 - $50,000 each for nine infringements and $20,000 each for three infringements).

1264 17 U.S.C. § 504(c)(2).

1265 17 U.S.C. § 504(c)(1).

1266 17 U.S.C. § 512.

1267 *See* Fonovisa, Inc. v. Cherry Auction, Inc., 76 F.3d 259 (9th Cir. 1996) (this case dealt with sale of pirated tapes at a swap meet, but the concepts of liability extended to the owner and organizer of the swap meet who provided space to sell the tapes could be applied to an OSP that provided online technology space).

1268 17 U.S.C. § 512(a) (limits liability of OSPs that transmit information at request of subscribers).

1269 17 U.S.C. § 512(b) (limits liability of OSPs that retain copy of online material placed there other than by OSP and then transmitted to a subscriber).

1270 17 U.S.C. § 512(c) (exempts OSP from liability if, upon notification by copyright owner of infringement, it removes or blocks access to infringing material).

information location tools,[1271] it also limits liability for nonprofit educational institutions.[1272] The infringing activities of faculty and students cannot be imputed to their institutions if online access has not been provided as part of required course materials during the preceding three years, the institution has not received more than two notifications of infringement during the prior three years, and the institution provides all system users with notice of copyright law compliance.

Agreement on Guidelines for Classroom Copying in Not-for-Profit Educational Institutions with Respect to Books and Periodicals

The purpose of the following guidelines is to state miminum and not the maximum standards of educational fair use under Section 107 of H.R. 2223. The parties agree that the conditions determining the extent of permissible copying for educational purposes may change in the future; that certain types of copying permitted under these guidelines may not be permissible in the future; and conversely that in the future other types of copying not permitted under these guidelines may be permissible under revised guidelines.

Moreover, the following statement of guidelines is not intended to limit the types of copying permitted under the standards of fair use under judicial decision and which are stated in Section 107 of the Copyright Revision Bill. There may be instances in which copying does not fall within the guidelines stated below which may nonetheless be permitted under the criteria of fair use.

<u>Guidelines</u>

I. Single Copying for Teachers

A single copy may be made of any of the following by or for a teacher at his or her individual request for his or her scholarly research or use in teaching or preparation to teach a class:

A. A chapter from a book;

B. An article from a periodical or newspaper;

[1271] 17 U.S.C. § 512(d) (exempts logical access providers, including web search engines, on same basis as OSP).

[1272] 17 U.S.C. § 512(e).

C. A short story, short essay or short poem, whether or not from a collective work;

D. A chart, graph, diagram, drawing, cartoon or picture from a book, periodical or newspaper.

II. Multiple Copies for Classroom Use

Multiple copies (not to exceed in any event more than one copy per pupil in a course) may be made by or for the teacher giving the course for classroom use or discussion, provided that:

A. The copying meets the tests of brevity and spontaneity as defined below; and,

B. Meets the cumulative effect test as defined below; and,

C. Each copy includes a notice of copyright.

Definitions of Brevity

1. Poetry: (a) A complete poem of less than 250 words and if printed on not more than two pages or, (b) from a longer poem, an excerpt of not more than 250 words.
2. Prose: (a) Either a complete article, story or essay of less than 2, 500 words, or (b) an excerpt from any prose work of not more than 1,000 words or ten percent of the work,whichever is less, but in any event a minimum of 500 words.

   (Each of the numerical limits stated in 1 and 2 above may be expanded to permit the completion of an unfinished line of poem or of an unfinished prose paragraph).
3. Illustration: One chart, graph, diagram, drawing, cartoon or picture per book or per periodical per issue.
4. "Special" Works: Certain works in poetry, prose or in "poetic prose" which often combine language with illustrations and which are intended sometimes for children and at other times for a more general audience fall short of 2,500 words in their entirety. Paragraph 2 above notwithstanding such "special works"

may not be reproduced in their entirety; however, an excerpt comprising not more than two of the published pages of such special work and containing not more than ten percent of the words found in the text thereof, may be reproduced.

Definition of Spontaneity

1. The copying is at the instance and inspiration of the individual teacher.
2. The inspiration and decision to use the work and the moment of its use for maximum teaching effectiveness are so close in time it would be unreasonable to expect a timely reply to a request for permission.

Definitions of Cumulative Effect

1. The copying of the material is for only one course in the school in which the copies are made.
2. Not more than one short poem, article, story, essay, or two excerpts may be copied from the same author, nor more than three from the same collective work or periodical volume during one class term.
3. There shall not be more than nine instances of such multiple copying for one course during one class term.
   (The limitation stated in 2 and 3 above shall not apply to current news periodicals and newspapers and current news sections of other periodicals.)

III. Prohibitions as to I and II Above
Notwithstanding any of the above, the following shall be prohibited:

A. Copying shall not be used to create or to replace or substitute for anthologies, compilations or collective works. Such replacement or substition may occur whether copies of various works or excerpts therefrom are accumulated or reproduced and used separately.

B. There shall be no copying of or from works intended to be "consumable" in the course of study or of teaching. These include some workbooks, exercises, standardized tests and test booklets and answer sheets and like consumable material.

C. Copying shall not:
1. Substitute for the purchase of books, publishers' reprints or periodicals;
2. Be directed by higher authority;
3. Be repeated with respect to the same item by the same teacher from term to term.

D. No charges shall be made to the student beyond the actual cost of the photocopying.

Immigration and Reform Control Act (IRCA)

Enactment of IRCA[1273] has had the effect of making all employers part of the Immigration and Naturalization Service (INS) process by requiring all employers within three business days of hire to establish through examination of appropriate documents both the identity and the work authorization of the employee.[1274] Documents which establish both identity and work authorization are:

(1) United States passport;

(2) Certificate of United States citizenship (INS Form N-560);

(3) Certificate of Naturalization (INS Form N-550);

(4) Unexpired foreign passport if the passport reads "processed for I-551" or has attached a form I-94 bearing the same name as the employment authorization stamp and has not yet expired;

1273 8 U.S.C. §§ 1324, 1324a, 1324b.

1274 8 U.S.C. §§ 3124, 1324a, 1324b.

(5) Alien Registration Card (Form I-551) contain ing bearer's photograph;

(6) Temporary Resident Card (INS Form I-688) or Employment Authorization Card (INS Form I-688A) containing bearer's photo graph.[1275]

If an applicant or new hire does not have documentation from one of the above categories, then separate documentation will be required for identity and work authorization. The following documents establish identity of the individual only:[1276]

(1) state driver's license with a photograph;

(2) state-issued identification card with a photo graph for individuals without driver's licenses or individuals in states without photographs on driver's licenses.

The following documents evidence employment authorization only:[1277]

(1) Social Security account number card as long as the card does not state on its face that the individual is not authorized for employment;

(2) Certificate of Birth in the United States issued by a state;

(3) Certificate of Birth issued by Department of State (Form FS-545);

(4) Certificate of Birth abroad issued by Department of State (Form DS-1350).

Although not specifically mentioned, a current I-20 form for full-time foreign students would be acceptable employment authorization for on-campus employment.

[1275] 8 U.S.C. § 1324a (b) (1) (B).
[1276] 8 U.S.C. § 1324a (b)(1)(D).
[1277] 8 U.S.C. § 1324a (b)(1)(c).

The above information is part of the documentation required for a new employee in completing the employment verification form called an I-9. The I-9, along with copies of verification documents, must be retained at least three years after the hire or one year after discharge, whichever is longer.[1278] The I-9 forms are subject to inspection by INS or Department of Labor agents upon no more than three days notice without having to secure a subpoena or warrant.[1279] If confidentiality of employee records is at issue under state law, then the employer would be advised to keep all I-9 forms in a location separate from personnel files.[1280] Since I-9 forms have no statutory value beyond the maximum retention date, there would be nothing wrong with educational institutions periodically destroying I-9 forms no longer required to be retained. Penalties for failure to comply with IRCA include fines up to $3,000 and six months imprisonment for each violation.[1281]

IRCA also addresses problems attendant to student reception of Title IV funds.[1282] To be eligible for Title IV funds, each student must declare under penalty of perjury in writing to the institution whether he is a U.S. citizen and, if not, that he is in an immigrant status that does not make him ineligible for grants, loans, or work assistance under Title IV. The following procedures are mandated:

(1) a student, who is not a U.S. citizen or national of the United States must present to the institution "alien registration documentation or other proof of immigration from the Immigration and Naturalization Service that contains the individual's alien admission number or alien file number (or numbers if the individual has more than one number)"; [1283]

(2) the institution must verify with INS the individual's immigration status; [1284]

1278 8 U.S.C. §§ 1324a (b)(3).

1279 *Id.*

1280 IRCA permits the copying of any identity or authorization documents for purposesof complying with the statute, notwithstanding any law to the contrary which prohibits such copying.
8 U.S.C. § 1324a (b)(4).

1281 8 U.S.C. § 1324a (f)(1).

1282 *See* 20 U.S.C. §§ 1070-1091.

1283 20 U.S.C. § 1091(c)(2)(A).

1284 20 U.S.C. § 1091 (c)(3).

(3) where documentation under (1) is not presented or, if presented, has not been verified under (2), the student shall have a "reasonable opportunity to submit to the institution evidence indicating satisfactory immigration status" and until such a reason able opportunity is provided, the student's eligibility for Title IV funds cannot be delayed, denied, reduced, or terminated;[1285]

(4) if the institution receives documentation which it determines constitutes reasonable evidence of employment status [other than the documentation in (1)], photostat copies must be sent to INS for verification and, pending verification, the student's Title IV eligibility cannot be delayed, denied, reduced, or terminated;[1286]

(5) where the institution determines a student is not in a satisfactory immigration status, the institution must deny eligibility or terminate the student's assistance and make available a statutory fair hearing process.[1287]

Where an alien student has improperly received Title IV money, the educational institution is protected from imposition of penalty by the Secretary of Education if the institution relied on INS verification of eligibility, was waiting for student documentation or INS verification, or was in the process of conducting a fair hearing.[1288] In the case of a guaranteed student loan, the guarantee is not voided or payments nullified if made prior to prompt notification by the educational institution of ineligibility to the entity making the loan.[1289] The purpose of these Title IV provisions appears to be standardization among

---

1285 20 U.S.C. § 1091 (c)(4)(A).

1286 20 U.S.C. § 1081 (c)(4)(B).

1287 20 U.S.C. § 1091 (c)(5) and (6). *See* Taka v. Immigration and Naturalization Serv., 828 F. Supp. 362, 365 (E.D. Pa. 1993) (Temple University could not be liable to student whose federal financial aid had been canceled because student could not prove she was "citizen or national of the United States, a permanent resident of the United States, in the United States for other than a temporary purpose ... Temple University cannot be liable to plaintiff for following the eligibility requirements mandated by Congress." *See also* 34 C.F.R. § 668.7.

1288 20 U.S.C. § 1091 (d).

1289 20 U.S.C. §1981 (e).

all forms of student assistance and the establishment of more detailed requirements to prevent the award of aid to nonqualified aliens.

IRCA has added a new section to the immigration statute prohibiting discrimination based on national origin or citizenship status. Employers of more than three employees are prohibited from discriminating in hiring or discharge of employees because of an individual's national origin or because the applicant is a U.S. citizen or intending to become a citizen.[1290] An "intending citizen" categorization applies to aliens admitted for permanent residence or as refugees and to those granted asylum or having completed a declaration of intention to become a citizen. However, aliens must satisfy certain time limits for receiving naturalization or they will lose the statute's protection.[1291]

Bankruptcy Act and Student Debts

In an era of rising consumer debt, most nonpublic schools can reasonably anticipate that some parents or students will seek to adjust their indebtedness by filing a petition in bankruptcy. Debtors have a choice of three kinds of bankruptcy: Chapter 7 in which nonexempt property is liquidated, proceeds are distributed among the creditors, and unpaid debts are discharged;[1292] Chapter 11, in which the debtor's financial affairs are reorganized under a court-approved plan;[1293] and Chapter 13, in which debtors have regular income, a portion of which is devoted to paying off debts.[1294]

Educational institutions will normally be the objects of Chapters 7 and 13 petitions in bankruptcy and as unsecured creditors,[1295] schools can expect that their debts will have a low priority in payment. Unless an institution files appropriate and timely objections (an adversary proceeding against the debtor),[1296] it will be bound by the debt discharge under Chapter

---

1290 8 U.S.C. § 1324b.

1291 8 U.S.C. § 1324 b (a)(3).

1292 11 U.S.C. § 523.

1293 11 U.S.C. § 1129.

1294 11 U.S.C. § 1324. Debts not covered by the plan will be discharged by the court. 11 U.S.C. § 1328.

1295 The bankruptcy court must determine in a Chapter 13 confirmation plan hearing whether the value, as of the effective date of the plan, of property to be distributed under the plan on account of each unsecured claim is not less than the amount that would be paid on such claim if the estate of the debtor were liquidated under Chapter 7 of this title. 11 U.S.C. § 1324 (a)(4). *See In re* Safka, 18 B.R. 196 (Bkrtcy. D. Vt. 1982).

1296 *See* Matter of Love, 577 F.2d 344 (5th Cir. 1978).

13. Much of bankruptcy litigation involving educational institutions revolves around whether denial of discharge under Chapter 7 would represent "undue hardship on the debtor"[1297] and whether a Chapter 13 plan makes a good faith effort to repay the unsecured creditors, which includes educational creditors.[1298]

Educational institutions (as creditors) are affected in the following ways under automatic stay provisions[1299] when a debtor to the institution files a bankruptcy petition, listing as a debt his educational obligation:

(1) The institution is prohibited from taking any action to recover. These automatic stay provisions tend to be interpreted broadly; thus, even continued send ing of bills to the debtor may be a basis for a contempt summons as harassing the debtor or as seeking to acquire an unfair advantage in debt collection.

(2) Educational institutions are prohibited from recovering any discharged debts.[1300]

(3) Educational institutions cannot deny admission, readmission, or access to classes for a student whose

---

1297 11 U.S.C. §523 (a)(8)(B). *In re* Plotkin, 164 B.R. 623 (Bkrtcy. W.D. Ark. 1994) (even though student still in college, hardship demonstrated where student suffered from severe osteoporosis, scoliosis, anorexia and gall bladder tumors and where future financial resources would only be able support debtor and dependents at subsistence level); *In re* O'Brien, 165 B.R. 456 (Bkrty. W.D. Mo. 1994) (discharge appropriate where debtor diagnosed with chronic fatigue syndrome and currently unemployed with no employment for past eighteen months); *In re* Price, 25 B.R. 256 (Bkrtcy. W.D. Mo. 1982); Matter of Powelson, 25 B.R. 274 (Bkrtcy. D. Neb. 1982) (hardship demonstrated by great dollar disparity between net income and debts); *In re* Norman, 25 B.R. 545 (Bkrtcy. S.C. Cal. 1982) (hardship demonstrated in discharging educational loans because college graduate could find only temporary or part-time work). *Contra In re* Bethune, 165 B.R. 258 (Bkrtcy. E.D. Ark. 1994) (discharge inappropriate where debtor's income for foreseeable future sufficient to support debtor and her dependents and to repay student loans); *In re* Albert, 25 B.R. 98 (Bkrtcy. N.D. Ohio 1982) (discharge denied where debtor's income was increasing and was expected to improve in the future).

1298 Wright State Univ. v. Novak, 25 B.R. 459 (Bkrtcy. S.C. Ohio 1982) (Chapter 13 plan denied where debtor proposed paying less than one percent of $2200 debt over thirty-six months); *In re* Miller, 24 B.R. 786 (Bkrtcy. E.D. Pa. 1982) (Chapter 13 plan denied where it proposed paying only nine percent of debtor's unsecured claims, sixty-nine percent of which consisted of outstanding student loans).

1299 11 U.S.C. §§ 362 (a)(6) and 1301 (the bankruptcy code specifically provides an automatic stay of action against any debtor from the moment of filing the bankruptcy petition).

1300 11 U.S.C. §524 (a)(2).

debts to the institutions are included in a bankruptcy petition.[1301]

(4) Educational institutions cannot refuse to send official transcripts as requested by the debtor-student while a petition in a bankruptcy is pending or after discharge of a debt.[1302]

Family Educational Rights and Privacy Act (FERPA)

All nonpublic educational institutions receiving funds distributed by the U.S. Department of Education must comply with the requirements of FERPA. However, generally only nonpublic higher education institutions will be subject to FERPA since the most common Department of Education funds are those under Title IV (e.g., Pell, GSL).

FERPA has two important functions: access by students to their own educational records; and control of access by others to student records. The key concept is "education records." "Education records" are records that are:

(1) Directly related to a student; and

(2) Maintained by an educational agency or institution or by a party acting for the agency or institution.[1303]

Excluded from the definition of "education records" are records that meet the requirements of the student as an employee of the educational institution;[1304] medical records;[1305] and law enforcement records.[1306] A record means "any information recorded in any way, including, but not limited to, handwriting, print, film, microfilm, and microfiche."[1307]

1301 *In re* Parkman, 27 B.R. 460 (Bkrptcy. N.D. Ill. 1983); *In re* Lanford, 10 B.R.132 (Bkrptcy. D. Minn. 1981); *In re* Ware, 9 B.R. 24 (Bkrtcy. W.D. Mo. 1981).

1302 *In re* Scroggins, 209 B.R. 727 (D.Ariz. 1997); Parraway v. Andrews Univ., 50 B.R.315 (W.D. Mich.1984); *In re* Lanford; Handsome v. Rutgers Univ., 445 F. Supp. 1362 (D. N.J. 1978).

1303 34 C.F.R. § 99.3.

1304 34 C.F.R. § 99.3 (b)(3).

1305 34 C.F.R. § 99.3 (b)(4).

1306 34 C.F.R. § 99.3 (b)(2).

1307 34 C.F.R. § 99.3.

Disclosure of education record information, either to the student or to someone else, means "to permit access to or the release, transfer, or other communication of education records, or the personally identifiable information contained in those records, to any party, by any means, including oral, written, or electronic means."[1308] The important concept of "personally identifiable information" is a way of protecting educational information concerning a student (such as posting of grades) by prohibiting identification with a particular student with such items as the following: the student's name; the name of the student's parent or other family member; the address of the student or student's family; a personal identifier such as the student's social security number or student number; a list of personal characteristics that would make the student's identity easily traceable; or other information that would make the student's identity easily traceable.[1309] However, in order to facilitate the normal business of the educational institution that could otherwise be restricted if permission had to be secured from each student for every publication of information concerning students, a separate classification called "directory information" has been created. As long as the institution notifies the student each year as to the categories included within "directory information,"[1310] permission need not be secured from students to reveal the information provided a student has not notified the institution that certain kinds of directory information are not to be revealed without prior permission.[1311]

FERPA provides a process by which a student can challenge the content of an education record[1312] and also identifies a number of conditions under which an institution can reveal personally identifiable information without securing student consent, the most important of which are disclosures in connection with application for financial aid, disclosures to

---

1308 34 C.F.R. § 99.3.

1309 34 C.F.R. § 99.3.

1310 34 C.F.R. § 99.3. Directory information can include "the student's name,address, telephone listing, date and place of birth, major field of study, participation in officially recognized activities and sports, weight and height of members of athletic teams, dates of attendance, degrees and awards received, and the most recent previous educational agency attended." 34 C.F.R. § 99.6 (a)(6) requires that the institution specify the kinds of information considered to be directory information.

1311 34 C.F.R. § 99.37.

1312 34 C.F.R. § 99.21.

comply with a court order or subpoena, and disclosures pursuant to an accreditation review.[1313]

Some states, in order to facilitate statewide assessment of school districts, have set up data collection systems. A number of Ohio public school districts challenged the state's Educational Management Information System (EMIS) on the ground that FERPA's confidentiality requirements preempted the state system. However, a state appeals court ruled that FERPA had not preempted the collection of education information about students.[1314]

An educational institution must comply with a request for education records within forty-five days and cannot destroy records once a request has been made.[1315] The institution can charge a fee for duplication of the requested records unless "the imposition of a fee prevents [an] ... eligible student from exercising the right to inspect and review [his/her] education records...."[1316] When personally identifiable information has been disclosed, the party to whom the information has been disclosed cannot then disclose the information to any other party without first securing the student's consent.[1317]

Enforcement of FERPA is declared in the Act as the responsibility of the Family Policy Compliance Office of the U.S. Department of Education.[1318] The Act provides that students can review their records, request changes in information in the records, and, if not satisfied, file a complaint with the Department of Education. Inevitably, students would seek a more direct redress through the courts. Earlier cases indicated that FERPA did not permit a private cause of action,[1319] but more recently, courts have recognized a private cause of action. Once information is part of a student's education record, courts have tended to permit claims to remediate violations of FERPA or its

---

1313 34 C.F.R. § 99.31.

1314 Princeton City Sch. Dist. Bd. of Educ. v. Ohio State Bd. of Educ., 645 N.E.2d 773 (Ohio Ct. App. 1994).

1315 34 C.F.R. § 99.10.

1316 34 C.F.R. § 99.11.

1317 34 C.F.R. § 99.33.

1318 34 C.F.R. § 99.60.

1319 Rothman v. Emory Univ., 828 F. Supp. 537 (N.D. Ill. 1993) ; Norwood v. Slammons, 788 F. Supp. 1020 (W.D. Ark. 1991).

regulations. In *Lewin v. Medical College of Hampton Roads*,[1320] a student who was denied an opportunity to challenge scoring errors on a test stated a FERPA cause of action. However, FERPA does not permit a student to challenge the underlying grading of an exam.[1321] In *Brown v. City of Aneonta*,[1322] a university that had supplied the names of black male students to police in response to a general request concerning criminal activity provided the students with a cause of action of conspiracy to violate FERPA. Some courts have recognized that a claim under Section 1983 is possible for FERPA violations.[1323]

In terms of possible lawsuits by disgruntled students, virtually no nonpublic schools will be subject to Section 1983 actions because of the absence of state action. However, nonpublic educational institutions that receive federal assistance may now be subject to private actions under FERPA for violations. Regardless of possible legal remedies, all nonpublic schools would still be subject to administrative enforcement through the Department of Education.

Even though many K-12 nonpublic schools may not be subject to the FERPA requirements, they should give serious thought to meeting the spirit, if not the letter, of the statute. Providing access to student records by students or their parents (where students are elementary or secondary age) is a good way of making certain that records do not contain inaccurate or irrelevant material. There seems to be no justification for maintaining information in student records that is not accurate, especially if the information as revealed to others could be harmful to the student. Student files need to be regularly reviewed and even information that might have been useful at one time may cease to be relevant as the student progresses through school. Anecdotal comments about a student's problem behavior in sixth grade may not seem particularly relevant when the student has demonstrated good conduct in high school and is ready to graduate. Release of student information pursuant to the standards in FERPA may be the best protection for a nonpublic school against charges of improper access by inappropriate persons to the student's

---

1320 910 F. Supp. 1161 (E.D. Va. 1996).

1321 Lewin v. Medical College of Hampton Roads, 931 F. Supp. 443 (E.D. Va. 1996).

1322 911 F. Supp. 580 (N.D.N.Y. 1996).

1323 Maynard v. Greater Hoyt Sch. Dist. No. 61-4, 876 F. Supp. 1104 (D.S.D. 1995); Krebs v.Rutgers, 797 F. Supp. 1246 (D. N.J. 1992).

records. Treating information in student records as solely the property of the school to be released at the discretion of school officials is a dangerous practice that may result in the nonpublic school and its officials facing an invasion of privacy or intentional infliction of emotional distress action, especially where the information released is inaccurate.

Fortunately, virtually all nonpublic students, regardless how unruly they may have seemed to have been during their school days, tend to grow up to be mature and responsible citizens; nonpublic schools can little afford to appear to demonstrate a spirit of vindictiveness by denying student access to information that may be inaccurate or irrelevant. At the very least, students should be permitted to submit responses to challenged information in their files, at which point school officials may want to rethink whether maintaining the information is really necessary.

Table of Cases

Index